The Life of St. Alphonsus Liguori

The Life
of
St. Alphonsus Liguori

BISHOP, CONFESSOR, AND DOCTOR OF THE CHURCH

FOUNDER OF THE CONGREGATION OF THE MOST HOLY
REDEEMER.

BY
A MEMBER OF THE ORDER OF MERCY

AUTHORESS OF "THE LIFE OF CATHARINE MCAULEY," "ANGEL
DREAMS," "GLIMPSES OF PLEASANT HOMES," "HAPPY HOURS OF
CHILDHOOD," "BY THE SEASIDE," ETC.

At the first sound of the bell, the villagers hastened to the Church: "Let us
go," they cried out, "let us go to hear our Saint that loves us and that
smooths our path to heaven!"
– Tannoia's MEMOIRS.

"Would that sweet spirit, Saint Alfonso, have been half as lax, had he been
but half so holy?"
– Faber.

"Lord, Thou knowest that all I have thought, said, done, and written, has
been for souls and for Thee."
– St. Alphonsus.

2024
Slaying Dragons Press Classics

www.SlayingDragonsPress.com
2024

To
"That Sweet Spirit,
St. Alfonso,"
This Feeble Attempt To Portray
His Labors
And His Sanctity,
Is Affectionately Inscribed;
In Gratitude For The
Edification And Instruction Imbibed In
The Perusal Of His Works,
And The Graces Received
Through His Powerful Intercession.

~~~

APPROBATIONS.

~~~

Having submitted to a careful examination the works, original and translated, of a member of the Order of Mercy residing in our diocese, we cordially and earnestly recommend them to the faithful under our charge.
+Napoleon Joseph,
Archbishop Of New Orleans, La.

New Orleans, January 10, 1873.
The book entitled "Life of St Alphonsus Liguori," by a member of the Order of Mercy, authoress of "The Life of Catharine McAuley," etc., having been carefully examined by learned priests, who have given me a perfectly satisfactory account of it, I recommend it to all classes of readers, as useful both to the members of the clergy and to the faithful at large.
+N. J. Perché,
Archbishop Of New Orleans, La.

We cheerfully concur in the above approbation of the most Rev. Archbishop Perché.
+Aug. Maria, Bishop of Natchitoches, La.

+WILLIAM HENRY, Bishop of Natchez, Miss.
+JOHN QUINLAN, Bishop of Mobile, Ala.
+C. M. DU BUIS, Bishop of Galveston, Texas.
+EDWARD FITZGERALD, Bishop of Little Rock, Ark.
+JAMES F. WOOD, Bishop of Philadelphia, Pa.
+S. H. ROSENCRANS, Bishop of Columbus.
+R. GILMOUR, Bishop of Cleveland, O.
+JOHN, Archbishop of New York.
+LOUIS DE GOESBRIAND, Bishop of Burlington.
+JOHN J. CONROY, Bishop of Albany, N. Y.
+W. O'HARA, Bishop of Scranton, Pa.
+LOUIS M. FINK, Coad. of Vicar Apostolic At Kansas.
+JOHN, Bishop of Brooklyn.
+WILLIAM, Bishop of Scranton.

Richmond, January 12, 1873.
I cheerfully unite with the most Rev. Archbishop Perché in recommending to the Catholic public the new life of St Alphonsus, written by a Sister of Mercy, and carefully examined by two learned priests of New Orleans.
+JAMES GIBBONS, D. D., BISHOP OF RICHMOND, VA., AND ADMINISTRATOR APOSTOLIC OF NORTH CAROLINA.

Savannah, August 21, 1873.
It affords me very great pleasure to unite with Monseigneur Perché in recommending to the public the Life of the latest Doctor of the Universal Church, St Alphonsus Liguori — just written by a Sister of Mercy.
+WILLIAM N. GROSS, C.SS.R., BISHOP OF SAVANNAH.

With full confidence in the judgment of the most Rev. Archbishop of New Orleans, and the priests deputed by him to examine the aforesaid work, I earnestly concur in recommending it to the Catholic public.
+RICHARD V. WHELAN, BISHOP OF WHEELING

I yield very willingly to the request to add my name to the foregoing approbations of a good book.
+J. B. PURCELL, D.D., ARCHBISHOP OF CINCINNATI, O.

A new Life, in the English language, of the great Saint, illustrious missionary, and eminent Doctor of these modern times, cannot fail to prove exceedingly interesting to every lover of our Holy Church, and it affords me great pleasure to recommend it to the faithful.
+AUGUSTIN VÉROT, BISHOP OF ST AUGUSTINE, FLA.

I take great pleasure in recommending to Catholics the "Life of St Alphonsus Liguori," written by a Religious of the illustrious Order of Mercy, and approved by the learned Archbishop of New Orleans
+WILLIAM, BISHOP OF LOUISVILLE

From the approbation given by the most Rev. Archbishop and suffragan Bishops of the Archdiocese and Province of New Orleans, I have no hesitation in recommending the "Life of St. Alphonsus Liguori," by a member of the Order of Mercy, and authoress of the "Life of Catharine McAuley," etc., as a work edifying and instructive both to clergy and people.
+STEPHEN VINCENT, BISHOP OF BUFFALO, N. Y.

San Francisco, Sept 12, 1873.
Any good work on St Alphonsus should be dear to every Catholic; I therefore take great pleasure in giving my approbation to the Life of the Saint, by a Member of the Order of Mercy, authoress of the "Life of Catharine McAuley," etc., relying on the recommendations it has received from the learned and most worthy Archbishop of New Orleans, and other high dignitaries.
+JOSEPH S. ALEMANY, O.P., ARCHBISHOP, SAN FRANCISCO.

Marysville, Cal., Sept 27, 1873.
Dear Sister in Christ: You honor me highly by asking my approbation of your forthcoming "Life of St. Alphonsus Liguori," the last, but not the least illustrious Doctor of the Catholic Church. Let me assure you, dear sister, that I hail your Life of St Alphonsus as much as I do the admirable "Vindication" of his Theology by the Redemptorist Fathers; convinced as I am that both these works will put the great Doctor's sanctity and learning in a clearer light, and promote throughout this country the devotions which your favorite Saint had so much at heart,

I remain, dear sister,
Your obliged servant in Christ,
+E. O'CONNELL, BISHOP OF MARYSVILLE.

Extract from a letter to the Authoress, approving the "Life of St. Alphonsus."

St. Joseph, Mo, Oct 25, 1873.

My dear Sister:
I hope your book will soon be out of press. I could not hesitate to write my name in recommendation of anything coming from your pen; for you have already very much surprised and edified myself and many others by your successful labors, in which 1 am glad to learn that you are persevering. I have read all your books, and some of them several times over.
I remain.
Your most devoted servant in Christ,
+JOHN J. HOGAN
BISHOP OF ST. JOSEPH

Table of Contents

Measures of his parents. — His resolutions. — His opinion of the legal profession. — Why he renounced it.

brother. — The saint dissuades him. — Persecution in Nocera. Alphonsus appeals to Mgr. Falcoia. — St. Michael.— Death of Bishop Falcoia.

Mildness of the saint — His Firmness.— Funeral of an excommunicated man.

CHAPTER XLIII.

Episcopal visitation. — The Seminary. — Judicious Regulations made by the saint. — His rigid discipline. — Examples. — His severe but just censures of Genovesi. — He prohibits the use of his work in the Seminary.

CHAPTER XLIV.

Spiritual exercises of the Seminarists. — Mortifications. — Vigilance of the saint. — The Seminary becomes a model. — Liberality to poor students. Solicitude of the saint with reference to penance and the Holy Eucharist. The elaborately-curled wig straightened out by the saint.— Minute regulations. — Neatness of the churches. — Dangerous illness of the Bishop. — Cases of conscience. -- Confraternities. — Mental prayer. — New Books.

CHAPTER XLV.

The saint's mode of progress through his diocese. — Apt rejoinder.— He refuses a carriage. — Compares himself to a vender of fowls. — Kindness to a servant — Accident. — Miraculous cure. — Magnificent hospitality of the Prince of Riccia. — "The saint that smooths our way to heaven." — The little monk. — The saint's kindness to children and young people. — His vigilance. — His charity to the poor.

CHAPTER XLVI.

Count Hercules Liguori marries a second time desiring to have heirs. Letters. — The saint's present to the bride. — The bridegroom's indignation. — Preaching. — Sermons. — Ecstasy. — Periodical missions. Rigor more hurtful than indulgence. — Style. — Extraordinary meekness of the saint. — "Poor Jesus Christ" — The Famine. — Heroic Charity.

CHAPTER XLVII.

Alphonsus presides at a General Chapter of his Congregation — His old opponent Patuzzi again attacks him. — Alphonsus dedicates his Defence to the reigning Pontiff. — Want of courtesy in Patuzzi. — Apology. Proposed Synod. — Decrees issued. — New arrangement of parishes.

CHAPTER XLVIII.

Dangerous Illness of the saint. — 'Non recuso laborem.' — Miracle. — The saint refuses to play on the harpsichord. — At Nocera. — Impatient to return to St. Agatha. — Letter. — Bad books. — The saint's measures against their circulation. — His Prophecy regarding the Free Masons. Papal Infallibility. — The assembly. — Society of Jesus. — Circular Letter. — He endeavors to resign.

CHAPTER XLIX.

Nuns of the Most Holy Redeemer. — Remarks of Archdeacon Rainone. The Church of St. Nobody. — Sister Mary Raphael of Charity. Additions. — Grand Reception. — Our Saint's Attention to the Wants of

occasion of sin.— His privileged poor. — His charity to pilgrims and strangers — To members of his household. — Testimony of an eye-witness. Prisoners. — St. Misery. — Mario. — All misfortune appeals to the saint. Letters. — Indignation of the saint at the imprisonment of one of his servants. — The smuggler. — The Albanian soldiers.

retires from office. — De Leon's animosity. — His ironical prediction fulfilled. — "Time is a courteous gentleman." — Honor done to the missionaries. — Letters. — Circular. — Untimely death of two of the saint's persecutors. — The Baron of Ciorani ceases to afflict God's servants. Alphonsus victorious over all his enemies.

the Church till death." — The Pope's words absolute. — He reads the Life of St. Joseph Calasanza. — He will not allow his sons to appeal to the king. The respect and obedience he compels them to evince towards the Pope.

men of ninety. — Foreshadowing. — Interesting details. — The saint is visited by his absent children. — "By thy words thou shalt be justified." Visit of Count Joseph Liguori. — "Save your soul." — Parting benedictions. Brother Gerard. — Delicate attentions of the Neapolitan bishops. Universal grief for the hopeless condition of the saint. — Miracles.

PREFACE

The great bishop of St. Agatha appears wonderful even among the Saints of God, yet it would scarcely be possible to select a biography more instructive, and even interesting, to readers of every class and condition. A transcendent model for laymen, priests, religious and secular, superiors of communities, and rulers in the Church of God; a man who was a hero to his valet, of whom his own officials affirmed that "a hundred bishops would not do what he did alone;" of whom Clement XIV said, when refusing to accept his resignation of the mitre: "He can govern the diocese from his bed; his very shadow is sufficient to govern it;" a missionary through whom the Holy Ghost spoke so forcibly that some of his auditors actually died of the grief and contrition his burning words inspired; a Founder, whose sons still recall to our minds his lineaments, and, thanks to God, his virtues, his contagious simplicity, his ardent love for the Blessed Sacrament and the Blessed Mother; a contemplative who passed whole nights kneeling absorbed before his Love; an author who has enriched Catholic theology with over a hundred works, sufficient to earn for many a well-merited immortality; a scholar who has quoted in his writings nearly eight hundred Christian authors — Italian, Spanish, German, Irish, English, Scotch, African, and American; a preacher whose zeal never flagged, who was often known to preach several times a day; a confessor who was always the first to enter the confessional and the last to leave it; and, most wonderful of all, a man who, having lived over ninety years, "returned to his Creator, without a spot, the stole of innocence he had received in baptism.," as the acts of his canonization attest.

When we add his many foundations, missions given and repeated in almost every town and hamlet in the kingdom of Naples, innumerable souls guided in the higher paths of the spiritual life, conventual and educational establishments founded or reformed, we may well revert to the marvellous industry of the earlier monastic founders, which our saints alone have been able to rival in modern times, — to Columbanus, who ordained that his monks should go to rest so fatigued as to fall asleep on the way, and get up before they had slept enough; for, what was the whole life of our saint but an heroic and successful effort to keep religiously the appalling vow by which he bound himself *never to waste a moment of time.*

This work, undertaken through obedience, has been for us a labor of love and devotion. It is hoped that it will become, if we may so speak, a popular life of the great Doctor, the size and price of which will place it within the reach of the multitude. In its preparation, we have used "Tannoia's Memoirs," Cardinal Villecourt's "Vie et Institut de Saint Alphonse," "The Oratorian Life of Saint Alfonso," A Life of Saint Alphonso by a Redemptorist Father, Life of the Saint, by Rispoli, the rule, the letters, and other works of the Saint, most of which have not yet appeared in English.

We give, as an appropriate introduction, the admirable *Etude* entitled MERCY AND LOVE, published by Léon Gautier, in L'Univers, on the publication of Cardinal Villecourt's Life of our Saint, in 1863.

St. Alphonsus' Convent of Mercy, New Orleans,
Feast of St. Alphonsus, 1873.

INTRODUCTION

MERCY AND JOY

It is not without a special design that God places each of His saints on the theatre of this world at one epoch rather than another. In the Divine economy nothing is abandoned to chance. Wherever the Church approaches a crisis, and seems menaced with a defeat, God gives a saint to earth. And such a saint — in himself alone a magnificent gift of Providence — is invariably endowed by heaven with the graces peculiarly necessary at that precise moment for the healing of the world and the victory of the Church.

Against Arianism, God raised up an Athanasius, a Hilary of Poictiers; to counteract Roman decadence, God sent St. Benedict and his legions of toiling monks; to the hypocritical poverty of the Manichean Albigenses, God opposed the sincere and most magnificent poverty of Francis de Assisi; the verbosity of the heretics He neutralized by the eloquence of a Dominic and the science of a Thomas Aquinas; against the perpetual militia of Protestantism there came forth from the soil of Catholicism the standing armies of St. Ignatius and St. Vincent de Paul.

Finally, and to come to our subject, at a time when the Christian world was in danger of becoming Jansenist; when Mercy and Joy were banished as foreign from almost every country and every hearth; when confessors armed themselves with iron sternness against weak and shuddering sinners; when frequent communion began to be regarded as an impossibility, if not a crime;[1] when the heretics would have effaced from our Sacred books, whose every page they replenish and illuminate, the words *Gaudium et Laetitia*; at the critical period between the seventeenth century, which commenced universal secularization,

---

[1] Interesting details about Communion and joy

and the eighteenth, which was about to consummate it, God sent into this world a saint destined to take *Mercy* and *Joy* by the hand, and render them victorious in every Christian household; a saint who would rob confessors of the heavy armor which suppressed the beatings of their hearts and rendered their aims powerless to embrace sinners; a saint who was to make frequent communion the cherished practice of new Catholic generations; who would love, and cause others to love, the words *Joy* and *Gladness*, and would make Sweetness, Unity, and Love triumph for many ages, perhaps forever!

Who this saint is, our leaders have already conjectured. It is Saint Alphonsus Maria di Liguori, who was born September 27, 1696, and died August 1, 1787, aged ninety years, laden with virtues and resplendent with miracles.

We will now speak of Alphonsus as being in a peculiar manner the destroyer of Jansenism.

I.

St Alphonsus was gifted with a most ardent temperament, and expressed his thoughts with a happy vivacity. More than once he turned the fire of his eloquence against the Jansenist sectaries: "That meeting which took place at Bourg-Fontaine was less an assembly of men than of demons." And again: "What good have the French Jansenists effected by making God SEEM LIKE A TYRANT?"

These words show the fixed sentiments of our saint, and he was not among those who change their sentiments every day. But previous to refuting these heretics in his books, he had already refuted them by his acts. The most beautiful *Treatise against Jansenism* is the Life of St. Alphonsus!

Scarcely had he been admitted to Holy Orders, when the ruling passion of his life became manifest, with all its ardor, with all its enthusiasm — his passion for great sinners. He put himself in their way; he met them everywhere; he pursued the most wretched; he attracted them; he heard their confessions and absolved them. "He could not endure," says Cardinal Wiseman,[2] in his beautiful panegyric on our saint, "those confessors who received their penitents with a discouraging, supercilious air; or who, having heard them, sent them off disdainfully, as unworthy or incapable of the divine mercy. His whole life was a protest against proceedings of this nature, and towards the close of his career, he could use those magnificent words which are the confirmation of his glory, and which should be written in letters of diamond: 'I DO NOT REMEMBER THAT I EVER SENT AWAY A SINNER WITHOUT ABSOLUTION'."

In fact, the great honor of St Alphonsus is that he restored *Mercy* to its true place in the Church. God had been regarded as a sort of giant, harsh and terrible, before whom men trembled, pale, ghastly, devoured by fear. Our saint annihilated these unworthy representations — dangerous and stupid pictures, which distorted the lineaments of the true God. He has shown us what is really the divine aspect; he has pointed out Jesus weeping over sinners, and lovingly extending His arms towards them. The Jansenists suppressed the paternity of God. St Alphonsus is among those who have restored to Him His character of Father, that is to say, His goodness.

And when our saint took up his pen, his doctrine was not at variance with his practice. In his "Praxis Confessarii," the great bishop of St. Agatha lays it down that the confessor is at once a *father*, a *physician*, a *teacher*, and a *judge*. Well, the procrastinating Jansenists would not agree to all this. Here is a great sinner, who, with trembling knees and shame-stricken countenance, comes to make an agonizing confession of twenty or thirty years' infamy. "Will you," asks the saint, "terrify him, and turn him off from month to month, according to the present régime? No, no; it is a Jansenist doctrine thus to defer absolution." And with a countenance almost terrible, he adds: "It is not difficult, then, to say to your brother: 'Go off, you are damned; I cannot absolve you.' But if we consider the value of the Blood of Jesus Christ, we should hold such conduct in abhorrence!"

Thus speak the saints: those who have least need of mercy for themselves dispense it most freely to their brethren. True

---

[2] Cardinal Wiseman's birthday was the Feast of St. Alphonsus, to whom, as the Apostle of the Sacrament of Penance, and of the spirit of benignness to sinners, he had an especial devotion — Dr. Manning's Sermon, *Omnia pro Christo.*

physicians, they do not say to the sick, "Wait; in some days I may dress your bleeding wounds." True fathers, they do not say, "Wait; after some months, I shall open my arms to embrace my repenting son." True teachers, they do not refuse to give decisions, and leave poor souls to perish in the dark. True judges, they do not inflict on the accused a horrible suspense, broken by sobs and watered with tears. The Jansenists, in being very severe, imagined themselves very wise; but what did they do? What use to say to penitents, "Come back tomorrow." The penitents did *not* come back. They made humanity loathe pardon by selling it so dear; and peace, being so tardy in bestowing it. I know that some will object to us the *probabilism* of St. Alphonsus; they will affirm that he sinned by an excess contrary to that of the Jansenists; they were too severe, he was too lenient. The Saint, with an elevation of principle which is well known, a thousand and a thousand times proclaims that "it is always necessary to act with moral certitude." He contents himself with adding "of two probable opinions, one is not obliged to adopt the more rigid." Is this, then, laxity? Or do you prefer the Jansenist proposition: "Some commandments of God are impossible to man?" Morose, forbidding, and austere, the Jansenists pointed out the way of salvation, but they strewed it with difficulties almost insurmountable — angular stones, sharp blades, and burning coals; all these must be encountered.

"My brother," says a sweet voice, "begin by walking in the path before you; it is uneven, stony, rough, but you can tread it, and you will even find thereon some flowers which the goodness of God scatters, to cheer and console you. Later on, you may enter on more difficult ways, but you must not despair in the beginning. God is good!" Thus speaks Alphonsus, and man takes courage. "Always acting with moral certainty, but not always adopting the more rigorous sentiment," he has confidence in mercy, he experiences some joy, he looks hopefully toward God. And not only does he attain salvation, but often goes farther, and acquires perfection. This is the work of our Saint, of his writings, of his actions. Yet more, he has been the consoler of desolate humanity.

II.

It is well Alphonsus has triumphed. He has made the confessional a consolation; he has installed therein goodness instead of indignation; the Father, in a word. But his mission is far from being fulfilled. In our churches reigns a timid, or rather, affrighted silence; eyes are no longer lifted to the tabernacle; the Eucharistic Majesty is dreaded; once a year the faithful are admitted, after a protracted and austere preparation, to approach the terrible altar; once a year the banquet of the heavenly Father is spread before them; once a year they may receive their God. During the remainder of the year, they can only remember or expect Him. Mothers in tears cannot unite themselves to the Consoler of their sorrows; sinners cannot more frequently draw from the tabernacle the strength their weakness so often needs; the children cease to remember the Eucharist. On the door of the tabernacle, the icy finger of implacable Jansenism had written: "Love is not permitted to descend into the hearts of men oftener than once a year."

Arnauld's book, "Frequent Communion," has accomplished a mischief that can scarcely be undone. It has plunged Catholic souls into a lethargy — those souls that God created to be everlastingly awake. The very movements of our hearts are arrested by the chilling touch of Jansenism. Hearts must not beat, love must not appear — fear, terror, awe — these alone are authorized. Mercy no longer dwells on our altars; the terrible God enthroned on them is always ready to hurl his thunderbolts. Frightful doctrines, which Alphonsus alone was able to undermine.

This great man enters our churches; with energetic zeal he opens a passage to our altars; he ascends the steps; a finger is lovingly pointed toward the tabernacle, and a powerful voice cries out to all Christian people, "Come, come; Love suffers strangely from your absence; Love is left alone." Then they come. The beautiful books of the Saint have reassured all souls. And these are only echoes of the words of all the saints. Alphonsus is in perfect accord with St. Charles Borromeo and with St. Vincent de Paul; with Popes and with Councils; with Jesus Christ, above all. He has expanded, he has dilated souls. Our hearts are more vast since his day. A moment ago, we said that he had raised MERCY to its rightful position among men; the same he has done with LOVE.

Who can sum up the incomparable prayers, the effusions of love, the crimes prevented, the virtues acquired or preserved, through the influence of our Saint? He has augmented Communions by hundreds of thousands; by hundreds of thousands then must we count up the wonders of purity, innocence, and virtue, which he has really produced in the world of souls.

III.

There are certain men who, in closing their eyes on the sun of this world can bear themselves this magnificent testimony: "I have always loved what is great." Well, on the bed of death every Jansenist might have said: "I have always loved what is little." I cannot imagine a Jansenist having an elevated thought. We have seen them dry up the sources of Mercy and Love; nor did their harshness stop here, they must dry up the very sources of salvation. Their hideous doctrine of grace drove *Love* not only from earth, but even from heaven; so that poor, stolid humanity with tearful eye and riven soul, knew not where to find it. "Jesus Christ did not die for *all* men," said the Jansenist murderers of Love; God wills to save only the predestined, and these are necessitated to do right, since man cannot resist interior grace.

Here my heart rebels, my anger is enkindled. Such were the doctrines proposed to the Christians of the seventeenth and eighteenth centuries! And we are astonished that they became disgusted with such odious principles! We are astonished that humanity, to whom the smile of Mercy, the smile of Love, the smile of Hope, were interdicted, became Jansenist or revolutionary! I am no longer amazed at the excesses of the National Assembly, since I see so many Jansenists on its benches. Still less am I surprised at the excesses of the Revolution, since among its terrible actors figure so many ancient Jansenists. These men had hearts of steel! their actions were eloquent of the fatalism and despair of their doctrines!

Well, whom does God send to restore to men the hope of an easier and more universal salvation? Who will become the consoler of wretched humanity, and open anew the beautiful paths to beatitude? It is still St. Alphonsus. He begins by laying down the principle that "God wills with a true and sincere will, that all should be saved, and none lost — that Jesus Christ died for all men." Then, in his memorable book entitled "The Great Means of

Prayer," he establishes incontestably that, *"God, willing the salvation of all men, has given to each the graces necessary to attain it.* If He fail to give the efficacious grace, He at least gives the *sufficient grace* of being able actually to pray. And by prayer, *every one can obtain the efficacious grace to fulfil the law, and work out his salvation."*

The most culpable of the damned, had he wished to profit by the grace of prayer common to all, would have obtained by prayer the requisite grace, and *would have been saved.*

Ah! at last I breathe freely. No longer is hope deadened within me. I see heaven peopled; I see the ways of salvation frequented; I see that God is good. I can throw myself on my knees; God is not inexorable. Away with these odious Jansenist crucifixes, whose arms are so contracted; I must have wide arms, immense arms, capable of enclosing all the sinners in the world. Give me the Jesus Christ of St. Alphonsus, not him of Arnauld and Saint-Cyran.

IV.

A phenomenon which has always seemed strangely surprising to me is, that all revolutionists have been passionately attached to the Jansenists, and passionately beloved by them. It is nevertheless certain that the Jansenists were the most intolerant, morose, and illiberal of sectaries. It is equally true that we, Catholics, defended against them all human liberties, and at the same time, the cause of Mercy, Love, and Hope. But the Jansenists were rebels; that suffices for our adversaries. And above all, they were enemies of the Holy See; that explains everything. It cannot now be a matter of surprise to see among our opponents Michelet and Nicole, the *Siècle* and the *Provinciales*, the Socialists even, with Saint-Cyran and Arnauld. All rebellions are connected, and are true to each other.

Not satisfied with effacing from the world all ideas of love, goodness, and hope, the Jansenists wished also to blot out the idea of unity. They were the most ardent and the most dangerous of Gallicans. This fact is so notorious that it is unnecessary to demonstrate it. We may add that the Jansenists managed their revolt well. Yes, during two centuries a school existed in the bosom of the Church which affirmed that "a Council is above the Pope," in other words, that members are superior to their head, and can assume its peculiar functions. Yes, during two centuries certain theologians used their best efforts to annihilate the idea of Infallibility, an idea which is the grandest honor of the human race; for, as the good Bishop of Lille recently said: "Man is so great that he must have for his guidance on earth a perpetual Infallibility; and each of our little ones has a right to say to his master: 'Do not deceive me; be infallible'." For two centuries has been exhibited the strange spectacle of a crowd kneeling before the Roman See, and crying out to the sovereign Pontiff: "We see in you the Vicar of Jesus Christ, but a most fallible Vicar — perpetually fallible, necessarily fallible." Yet the Jansenists dared to assert that they preserved Catholic Unity. Yes, after the fashion of a branch which, though lopped off, still holds on to the tree by some vegetative fibres, receiving just enough of sap to save it from immediate death, and which droops mournfully with its withered leaves, from a tree, always green, always beautiful, always living.

The idea of Infallibility, the idea of Unity, had all but disappeared from the earth when St. Alphonsus came. It has been remarked that he was by excellence the Saint of Infallibility; it may be said with as much reason or more, that he was also the Saint of Unity. "The Declaration of the French clergy In 1680 was a thorn that pierced his heart." But do not some maintain in these days that Gallicanism was the distinctive sign, the essential adornment, of all great minds, and that we have nothing to oppose to their celebrity? What? Is not St. Alphonsus, in a literary point of view, equal to the most celebrated Jansenists, the most illustrious Gallicans? Listen! His sweet voice is changed into thunder when he vindicates the rights of the Pope. He styles him the Prince, the King of Theology, *Theologiae Princeps*; the Governor, the Moderator of the whole Church, *Ecclesiae Moderator*; the Preserver, the Supreme Defender of divine truth among men, *Divinae veritatis conservator et vindex*; the Sovereign Judge of all doctrinal controversy, *Unus controversarium Judex*, the Universal Doctor, and Infallible Interpreter of the divine will.

And since the days of Alphonsus — thanks to him — these epithets are as "household words" on the lips of Catholics. He has trampled on Gallicanism as on Jansenism; he has been doubly triumphant. And to come to the natural result of what has been said, he has restored Unity to the world, having previously restored to it Mercy, Love, and Hope.

V.

His task was not yet completed. A joy was still wanting to the Christian world; the Blessed Virgin had too poor a place in liturgical invocations, in prayers, in the heart. The Jansenists professed a peculiar horror of the Immaculate Conception; they obstinately insisted that some stains had sullied the whiteness of this mystic swan. Mary, being thus almost entirely riven from the devotion of humanity, Joy disappeared, for, as our liturgy says, the Virgin announces Joy to the whole universe: *Gaudium annunciavit universo mundo.* St. Alphonsus perceived this danger as he had perceived all the others, and he undertook to restore to the Mother of God the glories of which Jansenist hands had robbed her. God worked with him, and glorious miracles gave his doctrine a supernatural consecration. In presence of thousands of spectators, Our Lady more than once appeared to vindicate her own cause. And Alphonsus was encouraged to proclaim boldly and distinctly the Immaculate Conception of the Co-Redemptrix of the human race; to cry out always and everywhere that "all graces come through the hands of Mary." Now let us open our eyes and ears. What language do all Christians now hold of the Blessed Virgin but the language of St. Alphonsus? Has not the dogma of her Immaculate Conception, so dear to him, been solemnly defined? Have not his works on the Mother of God become standard? Verily, our Saint triumphs.

Even in the bosom of the family, the Jansenists had acquired an influence truly deplorable. They drove out Joy. We know what Jansenist education meant. The little children were sternly treated. They must not jest or laugh too loud, or show their pretty little teeth in smiles. They were forced to submit to sacrifices which, to be meritorious must be voluntary and free. Their parents rarely mingled with them, *e loninquo auctoritas.* Their home was gloomy. The feasts of Our Lady and the Saints were diminished in number. The little ones were taught to enter a church in fear and trembling – *pavete ad sanctuarium meum;* their sweet little eyes must not presume to wander toward the tabernacle. Such an education, I tell you, was cold, dismal, and desolate.

The doctrine of St. Alphonsus has yet to triumph in the family, where a contrary system has replaced the Turkish regime of the Jansenists. Today we are in the opposite extreme; we make our children our companions; the Jansenists wished us to make them our slaves. Between these, extremes is true Christian education, grave but cheerful, austere but joyous, paternal and maternal — peals of laughter mingled with noble teachings, plays with lessons. St. Alphonsus has not yet wholly triumphed over the false austerity, the gloom of the Jansenists. But he who has brought back among us Love, Hope, and Goodness, will assuredly restore to us Joy. Melancholy was regarded in the Middle Ages as the eighth capital sin; Joy is a great virtue, and the Church incessantly says to us: *Rejoice, again I say to you, rejoice. Gaudete, iterum gaudete!*

LEON GAUTIER.

Chapter I.

THE LIFE of St. Alphonsus Mary di Liguori is a mirror of every virtue; well known and deeply meditated, it cannot fail to inspire a holy ambition to walk in his footsteps. He was exemplary in the world; as a priest, he has become the great model of evangelical workmen. Founder of a congregation of missionary priests, he perpetuates in his children his piety and zeal for souls. As a bishop, he proved himself worthy of companionship with the apostles; as the author of numerous works, inspired by his faith, his charity, his devotion to the Church, *being dead, he yet speaketh* to the incredulous who run blindly to perdition, to heretics who despise their true mother, to moralists tempted to the extremes of laxity or rigorism: in short, his writings have won him a place among the Doctors of the Church.

It were superfluous to enlarge on the antiquity and nobility of the family of our saint, a family whose origin is anterior to the Neapolitan monarchy; this would be absurdly out of place in the biography of one who so thoroughly despised mere worldly grandeur.

Happily, his family was ennobled by virtue as well as by rank. His father, Count Joseph di Liguori, of the Royal Neapolitan Marine, was remarkable for his sincere piety. When at home, he frequented the churches, and at regular intervals approached the sacraments; while at sea, he decorated his berth with so many pious emblems and pictures that it seemed like the cell of a religious. He would not allow an unseemly expression to be uttered in his presence, and he never submitted himself to that false code of honor by which so many noblemen of his age were unhappily governed. He was specially devoted to the passion of Christ.

The mother of Alphonsus was the Lady Anne Catherine Cavalieri, a matron of extraordinary merit and virtue, who loved prayer, was devoted to the poor, and excelled in every quality esteemed in a truly Christian wife and mother. Penances and mortifications were her delight; she was never to be seen at the theatre; worldly society was burdensome to her; secluded in her palace, she occupied herself chiefly with God, her soul, and the Christian education of her children. Such were the parents of the holy Doctor whose life we write. God willed to consecrate to himself in a peculiar manner the first of their holy union.

Alphonsus was born on September 27, 1696, the feast of the glorious martyrs, Cosmas and Damian, at seven o'clock in the morning, at Marianella, the country house of his family. He was baptized in the parochial church of St. Mary at Naples, September 29, under the auspices of St. Michael; and the names, Alphonsus, Mary, Antony, John, Francis, Cosmas, Damian, Michael, Gaspard, were given him in memory of the most illustrious of his ancestors, and to honor the saints on whose respective days he was born and baptized.

From the moment of his birth, he was placed under the special protection of the Blessed Virgin, that she might adopt him as her son, and be to him in all his necessities an advocate and a mother; hence he was always called Alphonsus Mary.

Three other sons, and three daughters, were born to Count Joseph Liguori: Benedict, who became a Benedictine, and honored the religious habit by a holy and mortified life; Cajetan, who chose the sacerdotal state, and lived like a hermit in his father's house; Hercules, who embraced the married state; Mary Louisa and Marianne, who became nuns; and Teresa, who espoused the Duke of Presenzano and led a saintly life in the world.

The birth of Alphonsus filled the hearts of his parents with the most lively gratitude to God. In testimony of this, they resolved to watch so carefully over their precious child that he should never lose the divine grace which had regenerated him.

Even in infancy, this predestined babe seemed endowed with the germs of those rare qualities which afterwards attracted the admiration and secured the reverence of all who knew him. When the countess presented her fair child to St. Francis Jerome, who happened to visit her, for his benediction, the saint, looking with loving eyes on the little Alphonsus, blessed him, and, illumined with the spirit of prophecy, exclaimed: "This little one will not die before his ninetieth year; he will be a bishop and do great things for Jesus Christ." The happy mother, struck by this prophecy, received her child from the arms of the saintly Jesuit, as a special gift from heaven; a child who would increase in wisdom and grace as in age, and one day become a powerful agent in the hands of God, to promote his glory by procuring the salvation of innumerable souls.

It is a singular coincidence, that the prophet and the subject of the prophecy were canonized on the same day, May 26, 1839, by Pope Gregory XVI; upon which auspicious occasion St. John Joseph of the Cross, St. Pacificus, and St. Veronica Juliana were also raised upon the altars of the Church.

CHAPTER II.

THE MOTHER of our saint cheerfully assumed the charge of her son's education, a burden rendered light indeed by her love for her precious first-born, and the ardor with which he advanced in virtue, far beyond her most sanguine expectations. Every morning she gave him her maternal benediction, and then heard him recite his prayers; every evening she instructed him, as far as his childish capacity would admit, in the sublime truths of our holy faith. When other children were born to her, she adopted a similar course with them, and it was delightful to see her surrounded morning and evening by those fair olive branches which the Divine Husbandman had given her to prune and nurture for his heavenly vineyard.

The seeds of virtue cast into the young heart of Alphonsus, did not fall on sterile ground; piety seemed, as it were, natural to him. The ordinary amusements of childhood pleased him not; but he loved to decorate little altars, to celebrate in his own fashion the ever-recurring festivals of the saints, and to imitate the beautiful ceremonies of the Church. Already he began to taste those celestial joys which are the portion only of souls far advanced in the ways of God. As soon as he was old enough, his mother prepared him for his first confession, and placed him under the spiritual direction of Father Thomas Pagano, an Oratorian of the church of St. Jerome, her own director, and a relation of her family.

Father Tannoia, who has left us such copious memoirs of the blessed founder, and several of the earlier members of the Congregation of the Most Holy Redeemer, was well acquainted with the noble and pious lady who formed the plastic heart of Alphonsus to every virtue. He loved to compare the Countess Liguori to that royal mother who directed the religious education of St. Louis, and planted in his infant mind the germs of every kingly and Christian virtue. As Queen Blanche desired that her dear Louis should be all for God, so the mother of Alphonsus had no desire in connection with her children but that they should become saints.

This was the great object of her zeal; and hence she inspired them with a tender love for Jesus, and a filial confidence in Mary. All her children eagerly responded to her pious care. Indeed five of the seven consecrated themselves to God in the ecclesiastical or religious state; but in this holy family Alphonsus was ever preeminently distinguished. As a boy, he closely imitated the piety of his mother, accomplishing with delight all the acts of devotion he saw her perform. His obedience was so prompt and perfect, that at the least sign from his parents he instantly executed whatever they desired.

The life-long zeal of our saint to instruct the faithful in the fundamental truths of religion, and to kindle in all hearts the love of Jesus and Mary, undoubtedly originated in the instructions of his excellent mother, who will assuredly be eternally recompensed in heaven for all the good her son will have produced in souls.

During the childhood of Alphonsus, the Oratorians of St. Jerome established at Naples a pious congregation to promote the spiritual welfare of the young nobility. Alphonsus was scarcely nine years old when his parents placed him under their care. The good Fathers soon recognized in their precocious pupil those rare virtues which excite the admiration of the good. Every Sunday he was among the earliest arrivals, and was so docile, so recollected during the spiritual exercises of the congregation, so eager to hear instructions and profit by them, that he was an example of fervor to the other young noblemen, and a source of comfort and edification to his superiors.

Every week he confessed to Father Pagano, and it was from his hands that this child of predilection received his first communion. It was an edifying sight to see him on his knees hearing mass with singular devotion; and whenever he approached the holy table, his fervor and piety, his diligent preparation and prolonged thanksgiving, excited a holy emulation in the breasts of his companions.

The solicitude of his good mother continually increased; she formed his heart to prayer, and instructed him in all the duties of a Christian nobleman. She inspired in his soul a horror of sin, even the slightest, because it offends our dearest Lord. Her language made the deepest impression on his young heart, and this zealous mother was delighted to find in her gifted son a rectitude of judgment and a docility of heart, which rendered all her instructions efficacious. Every one admired his constancy in his devotional exercises; when the time came for performing them with his mother, he was always ready to join her; nor was he less punctual with regard to the pious practices he imposed upon himself.

That he had already attained to sublime prayer even at the age of twelve, the following remarkable occurrence will show: — The Fathers were accustomed to take the young members of their congregation, every Sunday after Vespers, to some country house for recreation. On one of these occasions, while amusing themselves at the villa of the Prince de la Riccia, one of the boys suggested a play called "the game of oranges," and Alphonsus was invited to join. For a while, he excused himself on the plea of not understanding the game, but he was at length prevailed on to yield to their entreaties.

Fortune favored the young tyro to such an extent that he won thirty times in succession. His success excited the jealousy of his companions; and one of the oldest among them, the boy who had insisted the most on his joining in the play, exclaimed in a rage: "What! so you did not know the game!" adding in his anger an expression that was more than impolite. Alphonsus blushed when he heard it, and turning towards the other boys, exclaimed with severity: "How is this? Shall God be offended in this fashion for a few miserable cents?" Then throwing down contemptuously the coins he had won, he said: "Take back your money!" and immediately left his companions, his countenance still glowing with a holy indignation.

Ashamed and confused, the boys gazed on him as he retired to a distant part of the garden, but presently resumed their game which they continued till the fall of evening. When it was time to return to the city, they called him and sought him, but no trace of him was discovered. After a long and weary search, they finally caught a glimpse of him, kneeling behind a laurel tree. Coming closer, they found that he had suspended from one of the branches the picture of Our Blessed Lady, which he always carried about him. He was so absorbed and ravished in God, that he neither heard nor saw his companions for a considerable time. When the boy who had offended him, and who was really anxious to excuse himself, perceived the rapt and glowing countenance of his holy playmate, he exclaimed: "Alas! what have I done? I have maltreated a saint!"

Indeed Alphonsus was regarded in this light by all who knew him. One day when some one spoke of his virtues in presence of his friend Antony Villani, the latter tearfully exclaimed: "Ah, you little know the holiness of that great servant of God, who has been a saint from infancy!" Then, recovering from his emotion, he related the above incident, of which he had been an eye-witness.

CHAPTER III.

Studies of Alphonsus. — His musical and poetical talents. — Painting and architecture. — Evidences of his general knowledge of liberal arts and sciences. His success in jurisprudence. — He receives the degree of doctor. — His exploits at the chase, and fowling. — Lost time. — Increasing solicitude of his mother. — His love and gratitude towards her.

THE TALENTS and virtues of Alphonsus were a source of delight to all his friends, but chiefly to his parents. His father, proud of his rare capacity for acquiring knowledge, was determined to procure him the best possible education, that he might become a proficient in all the learning and accomplishments suitable to his rank and expectations. But partly through affection for his son, and partly to shield his innocence from the dangers to which it might be exposed in the public colleges, the Count resolved that the education of Alphonsus should be conducted under the eyes of his parents.

Accordingly, he engaged for him the most distinguished masters, men eminent in scholarship, and of irreproachable morals, that his boy's progress in virtue might not be retarded by his progress in learning. His quick and tenacious memory, his ripe judgment and extraordinary docility, rendered the office of his instructors a pleasure rather than a task. He soon attained considerable proficiency in the Greek, Latin, and French languages, and commenced the study of canon and civil law.

But his parents, desiring that he should become an accomplished gentleman as well as an able man of letters, procured him instructions in drawing, painting, and architecture, and in these arts he succeeded so admirably that, even in his old age, he executed pictures of Jesus Crucified and Our Lady with remarkable skill, and often designed and sketched the devotional emblems he was so fond of distributing among the faithful. He usually made the plans for the houses of his congregation, and when he had not sufficient leisure for this, he required the architects to submit their sketches to his criticism.

Specimens of our saint's skill in painting may still be seen in some of the older houses of his congregation. At Ciorani is a representation of the corpse of Alexander the Great, preyed upon by hideous vermin; the whole showing, more eloquently than any words, the utter vanity of all human greatness. In the refectory of Illiceto is an immense skeleton, painted by the hand of the artist-saint, with the usual doleful surroundings; and in the church of the same house hangs an ancient portrait of Our Lady which he entirely renovated. The beautiful landscapes and figures in oils that adorn the draperies of the grand altar, representing Jesus adored by the shepherds, give still more conclusive evidence of his artistic ability.

But the accomplishment in which his father was most desirous Alphonsus should excel was music. For three hours a day, the boy was obliged to practise under the eye of an able master, and the count was so passionately fond of music, that he generally assisted at the lesson himself; if business required his presence elsewhere, he would lock the door on teacher and pupil that it might not be abridged. The result of this severe discipline of the extraordinary musical talent of the youth was that he touched the harpsichord with the hand of a proficient before he had attained his twelfth year. He was equally successful in Latin and Italian poetry; and was accustomed even in old age to compose the beautiful hymns by which he sought to reanimate the devotion of the people, and set them to music.

In mature age, he often bewailed as lost the time he had devoted in youth to the study of music. "Fool that I was," he one day exclaimed, looking at his harpsichord, "to have wasted so much time on that! but my father would have me perfect myself in music, and I was obliged to obey him." His poetical genius would probably have taken a higher flight, had not his aim been rather to foster popular piety than to gratify the cultivated tastes of the few; yet many of his canticles are of rare and touching beauty, and give incontestable evidence of a high order of talent.

The numerous theological and metaphysical works published by Alphonsus furnished abundant proof that he was fully up to the age in philosophy, mathematics, and all the liberal arts and sciences. An astronomical instrument may still be seen at Illiceto, which shows that our saint possessed no mean amount of mechanical expertness. When head of a congregation, he himself gave the young clerics lessons in geography, cosmography, and kindred sciences, and it was to illustrate some scientific lecture that Alphonsus designed the ingeniously constructed instrument to which we have alluded.

His father, ambitious of seeing his precocious son raised to the higher offices of the state, made him apply diligently to the study of civil and canon law. This Alphonsus did with such success, that he received the doctor's gown in 1713, by virtue of a dispensation of three years and nine months, he being then little over sixteen years. He was still quite boyish in appearance and of low stature; consequently, the admiration his abilities excited did not hinder people from smiling as they noticed his doctoral gown trailing on the ground when he went to the courts. In after life, Alphonsus himself sometimes jested at the ludicrous appearance he made when a legal practitioner of sixteen: "My long cassock," said he, "perpetually twisting itself about my feet, provoked the laughter of every one I met in the streets."

Despite his youth, however, his success before the Neapolitan tribunals was prodigious. His father still kept him under the tuition of the ablest advocates and jurisconsults then practising in Naples, among whom were the celebrated lawyers, Perani and Jovene. Under these masters, he became so absorbed in his legal studies that he soon began to deny himself all kinds of amusements. He associated only with the pious and learned president, Dominic Caravita, whose house was a sort of academy for the most studious among the younger members of the bar.

Previous to this, however, he had indulged a little in the games then usual in good society, in which his mind found some recreation; and his father, who allowed him relaxation very sparingly, did not object to his spending an hour every evening at the house of his friend, Charles Cito, at which a few of the most virtuous and studious of the young nobility occasionally met, to enjoy a game of terzillio or ombre. Several times, however, he displeased his father by prolonging his visit; and on one of these occasions the count, wishing to punish his tardiness, removed from his table all books of study, substituting for them packs of cards. Awaiting his son's return, he greeted him thus: "Behold your studies; these are the authors that have made you so punctual in returning at the appointed hour to your home."

Alphonsus felt this mortification most keenly, but it had the desired effect. Henceforth he strove more earnestly than ever to obey his father's injunctions. In old age he mentioned, that, as a youth, he had been very fond of hunting and fowling, though he never indulged in these pastimes but on days on which he was excused from study. "The birds that had to do with me were fortunate," he added, "for, despite all my efforts, I rarely hurt one." Then seeming to regret a passing allusion to what he regarded as the follies of his youth, he would immediately pass from the subject of snaring birds to that of hunting for souls, remarking how dear to God, and becoming to apostolic men, is this burning zeal for souls.

His parents, especially his mother, kept anxious and unceasing vigilance over the morals and religious training of this wonderful youth. Dancing and fencing were not among his accomplishments, because they were considered dangerous to his soul.

Although Alphonsus always testified love, reverence, and gratitude to both these pious parents, his heart was particularly touched by the unwearied devotedness of his excellent mother. Even in extreme old age he blessed God because of her, and was wont to say: "If there was any thing good in me as a child, if I kept clear of wickedness, I owe it entirely to my mother." His father, being frequently absent on his naval excursions, was unable to give to the education of his children the constant surveillance which so grave a duty merited; hence it necessarily devolved entirely on his mother, a fitting instrument, in the divine hands, since she reared for the Church a family of saints.[1] "At the death of my father," said Alphonsus, on one occasion, "I refused myself the consolation of going to Naples to assist him; but when my mother is dying, if it be at all possible I shall watch over her last moments."

---

[1] Mother raised them, taught them, mostly herself as the father was often away. "raised a family of saints"

CHAPTER IV.

ALPHONSUS applied himself to the practice of law with so much success, that before he had attained his twentieth year his clients were numerous and often distinguished, and his merit had won him an honorable place among the leading advocates of the kingdom. His father had at that time friends and relatives among the principal senators, who, recognizing the superior ability of their young kinsman, promoted his advancement in every way which their friendship suggested. Nor was the young lawyer himself indifferent to public esteem. On the contrary, he knew so well how to attract it that, in a short time, the most important causes were confided to him. And his success was not undeserved; for if his talents and industry gained him universal admiration, his probity and disinterestedness made him universally respected. It is worthy of remark, that he gained all the causes entrusted to him from 1715 to 1723.

The following are the rules by which our young lawyer governed himself:

1. Never to accept an unjust suit.
2. To defend clients by lawful means only.
3. Not to burden them with unnecessary expenses.
4. To defend their causes with as much care as he would his own.

5. To study the details of a process diligently, that he might strike out the best line of defence.
6. To suffer no fault of his to retard the cause of his client, which would be contrary to justice.
7. To implore the assistance of God in order to succeed; He being the first protector of justice.
8. Not to load himself with causes which surpassed his talent and strength; nor to accept of any, of which he foresaw he would not have sufficient leisure to prepare the defence.
9. Justice and honesty should be the characteristics of a lawyer, which he must preserve as the apple of his eye.
10. A lawyer who loses his cause through negligence is obliged to make restitution for the losses of his client.
11. In the defence of a cause, it is necessary to be respectful, and to ground one's pleading, not on chicanery, but on sound logic.
12. Diligence, truth, fidelity, and justice are the qualities necessary in a lawyer.

Guided by such principles, it is not surprising that he gained so great an ascendency over all hearts, that his very adversaries often ranged themselves on his side, and that innumerable clients confided their interests to his care.

But if Alphonsus desired a brilliant career at the bar, he was not less anxious to render himself dear to God by increasing daily in virtue. Two years after receiving the gown, he passed from the congregation of young nobles to that of doctors, also directed by the Fathers of the Oratory. These good priests did not omit any thing calculated to promote the spiritual advancement of their pupils. Alphonsus responded to their pious care with ever-increasing ardor. He frequented the sacraments, visited the sick in the hospitals, practised prayer and mortification, and would never enter the courts till he had heard mass and finished his morning devotions. His confessor, Father Pagano, he regarded as a second Guardian Angel. To him he exposed his doubts and fears, and was always strictly obedient to his counsels. About this time, he with other brethren undertook to serve the sick in the hospital of Incurables; and a nobleman of Vitri, named de Senlis, has recorded that he remembered our saint making up the beds, though encumbered with his lawyer's gown, and feeding the patients with the greatest charity and compassion.

Every year Alphonsus, at the suggestion of his father, used to make a retreat of eight days, either in the house of the Fathers of the Mission, or that of the Jesuits. A retreat, conducted by Father Buglione, S. J., greatly affected him. "I was only eighteen at that time," said he, some years later; "but the sanctity of the preacher, the admirable order of the exercises, and the precious advantages I derived from them, remain indelibly engraved on my soul."

From this period, he began to entertain a special love for the virtue of holy purity. His modesty was, literally, known to all, and a word or gesture expressive of the slightest impropriety never escaped him, even when his father made him mingle in the gayest society. He composed himself to sleep, holding a wooden cross in his hands, a practice he continued to the end of his life. He continued always tenderly attached to the Congregation of St. Philip Neri, and, even during his episcopate, never failed to visit his ancient brethren whenever business brought him to Naples.

The edification resulting from such a pious life, will be fully known only in heaven; but we will cite one instance of it in these pages. His father, as captain of the galleys, had several Moorish slaves in his service, one of whom he selected to wait upon Alphonsus. He was not slow in manifesting an inclination to become a Christian, and when asked what had made him think of this, he replied: "The example of my young master. That religion cannot be false, which makes him lead so pure and holy a life."

Father Mastrilla of the Oratory commenced to instruct him gradually, but he soon became very ill. One night he eagerly requested to be baptized, saying: "I have seen Our Lady, St Joseph, and St. Joachim, and they told me I must be baptized now, because they want me in Paradise." The priest objected, that his illness was not dangerous, and that he was not sufficiently instructed. "Question me, Father, and you shall see," said he; and he answered correctly every question proposed to him. He was then baptized, and the priest having told him to rest a little, he said: "This is not my place of repose, for I must go immediately to heaven." The spectators smiled at this, but in a little while the poor slave, his countenance radiant with joy, surrendered his purified soul to his Creator.

CHAPTER V.

Matrimonial projects. — Teresina Liguori. — Birth of her Brother and consequent alteration in her prospects. — Negotiations abandoned and renewed. — Indignation of the young princess. — She enters a convent. Alphonsus becomes her biographer. — Indiscretion of our saint on one occasion. — Anger of his father. — Humility of the son. — Cooling of his fervor. — Testimony of Charles Cito. — Retreat. — Terrible incident. Effect on Alphonsus. — His devotion to the Blessed Sacrament. — His zeal for decorating altars. — His gratitude to his friend, the Duke of Casabona, and to the Fathers of the Mission. — Interesting letter.

ALPHONSUS was now almost twenty; and as he continued to make progress in every respect, his friends expected that with such powerful interest at court and such distinguished talents, he would speedily attain to the highest dignity in the magistracy. His expectations were known to be so great, his morals so irreproachable, and his manners and appearance so elegant, that the first families in Naples, having marriageable daughters, were desirous that he should form a matrimonial alliance with one of them.

The choice of his father fell on the beautiful and accomplished princess, Teresina Liguori, a distant relation, only child and heiress of Francis Liguori, Prince of Presiccio, then in her thirteenth year. The parents of the young lady esteemed Alphonsus so highly that the affair was considered as settled, though the nuptials were not to be celebrated until the bride-elect should have attained a more mature age. The parties, most deeply concerned, seem to have had no share in these arrangements.

Meanwhile, the Princess of Presiccio gave birth to a son, an incident which immediately changed the designs of the count, who no longer considered Teresina an advantageous match for his heir. But the infant, who had so inopportunely ruptured the plans of the worldly-wise father, dying in a few months, matrimonial negotiations were again renewed by the family of the proposed bridegroom, and favorably received by the prince and princess; who, though pained by the late desertion, were willing to overlook an insult, which, however, their daughter bitterly resented. With a firmness rare in Italian girls under similar circumstances, Teresina obstinately refused to listen to these renewed proposals. "No, no," said she with spirit; "when my brother was alive, I was not considered a suitable match for Alphonsus di Liguori. It is my fortune that is sought, not myself. I know enough of the world now, and I will have no more to do with it. I desire only Jesus Christ for my spouse."

The young princess kept her word. She took the veil in the convent of the most Holy Sacrament, at the age of sixteen, and died five years later, full of merits and good works, October 30, 1724. Alphonsus, at the request of her religious sisters, wrote the edifying life of her whom parental ambition had destined for his bride.

The rupture between Alphonsus and Teresina must be regarded as providential. Both, reserved by God to adorn higher paths than even the pride of their illustrious kinsfolks could covet for them, lived to attain eminent sanctity. It is probable that the example of Teresina had a powerful influence on Alphonsus. Certain it is, that her truly angelic life, and the odor of sanctity diffused by her early death, made an indelible impression on the mind of our saint, as is evident from the concise but beautiful biography he wrote thirty seven years later (1761) of his virtuous cousin, Sister Teresa Mary di Liguori; in which, however, the saint makes no mention of the relations in which the lawyer of twenty and the princess of thirteen once stood to each other by the mutual consent of their respective parents.

The following circumstance, which occurred about the time Teresina took the veil (1719), shows the docility of Alphonsus, and the submission his father continued to exact of him. One evening, the count having given a party, it happened that one of the servants, whose office it was to light the guests from the palace to their carriages, behaved with the most unaccountable stupidity, which so displeased the host that he could not cease reproaching him. Alphonsus, feeling pained for the poor servant, whose fault was quite involuntary, said: "What a noise you make about a trifle, father! once you begin to scold, you can never stop."

This indiscreet speech so displeased the angry nobleman, that he immediately replied by giving his son a blow on the face.

Humbled and confused, Alphonsus withdrew in silence to his room. As he did not appear at supper, his mother went to call him. She found him at the foot of his crucifix, weeping bitterly for the disrespect he had shown his father. Having earnestly besought her to intercede for him, he accompanied her back, and, kneeling, implored the count to forgive him. This he readily did, more affected by his son's humble repentance than he had been wounded by his late indiscretion. What reverence towards a father on the part of a son who was already eminent among the most distinguished lawyers of Naples!

Alphonsus confessed in his old age that at this epoch of his life his piety grew cold; he would omit his spiritual exercises on the slightest pretexts, and was in imminent danger of losing his soul. This decay of fervor is easily accounted for by the fact that his father compelled him to comply with all the requirements society seemed to authorize: besides being flattered and carressed in every direction, the compliments showered upon the elegant and successful barrister, were more than enough to turn the head of an ordinary individual. "I should have been lost," said he, "had all this continued much longer."

Yet it is possible that he spoke with an excusable exaggeration of his remissness at this period, for several who directed his conscience are of opinion that he never offended God grievously, though not always shielded from the occasions of sin. Indeed, he himself made the following acknowledgment: "I frequented the theatre, but, God be thanked, I never committed even a venial sin there, for the music absorbed all my attention, and was my sole attraction."

Even at this time, every one regarded him as a young man of irreproachable conduct; and his intimate friend, Charles Cito, being asked later on if he had ever perceived any levity of manners in Alphonsus, replied, bowing his head respectfully: "No; he was always most virtuous: I should blaspheme, if I spoke otherwise."

What is certain, however, is that his ardor had cooled to so great a degree that his most intimate friend, Francis, Duke of Casabona, beginning to be alarmed at his negligence, and desirous of reviving his own fervor, proposed that Alphonsus should join him in a retreat of eight days, to be given early in the Lent of 1722, at the house of the Lazarist Fathers. To this he cheerfully assented, and the retreat was conducted by the Superior, Father Vincent Cutica, so justly celebrated for his piety. When this man of God spoke of holy things, it was from the abundance of the heart. He made his auditors weigh well the shortness of time and the length of eternity; and painted striking pictures of the hideousness of vice and the ravishing beauty of virtue.

These exercises were productive of immense spiritual profit to all who made them, but particularly to Alphonsus. Faithful to grace which knocked at the door of his heart, he exclaimed: "The world which covets my heart has nothing solid to offer; nothing capable of satiating the yearnings of an immortal spirit: whereas, by sitting at the table of the Lamb, I can fully satiate the hunger and thirst which devour me."

With these salutary meditations, the divine light penetrated his soul, and immediately the seeds of piety began to germinate, despite the thorns of passion which had wellnigh choked them. He now bitterly deplored the moments he had sacrificed to dissipation, and solemnly resolved to renounce the follies which had lately occupied him. "Believe me," wrote he, many years after, "all is foolishness, – festivals, comedies, company, games: these are the joys of the world, but joys full of gall and bitterness. I have made the experiment and bitterly lament it." Thus did this great saint bewail his youthful wanderings, and, like the royal model of all true penitents, keep his sin continually before him.

What contributed to impress the pious youth still more deeply, was an account given by the preacher of an event that had recently occurred in Florence, during a retreat given by the fathers of St. Vincent de Paul. A gentleman who had been leading a scandalous life was suddenly converted; and, as the partner of his guilt had just died, he knelt to implore the divine mercy for her miserable soul. At the same moment she appeared to him, and said: "Pray not for me; I am damned." To convince him that it was no mere phantom of his imagination, she laid her hands on the table before which he knelt in prayer, and the parts which she touched were burned.

This table, which had been brought from Florence to Naples, was exhibited by Father Cutica to his audience in his sermon on hell; and so deeply moved was Alphonsus, that he instantly resolved to renounce marriage and all the vanities of the world, and give himself entirely to God.

This retreat our saint ever regarded as one of the greatest blessings of his life. Among the fruits he derived from it, was a special and tender confidence in Jesus present in the blessed sacrament. Henceforth he was wont to approach the holy table several times a week, and visit daily the church in which the Forty Hours' adoration was being made, when he would remain for hours kneeling in contemplation before his hidden Savior.

He loved to see the altar richly decorated, and often purchased flowers for his parish church; a pious practice he preserved during his whole life. In one of his hymns he sweetly says, that he envied those innocent creatures destined to repose night and day before their Creator, and breathe out their sweetest perfumes for him. In after life, he would procure the rarest seeds and cultivate them himself, to embellish the altars of the churches of his congregation; a practice he often recommended to the rectors of the houses, for he ever loved to see the altars adorned with the choicest and most fragrant flowers.

As a recompense for his tender devotion, the blessed sacrament became the source of all the graces bestowed on him through life: "If," said he, "I have abandoned the world to devote myself to God, I owe it entirely to Jesus in the most holy sacrament, though, alas! coldness and indifference have so frequently mingled with my devotion to him."

Alphonsus was accustomed during his after life to mention his friend, Francis, Duke of Casabona, in terms of the warmest gratitude. "Under God," he would say, "I owe it to him that I am not still the slave of the world, and a prey to my own passions." Nor was he less grateful towards the priests of the Mission. More than half a century later, he thus addressed the superior of that congregation, to whom he had just sent a copy of his translation of the Psalms: "Accept the profound respect of one who deems it an honor to be the son and servant of you and all members of your society; for it was in your house, during the holy exercises of retreat, that I learned to know God, and resolved to renounce the world."

CHAPTER VI.

Retreat of Alphonsus and his father. — Effect on the latter. — Another matrimonial project. — The interrupted duet. — Alphonsus gains his mother to his side. — The lost cause. — Emotions of Alphonsus. — Measures of his parents. — His resolutions. — His opinion of the legal profession. — Why he renounced it.

IN MARCH, 1723, Count Joseph and his son Alphonsus made a retreat in the house already mentioned, during which the latter was still more confirmed in his pious design of devoting himself to God. He determined to resign his birthright in favor of his brother Hercules, although he was as yet undecided as to whether he would abandon his legal practice. His father, knowing nothing of the extraordinary change which had just taken place in his heir, projected another marriage treaty. The lady was daughter of the Duke of Presenzano, and the proposals were at once agreed to by her father, to whom they had been made without the knowledge of Alphonsus. As he had not courage to speak his whole mind to his parents, with a view of temporizing, he visited the Presenzano palace, but so unwillingly, that afterwards he often said that in the amusements of which he partook he found only thorns, and longed only for the moment in which his martyrdom would end.

The count used all possible means to counteract the manifest indifference, or, rather, repugnance of his son. He expatiated on the singular good qualities of the princess, her superior education, her cultivated mind and elegant manners; arguments which could have no weight with one who had vowed celibacy to God. Yet the reluctant Alphonsus feared to refuse decidedly; his excuse was that weakness of the chest and tendency to asthma warned him not to think of marriage. His father, attributing his evident reluctance to mere bashfulness, continued to take him frequently to visit the young lady; but on these occasions he behaved with such circumspection, that no one could suspect him of going thither as a suitor.

One evening being invited to perform on the harpsichord, he willingly consented. The princess obligingly proposed to accompany him in a song, and rising, took her place by the instrument, her face turned towards the embarrassed performer. Alphonsus immediately turned his head in an opposite direction; and she, thinking it accidental, made a corresponding movement, but had no sooner done so, than he turned abruptly from her. Perceiving this, she was highly indignant, and immediately withdrew, remarking to the company: "That young gentleman has become moonstruck." Mortified though he was, he made neither apology nor explanation, preferring that the young lady should understand his real sentiments. Nor were the hints he gave her thrown away; she herself declared to her father her unwillingness to marry a man who would hardly look at her.

As his father was so obstinately bent on hastening the marriage he had projected that he would hear of no excuse, the son had no resource but to open his mind to his mother, who unfortunately happened to be just as eager for the alliance as her husband. She urged upon him the advantages the family would derive from the connection, the displeasure his refusal would cause; but to no purpose. He declared that nothing would induce him to settle in the world, and earnestly besought her to persuade the count to cease his importunities. The poor lady, knowing that her husband had set his heart on this union, was sorely puzzled; but she did not long resist the passionate pleadings of her beloved son.

A providential and most unlooked-for event soon changed the aspect of affairs, and demolished at one blow all the worldly hopes indulged by Count Joseph for his son. The tribunals of Naples were occupied in 1723 with a feudal process of great importance between the Grand Duke of Tuscany and one of the most powerful nobles of the realm. Six hundred thousand ducats depended on the decision. Alphonsus undertook the cause of the nobleman; and after an entire month devoted to a most careful study of the case, he believed it impossible that he should not gain the cause for his client so thoroughly had he mastered its salient points. Yet, despite his prolonged and severe study, he had completely overlooked one document, which was so important as to secure the victory to the adverse party. From the tenor of his speech, which was a masterpiece of erudition and eloquence, the opposing lawyer readily concluded that this important paper had entirely escaped him.

On the conclusion of his eloquent address, one of them rose, and sarcastically directed his attention to a certain document which would prove the right to be in quite a contrary direction. "Produce it, then," said Alphonsus with assurance; "the decision depends on the question: Was the fief granted under the law of Lombardy, or under the French law?" But on examination, it was found that the Grand Duke's advocate was correct. "You are right," said Alphonsus, generously, "it is I who have been deceived." But never was a discovery more unexpected. Every one could perceive his emotion. Fear of being suspected of unfair dealing filled him with consternation. It was in vain that the President Caravita, who loved him and relied on his integrity, endeavored to reassure him. He was perfectly inconsolable. Overwhelmed with confusion, his head sank on his breast, as he muttered: "World, I know thee now! Courts of law, you shall never hear me plead again!"

Even in old age, he could never understand how that important paper had escaped him. But Providence had permitted him to overlook it, that it might be an occasion of opening a more direct way for the accomplishment of God's designs on him.

He abruptly left the assembly, still repeating to himself: "World, I know thee now!" He entered his house, not knowing how he came there; and gaining his chamber by a sort of instinct, fastened the door. When dinner was served, he was absent: his mother, knowing that he had returned from the courts, though ignorant of his distress, went to call him. He said he would eat nothing. She returned with some of the family, but to their reiterated entreaties he would not even reply. Towards supper time, they insisted that he would at least open the door, but they insisted in vain. All the household were alarmed, for no one was aware of what had happened in the courts.

Next day, when his father who had been out of town came home, the countess informed him of the astonishing obstinacy of their son. He went straight to the room, but was refused admittance. Don Joseph could no longer dissemble his indignation; and while his wife wept and cried out, "My son is dying! my son is dead!" — "Well, then, let him die!" was the angry retort of her indignant husband.

For three whole days he continued deaf to all entreaties; but at last he opened the door to his mother, overcome by her tears. Even then he would not touch food, and it was with difficulty she forced him to take a slice of melon, which, he afterwards declared, seemed more bitter than gall.

This extraordinary and terrible emotion being somewhat calmed, a ray of divine light irradiated his bewildered soul, and showed him the utter vanity of all that ends with time. Obedient to the impulse of grace, he determined to break with the world for ever, and devote himself entirely to God; though something was yet wanting to the perfection of his sacrifice.

It was not, however, on account of the disgrace he imagined himself to have incurred in his last suit that he renounced the bar. "Law is a dangerous profession," he afterwards remarked to a friend, "and exposes one to an unprovided death. I renounced it because I wished above all things to save my soul, and must under all circumstances follow the dictates of my conscience."

CHAPTER VII.

Alphonsus begins to lead a life of seclusion. — The anguish of his father. Alphonsus refuses to transact the legal business of his family. — The birthday of the Empress Isabella. — Supernatural favor. — Final renunciation of the world. — Favorite church of our saint. — His devotion to Our Lady of Mercy. During his last visit to Naples he makes a novena in her church. — He acknowledges his indebtedness to the Mother of Mercy.

ALPHONSUS now renounced the bar in good earnest. When rest had somewhat calmed his troubled spirit, and when he had bewailed before God the transports of grief and indignation in which he had indulged, he politely dismissed his clients, and began to lead in his own house the life of a hermit. Grace acted more and more powerfully on his soul; his greatest pleasure was to divide his days chiefly between the church and the hospital of Incurables. When at home, he studied the lives of the saints, and entertained himself with God.

But his chief delight was to kneel before the Blessed Sacrament in the church in which the forty hours adoration was being made. There he might be daily seen for two or three hours together, kneeling immovable, and so absorbed in his devotions, as to be unconscious of all that was passing around him. He thus drew upon himself the admiration of the pious, especially of some priests who were greatly devoted to this adorable mystery.

The behavior of the son was a source of the greatest distress to the worldly-wise father. "What can he be thinking of?" said he to the mother; and the Lady Anna shared his uneasiness. They had a presentiment of the truth, but knew not how to baffle the projects of their son. One day, Count Joseph handed Alphonsus a process of much interest to the family, desiring him to examine it. "Give it to some one else," returned the youth, "the tribunals no longer suit me; henceforth I will occupy myself solely with my salvation." This reply fell like a thunderbolt on the ambitious father, and he began to weep bitterly. His wife offered all the consolation her tenderness suggested, and expressed a hope that, when the crisis was over, their son would resume his practice.

"No, no," sighed the Count, "Alphonsus is too obstinate; he will never waver;" yet he hoped against hope, that the event would prove him a false prophet.

Another altercation soon took place. It was the birthday of the Empress Isabella, wife of Charles VI (August 28); a day ever memorable in the annals of our saint. There was to be a grand fete at court, at which Don Joseph wished to assist with his heir. "What should I do there?" replied the latter, abruptly: "all that is but vanity." The Count, transported with rage, exclaimed: "Do what you like — go where you please!" Alphonsus, grieved that he had provoked him, said gently: "Do not be offended, dear father; I will accompany you to court." "Go where you will — do what you will," reiterated the count in a rage, and turning his back upon his son, he entered the carriage, and drove to his country house, where he gave free vent to his chagrin.

Deeply afflicted at seeing the vexation of his father, Alphonsus exclaimed: "My God! what shall I do? If I resist him, I do wrong; if I obey him, I do worse." In hopes of finding consolation by assuaging the miseries of others, he went to the hospital of Incurables. This refuge for the most grievous physical maladies, was to become a paradise to him. It was here that God awaited him, as he had awaited Moses in the burning bush. At a moment when the care of the sick completely absorbed him, he was suddenly surrounded with resplendent light. The house seemed to be shaken as by a violent earthquake, and a voice repeated: "Forsake the world, and give thyself entirely to me." Awed and amazed, he continued to wait on his patients; but when about to leave the house, just as he reached the staircase, the same light again encircled him, and the same solemn words resounded once more in his ears.

Alphonsus waited no longer. Like another Saul, he was perfectly converted to God. Weeping bitterly, he cried out: "My God! I have too long resisted thy grace. Here I am at last: do with me what Thou pleasest." Deeply moved, and, as it were, out of himself he proceeded to the church of our Lady of Mercy, — a church he loved to frequent, attracted at first by the magnificent statue of the Blessed Virgin which adorned it. He prostrated himself before the altar, and earnestly implored the protection of his Mother in heaven.

Environed with celestial light which radiated from his countenance, he consecrated himself unreservedly to God, renouncing the world and its vanities, offering generously the sacrifice of his birthright, and promising to enter the congregation of St. Philip Neri. As a pledge of his fidelity, he laid his sword on the altar of Our Lady of Mercy.

This memorable day was ever present to the mind of Alphonsus. He called it the day of his conversion, and never visited Naples without repairing to the church of Our Lady of Mercy, to thank the divine goodness for the multitude and greatness of the favors there showered on him, through the mediation of his divine benefactress.

In his last visit to Naples, he made in his favorite church the novena preparatory to Our Lady's Nativity, and went thither to pray as often as his occupations permitted. "Behold," said he to two friends, on one of these occasions, pointing to the image of Mary — "behold her who attracted me from the world, that I might consecrate myself to her in the ecclesiastical state."

CHAPTER VIII.

Evening of the memorable day. — Remark of Father Pagano.— Fervor of his penitent. — He remains three days without food.— Interior lights. — Holy impatience of the youth. — His father endeavors to persuade him to resume his profession. — Firmness of the saint. — Scenes between father and son, which disturb domestic tranquillity.

O N THE evening of this memorable day, our saint confided to his confessor what had passed; declaring that he was resolved to join the Oratorians immediately. "This is not a thing to be hastily decided," prudently observed Father Pagano; "I must think it over for a year before I can give you a decisive answer." "A year!" cried Alphonsus; "I will not wait a single day." The wise director admired his fervor and encouraged his design; and after suggesting several suitable reflections, concluded with these words: "Let us recommend the matter to Jesus and Mary." The youth returned to his father's house, but his heart and soul were in the oratory.

For three days after these remarkable occurrences, he tasted no food, eager to do penance for his delay in obeying the call of grace; but if his body languished for want of nourishment his soul was filled with heavenly manna. He discovered to Father Pagano the interior lights which irradiated his soul; the holy violence which grace exercised over his heart; the disgust he felt for all that this world values; and the holy impatience with which he sighed to consecrate himself wholly to God among the children of St. Philip. The pious director recognized in all this the evident and incontestable operation of grace, and mentioned to the Superior and other Fathers the vocation of the youth; but their unanimous opinion was, that this affair should be concluded very gradually so as to obviate, as much as possible, the grief it would cause the Liguori family.

His father, who had been absent while these events transpired, on his return learned with dismay that his son had not shown himself at table for three days. His vexation was excessive, yet he controlled himself so far as to plead, with all possible gentleness, that Alphonsus would renounce his present views and resume his practice, enlarging on the losses the course he contemplated would entail upon the whole family. But he pleaded in vain.

Similar scenes were daily repeated, and to such an extent, that the household was in constant commotion. Sometimes the affliction of Don Joseph became so violent, as to distress extremely both his wife and his son. Yet the resolution of the latter remained unshaken. Neither prayers nor tears had the slightest effect on him in this particular; he trusted in God, and bore sweetly, for his sake, the pains and penalties of his present state, imploring continually the divine aid to be faithful to the graces bestowed on him.

One day Don Joseph, unusually excited at the thought of his son's splendid talents being lost in inaction, exclaimed with unwonted bitterness: "Would to God that either of us was called out of the world, for I can no longer bear to look at you!" This urged Alphonsus to put his resolution in practice. "What!" said he within himself, "am I then an object of horror in the eyes of my father, that he beseeches God to separate us by death? Henceforth God is my only friend: I must be satisfied with him alone."

He then renewed his vows, offering himself to God a living sacrifice. Hitherto he had feared to declare his intentions, but now he felt courage to speak out manfully: "My father," said he, soon after, "it is I who cause your affliction, and therefore I must tell you that I am no longer for this world. God has called me to the Oratory; do not be offended if I follow my vocation, but console me with your benediction." These words froze the blood in Count Liguori's veins. In the utmost consternation he withdrew to his chamber, where his profound grief vented itself in groans and lamentations. But he did not remain long in this dismal solitude. Coming forth to the room in which his son was, he regarded him with an expression of unutterable contempt. Thenceforth he treated him with extreme severity, and went so far as to deny him the necessary clothing. Consequently his heir was seen abroad in torn garments.

This means proving ineffectual, the devil suggested a more dangerous one to the bewildered father: the most tender entreaties, the most pathetic exhortations, the mediation of friends — he would cloud the brilliant prospects of his brothers with the Austrian court — he would ruin their interests — he was not guided by a divine inspiration, but by a diabolical illusion: — even priests were against him. Father de Miro insisted that he was influenced by a melancholy humor, and urged him to obey his father. "Be assured, reverend sir," replied the saint, "God has called me out of the world: I must conform to His will, not to the wishes of my father."

Others were employed by his father to shake his resolution, but their efforts were fruitless. His constant reply was: "God has called me, I cannot resist him." At last, the unhappy old man threw himself on his child's neck, exclaiming in tones of anguish: "My son, my dear son, do not forsake me!" Terribly as these manifestations of paternal tenderness affected our saint, his resolution remained unshaken. Finally, his maternal uncle, Monsignor Cavalieri, Bishop of Troia, was commissioned, or, at least, entreated to use his authority with the obstinate heir.

But the pious prelate, convinced that his nephew only obeyed a divine call, replied: "What a beautiful commission you entrust to me! I myself renounced my right of primogeniture, the better to secure my salvation; and now you want me to risk my nephew's soul and my own."

Another distinguished ecclesiastic, yielding to the importunities of the inconsolable father, essayed to argue the youth out of a divine vocation, but he, too, was repulsed: "I have been the devil's advocate with Don Alphonsus," said he, later on, "but I could make no impression on him."

Amid these trials, Alphonsus had some defenders of his cause. Besides Monsignor Cavalieri, Father Vincent Cutica, superior of the priests of the mission, Father Pagano, the canon Peter Gizzio, also his uncle, and several other ecclesiastics, ably befriended him. These true friends of both parties at length succeeded in obtaining from the count a reluctant consent to his becoming a priest, provided he did not leave the paternal mansion. The Bishop of Troia advised him to submit for the present to this condition; and Don Joseph could no longer avoid presenting his son to the Archbishop of Naples, Cardinal Pignatelli. His

Eminence, struck with the firmness of the youth, exclaimed: "What! does Don Alphonsus Liguori want to become a priest?" "Would to God it were otherwise," replied the afflicted father, unable to conceal his agitation, "but his resolution is unchangeable."

Even after this decisive step, Don Joseph refused, on one pretext or another, to furnish ecclesiastical costume for his son; but Alphonsus found means to provide it himself, and on the 23d of October, 1723, renounced forever the livery of the world. When he appeared before the count in the garb of a cleric, the old man uttered a piercing shriek, and for a year after never addressed a word to his once idolized son.

CHAPTER IX.

His parents. — Former friends. — Maio changes his opinions. — Domini Bruno. — Newer and truer friends. — Cheering prophecy. — Zeal of our saint for little children. — Contrast between Don Alphonsus the successful lawyer, and Alphonsus the catechiser of little ones.

THE unhappy nobleman refused even to meet his son. If he chanced to perceive him at a distance, he would take an opposite route to avoid all contact with him. The heart of his mother, however, could not repudiate him. Far from it: she now recognized his vocation as the work of God, and cheerfully submitting to the divine will, endeavored to soothe the irritation of her husband, and second the intentions of her best-beloved child.

The world continued to condemn him loudly. Lawyers and senators, who were formerly proud to be in the category of his friends, now convicted him, unheard, of the most egregious folly. The President Maio, who had heretofore shown him the tenderness of a father, would not now tolerate him in his presence, and passed him by as a creature utterly beneath his notice.

Later, however, Maio judged differently. On his death-bed, when visited by Alphonsus, he cried out: "Oh, Don Alphonsus! how happy are you to have comprehended and followed your vocation! You have chosen the sure path: would that I had done likewise! Miserable wretch that I am, I must now appear before the tribunal of God, and render an account of all the judgments I have passed upon others. Alas! you were truly wise, but I was blind to my real interests."

One reads with pleasure the following little anecdote: — A celebrated advocate of the day, Don Dominic Bruno, who had recently been defeated by Alphonsus in an important lawsuit, met him clothed in the ecclesiastical dress, and having congratulated him on his choice, added: "God forgive you, Don Alphonsus, for not taking this step a year sooner. I should then be saved the disgrace and disappointment the loss of that suit caused me."

But if worldly friends deserted our saint, God was not slow to replace them by others more sincere, who had similar aims and aspirings. Among these was the Reverend Joseph Porpora. He had often been edified by the devotion of Don Alphonsus when he saw him prostrate for hours before the Blessed Sacrament; but he did not discover who this model of piety was, until after he had seen him in the ecclesiastical dress. He wished to make his acquaintance, but human respect restrained him. One day, however, seeing him conversing with a mutual friend, Reverend John Mazzini, he threw himself between them, unable to dissemble his feelings any longer, and cried out, "And I also wish to belong to you." Then embracing Alphonsus, he foretold the blessings Heaven would hereafter shed upon him and his followers, congratulated him upon his vocation, and declared himself his friend and companion. From that time the three friends were one. Every evening they might be seen before the Blessed Sacrament, in whatever church the forty hours devotion was being celebrated; and they continued to excite one another to advance in the path of perfection.

Having received the ecclesiastical habit, Alphonsus attached himself to the parish of St. Angelo. He immediately offered his services to the pastor, and every day afterward might be seen serving mass, and assisting at all the ceremonies. So remarkable was the modesty of his deportment, that the very world, which had lately proclaimed him a fool, now loudly applauded his generosity in sacrificing his brilliant prospects for the love of God. What excited the greatest admiration was, to see him going about, crucifix in hand, in search of children. These little ones he would lead to the church, singing simple canticles, often of his own composing, and catechise them with the greatest zeal, especially when preparing them for first communion. The contrast between Alphonsus the catechist, and Don Alphonsus de Liguori who had so frequently electrified the tribunals of Naples by his eloquence, was sufficiently strong to attract the attention, if not the admiration, of the whole city.

CHAPTER X.

Alphonsus applies himself to ecclesiastical studies. — He seeks the society of the most eminent churchmen. — His hymns become popular. — He becomes more austere. — He receives the tonsure and is ordained subdeacon. — New occupations. — He joins the congregation of the mission. — The rules he observed as a candidate for the priesthood. — His first sermon. — Illness. Miraculous recovery. — Rules for a priest.

ALPHONSUS had no sooner embraced the ecclesiastical state, than he sought to perfect himself in all the learning so holy a vocation exacts. Already well versed in *belles-lettres*, philosophy, civil and canon law, he now devoted his time to the study of the Holy Scriptures, and moral and dogmatic theology; the canon, Julius Torni, — afterwards bishop of Arcadiapolis, — a man eminent for learning and virtue, being his principal master. As, when a law-student, he had frequented the house of the President Caravita to increase his knowledge of jurisprudence, so now, having become an ecclesiastic, he sought out the most learned among the Neapolitan clergy, whose houses were soon transformed into academies for theological sciences. The elegant accomplishments he had already acquired, he consecrated entirely to the glory of God; and he had the satisfaction of seeing the beautiful hymns he set to music, replace, in many instances, the loose and dangerous songs which had unfortunately become popular.

From the date of his assuming the clerical habit, his life became more austere. His time was chiefly devoted to prayer and study; he crucified his flesh and refused his senses every indulgence: used the discipline, wore a hair shirt, and practised all kinds of penitential exercises. He fasted every Saturday on bread and water, in honor of the Blessed Virgin; his clothes were of the plainest description; for a while, to please his father, he tolerated

51

the attendance of a footman, but he soon dispensed with this incumbrance, and traversed the streets of Naples unattended, like the poorest of the priesthood.

In December, 1724, he received the tonsure from Monsignor Mirabello, Archbishop of Nazareth; and nine months later, September 23d, 1725, he was promoted to minor orders, in virtue of a dispensation from Cardinal Pignatelli. In December he was made subdeacon, and immediately after, entered as a novice in the Congregation of the Missions, which then counted among its members the elite of the clergy and the clerical nobility of the Neapolitan kingdom.

He at once applied himself diligently to the observance of the rules; he frequently accompanied the missionaries to country places and catechised the children. Nor did his zeal find full scope in this congregation. He also aided the Fathers of St. Vincent, and associated himself to a society called the Congregation of the White Monks, whose object was to procure the comforts of religion for condemned criminals.

We will here transcribe the rules he composed for his guidance as a candidate for the priesthood:

1. The cleric ought to frequent the society of holy priests, to be edified by their example.
2. He should spend at least one hour daily in mental prayer, that he may live in fervor and recollection.
3. He ought to visit the Blessed Sacrament frequently, especially during the time of exposition.
4. He should read the lives of holy priests, that he may imitate their virtues.
5. He must cultivate a special devotion to the Holy Virgin, the Mother and Queen of the clergy, and consecrate himself particularly to her service.
6. For the honor of the ecclesiastical state, he must be most careful of his reputation.
7. He ought to fly worldly conversation, and not be too familiar with the laity, especially women.
8. Seeing God in his superiors, he must obey them, because such is the divine will.
9. He should be modest, but without affectation, severity, or fastidiousness, and he should always wear the cassock and tonsure.

10. He ought to be quiet and gentle at home, exemplary in class, and edifying in the church, especially during the public offices.
11. He ought to confess every eight days, and communicate still oftener.
12. In short, the priest should have negative sanctity, that is, to live free from sin; and he ought to have positive sanctity, that is, to practise every virtue.

Edified by his sanctity, the Cardinal Archbishop conferred upon him deacon's orders on the 6th of April, 1726, by dispensation, and authorized him to preach in all the churches in Naples.

His first sermon was preached in the Church of St. John at the Latin Gate, from this text of Isaiah: *O, that Thou wouldst rend the heavens and come down! the waters would burn with fire.* His burning zeal and eloquence touched all hearts. He painted in glowing colors the wondrous love Jesus Christ bears us, and our monstrous ingratitude towards this divine and eternal Lover. So powerful were the effects of this sermon, that invitations to preach poured in upon him from all quarters. His favorite subject was the Eucharist, and he usually preached in the church in which the Blessed Sacrament was exposed. He spoke with vehemence of the hideousness of vice, and the injury it does to God; and the people, in their eagerness to hear him, deserted the other churches. Though only a deacon, the Fathers of the Mission sent him into various parts of the kingdom; and he preached with such unction and eloquence, as to promote in a wonderful manner the glory of God in the salvation of souls.

Don Joseph became more afflicted than ever, fearing that the young deacon would shorten his days by his excessive labors and austerities. The Lady Anna shared his sentiments: though she felt great consolation in seeing her son so devoted to the apostolic life, she could not bear to think of losing him. She wept continually, and conjured the Fathers of his acquaintance, especially his confessor, Father Pagano, to urge him to mitigate his astonishing labors and mortifications. The fears of the anxious parents were but too well realized. Mind and body, overcome by continued exertion, sank beneath an illness of so fatal a character, that the physicians, despairing of his recovery, sent one night in haste for a priest to administer the last sacraments to their exhausted patient.

In this extremity, experiencing an extraordinary sentiment of confidence in Our Blessed Lady of Mercy, he eagerly besought the attendants to go to the Church and bring him her statue, before which he had renounced the world. They did not refuse him this consolation: the miraculous image was brought to his room and placed upon his bed. He was immediately pronounced out of danger, so speedily was his confidence rewarded by Our Blessed Lady.

On the 21st of December, 1726, he was ordained priest; and from that date, his ardor and zeal redoubled. On descending from the altar, he seemed ready, like a lion, to pounce upon the strongholds of Satan, so amazing was the love that consumed him. Cardinal Pignatelli appointed him, almost immediately after his ordination, to give spiritual exercises to the clergy of Naples; and his Eminence had reason to congratulate himself upon his choice, for he saw in an unmistakable manner that God signally blessed the ministry of his servant.

Yet the cardinal was severely criticised for thus distinguishing the young priest. "There are some," said a person in authority, "who thrust into the ministry subjects wholly untried, heedless of the danger to which they expose them." Nevertheless, the prelate was right; ere many days elapsed, all Naples testified to the virtue of Alphonsus, and spoke with admiration of the apostolic spirit which animated him.

We will give here what Alphonsus wrote at this epoch on the obligations of a priest who wished to attain sanctity, merely adding that it was the rule by which he regulated his own conduct.

1. I am a priest, my dignity is above that of the angels. I should then lead a life of angelic purity, and I am obliged to strive for this by all possible means.

2. A God deigns to obey my voice. I ought with far greater reason to obey His, speaking to me through his inspirations, or my superiors.

3. The Holy Church has honored me; I must therefore honor myself, by sanctity of life, by my zeal and labors, etc.

4. I offer to the Eternal Father Jesus Christ, his Son; it is then my duty to clothe myself with the virtues of Jesus Christ, that I may become fit for my office.

5. Christian people see in me a minister of reconciliation, a mediator between God and man; consequently, I must always keep myself in the grace and friendship of God.

6. The faithful desire to see in me a model of the virtues to which they should aspire; I must then be edifying always and under all circumstances.

7. Poor sinners who have lost the light of grace, come to me to be spiritually resuscitated; I must therefore aid them by my prayers, exhortations, and good example.

8. Courage is necessary to triumph over the world, the flesh, and the devil; I must then correspond with divine grace, that I may combat these enemies victoriously.

9. To defend religion and fight against error and impiety, one must have knowledge. I will then strive, by every means within my reach, to acquire the necessary knowledge.

10. Human respect and worldly friendships dishonor the priesthood; I will then avoid them.

11. Ambition and self-interest have often caused priests to lose their faith; I must then abhor these vices as sources of reprobation.

12. Gravity should accompany charity in a priest; I will then be prudent and reserved, especially with regard to women, without being proud, rough, or disdainful.

13. I can please God only by recollection, fervor, and solid virtue, which nourish the holy exercise of prayer; I will then neglect nothing which may tend to their acquisition.

14. I ought to seek only the glory of God, my own sanctification, and the salvation of souls; consequently, I must achieve these ends, though it should cost my life.

15. Being a priest, it is my duty to inspire virtue in all with whom I come in contact; and to glorify Jesus Christ, the Eternal High Priest.

CHAPTER XI.

ALPHONSUS was no sooner invested with the sacerdotal dignity, than pastors entreated him to preach in their churches; congregations besought him to give them the spiritual exercises: and monasteries desired with avidity to share in the blessings inseparable from his powerful eloquence. Animated by the spirit of God, he preached Jesus Christ and him crucified, avoiding most carefully the vain ostentation which sometimes urges preachers to display their superfluous erudition, rather than convert and instruct their audience.

Every thing concurred to give effect to his preaching, — noble birth, rare talents, supernatural gifts; but what chiefly rendered his eloquence persuasive was his profound humility, his recollection, his contempt for this world. His sermons were not florid or pompous; he sought to make himself understood by the poor and the unlettered; yet all the nobility and intellect of Naples besieged his pulpit.

Sometimes his auditors left the church in tears, their heads bowed low upon their breasts, and their whole deportment eloquent of sorrow and compunction. Nicolas Capasso, a man celebrated for his vast knowledge, and dreaded for his powers of satire, was never absent from these sermons. One day he met the preacher, who remarked pleasantly: "You always come to hear me; should you not like to make me the subject of some new satire?" — "No, no," returned the satirist, "I listen to you with pleasure, because I see that you forget yourself to preach Christ crucified." So powerful is the gospel in the mouth of a man who illustrates it by his example.

Don Joseph now fully recognized the divine vocation of his son. One day, while Alphonsus was preaching in the Church of the Holy Ghost to an immense concourse of people, he happened to pass by as he was returning from the royal palace, and recognizing the preacher's voice, he felt irresistibly impelled to enter. He was soon moved to tears, and bitterly reproached himself for his past harshness and violence. Full of a salutary remorse, he returned home; and scarcely had Alphonsus entered the house, when he went to his room, and tenderly embracing him, exclaimed: "O my son! what do I not owe you? You have taught me to-day to know God! I bless you a thousand and a thousand times for having embraced a state so holy and so pleasing to God!"

The zeal of our saint for the souls of his brethren did not cause him to neglect his own. Every day he consecrated a few hours to meditation, and spent some time reading the Lives of the Saints, which he called "the gospel in practice." Not a day passed in which he failed to visit the Blessed Sacrament, in whatever church the "Quarante Ore" happened to be making: these visits were of considerable length. His morning mass, with preparation and thanksgiving, absorbed most of the forenoon, but this seemed little to his fervor. Before the Blessed Sacrament, hours scarcely counted as moments. From time to time, following the advice of his Divine Master, he would enter into his chamber, shut the door, and commune alone with his God. It was in these silent communings that he sought that "little repose" which Jesus Christ prescribed to his apostles.

He had, as we have already intimated, contracted an intimacy with several priests whose views and feelings were similar to his own. To cement their union, they were accustomed to take occasionally a little recreation at a country house owned by Don de Alteriis, one of their number. Once a month they retired thither, to spend a few days in penitential exercises and spiritual conferences. They arranged an oratory, in which they placed a beautiful statue of the Blessed Virgin, still devoutly preserved at Ciorani. Their repasts were frugal; a little image of the Infant Jesus was placed as if presiding at table; and each made to him an offering of some part of the food served him. Father Mazzini afterwards remarked that these meals were more spiritual than temporal, so abundant were the ejaculatory prayers. Their recreation was singing hymns, before they resumed their holy meditations.

Sarnelli soon rented a more solitary house, near St. Januarius, without the walls, and here they applied still more freely to their pious exercises. It was here that Alphonsus almost unconsciously formed the plan of the Institute which he afterwards gave to the Church.

It is not customary in Italy, as in France, to authorize priests to hear confessions immediately after ordination. They have to wait some years, during which they must give solid proofs of their piety and capacity, and finally submit to a rigid examination. Should they pass this successfully, faculties are given them for hearing the confessions of men; and on attaining a higher degree of maturity, they are allowed to hear those of women.

Alphonsus was scarcely a year a priest when Cardinal Pignatelli empowered him to hear the confessions of men and women, to the great joy of many who sighed for the moment in which they could open their hearts to him. He was quickly besieged by persons of every rank and condition, all of whom he received with the tenderest charity; and so devoted was he to this holy office, that he was the first to take his place in the confessional and the last to leave it. It was his constant opinion that the office of confessor is more profitable to souls, and less apt to produce vain glory in the priest, than any other sacerdotal function. For, by confession, sinners are immediately reconciled to God, and the grace of Jesus Christ superabundantly applied to their souls.

However severe towards himself, he was all mercy and compassion to sinners. The more a soul was degraded by vice, the more lovingly did he strive to snatch it from the fangs of Satan, and to place it in the ever open arms of Jesus Christ. He delighted in being surrounded by the beggars of Naples, and effected many remarkable conversions among them.

He received the vilest and most vicious with inexpressible meekness, instilling into their minds confidence in the precious blood of Jesus Christ shed for them on Calvary, and teaching them how to withdraw from sin. He never received poor penitents with a haughty, supercilious air, or dismissed them as unworthy or incapable of the divine mercy, and he has left us these beautiful words on this subject: — "The more deeply our fellow-creature is plunged in sin, the more tenderly should we cherish him, and the more strenuously should we endeavor to wrest him from the devil and place him on the bosom of his Savior. It is very easy to say to a poor sinner, 'Go away; you are damned; I will not absolve you;' but whoever dares to use such language has forgotten that souls are purchased by the Blood of Christ!"

In his old age he used these remarkable words: *I do not remember having ever sent away a sinner without absolution.* It was not, however, that he absolved indiscriminately all who approached him. No; but he received sinners with such unalterable mildness, instructed and admonished them with such extraordinary patience, and manifested for them such warm affection, that they were glad to return to finish their confession and make their peace with God, through the instrumentality of a minister who so well represented to them His mercy, goodness, and compassion.

"If a sinner is repulsed," said he, "he will never abandon sin;" and he was so particular in this matter, that even as sacramental penance, he would impose only what his penitents would cheerfully perform. "Let us beware," said he, "of overloading them with obligations they would accept with repugnance, and afterwards easily abandon. The penance should tend to inspire horror of the sin, but not of the penance." Thus he frequently enjoined the penance of returning to confess, of frequenting the sacraments, of hearing mass daily, of meditating on the Passion of Christ, or some eternal truth.

He also imposed as penances, visiting the Blessed Sacrament or some oratory of Our Lady; reciting the Rosary; and in case of heads of houses, he would have them recite it regularly with their families. As for fasting, disciplines, and hair-shirts, he might sometimes counsel, but he never commanded them. "If the penitent be truly contrite," he observed, "he will do these things of himself; but if they be made obligatory, he may neglect them and relapse." By this sweet but salutary conduct, he made penitents love the confessional, and easily withdrew them from sin.

Such was the system Alphonsus invariably followed during the whole course of his long and eventful career. This method full of sweetness, this direction wholly paternal, mild but salutary, won to our sweet Savior many hardened sinners, once slaves of the devil and their passions, but soon to be replenished with burning love for their Divine Master.

Two of these conversions were striking. One was Peter Barbarese, who, though young in years, was old in crime. A schoolmaster by profession, instead of enlightening the minds of his scholars, he corrupted their hearts. Fortunately he went to hear Alphonsus preach; and so deeply did the words of the saint sink into his soul, that, full of sincere repentance, he cast himself at his feet. Received with utmost kindness, he at once forsook sin, devoted himself to the service of God, and embraced a life of penitence. He now earnestly strove to undo the evil he had done: he awaited his children early at the school, conducted them to church, taught them to meditate on some eternal truth, finishing these morning devotions by acts of faith, hope, and charity. In the evening he took his children to visit the Blessed Sacrament and Our Lady, choosing the least frequented churches, to avoid all display, being penetrated with repentance and confusion for the scandal he had formerly given. Once a week he brought his scholars to confession, disposed the more advanced for communion, and during mass suggested acts of contrition, faith, hope, and charity. After communion he pronounced aloud the acts of thanksgiving; a pious custom still observed in the Neapolitan churches.

The other remarkable conversion was that of Lucas Nardone, who had long led an irregular life as a soldier. Several times he had deserted, and his last desertion had been so audacious that death might have been the penalty, had not his brother, an officer of the royal guard, interceded for him. He was, however, expelled the army as an incorrigible wretch. One day he happened to hear Alphonsus preach, and immediately grace touched his hardened heart. He knelt before our saint, confessed his innumerable crimes, and, consoled and encouraged by Alphonsus, began to lead so holy a life that he edified all, and attracted many souls to Jesus Christ.

Alphonsus never used far-fetched or studied language to dispose sinners to repentance; and yet his words were so efficacious that they overcame the most obstinate. All his auditors attested that his appeals were accompanied by a special influence of the Holy Spirit, which urged sinners to repentance; often he had no sooner opened his mouth than compunction penetrated their hearts.

A young gentleman once accused himself in confession of several enormous crimes, in a tone of the utmost indifference; when he paused, Alphonsus asked if he had any more to say. The youth answered in the negative. "What!" returned the saint, "is that all? Now do you not see that the only thing required to make you a Turk is the turban? Tell me now, my son," he continued, in accents of touching tenderness, "what evil has Jesus Christ done you?"

These words went directly to the heart of the sinner, and, filled with confusion, he said to himself, "Have I then committed such crimes that there cannot be greater?" and in sentiments of the deepest contrition, he bewailed his past disorders, and having placed himself entirely under the guidance of Alphonsus, ever after led a most exemplary life.

The means our saint employed to lead his penitents to perfection were chiefly two: meditation or prayer, and mortification of the passions. Meditation, as the mirror in which the soul sees her own deformity; and mortification, as a knife to cut or prune all the excrescences of nature. "There is no true prayer," he affirmed, "without mortification, nor is there any true mortification without the spirit of prayer."

But above all remedies, he prescribed frequent communion and daily visits to the Blessed Sacrament. In his admirable little book of "Visits to the Blessed Sacrament," he acknowledges that this devotion had been in his regard the source of all the graces he had received while living in the world. "O what exquisite happiness," he would exclaim, "to converse familiarly with Jesus in the Blessed Sacrament, asking pardon for our sins, exposing our wants as a friend does to a friend, and begging his love with its abundant graces! Can any thing be sweeter to a faithful soul?"

While in Naples, he always advised his penitents to pay their court to Jesus in the church when the Blessed Sacrament was exposed during the forty hours adoration. There might he himself be seen in an ecstasy of devotion for several hours, encircled by his faithful penitents.

He inspired them likewise with a filial confidence in the divine mother, Mary. "As all good comes to us from the celestial

Father though the mediation of Jesus Christ; so all good comes to us from Jesus Christ, through the medium of Mary." He wished all to recite the Rosary daily in her honor, visit her altar in some church, and place her picture at the head of their bed. With his penitents, each of her feasts was a day of general communion; and he was careful to propose some devout exercise for her novenas, to dispose them to receive her favors. He used to fast in her honor on Saturdays and the eves of festivals, and he frequently recommended to others the same salutary practice.

CHAPTER XII.

ALTHOUGH our saint preferred to devote himself to the poor, he did not refuse to hear the confessions of people of the highest rank, well knowing how powerful their example is for good or evil. But his chief delight was to evangelize the poor. So great was the crowd that applied to him for spiritual direction, that he judged it expedient to assemble them during the summer evenings in some solitary place, and give collectively the instruction he had not leisure to bestow on individuals. His audience consisted of nobles and lazzaroni, with many laborers who, after the day's toil, walked a considerable distance to hear him; and it was remarked that, the lower the condition of the auditors, the more friendly was their reception. Other priests took part in the good work, among whom were Fathers Porpora, Alteriis, Mazzini, and Sarnelli. Alphonsus preached daily to this motley assemblage, enlarging particularly on the loathsomeness of vice and the sublime beauty of virtue.

There were some individuals residing in the neighborhood to whom these meetings seemed not a little strange, they taking it for granted that, because they were somewhat novel, they must necessarily be evil. In hopes of confirming their suspicions, they concealed themselves behind their windows to hear what was going on. Now, some of the poor people were so eager to do penance, that they fasted far more rigorously than our saint would allow; and one artisan, though obliged to work hard for his family, had already begun to live on roots and raw vegetables. Alphonsus reprehended him severely for this excess, and forbade him to continue it. Father Porpora, happening to be present, remarked that God wills we should eat in order to live; and he added laughing: "If any one gives you a few cutlets, eat them without scruple, and much good may they do you." The audience were highly amused at this, and passed the joke from one to another. The listeners, catching only the words, "cutlets" and "eating," put an ill construction upon the whole, and ranked all concerned in the category of libertines or Molinists.

This was not all; they reported their conjectures to Cardinal Pignatelli as facts; and as the accusation was lodged against nocturnal assemblies, His Eminence was ready to believe the worst. Information was conveyed to the Governor of Naples, who immediately ordered a captain of the guard to attend one of the meetings, in disguise. They were then making the novena of the Nativity of Our Lady; and Alphonsus, to illustrate some truth he wished to impress upon his simple auditors, happened to mention some articles necessary for an infant's wardrobe. The captain was completely mystified. He immediately reported to the governor that he had heard a *melange* of things good, bad, and indifferent, but was wholly unable to infer from them the purport of the meeting.

His Excellency at once leaned to the opinion, that it was composed of evil-minded persons; and he the more readily acted on his suspicions, as some bands of Lutheran soldiers had lately created considerable disturbance in the city. He therefore, in conjunction with the cardinal, ordered the arrest of all, preachers and people.

Next morning, Alphonsus, calling by chance on the archbishop, happened to hear of this order, and suspecting that it referred to his own assemblies, hastened to warn his penitents not to go to the usual meeting-place. It was impossible to reach all. Consequently, those who lived at a distance came, and among them were the fervent penitents, Peter Barbarese and Lucas Nardone.

They had scarcely arrived when they were surrounded by archers and soldiers, and carried off to the guard-house, whence they were cited before the fiscal procurator. "Comrade," said Lucas to Peter, "I would like to know whether this courtesy is to your taste." — "I am perfectly satisfied," returned Barbarese; "they treat us much more civilly than the Jews treated our Lord. His arms were bound with ropes, and mine are bound only with a pocket-handkerchief."

The procurator having ordered them to specify their nocturnal proceedings, they replied: "As we are poor ignorant creatures, Don Alphonsus Liguori and other priests instruct us in our duties as Christians." On hearing the name of Liguori, the representative of the law exclaimed: "May God forgive you! you have alarmed two courts, the ecclesiastical and the civil."

The governor, in whose house they were, took pleasure in questioning them about the pious practices they had been taught; but, as he proceeded, they heard the sound of bells announcing that the Holy Viaticum was being carried through the streets; they immediately prostrated themselves upon the balcony, crying out: "It is our Divine Spouse! it is our Divine Spouse!" The governor asked no more questions, but dismissed them with tears of tenderness and consolation.

Alphonsus, upon hearing of this arrest, went to the cardinal, and acknowledged himself alone as guilty of whatever might be considered reprehensible in the meetings. His Eminence quieted him, by expressing satisfaction at the good he had done, but nevertheless advised him to discontinue these meetings. "The times are too critical," said he; "we must be careful that wolves in sheeps' clothing do not do harm under the shadow of your name."

Yet a false report spread through Naples, and Alphonsus and his companions were constantly asked to offer their prayers to God for the conversion of the heretics! One of the Camaldolese Fathers one day asked Father Mazzini, who had just said mass in their convent, whether any thing else had been discovered touching the new sect that had lately appeared. "What sect?" asked Mazzini. — "The sect of *Cutlets*," returned the monk, and he volunteered the following particulars: "We have heard that certain priests every evening meet certain people at the Place of the Star — they form a species of club. Some think them Molinists."

Mazzini reassured the good Brother, saying pleasantly that no great danger was to be apprehended from the new sectaries. Alphonsus, however, had already done immense good by his conferences; many of those who heard them, ever after led the lives of saints. Some entered religion, others remained in the world, but adorned it by their virtue. The most remarkable among the latter were Antonio Penino, who sold eggs through the town, yet found means, while pursuing this trade, to draw many souls from perdition; and Leonardo Christano, who went through the streets with his ass, and sold chesnuts. Both of these traders wrought miracles during their lives and after death.

CHAPTER XIII.

Barbarese continues the work of the conferences. — Reminiscences of Brother Angiolo. — The seed bears fruit. — Sentiments of our saint. — Exercises of his penitents. — He establishes a school for women. — Labors in the hospital. Exercises for the patients. — Perseverance of Barbarese. — Meeting between him and Alphonsus. — Death of this good man. — Death of Nardone.

ALPHONSUS, being prohibited his favorite conferences, endeavored to defeat the machinations of the devil, by suggesting to his docile disciple, Barbarese, that he and a few others might instruct the lazzaroni and other poor people, taking precaution to select for the purpose places remote from public observation.

Barbarese, thus encouraged, began to instruct the little errand boys of a neighboring barber's shop. A priest, who noted the good he effected, advised him to assemble his little flock in a chapel hard by. He did so; and every evening some sixty young people attended, as well as several of more mature age.

Lucas Nardone and several others pursued a similar course in various quarters of the city and Alphonsus frequently visited these reunions, to animate the zeal of his penitents and excite them to walk in the footsteps of Jesus Crucified.

Brother Angiolo, a saintly religious, of the order of St. Peter Alcantara, used, in old age, to describe one of these meetings which he attended when a boy. A wool-carder by trade, he one day strolled into a barber's shop, and seeing several persons enter the inner part of the house, he became curious to know their business.

Following the last comer, he found within several persons, some sitting, some kneeling before an image of Mary, and on his inquiring the meaning of all this, a man answered: "It is here Don

Alphonsus instructs us in the science of salvation; and when he does not come, our host takes his place."

Alphonsus not appearing, the barber fulfilled the function of catechist, after which all performed various acts of piety. The wool-carder was so touched by this spectacle, that he never after missed a meeting, till, touched by grace, he embraced an austere rule, under the name of Brother Angiolo.

Peter Barbarese presided over the most numerous flock. One evening, Canon Romano was taking a walk in the vicinity, when a friend met him and said: "Come with me, and I will give you an agreeable surprise." On seeing the canon, Peter rose and courteously offered him a seat.

Delighted with what he saw and heard Romano could not help telling the whole to the cardinal, who was so much pleased that he suggested to his informant to instruct the people himself. Peter gladly resigned his post, and immediately began to assemble the porters and lazzaroni of another district. Thus did the grain of mustard seed multiply, till, in every quarter of Naples, the fervent penitents of Alphonsus might be seen instructing and catechising the ignorant.

In after times, Alphonsus never came to Naples without visiting those favorite haunts, and exhorting all to persevere in the divine service, and in gaining conquests to Jesus Christ. He was particularly consoled by the thought, that the overthrow of one good work had been the very means of establishing another, far more important and more glorious to God.

Very soon these assemblies, protected by the cardinal, emerged from shops and back alleys, and were transferred to churches and oratories. Every evening, at the Angelus bell, the associates commenced their devotions and continued them for about an hour and a half. Rosary, acts of faith, hope, and charity, half an hour's instruction on some Christian duties, fully occupied their time. Every Saturday zealous priests heard their confessions, and on Sundays, after a half hour's meditation on the sufferings of Christ, they heard mass and received holy communion, a priest pronouncing aloud the affections and thanksgivings, all concluding with Benediction.

Such is the origin of the *Chapels* established in Naples by Alphonsus and his penitents. Their number continued to increase. In 1734, they amounted to one hundred, in each of which over three hundred persons of the working classes assembled. There is no tax to pay, no special office, no formality of association, the doors are open to all; and the working has been such, that the archbishops of Naples have derived the greatest satisfaction from these humble gatherings.

Alphonsus established similar meetings for women, but this good work lasted no longer than the life of the worthy lady whom he selected to preside over it.

The members of these assemblies afterwards agreed to visit the public hospitals on Sundays and Thursdays. They made the beds, swept the floor, attended to the spiritual wants of the patients, exhorted them to patience, and prepared them for the sacraments. When every thing was arranged for the comfort of the patients, a zealous priest exposed the Blessed Sacrament on a gallery prepared for it, and having spoken for a short time on some Christian truth, carried it through all the wards to bless and console the suffering.

Barbarese and Nardone lived to an advanced age, and persevered to the end in their pious labors. The only visit Alphonsus made to the capital during his episcopate, was an occasion of holy joy to Barbarese. Eager to hear him once more, the affectionate disciple hastened to the hospital of the Annunciation, where he met his old master. "What are you about here?" asked the latter, smiling. "Come to hear the Holy Ghost," was Peter's quick rejoinder.

This worthy man died on Saturday, September 19, 1767, the eve of the Seven Dolors. He left behind him a great reputation for sanctity; in fact his body was deposited near the high altar of the Church, as though he were a saint. We are ignorant of the particulars of Nardone's death, though he, too, died in the odor of sanctity, and his remains were laid in the place of honor in the church of St. Matthew.

CHAPTER XIV.

The Chinese College. — Alphonsus in his new abode. — Privations and penances. — Spiritual dryness and obscurity. — Zeal for souls. — Father Ripa's testimony. — Extraordinary gifts of Alphonsus as a confessor. — His penitent Mary. — Incessant labors of Alphonsus. — The epidemic of 1731. Illness of our saint. — The earthquake at La Pouille.

A LPHONSUS failed to find in his father's palace the solitude for which he sighed, and which he experienced in the monthly retreats he made with his companions, in the country house already mentioned. It happened about this time that the celebrated missionary, Don Matthew Ripa, returned from China accompanied by a Chinese doctor and four zealous young men, with the intention of founding at Naples a college for the Chinese.

God blessed the enterprise, and on the 14th of April, 1729, they opened the house of the Chinese mission, to the great satisfaction of the founder, the Pope, Benedict XIII, and the King, Charles VI. Alphonsus, struck with the excellence of this work, the rare merits of its founder, the great fervor which reigned in the house, and the poverty and privations which both Neapolitans and Chinese joyfully endured for love of God, resolved to join Father Ripa, who knew how to appreciate so invaluable a subject. He entered the college in June, 1729, to the great mortification of his father, who grieved to lose one whom he regarded less as a son than as an angel; yet he did not oppose so laudable a design.

No sooner did our saint find himself freed from the anxious watching of his parents, than he redoubled his former austerities. His garb was sackcloth, and chains of iron bound his loins. Several times a day he disciplined himself to blood. Scanty and miserable as was the food he took, he seasoned it with myrrh, aloes, and wormwood, and he generally ate in a kneeling posture. In his chamber he would not allow himself a chair, but stood while he studied, and even put little stones in his shoes. The Bishop of Cassano affirmed that his penances surpassed even those of St. Peter Alcantara.

Besides these voluntary penances, he cheerfully bore the privations common to all, and these were neither few nor slight. The rule limited them to the use of vegetables and a little boiled meat, but they frequently had no meat, and were obliged to dine on a salad of mushrooms. Sometimes they could afford to buy only bones, from which they strove to extract a miserable soup. During Lent they scarcely ever had fish, and when they had, it was always of the poorest and cheapest description. They sowed radishes in a little plot of ground near the house, and for months they lived on these roots. Their evening repast usually consisted of the remnant of the dinner, boiled with a few coarse biscuits. And far from ever showing the slightest repugnance to all this, Alphonsus rejoiced, and encouraged the others to suffer with pleasure, that they might become more holy and pleasing to God.

Through all this he was sustained by prayer and by the example of the saints. By reading their lives, he studied their virtues and imbibed them. He burned with an ever-increasing desire to love God and give proofs of his love. Besides the community meditation, he daily spent at least an hour and a half before the Blessed Sacrament. The very rest nature claimed was given grudgingly, and not without many contrivances to render it as disagreeable as possible: he often lay on the bare ground or on a hard table.

It might be surmised that these pious practices and austerities, undertaken and endured solely to please God, would procure for our saint a foretaste of heaven, which nothing worldly can either give or take away; but this was not the case with Alphonsus. God permitted him to share in the anguish of our dear Lord when he exclaimed: "My God! my God! why hast thou forsaken me?"

Deprived of all the favors which make the cross light and easy, his heart enjoyed no consolation. He believed he had lost all devotion: "I go to Jesus," said he, "and I am repulsed by him. I have recourse to the Blessed Virgin, and she will not listen to me." During these trials, he acted entirely by faith which made him resolve to please God in all things, even though there were no hell to punish his sins, or heaven to reward his virtue.

While he remained in this college, he gave proofs of an extraordinary zeal for souls. Crowds besieged his confessional and pulpit. Every Friday he preached on the glories of Mary, and recited with his audience the chaplet of her sorrows. During the year he celebrated several novenas, and gave retreats which attracted immense concourses. So devoted was he to his penitents that he scarcely took time to eat, but remained in the church as long as they required, often till late at night.

Father Ripa in his Memoirs of this congregation, writes as follows of our young apostle: — "We had with us the Count Alphonsus de Liguori, a priest eminent not only for his birth, but still more for his holy life, and wonderful qualifications as a missionary. He was in the house almost from the first, and though not aggregated to the Mission, he held himself in readiness to preach the gospel in China, as he more than once declared to his director. Assured of his zeal and talents, I gave him entire charge of our church in what regards the confessional and preaching, and he discharged these duties to the great advantage of souls."

It is impossible to enumerate the obstinate sinners his sweetness attracted to the love of Jesus Christ. He possessed a peculiar gift in the confessional of inspiring sinners with contrition. A famous courtesan whom he converted, became, under his guidance, a model of sanctity. This was but one instance in hundreds. At his feet sinners were touched with sorrow, and persons of ordinary virtue were inspired with the desire of giving themselves entirely to God. In short, to kneel to him and to feel compunction — the latter seemed a natural consequence of the former. This enables us to understand that wonderful saying of a later period of his life, that *he had never sent away one penitent unabsolved.*

The first sermon of a retreat he gave in the Chinese college, inspired fifteen young persons with a generous desire of consecrating their virginity to God. When he spoke of the beauty and dignity of virginity, the most indifferent among his hearers were forced to love and admire it; and frequently, inflamed by his words of fire, the gay, the beautiful, the talented, renounced the fading pleasures of earth, and devoted themselves under his direction to amassing the imperishable riches of heaven.

A young lady named Mary, whose heart was completely eaten up by the vanities of the world, was recommended by her anxious mother to the prayers of our saint, and soon began to reform a little; but her reformation was of a very temporary nature. Again the poor mother had recourse to the saint, who, at her earnest entreaty, spoke seriously to the girl, representing strongly the danger of her position. This happening in the church, the girl was touched to the heart, and going into a corner, began to bewail her sins most bitterly. Alphonsus, seeing this, called her to his confessional, and said, "Mary, will you sincerely give yourself to God?" — " Yes," was the quick reply. "But with your whole heart, and without the slightest reserve?" — "With my whole heart, and without the slightest reserve," repeated the poor girl energetically. "Then," said he, "go instantly, cut off your hair, and become a Carmelite." She obeyed, and died a saint. God sent her many severe trials to produce this result; for several years she was sensibly tormented by the devil. She made a most edifying end, and, being invoked by many, wrought several miracles after her death.

We find some particulars of this privileged soul in a letter addressed by Alphonsus to Mother Angela, superior of the monastery of the Holy Savior at Scala. "I beseech you pray, and procure prayers, for my poor penitent Mary; I really know not what to do for her; the more I speak to her, the more I increase her inquietude. Her temptations are fearful, yet they are *but* temptations … I tell you all this, that you may have compassion on this desolate soul. She consoles me, nevertheless, by her prompt obedience, even in the most difficult matters. Pray, and cause the community to pray, I entreat you, at least during the next three days, that our dear Lord would give me light, and to her strength to obey, and to support her terrible trials." Many similar souls were under the direction of Alphonsus.

At this period of his life, his labors were incessant: preaching, giving retreats, hearing confessions, going on missions to neighboring towns, which fully occupied him. Yet the saint, who, later on, made a vow never to lose a moment of time, found leisure for all without encroaching on his studies or devotions. "I never remember," said Father Fatigati, "to have seen Alphonsus waste a moment when he lived with us; he was always preaching, or hearing confessions, or at prayer or study."

In 1729, Naples was ravaged by a frightful epidemic. This gave our saint occasion for still more heroic self-sacrifice; he was ever foremost in anointing the sick. Besides, he opened a mission in the great Church of the Holy Ghost, and turned the common calamity to advantage, by using it as an argument to withdraw souls from the power of Satan.

In consequence of his great fatigues, he was seized, the following year, with a pulmonary complaint, which brought him to death's door; but again his beloved Mother wrought a miracle in his favor.

In the spring of 1731, La Pouille and the adjoining provinces were desolated by an earthquake. The bishops, not to lose this opportunity of calling their flocks to repentance, invited the missionaries to preach to them. Alphonsus, as usual, produced miraculous effects. The nuns of St. Clare, hearing several speak of him, entreated their superior to procure them the gratification of hearing him even once. Their request was granted, and they afterwards said that, in listening to him, it seemed as if a seraph were speaking: his words penetrated their inmost hearts.

CHAPTER XV.

Our Lady of Foggia. — The apparition. — Alphonsus preaches a novena. Success. — Our Lady appears to him. — Picture of the Vision. — Alphonsus visits Mount Gargano. — He is reprimanded by Canon Torni. — His sweetness and gentleness.

FOGGIA suffered more than any other town from the earthquake, little more than a mass of ruins being left of it; but God, who smote his people, would also comfort them, by giving them a miraculous proof of his love. In Foggia, was venerated a very old and miraculous picture of the Blessed Virgin, which was glazed and curtained, its colors being almost obliterated by age. Terrified by the repeated shocks of the earthquake, the people came in crowds to place themselves under the protection of the Mother of Mercy. On the morning of the 22d of March, while the multitude were kneeling before this picture, the Holy Virgin showed herself to them under the appearance of a young woman, and this miraculous manifestation was repeated for several days, and seen by all who came to venerate the picture.

This apparition made an extraordinary sensation throughout the kingdom; and at the conclusion of the mission, Alphonsus and his companions went to visit the miraculous picture. Monsignor Falcoia, the bishop, insisted that he should give a novena in honor of the Blessed Virgin. He at first demurred, having no permission to prolong his stay, but finally yielded to circumstances, the bishop promising to assume the responsibility of his delay. So immense was the concourse, that the greater portion could not find room in the church; a pulpit therefore was erected near the door, beside which was exposed the miraculous picture. The effects were wonderful. Numerous as were the priests, they were not sufficient to hear the confessions of the crowds who, touched to the heart by the discourses of our saint, turned from their wickedness and sought to be reconciled with God.

One day, after the people had left, the image having been replaced in the church, he ascended the altar over which it was placed, to examine it more closely. Scarcely had he placed himself in front of it, when he fell into an ecstasy which lasted nearly an hour. The Holy Virgin would fully satisfy his devotion by showing him her face, radiant with celestial beauty. When the vision disappeared, he came down, inebriated with joy, singing the *Ave Maris Stella*. He afterwards attested that he had seen the Virgin Mother, under the form of a girl of thirteen or fourteen, wearing a white veil. Next day he described to a painter what he had seen, and the picture executed on that occasion is still preserved in the house of Ciorani. Throughout the Congregation of the Most Holy Redeemer, the feast of our Lady of Foggia is celebrated on the anniversary, March 22d; the regular and secular clergy of Foggia celebrate the same feast on the same day.

From Foggia, Alphonsus proceeded home by Mount Gargano, where he desired to render homage to the Archangel Michael. At Manfredonia, the archbishop and his chapter came to meet him, accompanied by the most distinguished people in the town. They besought him to preach, but he declined, on the plea that he had no leave from his superiors. Next morning he said mass at the altar of the Archangel, with a devotion that attracted the gaze of all.

On returning to Naples, about the middle of May, he found that his fears of being blamed for delaying to preach the novena, were to be realized. The Canon Julius Torni, either because he disapproved of what he had done, or wished to exercise his humility for his spiritual profit, reprimanded him severely in presence of the whole Congregation. Alphonsus received the rebukes of his superior with his usual gentleness and sweetness. Far from excusing himself, he rejoiced to see himself mortified and humbled before so respectable an assembly.

CHAPTER XVI.

Alphonsus retires to Amalfi. — Proposal of the Vicar of Scala. — Alphonsus and his companions evangelize shepherds and goat-herds. — Sermon.

WORN out by his labors and austerities, the friends of our saint began to feel serious apprehensions regarding his health, and it was determined that he should repair to the country to regain his strength. Amalfi was the place selected. Here there was a hermitage on a hill opposite the sea. Several of his co-laborers accompanied him.

On their arrival, after a rough voyage, they went to pay their respects to the Archbishop, Monsignor Scorza. Meeting the vicar-general, he strongly urged them to go to a more convenient hermitage at Scala, where they could benefit the poor goatherds of the vicinity, who were destitute of spiritual aid. "Only go," he urged, "I will give you full powers."

The proposal was joyfully acceded to, and they established themselves at Saint Mary's of the Mount, as the hermitage was called. The Blessed Sacrament was placed in their oratory, and while our saint was recovering his bodily health, his soul gained new strength in the presence of his beloved Savior.

They began to catechise the shepherds and goatherds of the Mount, and the inhabitants of the adjacent country, and to hear their confessions. It was now that Alphonsus learned the extreme spiritual destitution of the scattered population of this district, many of whom had to be instructed in the rudiments of faith before they could make their confession. He met with many who were entirely ignorant of the essential truths of religion, deprived of the sacraments and the word of God. These poor people he instructed with his wonted gentleness, and their progress was to him a source of indescribable consolation.

The people of Scala, hearing that the celebrated missionary was in their environs, were very desirous of hearing him preach, and the bishop besought him to gratify their pious curiosity. He preached one sermon to them, which had the full effect of a regular mission. He spoke so powerfully of the love of Jesus in the Blessed Sacrament, and the pressing motives which oblige us to return him love for love, that the entire congregation wept and sobbed, their groans resounding through the whole neighborhood.

The superioress of the nuns of the Holy Savior entreated him to preach in their church, which he did with his usual unction; and the bishop was so delighted at the success of his labors, that he engaged him to preach a novena in the cathedral, preparatory to the feast of the Holy Redeemer, celebrated in September.

Having continued his labors among the shepherds till the appointed time, he returned to Scala, accompanied by his inseparable companion, Father John Mazzini. During the novena, he conducted a retreat for the nuns of the Holy Savior. There was among them a religious of great sanctity, eminent for many supernatural gifts. Being in an ecstasy on the 3d of October, she saw a new Congregation of priests evangelizing thousands of the hitherto neglected inhabitants of remote villages and hamlets, and at the head of it she saw Alphonsus, and heard a voice which said, "It is this soul I have chosen to be the instrument of my glory in this great work."

In a conversation subsequently held with him, she made known what she had seen in spirit, and what God required of him. Although her sentiments perfectly coincided with his own, and although he had frequently besought our dear Lord, even with tears, to raise up an apostle for the most abandoned, and gather their precious souls into his fold, he now reproved the nun and treated her as a visionary. Yet struck by the conformity between her vision and his own reflections, he at first regarded it as coming from God. The more he repulsed the good religious, the more firmly did she maintain that God had chosen him for a sublime mission.

He returned to Mazzini, terribly agitated, and on his hesitating to tell the cause, his friend said, "I know you have been disputing with one of the nuns, for I overheard you speaking rather loudly." At length, Alphonsus essayed to tell him what the nun had said, and this Mazzini treated very seriously. The sanctity of the nun was undoubted: "Besides," argued he, "an institution of this nature is greatly needed in the country, and who knows what designs our dear Lord may have upon you?"

"I highly approve of such an institution," returned Alphonsus, "and I foresee its glorious fruits; but what can I do alone? Where are my companions?" — "Here I am for one," answered Mazzini, "and I am sure other priests will not be wanting to consecrate themselves to an enterprise so fraught with the interests of God's glory."

While he was weighing this matter in his mind, Mgr. Falcoia, bishop of Castellamare, arrived at Scala. He was a man of well-tried sanctity, skilled in spirituality, who had been intimately acquainted with Alphonsus in the Chinese College. Mazzini induced his friend to open his mind to this estimable prelate, and to the Bishop of Scala, who was nowise his inferior in virtue. After several days spent in closely examining the subject, these prelates agreed that the inspiration came from God, and the vision of Sister Celestina only strengthened their belief, she being a person of extraordinary sanctity. Mgr. Falcoia, in particular, admired in this incident a special mark of God's providence; for, ever since his elevation to the episcopal dignity, he had desired the establishment of a work of this nature, having had proof of the extreme spiritual destitution of remote hamlets and villages. On learning that Alphonsus felt moved to undertake it, his heart was filled with consolation, and he urged our saint to hasten the execution of the project. But Alphonsus still demurred, and finally consented to refer the decision to his own director, Rev. Thomas Pagano.

CHAPTER XVII.

Conflicting sentiments. — Opinions of Pagano. — Cutica and Manulio agree with him. — Opposition. — Gizzio and Torni. — Others deride our Saint. The nun of Scala, Sister Celestina. — A miracle. — Father Fiorillo. — His letter to Alphonsus. — Embarrassment of our saint. — He shows the letter. Letter of Mgr. Falcoia.

THE interior light which illumined the soul of Alphonsus, strengthened by the advice of holy and experienced individuals, should have been for him a powerful motive of confidence; but when he considered his own weakness and incapacity, he was filled with indescribable anguish. He feared to oppose the divine will, and he feared, on the other hand, to engage in a rash enterprise.

Father Pagano, after a careful consideration of some days' duration, declared that the institution in contemplation must tend to the glory of God and the salvation of souls; but through a holy diffidence in himself, he forebore to give a final decision, and referred his penitent to Father Vincent Cutica, and Father Manulio, a Jesuit. Their opinions coincided with that of Pagano, and they urged Alphonsus to begin the good work at once. Several other religious, equally estimable, were of the same mind, so that he could no longer hesitate.

He now took courage, for he felt that he knew for certain God's will in his regard. He therefore gave himself unreservedly to God, sacrificing his love for his native city, and offering to spend his life in villages and remote districts among the poorest and most neglected class.

As soon as our saint's determination became known, all Naples exclaimed against him; some hinted that his brain was affected, others treated him as a madman; not a few considered him a visionary, and a respectable quota of the more rational adversaries judged that the promising young priest had been spoiled by too much praise. His brethren of the Chinese College were his most uncompromising opponents. Father Ripa used his most strenuous endeavors to persuade him that his designs were impracticable. This good priest had dearly loved our saint, and had from their first acquaintance regarded him as the firmest pillar of the college. Now he chose to believe him the victim of a lamentable delusion, and publicly and privately reproached him for his extravagance.

Having heard of the vision of the nun, the Fathers of the Propaganda imagined it to be the sole basis of his plans, and were shocked that a man of his ability and good sense should allow himself to be led astray by such reveries. What afflicted him most was, that these opinions were shared by his uncle, Matthew Gizzio, Rector of the Seminary, and his friend and professor, Julius Torni. When assailed by such respectable adversaries, he meekly replied that he would do nothing without the consent of his director.

"It is not God who directs you," said Gizzio, bluntly; "you are guided by the reveries of a young nun, and you will not see that you are deluded." — "I do not regulate my conduct by visions," returned our saint, gently, "but by the Gospel."

One day, Gizzio jeeringly asked if he ever expected to realize that brilliant scheme of his. "He who trusts in God can do all, and should hope all," returned Alphonsus.

Finally his uncle treated him as a fool, saying that his brain had been turned by self-conceit. On one occasion, as he entered the sacristy of the cathedral, several persons of rank began to insult him: "Keep to your word now," said they derisively; "be quick and show us these new institutions which you have promised the Church." — Alphonsus humbled himself interiorly, but would not utter a word in his own defence.

Gizzio had for his director Father Louis Fiorillo. "Why," said he one day to his nephew, "why do you not guide yourself by the counsels of Fiorillo?" — "I am directed by Father Pagano," answered Alphonsus. But Father Pagano himself referred his saintly penitent to Fiorillo; and the moment Fiorillo saw him, he said: "God is not yet satisfied with you; He wishes you to be entirely his, and expects great things from you."

At these words Alphonsus seemed to breathe more freely, and felt his heart penetrated with new life. Thus encouraged, Alphonsus opened his whole soul to the good Dominican, and it was agreed that he should continue to consult him. He began to perform the most severe penances, that the Father of Light would enlighten his servant Fiorillo, upon whose decision the affair seemed to depend. He recommended himself to the prayer of many holy persons, but above all to the nun of Scala. All the other nuns of her monastery joined her in prayers, fasts, and mortifications, to beseech God to enlighten our saint's directors. An occurrence which must be considered miraculous, confirmed the opinions of those who believed Alphonsus to be called to establish a new Congregation. One day, when the nuns were speaking for and against the project, Sister Celestina exclaimed in ecstatic transport: "It is the work of God, and you will see it accomplished!" — "Yes," returned one of the most incredulous, "I will believe it when Sister Magdalen is cured." Hardly were the words uttered when this poor Sister, who had been deranged for many years, perfectly recovered her senses.

When Alphonsus made known to Father Fiorillo the lights he had received from God at Scala, and the lights he still continued to receive, the man of God replied: "In a similar conjuncture, St. Louis Bertrand asked six months from St. Teresa to reflect before giving an answer: I ask the same of you." — "Not six months only," said Alphonsus, "take a whole year."

Some days after however they met again, and the venerable man, tenderly embracing him, said: "Be of good courage, for this work certainly comes from God. Throw yourself into his arms as a stone falls into a valley. You will encounter contradictions, but be of good cheer; have confidence, God will help you."

But having other good works on hand, and fearing to offend the clergy who might cease to aid them, he begged Alphonsus to conceal his approbation and not to visit him again. Fully satisfied that he was but fulfilling the divine will, the saint now began in earnest to look out for companions, Fathers Cutica and Manulio also authorizing him. He wrote to Fiorillo, asking him to point out some suitable individuals.

The reply was as follows: — "Do not suppose I forget you in a matter so intimately connected with the divine honor. I have your interest more at heart than ever. Be tranquil, and place all your confidence in God. He will aid you in a work so dear to his Heart. At this moment I have no subjects to offer you, but should I meet with any, I shall be happy to present them. Would that I were young myself! I would gladly follow you, were it only to carry your baggage. Fear not because your disciples are few; they will be strengthened to do the work of many. A small number of perfect men can do more than an army of the ordinary stamp. I bless you in the name of Jesus and Mary, and embrace you tenderly and with humble respect, in the charity of our Lord."

Meanwhile, nothing was talked of in Naples but the new Congregation and its presumptuous founder. The missionaries of the Propaganda were the first to prepossess the public mind against Alphonsus. They publicly regretted that he had ever been of their number, and bitterly resented the slur they imagined he cast upon them. "Do you not yet perceive that you are a visionary?" said Gizzio to him one day, on which he had accidentally met him in the church; "all are against you; neither Pagano nor Fiorillo is with you, and you obstinately persist in your own notions, submitting only to the reveries of a nun! Fool that you are! can you not see that you act the part of an idiot?"

"Say what you please, Uncle," said the founder with his accustomed gentleness; "I assure you, nevertheless, that I am not acting in consequence of any one's reveries, but am ruled by the word of God, and guided by those to whom I ought to submit."

Naturally, his embarrassment was great at this period: he was bound not to betray Fiorillo, who was then absent; and, on the other side, the scandal and astonishment of the people were on the increase. Pagano advised him to keep the secret no longer; the bishops of Cassano and Ischia agreed with Pagano; and, after several consultations with them and others, he determined to obey his director.

Hardly had he entered his uncle's abode, when that dignitary and Canon Torni attacked him with more than ordinary rancor. "You are deceived," said he calmly; "my conduct is the result of the counsels of Father Fiorillo." He then placed a copy of Fiorillo's letter in his uncle's hand. "But," said the cautious Torni, "I would see the original." Alphonsus presented it: "Now," said he, "I want no other testimony; this is sufficient for the honor of my Congregation."

After this, Alphonsus expected some respite; but his brethren of the Propaganda refused to be reconciled with him, and threatened to expel him ignominiously from their congregation. But Cardinal Pignatelli, although he had been prejudiced against the founder, warned Torni to beware how he took any steps against Alphonsus de Liguori.

Father Ripa, far from withdrawing his opposition on learning that Alphonsus was acting under the advice of Father Fiorillo, became more violent than ever, accusing the saint and his director of being duped by a nun's reveries. He believed himself justified in opposing schemes which would withdraw Alphonsus from Naples, and deprive the Chinese College of some of its most zealous subjects; for Januarius Sarnelli, son of the Baron of Ciorani, and Vincent Mandarini had signified their desire of following him. He called the plan a suggestion of the devil. He quarrelled with Pagano and Fiorillo, and wrote a very bitter letter to Mgr. Falcoia, whom he suspected of being in some manner the inventor of the vision connected with the name of the pious nun of Scala.

The reply is too admirable to be omitted here: — "Your esteemed letter has just been received, and, despite the bitterness it displays, it is still dear to me as coming from you. I reply immediately, because I would not have your annoyance continue a moment if I can help it. You know it does not belong to a spiritual father to give his penitents any vocation which may happen to please himself. This is the province of Almighty God, who has prepared niches in Paradise for the statues He fashions here below. On earth He establishes different studios, and is daily opening new ones, where these rational statues are to be moulded to perfection according to his will, ever most holy, that they may be prepared for their position in eternal glory. But that all may not be crowded together, God has destined one to be sculptured in one studio, and another in another. It is not the province of a spiritual father to do any thing but approve or disapprove.

"When a soul is faithful to God and his holy words, — 'He that heareth you heareth me' — we may believe she cannot wander. You may argue that a spiritual father can be deceived; but I would reply that God, who is always faithful, will not fail to communicate his will to those whom He has appointed to enlighten others. Were it otherwise, what security could we have in deciding what was God's will?

"Now, inasmuch as Alphonsus has followed this rule, he cannot go astray. I see from your letter that you condemn me as one who would overturn your Congregation, and ruin a valuable work which owes all to your labors. But fear not. Is the arm of God shortened? is he not able to sustain your Congregation and many others at the same time? Let God perform his own work, for a work that comes from him may aid, but cannot destroy, another equally divine. But this enterprise, you say, will dissipate itself. If so, you will lose nothing; but, according to my view, the project comes from God, who will not permit it to perish if he who is charged therewith continues faithful. To oppose it, therefore, is to oppose the divine will.

"'But,' you persist, 'we shall lose our subjects.' I wish, dear Father, we all had more confidence in God and less in man. When the Congregation of the Pious Workers was established, four of its most useful members left and founded four different Congregations. Yet the venerable Fathers Carafa and Colellis were not disturbed by their secession, nor was their Congregation ruined; on the contrary, new arrivals filled up the vacant places. Be persuaded that the work which Don Alphonsus is about to undertake has not been suggested by the devil; on the contrary, the devil opposes it, as he has always opposed every good work calculated to injure his empire on earth."

Despite this reasoning, strong and supernatural, Father Ripa continued to blame our saint; and, in his memoirs of his Congregation, bitterly inveighs against Alphonsus di Liguori, and all who approved or forwarded his projects, though he never ceased to regard him as a dear friend.

CHAPTER XVIII.

Fathers Pagano and Fiorillo decline the direction of Alphonsus. — Alphonsus places himself under the guidance of Mgr. Falcoia. — Canon Torni endeavors to shake the resolution of Alphonsus. — Retreat for the Clergy. — Missions. Letter. — First disciples of Alphonsus.

WHEN Fathers Fiorillo and Pagano saw that the tempest, instead of abating, rather increased, they began to fear for the success of their own immediate affairs, if they continued to bear the blame of directing Alphonsus. They therefore strongly urged him to place himself under the guidance of Mgr. Falcoia, a prelate of extraordinary sanctity, and particular light in what concerns the religious state, and venerated by all Naples.

Alphonsus was unwilling to leave Father Pagano who had been his director from childhood, but he determined to seek help from his Blessed Mother; and for this end commenced a novena, the feast of the Assumption being at hand. The Divine Mother listened to her favored child, and filled his soul with light as to his future course. He then placed himself in the hands of the holy old prelate, and never was child more obedient to a parent.

The Canon Torni, though convinced of the wisdom of those who directed Alphonsus, and aware of the approbation bestowed on his projects by persons of the most respectable character and position, could not bear to think that his services would be lost to Naples. He therefore began an indirect opposition, in his capacity of Superior of the Propagandists. He charged him with several important matters, hoping that, when he saw the good he was effecting in the capital, he would relinquish the idea of going elsewhere.

91

In October, he commanded him, in the name of the cardinal, to give a retreat to the clergy of Naples. He obeyed, despite the repugnance he felt to appear before priests, many of whom had interpreted his intentions in a manner contrary to charity; but the will of his superior was always for him as the will of God. The divine blessing rested abundantly upon this retreat. Most of his auditors were touched to the heart, despite their prejudices against him. The cardinal himself was so moved that he exclaimed: "One may easily see that he is a vessel of election, for the Holy Ghost speaks by his mouth."

Several of the clergy, who had heretofore been cold and indifferent, became zealous and fervent pastors. No sooner was the retreat finished, than he was ordered to give missions in three other churches. From all parts of the city multitudes crowded to hear him, and his confessional was besieged from morning till night. But, notwithstanding this abundant harvest, our saint longed for the moment when he could set out for Scala, to establish there the cradle of his new Congregation.

Mgr. Falcoia, either because the opposition was rather on the increase than on the wane, or because he wished to test still more the constancy of our saint, delayed to give his parting benediction. "Father," wrote Alphonsus, "I beseech you hasten to call me hence; I am dying with anxiety to set out; release me from the obedience to remain at Naples. The devil is doing all he can to delay us, but let us hasten to the work, and obstacles will vanish; all will succeed wonderfully. I am on the eve of the last day of the retreat I was directed to give, and I must speak to-day of my Mother in heaven, the glorious Virgin. Pray for me always, always, and for the glory of our dear Lord begin the work at once."

The more dearly Fathers Ripa and Gizzio loved the saint, the more they imagined themselves obliged to counteract his designs. Heaven sometimes permits similar delusions even among the most fervent. Later, however, when the blessings of heaven descended on the institute, now only in contemplation, his most bitter opponents applauded the work, and gained the rising institute many sincere friends and not a few disciples.

Even now several distinguished ecclesiastics offered themselves to follow our saint; but when the moment came for executing their good resolutions, the majority withdrew under different pretexts.

His first companion was Vincent Mandarini, a nobleman of Calabria. Like Alphonsus, he was a pensioner in the Chinese College, an excellent theologian, and a man of singular learning and virtue. He was followed by his bosom friend, Sylvester Tosquez, who, though still a secular, was well versed in theology and jurisprudence, and had an ardent zeal for his perfection; by Don Januarius Sarnelli, also of the Chinese College, son of the baron of Ciorani, a priest of eminent sanctity; by Don Peter Romana of Scala, Dr. Sportelli of Aquaviva, Don Jerome Manfredi, Don John Baptist Donato, Don Joseph Banza; and by two others whose names have not reached us. These formed the catalogue of the first disciples of Alphonsus.

These, as became corner-stones of a new edifice, were all animated with lively zeal for the glory of God, and devotion to the cause they had espoused. But our saint placed all his confidence in God and in the protection of our Lady. A gentleman named Vitus Curzius, whose vocation was evidently miraculous, was the first lay-brother. He had been secretary of the Marquis of Vasto, and was very intimate with Sportelli, of whose vocation, how ever, he knew nothing. One day he mentioned to him a dream he had the preceding night. "I thought," said he, "that I stood at the foot of a high and steep mountain which many priests were trying to ascend. I wished to follow them, but at the first step was thrown backwards. Unwilling to give up I tried to ascend several times; but to my great annoyance, I aways slid back, till a priest, moved with compassion, reached out his hand and helped me." Towards noon, as they walked to the Chinese College, they met Alphonsus. Curzius, who had never seen him before, struck with astonishment, exclaimed: "There is the priest who gave me his hand last night!" Sportelli now understood the dream, and mentioned the design of the founder, whereupon Curzius instantly begged to be admitted among the disciples of the saint, but in quality of lay brother. His request was granted.

CHAPTER XIX.

The germs of the new Congregation. — The missionaries in Scala. — Touting incidents.— Penitential life of the missionaries. — Alphonsus signalizes himself even among saintly men. — Pious customs he introduces. — Consoling Letter of Canon Torni.— New Persecutions. — The Archbishop defends the saint. — The flame of resentment is arrested but not extinguished. Gratitude of Alphonsus towards his defenders.

THE YEAR 1732 was destined by God to give birth to the Congregation of Our Most Holy Redeemer. Clement XII then occupied the Chair of Peter, and Charles VI the throne of Naples. After receiving the benediction of Fathers Pagano and Fiorillo, Alphonsus, without acquainting either friends or relations, hired a wretched donkey and set out for Scala, November 8. Mgr. Santoro, who impatiently expected him, received him as an angel from heaven, and blessed God that he had lived to see so happy a day. The dwelling prepared for the missionaries pleased them in every respect. It was a hospice belonging to a convent, almost destitute of furniture, poor and inconvenient. The day after their arrival they assembled in the cathedral, and after prolonged meditations, chanted the mass of the Holy Ghost, in thanksgiving for the establishment of the Congregation, and to beg God's blessing upon the work. They styled it "Of the Holy Savior," placing it under the protection of the chief of all missionaries. The founder hoped to form a company of priests animated with great zeal, who would willingly embrace a kind of apostolic life, poor and humble, despising all earthly things.

Alphonsus, on leaving Naples, had entirely broken with the world. The August previous, he had returned home to adjust his business. It was then that Count Joseph made a last appeal to this cherished son. One day when Alphonsus had lain down to take a little repose, the wretched father entered the room, and throwing himself on the bed beside him, exclaimed in piteous accents: "My son, my son! why will you abandon me? I do not deserve that you should cause me such misery!" For three hours this scene lasted, the father embracing him and passionately repeating: "My son, my son, do not abandon me!" — Alphonsus afterwards spoke of this trial as the most terrible he had ever endured.

The newly established missionaries applied themselves seriously to prayer and penance, their hearts overflowing with gratitude and love. Even their repasts they signalized by penitential exercises. Some kissed the ground; others knelt and remained for some time with their arms extended in the form of a cross. They ate kneeling or in some other penitential posture, and some hung heavy stones about their necks. Their scanty food they seasoned with bitter herbs, so that the very beggars refused to partake of what was left.

The end which Alphonsus proposed to himself was to unite in one body zealous priests who had but the glory of God and the salvation of souls in view. They were to lead an apostolic life, conforming themselves to Jesus Christ in poverty, humility, and self-abnegation. Prayer and penance were conspicuous in Alphonsus and his disciples; they were so inflamed with divine love, that they could scarcely think but of God. To their bodies they refused every comfort.

Alphonsus signalized himself in this holy assembly. He was ever to be found with God in prayer, or with God in works undertaken for his glory. Never was he seen to waste a moment of time. After a lengthened preparation, he daily celebrated the holy sacrifice of the Mass; after which he made a most devout thanksgiving. No sooner did business leave him free, than he prostrated himself before the Blessed Sacrament, to satiate his love in that source of love.

Besides laboring most zealously for his own perfection, he endeavored to convert or sanctify the people of Scala. He introduced the custom of giving a meditation every morning in the cathedral, and of making visits to the Blessed Sacrament and the Blessed Mother every evening. Every Thursday he gave a sermon and exposition of the Most Holy Sacrament. On Sundays and Feasts he instructed and catechised the people. He established two confraternities, one for noblemen, the other for artisans, and similar associations for the other sex; and to each of these he gave a particular instruction every Sunday. In a word, Scala was soon thoroughly reformed, to the great satisfaction of its zealous bishop. Ably seconded by his companions, Alphonsus gave missions in various town and villages adjacent; so that the renown of the new Congregation began to spread everywhere, and bishops were constantly beseeching the founder to evangelize their flocks, and even to accept of establishments in their respective dioceses.

In a letter, dated December 29, 1732, addressed to Mgr. Falcoia, we find the following: — "The Bishop of Caiazzo expects us, and counts the moments till our arrival. It is the same with the Bishops of Cassano and Salerno; but for this, experienced subjects are necessary, and it takes time to form them. What is of the utmost importance is, to have men who are all animated by the same spirit."

While matters were progressing so favorably at Scala, the fathers of the Propaganda in Naples became more and more embittered against their late companion. Their conduct so deeply grieved our saint that he wrote to their Superior, Canon Torni, who comforted him by the subjoined reply: — "I could not restrain my tears on reading the letter with which you honored me, and in which you make known to me the afflictions that assail you on all sides. Wherefore I have not ceased to pray to our Lord that he might deign to bestow on you the fortitude you so greatly need to bear the trials to which his all-wise Providence has willed to subject you, and to communicate to you with ever-increasing abundance light to see his holy will.

"Do not imagine that I entertain for you sentiments of aversion: such would be impious in my eyes. I have always loved you with the tenderest affection, and now more dearly than ever. You may then write to me whenever you think proper; your letters will always be most welcome.

"Our Congregation has not ceased to regard you as one of its most cherished members. We shall take no step in your regard but by order of his Eminence; and you may be sure that while I remain Superior, so far as depends on me, nothing will be done against you."

Notwithstanding the friendly sentiments of Torni, he was finally forced to yield to the importunity of his subjects, and permit them to affix to the door of their house the following notice: "According to the order of the Superior, on the 23d of February there will be a general investigation touching the following questions: Whether the brother Don Alphonsus Liguori should be expelled from the Congregation? And whether he ought to be deprived of his chaplaincy?"

Canon Torni, who had submitted so reluctantly to the dictation of his unworthy disciples, was determined to frustrate their iniquitous designs. Therefore he secretly informed the cardinal of their proceedings, and spoke strongly of the injustice contemplated against Alphonsus. "One may see," said he, with a burst of generous indignation, "that it is nothing short of madness. Not content with blasting his reputation, they would deprive him of the means of subsistence."

The cardinal was exceedingly annoyed, but he would not hinder the convocation: "Let them deliberate," said he, "but fear nothing." They did deliberate, and with incredible rancor. They unanimously decided to expel him, and deprive him of his benefice; and to prevent interference in his favor, all was conducted with the utmost secrecy. One of the members, probably his uncle Canon Gizzio, delivered himself as follows: "I have never given a vote of expulsion in this Congregation, but to-day I do it with pleasure." Don Buonacquisto, who related the above, added that the scene reminded him forcibly of the last judgment.

Gizzio and the other principal members went to implore the cardinal to ratify what had been done. But his Eminence showed intense displeasure: "Why," asked he, "do you proceed to such extremities? Either God will bless the enterprise of Don Alphonsus, and it will prove glorious to you; or He will overthrow it, and nothing worse can be said than that a good work was attempted, but did not succeed. In any case, I see no dishonor in it." He added in a tone of authority: "I am Superior of your Congregation; I desire that Don Alphonsus de Liguori be reinstated, and that he continue to enjoy his chaplainship; and I forbid you to take any steps against him, unless authorized by me to do so."

This generous conduct arrested the flame, but did not extinguish it. The deputies were silenced indeed, but they retired more determined than ever, never to recognize Alphonsus as a member of their Congregation.

Alphonsus wrote to the cardinal and to the canon in terms expressive of the most lively gratitude; but it is remarkable that in these letters not a word escapes him with reference to the cruel treatment he had received from his brethren; neither does he justify himself or declare his innocence, but suffers all with admirable sweetness and resignation.

CHAPTER XX.

His severest trial yet — Odd Proposals. — Firmness of the saint Withdrawal of Mandarini — Letter. — Modest proposal of Mandarini. Secession. — Grief of St. Alphonsus.— Freezing reception accorded by Bishop Falcoia.— Temptations. — Terrific struggle. — The pulpits resound with anathemas. — Deserted by all — In Naples. — At Scala again.

THE STORM was subsiding at Naples, and Alphonsus was living in profound tranquillity at Scala, when God, to try His servant more severely than ever, permitted discord to appear in the new-born Congregation. Alphonsus wished that his brethren should be occupied only in promoting the sanctification of clergy and laity, giving spiritual exercises in convents, and instructing destitute souls by means of missions. Mandarini would add colleges to the plan; and each giving his individual opinion Tosquez maintained that, as the end of the Institution was to imitate Jesus Christ, it would be necessary to dress in a dark-red cassock and a mantle of celestial blue, these being the colors our Savior was said to have worn!

Some disliked the recitation of the office in common; others objected to sleeping on straw; a few saw no necessity for rigorous poverty; and the perfect community life to which the founder persistently held, was not pleasing to all. Tosquez, who seems to have had a wonderful liking for extremes, insisted that the brethren should embrace the reform of the most austere mendicant order, having previously sold their estates and laid the price thereof at the feet of the Superior.

Alphonsus could not forbear smiling at the proposal of Doctor Tosquez: "Would it not be absurd," said he, "for simple priests to appear in masquerade, by adopting a blue and red costume?" And with regard to the other proposal, he pleasantly added that he feared the Ananiases would be so numerous, that it would be impossible to bury all who would come forward with a lie in their mouth.

He approved of establishing a choir, as being a good means of reciting the office well; and insisted on the vow of poverty, without which it would be impossible to observe community life. "If," said he, "the words *mine* and *thine* are heard among the brethren, great inconveniences will result; they will go on missions not for God and souls, but for mere temporal emolument."

These conflicting sentiments were well calculated to disturb his serenity: he spoke, he supplicated, he had recourse to prayer; he consulted Mgr. Falcoia, Father Pagano, and Canon Torni, who all looked upon it as a stratagem of the devil. Finally, Mandarini, refusing to yield to the founder, withdrew, accompanied by all the disciples of his master, except Sportelli.

Previous to this sad separation, Mandarini's conduct and influence had been but too instrumental in causing coldness and misunderstanding to creep into the little community. Nor was Alphonsus slow to perceive this: "O my father!" wrote he to Mgr. Falcoia, in the bitterness of his soul, — "you know not how painful it is for me to associate with Don Vincent Mandarini. It is only the love of Christ that has enabled me to keep up friendly relations with him. Thank God, who gives me grace to endure these storms. See what I have deserved for obeying God, renouncing my family, and making light of the reproaches of friends and relations. Still you encourage me to put my confidence in God, even though all my companions should desert me. Ah, my father, do not abandon me! Command and I will obey. Have pity on me, your unworthy son."

The withdrawal of Mandarini and his companions took place in March, 1733, just four months after the auspicious opening at Scala. Yet almost alone as Alphonsus was, he continued to labor for souls with extraordinary zeal and success. Mandarini coveted his zeal and abilities for his own projects: "If your Reverence would only come to us," he wrote from Naples, "we all most earnestly desire a reunion; but if, as I will not believe, you persist in remaining, it will be for us the greatest misfortune."

With this modest request of his late novice, Alphonsus, as will be readily surmised, declined complying. "With God, one is a majority," says a representative man of our day; but St. Teresa had already said as much and in stronger terms. No doubt St. Alphonsus felt this when he was forsaken by the men of learning and prestige, who had renounced the world and undertaken a glorious enterprise at his bidding. Yet Mandarini seems to have been sincerely attached to him: "Command me," he wrote, "if I can ever be of the smallest service to you; for, though absent in body, I am with you in spirit."

The paths of these men diverged from the first separation. Mandarini founded a Congregation which embodied all his plans; and though, later on, he was willing to adopt the views of St. Alphonsus and affiliate his foundation to the order of the Most Holy Redeemer, our saint wisely declined his proposals.

This separation was a terrible trial to the tender heart of the founder. Gloomy thoughts filled his troubled mind; and the rocks of Scala, once so dear to his heart, now seemed to frown upon his projects. In imagination he heard taunts and jeers uttered triumphantly in the salons of Naples when it was announced that his enterprise was a failure, and he shuddered at the scorn the world would lavish on him. Unable to bear up any longer, he sought Mgr. Falcoia, sure of finding in him a friend who would at once strengthen and console him. But God permitted him to be grievously disappointed. The bishop, who had heretofore zealously defended him against all opponents, felt wounded at the disgrace which must necessarily fall upon himself from the failure of the scheme, and received him with marked coldness. "God has no need of you or your companions," was his greeting to his disconcerted *protégé*: "if He wills you to go on, He will raise up other disciples for you." — "My Lord," returned Alphonsus, regaining his courage, " I am well aware that God has no need of me or of my labors; nevertheless I believe it to be his will that I should proceed in this work, and, deserted as I am, I shall yet succeed. I have not left Naples, I have not renounced the world, to gain the glory of founding a new order, but to do the will of God and promote his glory." This reply deeply affected the prelate, who suddenly changing his manner, said: "Put your confidence in God: He will certainly bless your good intentions."

He returned to Scala, much comforted by this interview, but the devil would not leave him in peace. Don Sportelli was necessarily absent frequently; and when Alphonsus found himself alone on this desert mountain, disgust, anxiety, and depression assailed him more strongly than ever. One day, when these temptations were at their height, he fell on his knees and solemnly vowed to consecrate himself to destitute souls, even though he should be left entirely alone. God blessed this heroic act; his fears and anxieties vanished, and he was filled with courage, hope, and consolation.

Even in his old age, our saint could not remember without a shudder the terrific struggle he had sustained on that occasion; and he told his director, Father Dominic Corsano, that this, and his separation from his father, were the two most dreadful trials he had ever undergone.

No sooner was it known that the new founder was abandoned by his companions, than every one in Naples ridiculed the whole affair, condemning the fanaticism of the would-be head of a Congregation who had blindly lent himself to the fancies of a visionary nun. Some even affirmed that the Pope himself had interfered to prevent the establishment of such a Congregation. The very pulpits resounded with anathemas. Preachers showed how even the most favored individuals can go astray, when they allow themselves to be ensnared by the devil, and neglect the practice of humility; and they pointed at Don Alphonsus Liguori as an illustration of their theories.

Even his friends were silenced by the mockery and contempt which everywhere greeted them. Not one was to be found in the city of his birth to say a word in his defence. Father Fiorillo, indeed, felt sure that the devil had raised this storm, and that God would uphold his own work. The cardinal pitied him: "After all," said he, "there is nothing reprehensible in his projects; but who can know the judgments of God?" Embarrassed, however, by an infinity of conflicting reports, he desired Canon Torni to recall Don Alphonsus to Naples.

The reception that awaited him may well be imagined. Canon Gizzio refused to see him or hear his name mentioned. Father Ripa would have no further connection with him, and his example was followed by others who had once held him in the highest esteem.

He at once visited Cardinal Pignatelli, accompanied by Canon Torni. His Eminence was grieved to hear the number of false reports that had been circulated concerning him. The canon, eager to retain his friend in Naples, remarked that, if the work had been pleasing to God, He would not have withdrawn the means of carrying it into execution. To which Alphonsus replied with entire confidence: "We have reason to be convinced that the devil is the author of what has happened at Scala; but do not imagine that I am conquered because the devil has crossed my path. If my first companions have deserted me, other zealous priests can be found; but I should not hesitate to devote myself alone to the salvation of the destitute souls of this kingdom."

The cardinal, unable to refrain from admiring this speech, turned towards Torni and said: "It will not do to abandon Scala just yet; let us have recourse to God, to learn his holy will." Then, to encourage Alphonsus, he said to him: "Trust in God; place no confidence in man, for it is God who will help you." He approved his constancy, and advised him to decline all overtures of reunion with those who had forsaken him.

Consoled by the sentiments of the cardinal, Alphonsus returned to Scala, full of hope. Meanwhile, the opinions expressed by his Eminence reduced to silence those who had previously railed against him. The germ of the future Congregation of the Most Holy Redeemer consisted of the founder, Don Sportelli, still a layman, and Vitus Curzius, a lay-brother. Alphonsus soon had the consolation of seeing his solitude peopled by promising subjects. "Our novices," wrote he, in the fulness of his joy, — "our novices think neither of country nor friends, nor even of suffering: all their desire is to love God, and conform perfectly to his will."

About this time (July, 1733), they left the hospice for a dwelling equally poor, which an eye-witness has described in the following terms: — "There was one small parlor, in which Alphonsus had made an oratory and set up a crucifix so beautifully carved, that it drew tears from the spectators. A square apartment under ground, more like a vault than a chapel, answered for their church. Poverty reigned supreme; they had not even a tabernacle for the Blessed Sacrament, which Alphonsus was obliged to place in a box decorated by himself. The altar was poor, but they endeavored to hide its poverty under bouquets and garlands of flowers. The greater part of the night they passed before the Blessed Sacrament, taking their scanty repose on the bare ground before it."

CHAPTER XXI.

The grotto near Scala. — Prospects brighten. — Don Xavier Rossi. — A foundation after the saint's own heart. — An incident — Father Mazzini. Loss of a Novice. — The wonders of the Thebaid renewed. — Tosquez becomes a financier. — Mandarini endeavors to make reparation.

AFTER THE departure of Mandarini and his companions the spirit of prayer and penance resumed its sway at Scala. All breathed self-denial and mortification, Alphonsus, as usual, signalizing himself above the rest. Close by the house was a half-ruined grotto, where every day he inflicted on his body the most rigorous penances. There is a tradition among the inhabitants that, while practising self-mortification, our Blessed Lady appeared to him, and bestowed upon him many spiritual favors. Even in extreme old age he was wont to sigh after this beloved spot, and cherished the hallowed remembrance of the graces received therein. Whenever he came to Scala, he visited his beloved grotto, exclaiming, "O my grotto, my cherished grotto! why cannot I possess thee now as in bygone days!"

Four months had scarcely elapsed, when our saint was enabled to resume his missions. Meanwhile he had been joined by Don Sarnelli of Ciorani, a priest; and in the following January, yielding to his pressing solicitation, accompanied him to that territory. The inhabitants never lost the remembrance of this first visit, in which they were edified no less by the holy example of these two friends, than by the instructions they gave. After a few days they were invited by the bishop of Cajazzo to give a mission in his diocese. The general reformation which followed excited in the people an ardent desire to have a house of the Order in their midst, but the Fathers were not as yet sufficiently numerous to form a new establishment.

At Formicola, there was a house well suited to the Congregation, with a church adjoining. Among those most anxious that the Fathers should effect a settlement in the town, was Don Xavier Rossi, a young nobleman who had already taken priest's orders. He exerted himself to the utmost, commissioned an architect to make the necessary alterations and repairs, and ordered that all should be done at his expense.

Alphonsus, delighted with the purity of soul he found in Rossi, one day addressed him thus: "Don Xavier, it is yourself God wishes to have, and then this foundation." This saying was a prophecy. At that time, however, Rossi, though filled with admiration for Alphonsus and his companions, had not the courage to imitate them. But, after a while, a sudden movement of grace impelled him to go to Alphonsus, and even in spite of himself to join his little band. He served his mass, and was wont to remark, that it was not a man but a seraph that offered the holy sacrifice. The founder, perceiving his emotion, earnestly entreated the Heart of Jesus to captivate the young patrician; and so effectual were his prayers, that, the moment mass was over, he knelt before Alphonsus and begged to be admitted among his sons. To prove his sincerity, the saint counselled delay; but he gave such incontestable proofs of a strong vocation, that he was speedily admitted to the novitiate. Xavier became a corner-stone of the new Congregation; and having rendered it the greatest services, departed to our Lord in the odor of sanctity.

This foundation was precisely what our saint desired. Situated on the confines of four dioceses, the adjacent country was very thickly peopled, and villages were scattered in every direction. Poverty reigned among the founders of this institution; one carlino (about eight cents) was assigned to each Father for his support. Only a belfry distinguished their dwelling from the surrounding houses. While the building was in progress, the people piously assisted. The neighboring nobles might be seen mingling with the neighboring plebeians, carrying materials. Alphonsus labored like a common workman; and, when the gentlemen endeavored to dissuade him, he said: "I wish to have my share in the merit as well as the rest."

One day, while a poor woman was carrying a large stone, another equally large fell from the scaffolding on her head. Every one thought that the blow was mortal, but Alphonsus addressed himself to our Lady: his prayer was heard, the woman rose up unhurt. No one evinced greater zeal than the young novice Rossi. Not only did he bestow on the good work all he could call his own, but he went about the country begging alms for it, regarding neither the excessive heat, nor the streamlets overflowing from recent rains, that obstructed his passage.

Alphonsus remained here until August, and it was here he had the happiness of receiving Father John Mazzini. Already had this priest attained a high degree of virtue; and such was the opinion the founder entertained of his sanctity, that he made him rector of the new house.

The consolation he derived from this acquisition was neutralized to some extent by the grief he felt at the loss of a promising cleric, Michael Alteriis, whose friends violently forced him away.

Michael had lately joined the Congregation, much to the indignation of his father, who came to the house accompanied by a body of police to carry him off. Alphonsus helped him to escape during the night; but his enraged relations appealed to the cardinal, who advised our saint to let him go.

"This victory will cost them dear," was the comment of Alphonsus. Hardly had the youth returned home, when the eldest son died quite suddenly. In his bereavement, the unhappy father exclaimed: "I have carried off one from God, and God has carried off one from me." However, God blessed Don Michael, because he had always obeyed the voice of his superiors. He subsequently returned to the service of God, and became an infatigable laborer in the vineyard of the Lord; and, after a useful and holy life, died in the odor of sanctity.

The life which our saint led with his dear brethren, renewed the wonders of the Thebaid. He ate sometimes on his knees with a heavy stone suspended from his neck; his food usually consisted of pottage which he seasoned with bitter herbs. He took the discipline in private as well as in common, wore a heavy haircloth, and reposed, it may be said, on the boards, so thin was his poor mattress. His humility was extraordinary; before and after meals he would frequently kiss the feet of his spiritual sons, placing himself in spirit beneath the lowliest of them. His cassock was so worn and mended, that there remained scarcely any of the original garment. On his journeys he would never use a horse, but went on foot or mounted on a sorry mule.

A profound silence reigned throughout the house. Towards evening all assembled for recreation, which was in their case little more than an interchange of sentiments on spiritual things. Besides the meditations made in common, our saint was in continual prayer, and spoke only when necessary.

Many priests and able young men were attracted to the rising Institute; and these, charmed and edified by the sweetness and sanctity of Alphonsus, drew others after them. But if subjects came in crowds, unfortunately they withdrew in crowds, for few could endure a life so painful to flesh and blood.

From a missionary and projector of an order of men to be dressed in red and blue, Don Tosquez became a financier and minister of state. A brother of his having died at Vienna, he went thither to administer his estate. On the way, he visited Pope Clement XII, to obtain a dispensation to be promoted to the priesthood. But at Vienna he displayed such consummate business talents, that the Pope, on his return, made him inspector of all the ports on the Adriatic in the Roman States. Every week he had a private audience, which gave him admission to the Council of Cardinals charged with the administration of civil affairs.

He repented of the absurd projects he had once suggested to our saint, and frequently spoke of him with the greatest esteem to his Holiness, who in consequence took no small interest in his success as founder of an Order.

Mandarini equally regretted the division. He even went with Tosquez to the Pope, to render justice to Alphonsus. His Holiness was much delighted to hear such good tidings, and promised to do every thing he could for the founder.

Mandarini wrote to Alphonsus, begging him to come to Rome immediately and take advantage of the Pope's favorable dispositions. "The Head of the Church," wrote he, "being so favorably disposed towards your enterprise, I unite with all the others to beseech you to reunite the scattered sheep, that we may more efficaciously cooperate for the glory of God and the salvation of souls."

Although this letter rejoiced our saint, he did not judge the proposed reunion advantageous to his work. He therefore sent a polite but indecisive reply.

CHAPTER XXII.

Alphonsus preaches the Lent in the cathedral of Scala — Singular incident. Reception of the Fathers at Ciorani. — Abundant fruits of that Mission. Retreat for the nobles. — Villani joins the Congregation. — Trials.

W HEN THE new foundation seemed sufficiently consolidated, Alphonsus returned to Scala. He was greatly consoled by the good which Sportelli had effected in his absence; nor was his consolation abated on learning that many candidates had been awaiting his arrival with impatience. At the request of Bishop Santoro, he reluctantly consented to preach the Lent in the cathedral of Scala, after which he conducted retreats in several monasteries of nuns.

It happened one day that the bishop was preparing to assist at some representation, and, Alphonsus calling, the prelate invited him to accompany him. Our saint excused himself on various pretexts: "Oh, you are scrupulous!" remarked the prelate; "but where a bishop can go, missionaries may surely appear." — "It is not that" returned Alphonsus, "but I fear the platform will give way." — "Father Liguori," interrupted the bishop, "I know you are an excellent spiritual father, but I do not yet recognize you to be a prophet." — He then ordered the master of ceremonies to have chairs placed for Alphonsus and his companion. Our saint, no longer able to resist, begged the prelate to allow them to sit near the door. Scarcely was the prologue terminated, when the platform gave way and the play came to an end, in a manner painful to several present.

Father Sarnelli ardently desired to see a house of the Congregation in the territory of Ciorani, of which his father was baron. The pastor, Angelo Guadiello, learning the good done by the missionaries in the neighboring parishes, earnestly sought similar advantages for his own. Don Andrew Sarnelli, brother of J. Sarnelli, entered with spirit into the scheme; and persuading the baron of the immense advantages that would result therefrom, easily obtained his consent. By April, he had secured for their maintainance a rent of one hundred ducats, which was afterwards increased to two hundred, and finally to five hundred.

When the Archbishop of Salerno was informed of this, his joy was boundless. As soon as the necessary arrangements had been made, Alphonsus came to Ciorani with Mazzini and Rossi, in May, 1735. Four wretched donkeys formed their equipage. An immense concourse awaited them, among whom were the pastor and his curates. Hundreds of men appeared carrying muskets, which they fired off at intervals, *vivas* resounding in every direction. "Behold the saint! Behold the saint!" was the salutation which greeted Alphonsus on all sides. The bells rang out their most joyous peals, as the fathers led the way to the parochial church.

Inspired by the presence of so vast a multitude, Alphonsus ascended the pulpit; and taking as his subject the motive of his coming — the salvation of their souls — he preached with such powerful effect, that the hearts of his auditors were penetrated with compunction, and their eyes suffused with tears.

The baron asked him to become his guest, but on that day he sought no repose: the sick who were unable to leave their houses, sighed for a visit from the servant of God. Overflowing with charity, he would not delay to gratify their longings.

Next day, he received the felicitations of the pastors of the neighborhood and the noblemen of the country. In the evening he opened the mission, and the immense church was not capacious enough to contain the crowds that followed him. Seeing the saint so poor, so humble, so radiant with devotion, the most hardened sinners were touched, and the conversions effected were innumerable.

The house which the baron had given them consisted of a species of cellar or cave which served as a kitchen, and two rooms more spacious than those of Scala. He afterwards added two more rooms; but, in passing from one to the other, they were obliged to cross an open court, which was a great inconvenience, especially in winter. Planks formed the exterior wall of these apartments, admitting wind and rain through innumerable chinks. But these inconveniences were small, compared to that resulting from the fact, that the basement of their dwelling was occupied partly by a public house, and partly by a prison.

In one of these chambers Alphonsus, with the sanction of the archbishop, erected a small oratory, reserving the remaining room for a sleeping apartment. Far from having superfluities, necessaries were often wanting to the missionaries; but they rejoiced in these privations, happy to participate in the sorrows and sufferings of Jesus Christ. Their oratory was their heaven. There might the holy founder be seen in the stillness of the night, pouring forth his soul into the bosom of his God.

So great was the concourse of people that attended the mission, that the Fathers had scarcely time to eat or sleep. From morning till night the confessionals were thronged; but, as penitents came very early and disturbed the slumbers of the poor old pastor, Alphonsus undertook to repair the ancient church of St. Sophia, annexed to the baronial palace, and in future received the people there. As all the inhabitants of the neighboring villages could not come to Ciorani, Alphonsus sent missionaries on feast days, to preach in distant places and comfort the sick and aged.

Ere long, Ciorani was thoroughly reformed. Quarrels and dissensions were unheard of, the pious canticles of Alphonsus replaced the profane and licentious songs that had heretofore sullied the lips of the young people, and all emulated the virtues of the first Christians. When the inhabitants met, they saluted one another by saying, "Praise be to Jesus and Mary!" The little children, taught by their mothers, lisped this blessed salutation whenever they met the priests. So abundant were the seeds of salvation sown in this territory, that their fruits are still to be seen among the inhabitants.

Many persons of quality, seeing the effect produced on the humbler classes, ardently desired to have a kind of mission for themselves. The baron being then in Naples, Alphonsus obtained leave to give the mission in the great hall of the castle. Several ecclesiastics assisted at this mission, and the fruits were recognized in their redoubled zeal for souls. It was in this retreat that the young priest, Andrew Villani, a descendant of the dukes of Sacco della Polla, resolved to despise the transitory joys of this world, and consecrate himself to God in the new Congregation, of which he became so admirable an ornament

But while these works, so glorious to God, were progressing, the devil excited the jealousy of some neighboring curates, who, instead of emulating the zeal of the missionaries, regarded it as a reproach to themselves, and so embarrassed the archbishop with their complaints, that he began to think of suppressing the house. But this misfortune was happily averted, God permitting the opponents, both secular and religious, to be disabused of their error. Hence, on the 12th of December, 1735, his Grace, by a pastoral letter, definitely authorized the new foundation, to the general satisfaction of the whole province.

CHAPTER XXIII.

Imprudent Suggestion of Don Andrew Sarnelli. — Evil consequences.— The Archbishop defends Alphonsus. — Terrific incident.— Extraordinary success of the mission at Naples. — Interesting Conversion. — Mission at Santa Lucia. Violent Persecutions. — Punishment of the persecutors.

T HE HOUSE at Ciorani was prospering miraculously, when the devil again assailed it. Don Andrew Sarnelli, moved by an injudicious zeal, suggested to the archbishop that, as so many pastors profited by the labors of the missionaries, each should contribute a trifle towards their support. This measure was violently opposed by the pastors, several of whom demanded that the missionaries should be driven out of the territory. The pastor of Ciorani, on being invited to join the adverse party, indignantly exclaimed: "What! would you have me deprive my flock of the great help afforded by these holy priests who labor incessantly in my parish?"

They then represented to the archbishop, that the missionaries, under pretence of zeal and devotedness, sought to enrich themselves at the expense of the legitimate pastors. His grace smiled coldly and said: "I know Alphonsus di Liguori. Like myself, he is of noble birth. Vocation, not necessity, induced him to renounce the world. Whatever anxiety he has is to sanctify souls and himself, not to amass wealth."

As soon as the inhabitants of Ciorani heard of these complaints, they sent a deputation to the archbishop to vouch for the zeal and disinterestedness of the missionaries, and his Grace replied very graciously that he took the missionaries under his immediate protection, and approved of the works to which they had devoted themselves, as being most advantageous to the souls confided to his pastoral care.

This storm having abated like its predecessors, the priests who were most opposed to our saint were the first to profit by his labors.

In the course of a retreat he gave to priests about this time, the following terrible incident occurred: Speaking of the enormity of sin in the sacerdotal state, he quoted the words of St. Chrysostom: "In the priesthood, to sin is to perish." At these words, one of his auditors exclaimed, *Nego consequentiam*: "I deny this consequence." The unhappy man soon experienced the consequence. Next morning, on beginning the psalm, *Judica me, Deus*, "Judge me, O God!" — he dropped dead on the altar steps.

In October, 1737, at the pressing entreaty of the Superior of the Propaganda, he went to Naples to conduct the mission to be opened in the church of the Holy Ghost on the 26th of that month. The good which God operated by his ministry was so abundant, that volumes would be required to register the conversions he made on this occasion.

After this mission, he proceeded to Amalfi; and thence to Majuri. In this place, a poor woman whose son had been assassinated, had persistently refused to pardon the murderer, though urged by the most influential persons. But a sermon by our saint so touched her heart, that she immediately wrote a declaration to the effect that she had pardoned the murderer, and, bringing it to the church, publicly laid it at the foot of the crucifix.

He was now called by his uncle, Mgr. di Liguori, to the hamlet of St. Lucy, in the diocese of Cava. The inhabitants led very irregular lives; but where sin had abounded, grace did much more abound. Abuses were extirpated, restitutions were made, scandals were repaired; and so convincingly did he treat of the merit and dignity of chastity, that many left the world to consecrate themselves to God in religion.

The buildings at Villa dei Schiavi were nearly completed, and the house was filled with priests and candidates for the ministry, whom Alphonsus directed in the way of perfection. A congregation of artisans had been established, which already numbered more than two hundred brethren, whose zeal and fervor made them missionaries throughout the district. The frequentation of the sacraments became general, and many individuals were aiming at a high degree of perfection.

But again a storm arose which withered these blossoms, so full of hope for eternity. Under the pretext of defending the interests of the resident priests, a certain sower of discord began to declaim against the missionaries for coming hither to eat the bread of the inhabitants. The calumnies increased to such an extent, that their morals were attacked. Father Liguori himself was denounced as a hypocrite who made traffic of his affected sanctity.

Nor did the iniquity stop here. A wretched creature was suborned to defame Alphonsus, and she boldly showed presents which she declared she had received from him. But he took these slanders quite calmly, knowing that persecution is the inseparable accompaniment of works undertaken for God; he merely cautioned the community to be still more circumspect in behavior, and to recur more frequently to prayer and penance, as their great resource.

The promoter of these infamies finally succeeded in prejudicing the baron himself; and when our saint went to claim his protection, the irritated nobleman designated him as "one of these nasty hermits," and immediately dismissed him with many opprobrious marks of contempt.

This scene being widely noised abroad, filled his enemies with joy. They now even dared to solicit the Neapolitan tribunals to interfere, but without success. Finally, they had recourse to open violence. As one of the lay brothers was going to the church to ring the Angelus, a warden, accompanied by several disaffected persons, met him, forced the keys out of his hands, locked the church, and ignominiously drove him back to the house. To forestall any defence friends might be disposed to make, they placed men, armed with loaded muskets, on the belfry.

They next besieged the house, to which all communication with the outer world was sternly interdicted. The situation becoming every day less endurable, their friends at Naples advised them to abandon the place to its fate. The bishop wept with regret, the poor people were disconsolate, and the surrounding villages were in mourning. On the night of June 10th, 1737, the Fathers shook the dust from their feet, and left the hamlet they had come to evangelize.

God did not permit all this wickedness to go unpunished. The wretch who had accused the saintly missionaries had her tongue eaten by worms, so that she could not receive the Viaticum. Seized with the acutest remorse, she publicly confessed that she had uttered the most infamous calumnies. More terrible was the fate of other calumniators: one died in despair, littering the most frightful cries; another howled like a maniac, and died in that state; a third, who had suborned false witnesses and written down their testimony, had his hand withered; the death of an only son soon after caused him to become an idiot, and he died in indescribable misery.

A fourth, who had been bribed to attest all the slanders, died in impenitence. A fifth, a healthy young man, fell dead on the ground immediately after the departure of Alphonsus. The chief instigator remained deaf to all these warnings. During a tremendous storm a thunderbolt fell at his feet; it stunned him, and he remained for some time without sense or motion. Yet even this warning he failed to recognize. But, ere long, he fell into disgrace with his prince, was ill-used and persecuted, and within a year was found one morning a corpse under his bed, weltering in his blood. In a word, all who persecuted our saint and his children were made terrible examples of the divine vengeance, as all the ancient inhabitants of the place have testified.

CHAPTER XXIV.

Another mission. — Apparition of our Lady to Alphonsus.— Castellamare. The new house at Ciorani. — Scala relinquished. — Regret of the inhabitants. The rain at Aquarola. — Priests. — "The Apostle." — Wonderful cure. — The standard bearer of the Redemptorist Order.— Alphonsus writes his epitaph.

A VAST field was now opened for the labors of our saint. He gave numerous missions, everywhere reaping the most abundant harvest. In the little village of Ajillo, especially, God gave him extraordinary success. Scandals disappeared, the taverns were deserted, and the churches were filled. There was not a house in the place in which the rosary was not said in common every evening.

It was here, too, that the Blessed Virgin was pleased to give Alphonsus a public testimony of her love. One evening, while he was expatiating on her glories, he was ravished in ecstasy and raised some feet above the pulpit; at the same time rays of glory darted from a statue of our Lady and rested on the head of her chosen servant.

Shortly after, he visited Castellamare, a maritime town, in great need of spiritual succor. Eight companions shared his labors, and multitudes were converted. Smuggling was discontinued, and the magical practices common among the sailors given up. The churches were crowded, the sacraments frequented, and the whole town breathed an air of sanctity.

By this time the new house at Ciorani was finished, together with the small church, and the missionaries removed into it. Here, too, poverty predominated, and piety was the chief ornament. It was dedicated to the Blessed Virgin, and in it our saint placed the beloved statue of that dear Mother before which he had so often poured out his heart in the retreats he made with his companions

121

at the house of Don Alteriis. The conveniences which the new establishment afforded, drew thither numerous ecclesiastics and laymen, especially in the general missions, so that our saint and his sons, to practise hospitality, had frequently to sleep on the floor of an apartment which had formerly been used as an oven room.

It is doubtful whether Nitria or the Thebaide ever counted, among the solitaries that enlivened them with still life, more perfect models of every religious virtue than the Fathers of Ciorani. Not a superfluous word, no going out without necessity, profound humility, perfect obedience, no pretension, no repugnance, no jealousy, — each was content with his employment, the will of Alphonsus was regarded as the rule by his brethren and sons in the Lord.

But the more he endeavored to consolidate the new work, the more the devil sought to destroy it. Several individuals, having learned what had happened at the Villa began to murmur and to excite the jealousy of others. Alphonsus, to avoid new misfortunes, removed from Scala; a proceeding deeply painful to the good bishop and the inhabitants.

Hell rejoiced at this step; and, years after, Father Tannoia heard from a soul far advanced in perfection, that, on the night of the departure of the missionaries, the shouts and dancing of the evil spirits disturbed the repose of the inhabitants. No wonder: Scala had been thoroughly reformed. Two years later, when a mission was preached there by the Pious Workers, they scarcely found among the people a voluntary venial sin, and all sorts of pious practices were rigorously kept up. Yet calamities followed the departure of the missionaries. A few days after, a violent storm destroyed the chesnuts upon which the poor of that district chiefly live. But Alphonsus could not forget his beloved Scala. Absent in body, he was often present there in spirit, and every year either went thither himself, or sent some of his Fathers, to give the novena of the crucifix, that the nuns, who afterwards took the name of Religious of the Most Holy Redeemer, might not be deprived of their annual retreat.

The fields in which the holy founder labored during the following autumn and winter, were not less fertile in fruits of salvation. At Castiglione the concourse was so great, that people, desirous of hearing him preach in the morning, passed the night in the church. The name of Alphonsus had become so renowned in these parts, by reason of the wonders of grace operated by him, that people often walked a distance of seventeen miles to confess to him.

At Calvanico, the ecclesiastics to whom as usual he gave the spiritual exercises, were animated with such fervor, that they followed in his suite to assist at the missions, — a practice not unfrequent at present.

In the summer he returned to Ciorani, to give a little repose to the body overpowered with fatigue, and refresh the spirit in retirement.

In the beginning of 1740, accompanied by eleven brethren, he evangelized the country, shedding the benedictions of heaven on many villages in which great disorders had previously reigned. Having finished the spring missions he again returned to Ciorani to regulate the affairs of the Congregation, and reanimate his brethren by his example in the observance of the rules.

The country of St. Severino suffered from great drought this year. To obtain the divine mercy, the inhabitants of Aquarola invited Alphonsus to give a mission towards the end of July. Their fervor was rewarded: one day he foretold that at a certain time rain would fall. The day indicated set in without any appearance of rain, but all at once a very small cloud was perceived above Salerno. When our saint saw it, he extended his arms, as if to invite its approach; and then, prostrating himself on the ground, he besought the divine mercy in behalf of the people. Immediately clouds obscured the sky, thunder rolled, lightning flashed, and during the next five hours the rain fell in torrents.

In autumn he continued his missionary labors, with signal success. Among the thousands who owed their conversion to his zeal, were several bandits and murderers. Many ecclesiastics who had been cold and indifferent, now devoted themselves to God with admirable fervor. This rejoiced our saint exceedingly: "The conversion of a priest," he would say, "is more glorious to God than that of a hundred seculars; for no layman, though he be a saint, can perform the good works peculiar to the priestly office."

He had great consolation in revisiting two monasteries, whose inmates led lives of wonderful virtue. He strove to confirm them more and more in regular observance, love of prayer and recollection, detachment from the world, frequentation of the sacraments, and love of Jesus and Mary.

A zealous priest of Nocera, Don Nicholas Tipaldi, who had become acquainted with the Fathers at Ciorani, eagerly desired the blessing of their presence near his own home. Knowing that Contaldi, the Dean of Nocera, had resolved to endow a house of missionaries, he spoke to him and to the principal inhabitants of the virtues of Father di Liguori and his companions, and arranged that they should give a mission in the town. This had the greatest success. Numerous conversions were wrought among ecclesiastics and seculars, and Alphonsus was universally designated the "Apostle."

He certainly enjoyed many supernatural gifts: he knew how to touch all hearts. The spirit of prophecy and the gift of healing accompanied him; and he often cured the most grievous fevers, by merely making the sign of the cross over the patient.

While he lodged in the house of Don Nicholas, the mother of that priest who was subject to violent convulsions from acute pains in her arms, full of faith in the sanctity of her holy guest, wrapped herself in a shirt belonging to him, and was immediately cured. This made the people more anxious than ever to have the Fathers among them, but their hopes were not realized until a later period.

It was on the 18th of April, the same year, that God called to himself the first member of the Congregation, Joachim Gaudiello, lay-brother. He died in transports of joy, exclaiming: "It is I who carry the standard!" All the virtues seemed to have made their home in the beautiful soul of this good brother. As his portrait had not been taken before burial, the Fathers allowed his coffin to be opened eleven days after his death, in the hope that his body might still be incorrupt. The event justified their expectations: the sacred remains were found entire and flexible, as if still animated by the pure soul.

The holy founder himself wrote in Latin the epitaph of this dear and cherished son. We give a translation; —

"Brother Joachim Gaudiello, rich in every virtue, sighed only for perfect resemblance to Jesus Christ, assimilating himself in every respect to this divine model, especially by his patience in infirmity, and his sweetness under adversities. He was particularly remarkable for his obedience: always the same, his whole life was but a following of Christ. Not on the wood of the cross, it is true; but yet with the desire of the cross, and embracing the crucifix, the first member of our dear Congregation was crowned with celestial glory."

CHAPTER XXV.

Mission in Naples. — Disagreeable incident. — Firmness of the cardinal. Alphonsus' Christmas Hospitality. — Father Cafaro becomes a Redemptorist. Proposals of the cardinal. — Rejected by the saint. — He is mistaken for the cook. — His unselfishness.— Renewal of missions. — He originates the Novenas previous to our Lady's Feasts.

P ROVIDENCE had prepared for our saint yet another field to cultivate. In the spring of 1741 his Eminence Cardinal Spinelli, who had succeeded Cardinal Pignatelli, lately deceased, invited him to give some missions in Naples. He declined, on the plea that the capital was much better supplied with priests than the country, but the cardinal insisted, and he was obliged to yield; for the city of his birth had certainly some claim upon his services.

That his other missions might suffer but as little as possible, he took from his own Congregation only Fathers Sarnelli and Villani; but, in compliance with the wishes of the cardinal, he chose the *elite* of all the Neapolitan Congregations to assist him, his Eminence being anxious that others might learn from him how to conduct missions with success. A country house in the Barra was placed at the disposal of the missionaries.

The Superior of the Propaganda was exceedingly annoyed at this arrangement. He affirmed that his Congregation enjoyed precedence over all the other Congregations in the kingdom, and that therefore to him belonged the right of nominating the chief; but the real motive of his opposition was the unwillingness of the members of the Propaganda to submit to a priest whom they had endeavored to expel. But the cardinal would not admit their claims: "I am your Archbishop," said he, "I am Superior of all the missions in my diocese: if the missions depend on me, it is I who will regulate them, and not others."

In May, the missions commenced at Fragola, where Alphonsus opened three at once, in three parochial churches. As usual, he established the practice of morning and evening prayer in the church, visits to the Blessed Sacrament and the Blessed Virgin, exposition of the Blessed Sacrament, and protestation for a good death, once a month. To render the priests more skilful in the confessional, he instituted conferences to be held every eight days, in which were discussed cases of conscience. He established the Way of the Cross in each parish, and exhorted the faithful to the practice of this devotion, especially on Fridays, in memory of the sufferings of our Lord.

When the summer heats came, the holy founder dismissed the Neapolitan missionaries, and remained with his own Fathers at St. Agnello, where they continued to preach and hear the confessions of crowds who came from all quarters. On feast days they evangelized the neighboring hamlets, exhorting the people to repentance.

On these missions, they followed the rule established for the Congregation. Their bill of fare was rather frugal. Soup, vegetables, boiled meat, fish of the cheapest description, were the principal dishes, even when persons of distinction dined with them. This rule was but slightly relaxed even at Christmas. Persons attached to the household of the cardinal, who dined with the Fathers on that feast, jested about "the grand dinner" on their return. "Your Eminence is not aware," said they, "of the great treat Father di Liguori gave us at Christmas: forcemeat balls were added on that occasion, at the risk of ruining his household economy!"

Alphonsus, whether at home or on the missions, provided necessaries, but he had a horror of superfluities. He allowed the other missionaries to travel in carriages, because they were accustomed to it; but asses and mules served for himself and his brethren.

For a long time, Father Paul Cafaro, pastor of St. Peter's at Cava, had wished to join the Congregation; he was a man skilled in theology and canon-law, pious and full of zeal for the salvation of souls. Admitted by Alphonsus, much to the chagrin of Mgr.

Liguori, bishop of Cava, he ultimately became one of the principal pillars of the Congregation of the Most Holy Redeemer.

In November, the missionaries met again and resumed their labors. During Holy Week, 1742, Alphonsus, though in the service of Mgr. Spinelli, could not refuse to go to Nocera to give the exercises in honor of the Holy Sacrament, in the great church of Corpus Christi, the salutary effects of which were most consoling.

The cardinal, in view of the wonderful blessings that followed the labors of the Fathers, proposed to establish them in Barra, situated in the centre of his diocese. But Alphonsus objected. "When my missionaries," said he, "will be settled at Barra, and have ladies and gentlemen for their penitents, will they be willing to leave that place for hamlets and mountains? Who knows but that, fascinated by their noble penitents, they may fix themselves at Naples for the greater part of the year? Your Eminence is in no want of able workmen at Naples, but other bishops have not the same advantages. It is not from Naples that we can draw missionaries for the remote villages." — This reasoning appeared conclusive to the cardinal, who no longer insisted on the proposed foundation.

During the Octave of Easter, he resumed the country missions; and, before the close of the season, he had given seventy missions, besides the spiritual exercises. An eye-witness, speaking of the effects of his labors, says: "Were I to report all the facts that came under my observation, they would fill volumes. In the diocese of Naples, Father di Liguori banished scandals and abuses without number. No more unbecoming conduct in church; women no longer dressed in a manner calculated to give scandal, and occasion sin in the weak. Girls who formerly seemed ignorant of the very name of modesty, now behaved with becoming reserve. Taverns were no longer frequented, dangerous pastimes were abolished, and the licentious songs, so common in the harvest and vintage, now gave place to pious canticles."

Meanwhile, the labors of Alphonsus were extraordinary: mind and body were continually on the stretch. He managed to do what would have overpowered another, so that people said he lived by a miracle. He often preached twice, and sometimes even thrice a day. His meals were always frugal, or, rather, poor. He gave but little time to sleep. During his journeys and missions he never diminished his bodily austerities, although he made others take some care of themselves. He always travelled on an ass, and those who did not know him often mistook him for a domestic. One day, as he preached the opening sermon of a mission, the peasants, struck by his beautiful language, said to one another: "Well, if the cook can preach in that manner, what will it be when the others begin?"

He always reserved for himself the worst bed and the most incommodious chamber. Every thing came well to him, provided he was mortified and humiliated. At Casal Nuovo, he gave up to his companions the only three rooms to be had, and reserved for himself a miserable ruin, still pointed out as having once accommodated Father Liguori.

As the harvest time approached, our saint thought it best to confirm the good already done, before beginning new labors. He therefore sent missionaries in small numbers, and for a few days only, to those places in which missions had already been given. These renewals produced much fruit. They reanimated the fervor of confraternities, confirmed the people in their pious practices, raised up those who had fallen, and encouraged those who persevered in virtue.

During this summer, he labored incessantly to promote devotion to the Mother of God, giving retreats for nine days previous to each of her feasts. He thus originated the novenas, now so common in Naples and other places, and so beneficial to those who engage in them.

CHAPTER XXVI.

The Saint resolves to form his disciples into a regular community.— Reasons. Withdrawal of Father Majorino. — His letter. — Poverty. — Ecclesiastical Dignities. — Obedience. — Vow of Stability. — Dispensation. — The saint leaves Naples. — Father Sarnelli replaces him. — Interview with the Cardinal. He returns to Ciorani.

HITHERTO our saint and his companions had lived together, without binding themselves by vows; but, remembering that the spirit of religion is liable to decay rather than increase, he now determined to fix the spirit of piety by vow, and form his Congregation into a religious community.

He therefore represented to his companions the merit they would acquire when, by vow, they would have freely sacrificed their own wills, and despoiled themselves of worldly wealth. "The renunciation of our own will," said he, "procures more glory to God than all the good works we would undertake by choice. A delicious fruit is pleasant to him to whom we present it; but, if with the fruit we offer the tree that has borne it, the offering acquires far greater value. The vow will be as a buckler against the devil and our own inconstancy. It will confirm us in the service of God, and be as an anchor to preserve us secure, when beaten about by the winds of temptation."

Fathers Sportelli, Mazzini, Sarnelli, Rossi, Vilani, and Cafaro, were regarded as the foundations upon which the Congregation was built, not only because they were its earliest members, but also on account of their distinguished merit. No importunity was necessary to induce them to make this generous sacrifice; on the contrary, they incessantly besought the holy founder to permit them to make it. The decision was hastened by the withdrawal of

Father Charles Majorino, a zealous priest and a man of undoubted virtue, but who returned to the world through excessive tenderness for his relations.

Hardly had he left the Congregation — which he did without even acquainting Alphonsus — when he recognized his error; but, unhappily, he had not courage to repair it.

"My Father," he wrote to Alphonsus, "I condemn my inconstancy and my inordinate attachment to my parents. I have always praised the great virtues practised in your community, and shall ever continue to praise them. How happy you are! I weep, I shall always bewail my misfortune. I shall never cease to praise the virtues practised among you: whoever envies not your lot shows that he knows not God, or that he has lost his senses."

As the inconstancy of a man so exemplary as Majorino, was a subject of grief for his brothers, it was also for each of them a powerful incentive to consummate without delay the sacrifice they meditated for God.

Regarding poverty, it was determined that each, in preserving his wealth, should renounce the temporary use of it in favor of his relations; but when they did not require it, the revenues should be placed at the disposal of the superiors of the Congregation.

As to ecclesiastical dignities, it was agreed that they should refuse every thing of the kind, unless commanded by the Pope himself. No distinction of rank or merit was allowed, that the life might be perfectly in common; to the end, to unite them more closely to God and to one another.

Having by these regulations banished interest and cupidity, he desired above all to unite hearts, by the vow of obedience, to the will of one superior.

"Where obedience is wanting," said he, "true religious cannot live; and what would have been a paradise by concord, becomes a hell by diversity of feeling and sentiment."

He therefore ordained that there should be no will but that of the superior; and that, in the Congregation, reply and excuse should be unknown. He established by unanimous consent that every one, on the termination of his novitiate, should make a vow to live and die in the Congregation; but, in case of sufficient cause, dispensation could be obtained, but only from the Sovereign Pontiff or the Superior-General; while the Congregation would always be free to dismiss any member whose conduct should be disedifying, and who should prove incorrigible.

Distrusting his own lights, he had recourse to God, and consulted many pious persons, especially Mgr. Falcoia. His plans being approved by all concerned, it was resolved that the profession should take place on St. Mary Magdalen's feast, July 22, 1742, after three days of retreat. The Institute not being yet confirmed by the Pope, and Alphonsus having no legitimate character of superior, they agreed to make their vow of perseverance to Mgr. Falcoia, in his quality of bishop, as he took such a deep interest in the Congregation. All were filled with the most lively joy; and our saint, after giving thanks to God, and exhorting his brethren to be faithful to the grace of their vocation, returned to the Barra with Father Villani, to resume his labors.

Although convinced of the great good which resulted from his missions in the diocese of Naples, and the extreme satisfaction of the cardinal, it was with regret that he labored in the capital, knowing that his Eminence had many zealous missionaries at his own disposal, and that there were hundreds of other places in extreme spiritual destitution. He prayed, and besought his brethren to pray, that he might be delivered from Naples. He also entreated the Canon James Fontana, a man of great merit and very agreeable to the cardinal, to obtain leave for him to withdraw from these missions.

His Eminence was not pleased at this proposal, and peremptorily declared that, if Alphonsus left, he would discontinue the missions altogether. Fontana, however, persisted, and finally persuaded him that the missions could be carried on successfully without Alphonsus. But it was only on condition that Father Sarnelli should remain to superintend them, that the cardinal consented to part with Alphonsus.

Mounted on a wretched mule, Alphonsus traversed the streets of Naples, and alighted at the gate of the archiepiscopal palace. Some were edified by his humility, others laughed at him. He sat in a remote recess of the anteroom which was filled with ecclesiastics and other gentlemen. In a few moments the cardinal came out, and, not noticing the other visitors, went straight to the holy founder, took him by the hand, and led him into an inner room. He spoke of the missions, and thanked the saint for the zeal he had shown in the cause. He begged advice regarding all that could be useful to the people, and testified the greatest regret at losing him. Alphonsus thanked the good prelate for the favors received at his hands, and begged a continuance of his protection for the new Congregation.

He then proceeded to the Barra, where he had promised to make the novena of the Assumption; and, this being finished, he returned to Ciorani, accompanied by Father Villani.

CHAPTER XXVII.

The House at Pagani. — Humiliations. — Ambition of Count Joseph for his son. — Edifying letter. — A new foundation. — Miracle. — Wonderful fruits of the mission. — The Blessed Virgin sends a sinner to Father Liguori.

THE zeal of the dean of Nocera and the ardent desire of the inhabitants of Pagani were now about to be recompensed. Clergy and laity were equally desirous of having the Congregation established among them. The dean gave the house and furniture, promising to give at his death a further legacy of three thousand ducats. He expressed his intention of living in the house with them, and they promised to treat him as if he were one of themselves. The house was opened, October, 1742, to the great satisfaction of all. Father Sportelli was appointed rector, and Fathers Mazzini and Jourdan were to remain with him.

Having given up Naples, Alphonsus commenced preaching missions in the more destitute parts of the country. As usual, his apostolic labors were crowned with the most astonishing success. God furnished him with many occasions of exercising patience, meekness, and humility.

In one of the many villages which be evangelized, the abbot of a monastery refused him hospitality; and, when ordered by the archbishop to receive him, obeyed with a very bad grace. As soon as the mission was over, he declined to accommodate his saintly guest any further; and, though suffering from fever induced by excessive fatigue, Alphonsus left without uttering a word of complaint.

By order of the archbishop, he repaired to St. Thecla, although scarcely convalescent. Here, too, he was badly received, the pastor pretending he could not lodge him, and that he had sent a message to that effect. A notary who was present on this occasion, was so indignant at the language of the pastor, that he offered the saint and his companions the use of his own house, which they gratefully accepted.

Again at Carrea, the pastor would not allow him to give a mission, though the archbishop of Amalfi had commanded it, and positively refused to receive Alphonsus into his house. Not in the least disconcerted, he quietly took refuge in a corner of the church. A gentleman who had witnessed these inhospitable proceedings, received the missionaries into his own house, and God blessed their labors with signal success.

When Alphonsus, always more and more disgusted with the world, retired to Ciorani to pass his days in prayer, penance, and labors for its salvation, the world again beset him with its allurements. Don Joseph could not bear to see him devote his brilliant talents to poor shepherds and peasants, but longed intensely to see him raised to an eminent position in the Church. To compass this, he employed every imaginable artifice, but his blessed son was invulnerable to all his attacks. "Speak to me no more, dear father," he wrote, "about the episcopate; for, if you should succeed in obtaining it for me, I would refuse it. We make it a rule in our Congregation to refuse all such dignities and honors."

The count longed to have his son elevated to high rank on earth, but Alphonsus only coveted for his father the highest degrees of heavenly honor. "I beseech you, my dear father," he wrote, "to keep yourself more closely united to God. Confess often, and have your accounts ready, for our Lord will come when we least expect him. Think of your advanced age: who knows how soon you may be called from this world? Come the day will, whether we watch or not. I recommend you to hear mass daily, for I fear much for your eternal salvation. I hope the Blessed Virgin will assist you; but, without your cooperation, she will do nothing. Pray that I may accomplish the designs of God. I humble myself before you and kiss your feet, imploring your paternal benediction."

The affairs of the Congregation continued to prosper at Nocera. Mgr. Dominicis having represented to King Charles the spiritual destitution of his diocese, and the good that Alphonsus wrought in it by missions, the monarch wisely consented to the formation of a missionhouse. and letters of authorization were speedily issued. When the first stone of the establishment was laid, the chapter of the cathedral and four pastors attended, the dean himself giving the benediction. Hardly was the edifice commenced, when materials flowed in from all quarters, as if by miracle. Men and women strove to rival one another in contributing towards its erection; even ladies of quality divested themselves of their jewels in its behalf, and, like the gentlemen, worked with their own hands at the building.

When the people of Angri learned the good our saint was doing, they insisted on having a mission, the place containing about five thousand souls. He went thither in November, and was received as an apostle. The people strove each to procure some object he had worn or touched. He lodged in the house of one Lawrence Rossi, whose daughter Teresa obtained from a lay-brother a pair of stockings tinged with his blood. She preserved them devoutly till a religious reproved her for doing so, as the owner of them was not yet canonized; upon which she gave them away to a poor man whose legs were swollen by dropsy. Some days after he returned to the house entirely cured; and, when she expressed her astonishment, he replied, "From the time you gave me the stockings, the swelling disappeared."

Wonderful were the fruits of this mission. One hundred and twenty-eight abandoned women were converted, three hundred girls embraced the religious state, and a clergyman of scandalous life became a sincere penitent.

The mission of St. Matthew quickly followed. To inspire the people with devotion to the Blessed Virgin, he exhorted the faithful to erect a statue to our Lady of Dolors in the church. Immediately the women brought every thing precious they had in gold and silver; so numerous were the offerings that a considerable sum remained, which was given to the poor of the neighborhood.

Alphonsus was so devoted to the Blessed Virgin, that this glorious Mother testified her love for him, by operating the most extraordinary conversions at his intercession. The evening he arrived, an unfortunate young man arose in the night to engage in a sinful transaction; but feeling a repugnance to commit sin with the scapular on his neck, he took it off to place it in a hole in the wall, when, upon extending his hand, he felt himself drawn back, and fled from the spot in terror. The following night the Blessed Virgin appeared to him in a dream, and said: "Miserable being, thou hadst respect for my scapular, and thou hadst no horror of offending my Son! Tomorrow Father Alphonsus will come here to give a mission: go, confess to him, and amend thy life."

The young man had never heard of Alphonsus, and knew nothing of the mission; but next morning he went to a fortune-teller to have the dream interpreted. Before he opened his mouth, she exclaimed: "Do you not know that Father Alphonsus has arrived to-day to give a mission?" When he heard the words, "Alphonsus" and "mission" he was thunderstruck; he instantly went to the dwelling of Alphonsus, and recounted to him the whole story. "So then," murmured Alphonsus with emotion, "our good Mother has sent you to me." He heard his confession; and thenceforth the penitent led an edifying life under his direction.

CHAPTER XXVIII.

Obedience of Father Rossi. — A welcome postulant. — The saint is summoned to Naples. — His father comes to Ciorani to enter as a lay-brother. — The saint dissuades him. — Persecution in Nocera. — Alphonsus appeals to Mgr. Falcoia. — St. Michael.— Death of Bishop Falcoia.

THE house at Ciorani was much too small to receive the numbers of clergy and laity who came thither to make retreats. Alphonsus proposed to enlarge it; but Father Rossi, who was then superior, objected, on the ground of insufficient funds. "Father," said the holy founder, "we ought not to build as seculars do; they amass money and then begin. We should build, and look to Providence for what is necessary for our undertakings."

Animated by the confidence of the saint, Rossi commenced with one sequin; yet he never had cause to regret his obedience. Means flowed in upon him from all quarters. One day when prospects seemed unusually dull, a young man presented himself to be received as laybrother. On withdrawing after Father Rossi had received him provisionally, he slipped into the Father's hand some pieces of money wrapped up in paper, which, to the intense surprise of the recipient, contained a hundred gold ducats. He immediately called the youth back, but he never appeared before him again. One day Alphonsus directed the young students to get up a petition to Jesus Christ in the Most Holy Sacrament, for the success of the house in course of erection. This he deposited in the tabernacle, having added his own name to the names of the young clerics, his children.

Scarcely was this done, when he was summoned to Naples to assist at a council regarding the admission of several gentlemen

139

to the honor of knighthood. Arrived at the place of meeting, he descended from his well-known mule; and being about to enter, the guard, seeing his tattered garments, mistook him for a beggar and rudely repulsed him. The saint smiled at the mistake, and stood aside until the chevalier in waiting perceived him. This gentleman advanced to meet him and respectfully kissed his hands, to the great astonishment of the guard. On this occasion a sum of money so considerable was offered him, that it sufficed to finish the building. Having related this to his brethren on his return, he said laughing: "After that, how could I refuse my vote even to the son of a coalheaver?"

About this time Count Joseph Liguori came to Ciorani to visit his son, and scarcely had he entered the house when he was penetrated with deep devotion. He admired the edifying lives the Fathers led, the silence which reigned through the house, and the odor of sanctity that pervaded every thing. His mind became full of thoughts of a blessed eternity, and his heart wholly detached from earthly things. He pressed his son to his bosom, kissed him, and blessed God for the benedictions showered upon the house. Every day more in love with the humble, peaceful life of the Fathers, he resolved to renounce his rank and its accompaniments, and serve God under the wise direction of his saintly son, as a humble lay-brother. So intent was the old nobleman on making this sacrifice, that he begged for admission with tears.

The holy founder, though edified with the humility of his father, dissuaded him from his purpose: "This vocation," said he, "does not come from God; you must live in the world and edify it by your example as father of a family, in which condition God has placed you."

Don Joseph returned to Naples an altered man. Not content with being a pious nobleman, he endeavored to become a saint, living the life of an anchorite. He kept up a regular correspondence with his dear son, following his counsels in all that concerned the salvation of his soul.

Meanwhile, the house of Nocera began to experience persecution. The esteem of the bishop, the applause of the gentry, the concourse of people who frequented the church, gave umbrage to some curates, and excited their jealousy to such a degree, that they repented having given consent to the establishment of the missionaries. This operated to so great an extent, that it alienated the minds of many, and diminished the reverence felt for the missionaries. As they could not reproach them on the score of morals or regularity of life, they sought to blacken their motives. These evangelical laborers, who led lives so poor, were represented as grasping, covetous men, who would monopolize all the alms usually bestowed on the priests of the place.

There were but two priests in Nocera who were not opposed to the missionaries. A regular plot was now formed, and the first move was to endeavor to prejudice the king; but God showed his displeasure in an unmistakable manner.

The enemies of our saint had employed a celebrated lawyer to write out a memorial of their grievances. He took up a pen, but it would not write; he tried a second and a third, but all to no purpose; finally, he succeeded in writing a page, but unintentionally threw ink over it instead of sand. Struck by these mysterious accidents, he exclaimed: "Employ whom you will, I will do nothing against these Fathers."

They employed another, and God permitted him to arrange the memorial. They would fain have the bishop to concur in their views, but he indignantly refused; and to show how highly he esteemed the calumniated Fathers, he chose one of them for his confessor, and two to accompany him on his visitations and aid him in preaching to the people.

In spite of the bishop's friendship, the trials of the missionaries rather increased than abated. If any of the Fathers appeared in the town, he was instantly assailed with taunts and insults. One morning, while preparing to celebrate mass in the parochial church, a Father had the amice snatched out of his hands. Brother Antony, while digging one day in the garden, was grossly abused by a passer-by, who, irritated by the meekness of the Brother who continued to dig as though nothing disagreeable were taking place, dealt him a violent blow in the face.

The holy Brother not only showed no resentment, but knelt down and offered his other cheek.

During the stillness of the night, wretches would come howling under the windows, insulting the brethren by indecent songs and violent language. As soon as Alphonsus, who was then at Ciorani, learned what was going on at Nocera, he came thither with all possible speed. But how different his reception from what it had formerly been! One person addressed him as a vagabond, accusing him of coming with his companions to eat the bread of the inhabitants and ruin them. The gentle saint humbled himself before this vile adversary, whose audacity was but increased by his sweetness and humility.

The petition addressed to the king, was wholly unsuccessful. The same was the case with another, addressed to the viceroy while his majesty was absent in the Abruzzi. Defeated, but not disheartened, they went to Cantaldi, on whom our saint greatly relied. So successfully did vice personate virtue, that the dean began to regret what he had done, gradually withdrew the assistance he had given them, and, though living in the same house with them, never addressed them a word. Alphonsus, warned by sad experience that the new foundation was in danger, consulted God in prayer, and went to Naples to advise with those wise and enlightened friends who had so often helped him through difficulties. He also went to Castellamare to consult Mgr. Falcoia, who, while they were conversing, suddenly exclaimed; "It is the devil! hold firm, and continue to fight." Then casting his eyes on a small statue of St. Michael, he added, "God and St. Michael will protect you!" He then advised him to dedicate the house and church to the Archangel Michael.

Alphonsus, as has been already remarked, was directed to a great extent, both in what concerned his own conscience, and in what regarded the affairs of his Congregation, by Mgr. Falcoia: but this prelate having passed to a better life, April 20, 1743, he chose for director Father Paul Cafaro, a priest of saintly life, and well skilled in the guidance of souls. Alphonsus made a vow to obey him in all things as he had Mgr. Falcoia.

The death of this holy prelate was a great blow to the persecuted Congregation. He had loved the work of Alphonsus, and favored it to the utmost of his power. The last moments of this great man were sweetened by the presence and assistance of his spiritual son, Father Sportelli, and several other members of the Congregation. When at the point of death, he turned to the archbishop of Sorrento, and collecting his remaining strength, said: "My Lord," — here he pointed towards Father Sportelli, — "this is the work of God; he will bless the Congregation and propagate it as the grass of the fields."

CHAPTER XXIX.

The enemies of the Congregation. — Its friends. — The wicked triumph — but not for ever. — Cantaldi's sister. — Pope Benedict XIV charges Cardinal Spinelli to inquire into the affairs of the Congregation. — Advice of Mgr. Dominicis. — His death. — His successor.

THE tempest at Nocera, far from abating, continued to rage with increasing violence. The holy founder, while having recourse to human means, prayed and mortified himself, beseeching many holy souls, especially of religious houses to intercede with God on behalf of his persecuted family. His enemies wished to blot the Congregation out from the face of the earth.

But their intrigues and revilings at length aroused the zeal of several gentlemen of the place, who boldly declared in favor of the missionaries, and soon there was hardly a respectable family who did not side with them. When this manifestation of good feeling was reported to Alphonsus, he wept with joy on finding his labors appreciated by the most influential class. Yet this only embittered his enemies still more, and in June, 1774, they carried their complaints to Rome and Naples. Though the foundation had been made with the consent of the king, they pretended that its existence was unauthorized, and its members useless to the state and hurtful to religion. At Rome, they described it as a conventicle founded in opposition to canon law and the decrees of Sovereign Pontiffs!

When the saint saw that his enemies had determined to crush his Congregation root and branches, the lawyer rose up within him; and the nobleman who had formerly electrified the Neapolitan tribunals with his eloquence, now reduced his enemies to silence by an energetic statement of the circumstances under which a religious house could be considered lawful or illegal. At Rome, he confounded them by bulls of Sovereign Pontiffs and the authority of canon law, and showed that no institution had been definitely approved until after a period of probation, having been in infancy protected by episcopal sanction. These documents, wonderful for their profound legal acumen, satisfied the king at Naples, and obtained favor with the Pope and cardinals.

The malecontents now had recourse to the Sacred Congregation of Bishops and Regulars, alleging that the house in question was injurious to the welfare of religion, repeating all the former calumnies, and adding that the Fathers carried on a shameful traffic in crucifixes, beads, &c., and compelled the people to carry stones for the new building.

The gentlemen of Nocera, Pagani, Corbora, and St. Egidio, no sooner heard of this new attack, than they undertook the defence: thirty-six of them charged themselves with the management of the affair at Rome, whither they sent an advocate and procurators. Several pastors, the chapter of the cathedral, the clergy of Nocera, and twenty-three clerics of Pagani addressed the Pope, Benedict XIV, in favor of Alphonsus. His Holiness instructed Cardina Spinola to obtain exact information from the bishop of Nocera. In his statement, Mgr. Dominicis, after having shown that the complaints they had made were unfounded, and their accusations calumnies, proceeded to the most important point, namely, the end for which Father di Liguori had founded the Congregation. He concluded by an elaborate eulogium on the sanctity of the founder, and expatiated on the high esteem in which he was held by the cardinal archbishop of Naples and many other distinguished prelates.

Unable to obtain the suppression of the house, they sought to interrupt the erection of the church, and by bribing the underlings of office, they altered the words, "the king permits the erection of a house with a church," to "the king permits the erection of a house *without* a church," and showed it to the commissary who was thereby persuaded that Alphonsus had exceeded his limits. The commissary therefore dispatched an order to Nocera to discontinue the work.

This time the wicked triumphed; and our saint was in great embarrassment, not knowing how to proceed. He sent Father

Sanseverino to Naples to inform the Minister of State, Marquis Brancone, of the obstacle, and entreat him to remove it.

The marquis was astonished, for he remembered expressly having given leave for the erection of a church. He ordered one of the clerks of the Bureau to produce the paper, and wrote with his own hand "a house with a church." On the 21st of July an order was transmitted to the syndic of Pagani, to permit the building to proceed.

While God arranged the happy issue of this affair, He mingled bitterness with the sweetness. The good Father Sarnelli was called to a brighter world, and rendered his beautiful soul into the hands of his Creator, June 30, 1744, having spent himself in the service of God and his neighbor. All good people bewailed his loss; and the affectionate heart of Alphonsus, who loved this dear son most tenderly, could find no consolation but in the hope that the Congregation had acquired a new protector in heaven. Unwilling that the example of such sanctity should be lost to the future members of the Congregation, Alphonsus wrote an abridgment of his life, a labor of love to so loving a father.

Silenced at Naples and repulsed at Rome, the enemies of the saint employed the sister of Cantaldi to declare that the house given them by her brother was her private property. Accompanied by twenty-two persons, including two notaries, she forced herself into the house, her brother refusing to appear openly against the Fathers.

Greatly distressed, Alphonsus came to Nocera, but the bishop and other friends advised him not to yield. An able lawyer was engaged, and the pretended proprietorship of the sister was soon exposed, to the confusion of the plotters who, nevertheless, became more violent than ever. One day a person of rank and a priest said to him: "If you will act the thief and rob people by force, why do you not take to the highway?" "Blessed be God," rejoined the saint, "I have given up my own house to be treated like a robber at Nocera."

In August, they made another attempt, but warned by experience, they no longer attacked Alphonsus whose sanctity was venerated by all; their infernal rage expended itself on his companions. Accusations against them, however, Alphonsus always treated with contempt, well knowing their virtues and labors in the cause of God. The matter was again carried to Rome, and the most respectable inhabitants of Nocera took upon themselves the expense of defending the Congregation at Rome. Benedict XIV once more charged Cardinal Spinola to make inquiry anew of Cardinal Spinelli at Naples, and also of the archbishop of Salerno, Mgr. Rossi. All this happened in the designs of Providence, who willed that this great Pope should be made fully Aware of the merit of the saint and his works, and disposed in advance to approve an institute recommended by such estimable prelates.

Meanwhile Mgr. Dominicis attempted to arrange the affair by arbitration; but when Cantaldi offered to assume the debts, but made it a condition that the Fathers should leave the place, and, in case they refused, threatened to shut up their church and force them to live as simple individuals, the bishop indignantly broke up the meeting, and, turning to his clients, said: "Defend your cause at Rome and Naples; trust that Cardinal Spinelli will recognize the justice of your cause, for God is with you."

This worthy prelate, who was so deeply interested for the Congregation, died August 22, 1744, to the great regret of Alphonsus and his companions. The adversaries of our saint were rejoiced, because the Congregation had lost so ardent a protector; but God raised up for them a friend equally well disposed towards them, Mgr. Gerard Volpi, a prelate illustrious for prudence, zeal, and piety, and for every virtue that could adorn the episcopal character.

CHAPTER XXX.

Illiceto. — Alphonsus miraculously raised several feet from the ground. Early days at Illiceto. — Happy death of Brother Vitus Curzius. — Grief of Alphonsus. — New Trials. — Father Sportelli a match for his enemies. Right victorious. — Might defeated.

WHILE our saint and his companions suffered in their last foundation, God opened a new field to their labors. The Prince of Castellaneta, D. Mathias Miroballi, besought the holy founder to visit his fief of Illiceto, to give the people the instruction they so much needed. The Bishop of Bovino dispatched a canon of his cathedral to urge the prince's petition. This mission was crowned with success.

The canon had another object in view. In a wood called Vallin-Vincoli stood an ancient church dedicated to our Lady of Consolation. It had formerly belonged to the Augustinians. In it was a large painting of the Blessed Virgin, for which the faithful of the vicinity had a great devotion. There the canon had resolved to found a community. Alphonsus, however, hesitated, because the distance between the church and any human habitation was considerable; but, when visiting the picture, he was so captivated, that Fathers Cafaro and St. Severino easily persuaded him to accept the offer.

Near Illiceto, were vast domains of the crown where thousands were employed in keeping flocks and herds, and cultivating the ground. Touched by their destitution, Alphonsus sent Fathers to distribute to them the Bread of Life; and he looked upon the house in prospect as destined to supply spiritual succor to these abandoned people. The king gave his royal assent for this foundation, January 9, 1745.

Having arranged the affairs of this house, he departed for Madugno, where Don Dominic Fiori, professor of music in the Cathedral of Naples, had invited him to give a mission. This mission was an arduous one, and cost much labor and fatigue, lasting forty days. It was during its continuance that Alphonsus, while saying mass, was raised several feet from the ground, as many eye-witnesses attested. As for the foundation proposed by Fiori, our saint advised him to make arrangements with the Fathers of St. Vincent de Paul, having heard that the king had granted them an establishment in the neighborhood, and not wishing to interfere with them.

After their return, Alphonsus and his companions suffered much at Illiceto. A priest who was there that winter, said in a letter: "Their bread was of rye mixed with bran, black as coal and ill-baked. Sometimes they had none at all, and were obliged to accept the charity of an old man who lived by the produce of his goats and the cultivation of a small field near his cottage. They were regaled with meat only when some sheep or cow died of exhaustion. Wild chesnuts or crab apples were their ordinary dessert. They had no linen, and were almost shirtless. The house was a mass of ruins. The wind blew more keenly within than without, the windows were of oiled paper instead of glass, the roof was so bad that snow frequently formed their coverlets."

Amid these miseries or, rather, in consequence of them, Alphonsus had the misfortune to lose the good Brother Vitus Curzius. In July, he was sent out to beg a little corn. Although unaccustomed to traverse the country during the burning heats, he obeyed cheerfully; but one evening, being refused a lodging where he had applied for one, he slept in the field, and was seized during the night with a burning fever. Unable to drag himself to his convent, he was received into the house of a charitable priest, and, after forty-nine days of intense suffering, was called to receive the reward of his labors. This death deeply afflicted the tender heart of Alphonsus, though he was consoled by the reflection that his beloved son had passed away rich in merits and good works.

The Chapter of the Cathedral and many religious priests united with the missionaries in paying the last honors to the sacred remains of this poor lay-brother, once a wealthy and elegant gentleman, but who, like his Divine Master, had chosen to serve instead of being served. All the confraternities and numbers of the people assisted, but rather to implore his protection than to pray for his chastened soul. The holy founder sang mass, but was frequently interrupted by tears. He afterwards consoled his bereaved heart by transmitting to his children a faithful sketch of this tenderly loved brother, whose sanctity shone resplendent even among the companions of St. Alphonsus.

New plots were meanwhile being concocted to ruin the missionaries, God permitting his elect to be proved by extraordinary afflictions, that the strength of his omnipotent arm might be more triumphantly displayed.

Cantaldi now openly attacked them. He revoked the donation he had made them, and, in concert with his sister, cited them before the royal council. He pretended that the missionaries had deceived him by usurping the title of Congregation, and demanded that they should be forbidden to build, protesting he had made the donation, not for a religious community, but for a college of priests. But the council having accredited an auditor to verify facts, the missionaries were confirmed in possession of the property, the deeds having been found perfectly valid.

But the animosity of these unfortunate people was far from being abated. Going from bad to worse, they at last laid two barrels of gunpowder under the foundation, and had not one of their accomplices, stung by remorse, revealed the plot, all would have been destroyed. In future, Father Mazzini was obliged to keep a strict watch nightly.

Alphonsus was then at Illiceto. Far from being discouraged, these barbarities but increased his confidence of ultimate success. Meanwhile the Fathers remained as if in prison in Cantaldi's house, but such were the restraints and other miseries of accepting, or rather compelling, his hospitality, that they determined to quit it as soon as their own convent offered the merest shelter. Accordingly, the walls of the new building were scarcely finished when they removed thither, without heeding the dampness and other inconveniences. On the Feast of our Lady of Mercy, September 24, which occurs during the Octave of the Archangel Michael, protector of the Congregation, they entered their new abode.

When Alphonsus heard of their removal, he rejoiced exceedingly, and wrote from Illiceto to urge them to a stricter observance of rule, assuring them that God would bless and sanctify them only inasmuch as they observed their rules with strictness and fervor.

The malecontents, provoked to see the Fathers established in their new house, obtained an order from the council forbidding them to undertake any thing additional; intending thereby to hinder the completion of the little church in course of erection; and hoping that, by depriving them of every opportunity of exercising the functions of their ministry, they would ultimately force them to abandon the foundation.

Informed of all this, Father Sportelli prevailed on some friendly gentlemen of Nocera to detain the king's officer for one night. He then sent for the workmen, and despite the protestations of the architect, the scaffolding was removed, the earth smoothed, a portable altar erected, and a confessional arranged. The Fathers ornamented the altar and walls as magnificently as their poverty would admit, with garlands and tapestry. Permission having been previously obtained to bless the church, Father Sportelli celebrated mass therein at daybreak, preached, heard confessions, and gave Holy Communion.

The officer arrived early, and, calling Father Sportelli and the rest of the community, declared that by order of the king no one must have the temerity to attempt any thing new, at the risk of incurring the penalties mentioned in the royal decree. "We shall do nothing new," replied Sportelli; "nor shall we disobey the king's order. But I protest that this edifice is a church; the holy sacrifice has been offered in it, we have preached in it, and administered the sacraments to the people." The adversaries were again outwitted, but they did not yield the victory without a fierce struggle.

CHAPTER XXXI.

Missionary Project of Benedict XIV. — Terrible example. — Our saint's countenance is radiant with heavenly light. — Precious death of Count Joseph Liguori. — Illness of the saint. — A liberal benefaction. — Gratitude of the founder. — He is again invited to Foggia. — A new foundation. — An inhospitable noble. — The saint sees from one foundation what is done in another. — Signor Corona. — Prophecy fulfilled.

WHILE Alphonsus was at Illiceto, he received new encouragement to labor for the salvation of souls. Benedict XIV, convinced of the great good produced by missions, conceived the project of reforming, by this means, the whole kingdom of Naples. By a brief, dated September 6, 1745, he delegated Cardinal Spinelli to superintend this work, with full powers to send whom he would. Many bishops solicited him to send into their dioceses the holy founder and his missionaries; and when the vintage was over, they began to evangelize Foggia. Here occurred a terrible example of the divine justice, which served as a powerful warning to sinners. One of the Fathers happened to go through the public places to call the people to church. An unfortunate wretch, who had been indulging in deep potations,[1] holding up a glass, cried out, "Father, would you like to know my mission?" and putting it to his lips, he instantly dropped dead! An appalling incident, and the most powerful sermon ever given to the people of Foggia!

Another extraordinary incident, of a more consoling nature, confirmed the spectators in their high opinions of the sanctity of Alphonsus. One evening as he was preaching before the image of our Lady of the Seven Veils, exposed for the occasion, he appeared more like an angel than a man, as a ray of brilliant light darted

---

[1] Drinking alcohol, likely in excess.

from the image and was reflected from his countenance. Simultaneously an ecstasy came upon him, and he was raised several feet in the air. The people uttered cries of joy which brought crowds into the church. Over four thousand persons were the delighted witnesses of this miracle.

For forty days this mission lasted, and its effects were wonderful. The floodgates of charity were opened in the hearts of the rich, and they enabled their apostle to aid young and friendless girls whose poverty placed them in danger, and to procure asylums for the aged and for repentant sinners.

During the mission at Troia, as Alphonsus was about to ascend the pulpit, news was brought him of the death of his beloved father. He devoted a few moments to prayer, and then begged his auditors to recommend to Jesus and Mary the soul of his dear father. He had heard of his serious illness: but engaged in his apostolic labors, he denied himself the sad gratification of watching over his closing hours. Count Joseph di Liguori died laden with years and merits. He had led the life of a saint, especially since he had placed himself under the direction of his saintly son, and the memory of this illustrious and pious nobleman is still held in benediction.

This death was the first of a series of family afflictions which rent the tender and affectionate heart of our saint all the more painfully as his duties, no less than his sublime resignation to the divine will, forbade him to give vent to the bitterness of his grief.

While at St. Agatha, Alphonsus was seized with a violent fever, resulting, perhaps, from the depths of grief and affection awakened by his recent bereavement; but this did not impede the mission, and when he appeared in the pulpit, the mere sight of him produced compunction in the hearts of his audience.

After this mission, he was summoned to Illiceto, to the bedside of his friend Canon Casati, who lay dangerously ill; but, despite his haste, the dying man expired before his arrival. This worthy dignitary left his whole property to our Lady of Consolation, beneath the shadow of whose image his remains repose as he desired. Full of gratitude for this donation, the holy founder celebrated his obsequies with the utmost magnificence, and had one hundred ducats distributed to the poor for the soul of his benefactor.

152

Alphonsus was not yet rid of his fever when the inhabitants of Foggia, whose territory was desolated by a protracted drought, besought him to give them a novena in honor of the Blessed Virgin, who had always been so propitious to his prayers. Our saint hurried to the relief of his suffering children, and, probably as a reward for his zeal, the fever suddenly left him. Scarcely were the exercises begun, when rain fell in abundance. The seed was saved, and produced a rich harvest.

Meanwhile, a new foundation offered. Mgr. Nicolai, regretting to find himself at the head of a large diocese in great want of spiritual assistance, was one day lamenting his position in presence of two pious priests: directly they suggested the establishment of a Redemptorist Convent, and the archbishop eagerly embraced the proposal. Alphonsus, however, was not by any means anxious to bring the matter to a close, yet, at the request of Father Villani, he consented to give a mission in the place.

The joy and consolation his mere presence diffused among the population, seemed incredible. They regarded him as another St. Paul. His words seemed less words than arrows which pierced all hearts. During the mission he went with several gentlemen to inspect the church offered him. The situation pleased him, being in the centre of an archdiocese, surrounded by several dioceses, all in great spiritual destitution.

The archbishop being then at Calabritto, Alphonsus set out mounted on a mule to visit him. Hearing he was at dinner, and loath to disturb him, he retired to a small chapel in a wing of the palace, to say his office. While there, the eldest scion of the del Plato family, in which the prelate was staying, came to close the door, and seeing a man covered with rags, he took him for a vagabond come to beg from the honored guest. Fearing he might steal something, the youth ordered him out. "Would you have the goodness to wait till I finish vespers?" pleaded the saint. "No, no," was the uncourteous reply; "it was only yesterday we had a napkin stolen; it would be too much to lose another to-day." The saint instantly eased the mind of the inhospitable Don Xavier, and finished his vespers in the street.

After some time, he again presented himself in the palace, and the archbishop, hearing of his arrival, came out and received him with every mark of respect. Xavier del Plato's confusion increased, when he learned that our saint was a nobleman and superior of a Congregation. The conversation went on as though nothing unusual had happened, Alphonsus not noticing the young man's embarrassment. When the archbishop heard what had occurred, he was more than a little annoyed.

God showered his benedictions on this mission. The humility, modesty and self-contempt of which our saint's whole life was eloquent, touched all hearts. All this time he suffered such violent toothache as to produce convulsions; nevertheless, he sometimes continued his labors till so overcome with pain and fatigue, that he had to be carried from the church. Generally in his sermons he seemed ravished out of himself. One evening God showed him in spirit what was passing at Illiceto. "While we are occupied here with the mission," said he, "the devil is tormenting my poor children at Illiceto." Next morning a lay-brother came thence, and spoke with him for three hours of the afflictions they were there enduring.

The archbishop arrived at Caposele according to previous arrangement, and he was so deeply affected at hearing Alphonsus preach on the Blessed Virgin, that he shed tears of devotion. The priest, Don Salvatore Corona, a learned and influential man, came to oppose the foundation, and having entered the church, his mind filled with thoughts hostile to the Congregation, he was struck with apoplexy, as he approached our Lady's altar. He immediately recognized the divine hand, and said: "Mother of God, I protest I will no longer oppose this foundation." Scarcely had he uttered these words when he recovered, and his mouth which had been twisted on one side by the paroxysm, resumed its natural position.

True to his word, Corona advocated the foundation with all his eloquence; but on a sudden the archbishop was seized with indecision, and spoke of delay. Alphonsus declared that he had tome to give a mission, not to found a house, and that, his business concluded, he would depart. Whereupon, the Archpriest Rossi burst into a passionate fit of weeping, and casting himself before the feet of the archbishop, besought him to arrange matters at once. The establishment was finally decided on, June 4, 1746.

On hearing this, the people testified the most unbounded joy. Every house was illuminated, guns were fired, and fireworks displayed. A noble family in the neighborhood put their forests at the disposal of the missionaries, to supply wood for the buildings.

154

The inhabitants had no small consolation in the fulfilment of the prophecy of St. John Joseph of the Cross, that in twenty years a devout and zealous community of missionaries would be established among them. That period had just expired.

CHAPTER XXXII.

The foreign comedians. — Vision. — Our Lady sends a penitent to the Missionaries. — Removal of the Novitiate. — Our saint begins to publish. His devotion to St. Teresa. — His work on the episcopacy. — An opponent. He refuses the mitre. — He pleads his cause before the king of Naples. — He refuses to receive Mandarini. — Insults. — Instructions on various subjects. Sermons.

ANTALDI continued to harass the Fathers at Pagani,[1] but his machinations were powerless to hurt them. Alphonsus sympathized most deeply in their sorrows, and wrote from time to time to comfort and encourage them. He continued to give missions wherever he was invited, and in every instance success crowned his labors.

On one occasion, while giving a mission at Foggia, a town greatly devoted to him, he found that a company of foreign comedians had the start of him, and that certain gentlemen had bound themselves to support them. This, as a new occasion of sin, grieved him exceedingly. He endeavored to have them dismissed, but without success; so he left the town, and when the people urged him to stay, he replied: "We cannot serve God and the devil at the same time. Foggia will not hear me, but God will lay a heavy hand upon her and chastise her for her libertinism." Scarcely had he departed the town was shaken by an earthquake, to the great dismay of the terrified people.

The erection of the new house of Caposele now approached completion. The Blessed Virgin deigned to show her love of this establishment in a special manner. There lived in a neighboring village an unfortunate creature who had been confined to bed for three years by a most loathsome disease. Every night he saw the

[1] Pagani is a suburb of Nocera; the latter is often called Nocera del Pagani.

devil, under the form of a goat, place himself on his breast, and press his throat and sides until he was nearly choked. One morning the Blessed Virgin appeared in his chamber radiant with beauty, attended by two angels. "My son," said this loving mother, "how hast thou the audacity to live in sin? Change thy life. Tomorrow thou shalt see my children of the house of Mater Domina. Confess, repent of thy sins, and Jesus will pardon thee!"

The vision disappeared, and the sinner felt inspired to amend, but he knew nothing of the approaching mission. Next day he Heard the bells ringing, and on inquiry learned that the Fathers had arrived. Full of joy, he immediately sent for one of them. The Father, to whom he confessed with torrents of tears, asked if he had been in the habit of practising any devotion to the Blessed Virgin. He replied that he had made a vow to say the Rosary every day, and had religiously kept it. He died during the mission, giving evident signs of sincere repentance.

As yet, the Congregation had no regular novitiate. Only subdeacons were admitted, and these made their novitiate, following the founder from hamlet to hamlet. He soon commenced a novitiate at Illiceto, admitting young men not in orders. But because of the extreme poverty of the house, the young levites were discouraged. Some, not having courage to declare their weakness to Father Cafaro, the novice-master, fled secretly through the windows, the doors being shut. Finally, the novitiate was removed to Ciorani; and there were soon, under Father Villani, the new novice-master, some twenty novices, whose conduct caused the greatest consolation to our saint.

It was from Illiceto that Alphonsus first began to write and publish his beautiful works. Missions, fruitful as they were, seemed too narrow a field for his burning zeal. He desired that all Christians might profit by the reflections which consoled and animated himself. While he was still in the world, the Blessed Sacrament was the divine object of his dearest affections, and the prolific source of all the graces bestowed on him. He therefore arranged some of the beautiful sentiments which fed his devotion, in the form of visits for every day in the month; and as he knew not how to separate Jesus and Mary, he published at the same time prayers and reflections on our Blessed Mother, to excite the faithful to love and serve this powerful advocate of sinners.

This charming little work, so replete with the unction of divine grace, was joyfully welcomed by all pious Catholics. It circulated rapidly through the kingdom of Naples and the whole of Italy; and, in an incredibly short time, a French translation was made from the fiftieth Italian edition!

His next work was "Thoughts and Reflections on the Passion of Christ" "That man," said he, "has no heart or no faith, who is not moved at the sight of a crucifix." Since he had embraced the ecclesiastical state, he had chosen St. Teresa for his special advocate, and frequently indeed did he experience the efficacy of her intercession. Desirous of seeing her honored, he published meditations and prayers in form of a novena, which comprised every beautiful thing that could be said in her praise.

He next composed a book on the obligations of the episcopacy; he sent copies to all the bishops in Italy, and many of them responded with thanks and compliments. He published, too, his opinion regarding certain cases of conscience, but this work gave some offence. A certain priest, instead of discussing the question, wrote: "Who are you, coming out of the woods to set up for a doctor and lay down the law to others?" He then accused him of being a heretic and condemning vocal prayer; to which the saint gently replied: "How can I proscribe vocal prayer, I, who have made a vow to recite the Rosary daily, and exhort every family to do the same? Besides, is it not our practice to recite it publicly in all our missions?"

In April, 1747, Alphonsus repaired to Ciorani. He found the novitiate full of virtuous young men, and priests eminent for learning and sanctity. At Pagani, he was consoled in a similar manner. The success of these two houses made him shed tears of holy joy. But remembering that the argument constantly brought forward by his adversaries was, that the Congregation was not authorized by the king, he resolved to go to Naples and obtain the necessary authorization.

Having arrived at his destination, he immediately called on the Marquis Branconi, Minister of State. "The king has determined to make you a bishop," was the salute of the prime-minister. Confounded by this information, our saint instantly refused the proffered mitre, and when his Excellency would persuade him to accept, he said: "If you love me, never speak of such a thing. I have renounced the world: its dignities can inspire me only with horror;" nor would he desist, until the marquis promised to torment him no more on the subject.

Having recommended to him the interests of the Congregation, he begged of the chamberlain to procure him an audience with the king. This was speedily granted. One day, as he was saying his office in the cloisters of St. Catharine, he was told that the king awaited him. Introduced to his majesty in the usual patched cassock, he eloquently expatiated on the want of spiritual succor to which the poor were subjected, and the evils resulting to the commonwealth from the ignorance of so large a class. The missionaries, he said, had done more than their share to alleviate the deplorable effects of this state of things, but they could no longer endure the anomaly their present position: it was essential now that his majesty should recognize their institute for a regular Congregation.

He then presented the rules, and in a few words explained the objects of the Institute. The heart of the pious monarch was touched: he took notes with his royal hand, and placed the rules and the accompanying petition in the keeping of his grand-almoner.

All this coming to the ears of Mandarini, he became more pressing than ever for a reunion, and even went to Ciorani, and offered, on the part of his companions, to embrace unreservedly the rules of Alphonsus. Though deeply moved by this step, our saint feared to consent. "One who has been accustomed to possess and to command," said he, "will not like to find himself poor and deprived of his liberty. To-day he is ready to sacrifice his own will, to-morrow he would regret having vowed obedience to another. A reunion, without being beneficial to your subjects, might be hurtful to mine."

Mandarini applied to the grand-almoner, who signified his wish to Alphonsus that he immediately accept the humble proposal of Mandarini; but our saint by prayer, entreaties, and the influence of many distinguished friends, finally gained his point.

While these affairs were progressing, he hardly took time to eat or sleep. Overpowered with fatigue, he might daily be seen going from palace to palace. Some refused him admission, others listened with a cold, abstracted air. One day a princess who had formerly known him, happened to pass through the antechamber in which he was seated. Seeing him so poor and ragged, she exclaimed, "Oh, how dirty you are!" "I do not understand you," rejoined the saint. "Ah! then," said she, turning her back upon him, "you must be from Calabria."

The king, though temporizing, to say the least, about approving the Congregation, wished to adorn Alphonsus with the mitre. The see of Palermo becoming vacant, he exclaimed: "The Pope makes good selections, but I will make a better." He then ordered the prime-minister to notify the bishop-elect, that his majesty would take no refusal.

Foreseeing that the Pope would sustain the action of the king, he felt no repose day or night; he wrote to Father Cafaro, his director, that he would sooner hide in the depths of the forest than become a bishop. He charged all the houses to have special prayers offered up for him, and begged the same favor of all the holy souls he knew, redoubling, meanwhile, his own austerities. For a whole month, the king continued inflexible, but God was pleased ultimately to grant the desires of his servant. Quite unexpectedly the sovereign yielded to the reasoning of Marquis Branconi, who maintained that Alphonsus the missionary was much more useful to the kingdom than Alphonsus archbishop of the distant see of Palermo would be.

The refusal of Alphonsus gave offence to many, but, on reflection, all were edified by his humility. "The church," said he, "is not in want of bishops, but of men who will labor for souls in remote and abandoned places."

He now retired to Ciorani for some days. On his return, he was requested by his old friend and companion, Don Joseph Porpora, to preach the novena preparatory to the festival of the Assumption. Though wholly unprepared, having left his books and notes at Ciorani, he at once exclaimed: "Well; I will say every thing the Blessed Virgin will put into my mind."

He treated of the humility of Mary as contrasted with the pride of men, the ardent love of Mary and the coldness of men, the union of Mary's will with the Divine will, and the opposition of the will of men to the will of God. He depicted the precious death of Mary, and the help she affords her cherished servants in their last hour. Finally, on the day of the Assumption he enraptured his audience, by dilating on the glorious triumph of Mary crowned in heaven. During this novena, thousands awoke from sin, and, penetrated with lively sorrow, returned to God, by beginning a new life.

He was now invited by Canon Borgia, Superior of the Apostolic Missions, to give a retreat to his brethren. Our saint consented, and during the exercises, he expatiated chiefly on the obligation of preachers to make known Christ crucified, and not to preach themselves. He spoke vehemently against a celebrated preacher, lately deceased, who, by his style of preaching, had shown himself a traitor to the word of God. "Fill your discourses," said he, "with the truths of the Gospel, and do not fatigue yourselves, seeking for vain ornaments which produce no fruit. Ah! I pray that he to whom I now allude may not have to expiate his vanity in purgatory."

Several young ecclesiastics were offended at the apostolic boldness of the Saint: "To blame such a preacher!" exclaimed one, "and that publicly!" "One does not speak in public," returned Alphonsus, "when he addresses only ecclesiastics." Don Borgia was so delighted with this sermon, that he begged the saint to give another on the same subject, which was done, and in still stronger language. More than one of the audience was filled with a salutary confusion by the saint's remarks.

During his sojourn at Naples, as he was saying Mass in the Oratorian Church, when he turned around to give communion, he perceived a gentleman seated cross-legged in the choir. "Have you lost the use of your limbs that you cannot kneel?" was the indignant exclamation of the celebrant; whereupon the man sank on his knees, but, being excessively provoked, he began to cough and make all manner of noise. When Mass was over, he ran to the sacristy to inquire what wretched priest had said Mass. But when the name, Don Alfonso di Liguori, was uttered, he felt greatly ashamed, and was careful to retire before the saint returned to the sacristy.

For over three weeks Alphonsus suffered from violent toothache, but he never ceased a moment to apply himself to his ordinary avocations. At last he was obliged to have a tooth extracted, and for this purpose he repaired to a barber's shop, like the poorest laborer. Soon after, perceiving that Father Francis preserved the tooth, he asked to see it, and snatching it up, threw it into a ditch.

Towards the end of autumn, our saint returned to Nocera, to prepare for new labors.

CHAPTER XXXIII.

The saint repairs to Naples.— Tanucci opposes him. — Illness. — A strange calumny. — Renewed efforts to procure the confirmation of his institute. Mission. — Fortunate circumstance for Alphonsus. — Incessant labors. — He gives a retreat in the Cathedral. — Criticism.— Changes suggested.— Father Villani in Rome. — Ruse. — Graciousness of the Pope to Father Villani.

I N the beginning of 1748, Alphonsus having returned to Naples, Branconi informed him that the king was dissatisfied that the Council of State had refused to recognize his Congregation. Our saint therefore presented a new petition for the confirmation of his institute, declining to ask for a subsidy for its support, which, owing to the favorable dispositions of the king, would have been readily granted. His disinterestedness greatly pleased the marquis, but the chief minister, Tanucci, had political views not in accordance with the pious designs of the monarch, and the petition, though presented by Branconi, remained unnoticed.

Scarcely twelve days had elapsed since his arrival, when he was seized with an asthma so violent that he could not speak. For some weeks he was unable to say Mass, but though obliged to remain in bed, he directed all who came to him on affairs of conscience. Upon recovering, he resumed all his labors, and multitudes were converted by his discourses.

About this time he became the object of a most malicious calumny. Speaking of the love of Jesus in the Blessed Sacrament, and the readiness with which He receives us, he quoted these words of St. Teresa: "It is not thus with earthly kings, they give audience only a few times a year: and how much it costs to obtain an audience! Then no one dares to say all he wishes, while we can open our hearts to Jesus in the Blessed Sacrament with the fullest confidence at all times." These words a wretch present construed into an insult to the king; and to ingratiate himself with his majesty, he represented Alphonsus as a person who endeavored to sow discord between the monarch and his people. Tanucci, the minister, being unacquainted with our saint, believed the calumny, and threatened to banish him from Naples.

Six days later, Alphonsus learned the evil construction that had been put upon his words. He immediately informed the cardinal, who was extremely indignant at the calumny. Through the medium of that estimable prelate, the king and his minister were speedily undeceived, and from that moment held Alphonsus in higher esteem and veneration than ever.

He renewed his efforts to procure the confirmation of his institute, but was again unsuccessful, though the king graciously bade him rely upon the royal protection. He was now requested to give a retreat at the barracks of Pizzo Falconi. The exercises were attended by the prince and the state-major in command. Seeing the effect the spiritual exercises produced on the officers, he was asked to extend his zeal to the privates, which he gladly did. Scandals rapidly disappeared from among them. Our saint furnished them with a small library at his own expense. So thorough was the conversion of these men, that five quitted the service to dedicate themselves to God in religion.

Alphonsus now returned to Nocera, and here an event occurred which at last brought peace to that much-afflicted community. A dean in the neighborhood, who had been greatly prejudiced against the Fathers, had a relative who led a very bad life. Offended by the charitable warnings of his friend, the young wretch overtook him one evening, beat him, wounded him on the head, and left him for dead. Father Mazzini, hearing this, made haste to offer him the necessary spiritual and corporal aid, and, alternately with the other Fathers, nursed him with all possible tenderness and assiduity till he became convalescent. The poor dean was so grateful for this kindness, that he thought of nothing but how he could recompense his kind benefactors; and through his means, aided by the worthy bishop, the leaders of the conspiracy were convinced of the pernicious nature of their proceedings, and peace was soon restored.

Though the royal council had decided in favor of Alphonsus against Cantaldi, yet our saint, having the peace of his

Congregation more at heart than its temporal interests, persuaded the bishop to allow him to resign at once the donations made by Cantaldi. This disinterestedness was duly appreciated by all good men, and gained general applause throughout Naples. Mgr. Volpi contributed much to the establishment of peace, for he knew how to value Alphonsus and his companions. He consulted them in every emergency. He gave audiences at their house, and ordered many to come thither for spiritual exercises, instruction in the rubrics, and to reform their conduct. The esteem shown them by the bishop conciliated their enemies.

Alphonsus continued his warfare for God in every direction, his burning zeal allowing him no repose. "Who knows," said he, "what God requires of me? perhaps the predestination of certain souls may be attached to one of my sermons." He opened a mission in the church of St. Anne, and it seemed as if he had but to cast out his net to receive a miraculous draught of fishes. He continued his labors in the suburb of St. Anthony, to which the unfortunate women of the town had been compelled to withdraw through his exertions and those of Father Sarnelli. Many of these poor creatures, touched by grace, approached the tribunal of penance and were thoroughly converted. Of these fervent converts, some were placed in houses of refuge, and some were taken care of by charitable women. He also preached frequently in religious houses, to console and animate those consecrated virgins whom he regarded as the most precious portion of the flock of the Good Shepherd, and to inflame their hearts more and more with divine love. Besides, his room was almost always crowded with persons of distinction, lay and clerical, who daily repaired to him for instruction and direction, so that he could scarcely find time for his office and other devotions.

Cardinal Spinelli requested him to give a retreat in the cathedral, and that immense church could hardly accommodate his hearers. An eye-witness remarked that eternity alone can disclose the wonders of peace operated in the hearts of many, even of professed infidels.

At length he went to the country to distribute the bread of life among the poor peasants. At Victry, a daring fellow entered the church to criticise the preacher, but though "he went to scoff, he remained to pray." "The sermons of other preachers" said he, "speak to the mind, but the words of Father Liguori penetrate the heart." He immediately went to confession, and he persevered to the end.

In 1748, the new Congregation had already become rich in subjects of profound learning and eminent sanctity, and was approved by the episcopate of the kingdom. He therefore determined to apply for the approbation of the Pope. He addressed a petition to Benedict XIV, through Mgr. Puoti, a prelate honored with the particular friendship of his Holiness.

The Pope ordered Cardinal Gentili to charge Cardinal Spinelli to take informations on the subject. The rules were at once submitted to his Eminence, who, though admiring the wisdom of the general arrangements, thought that the health of the Fathers must fail, if so much fasting were joined to such fatigues, for a workman needs his health; also that it might be best to limit the number of consultors to six, Alphonsus having determined upon twelve, in honor of the twelve apostles.

Every one now advised our saint to proceed to Rome, but he concealed his humility under pretence of infirmities, and delegated Father Villani and another Father to act for him. Many bishops, besides those in whose dioceses the Congregation was established, wrote to give favorable testimony at Rome, and several noblemen and other distinguished persons wrote in their behalf to Cardinal Orsini and the Duke of Tora.

When the rule was presented to the members of the Sacred Congregation, they retrenched, as superfluous, the vow of placing themselves at the disposal of the Pope: "We suppose," said the cardinal, "that all religious orders are ever ready to obey a sign from the Holy Father."

Full of admiration for the rule, the cardinals unanimously approved it, though an auditor who had read the laudatory approbation of Cardinal Spinelli, regarding the good done by the institute in Naples, pretended that this meant that it ought to be confined to that kingdom. But the Cardinal answered that Alphonsus had applied for sanction for his Congregation throughout the whole Church, and added: "It is but just that a work of such magnitude should be universal."

Yet no decree was issued. Towards the end of February, Father Villani visited Cardinal Orsini, who thus addressed him: "Be comforted; this morning the Sacred Congregation has had one of its most difficult conferences." "But," said Father Villani, "what cannot be done in the Congregation might be done at the house of the cardinal-prefect?" "True," returned his Eminence, "and I will repair thither immediately. Recommend my business to God with yours." The same day the decree of approbation was given.

Father Villani, on being presented to the Pope, asked for a confirmation of the decree. Next day, His Holiness read the decree and the rule. He was particularly pleased that the offices of the Rector-Major and his councillors were perpetual.

"This," he said, "hinders parties and divisions among the Regulars." He then suggested that the Congregation should take the name of *Holy Redeemer*, instead of *Holy Savior*, the latter being already borne by a Congregation at Venice.

The Pope named Alphonsus perpetual Superior of the Congregation, but our saint piteously entreated to be delivered from so heavy a burden. "Your Reverence must have patience," wrote Villani in reply; "since you are named perpetual Rector, you must submit to the yoke. Speak no more on the subject, dear Father, for you are bound by duty, justice, and gratitude."

The devil, however, wished to thwart the work of God. There was at Naples a community, otherwise very respectable, which beheld with a jealous eye the progress of the Congregation, and sent one of its members to Rome to give Alphonsus all possible opposition. But he arrived too late. Yet, determined to effect some mischief, this envoy gained over one of the officials to pretend that the rules were approved, but not the institute. The Pope, seeing the *ruse*, was very indignant, and wrote with his own hand *Regulam et Institutum*; so that, to the confusion of the malevolent, Alphonsus had the satisfaction of receiving from Rome, February 25, 1749, the confirmation of the Rule and Institute.

When our saint heard this news he shed tears of joy, and prostrating himself on the ground with the other Fathers, thanked God for His mercies. The community bell was rung, and all went to the church to chant the *Te Deum*, after which Alphonsus exhorted his spiritual children to correspond to so great a grace by ever-increasing fervor in the exact observance of rule, and in the love of Jesus and Mary.

At the last audience accorded to Villani, His Holiness inquired whether he had any thing further to ask. The Father begged the apostolic benediction for the holy founder and all the members of the Congregation, which was freely accorded, with several special indulgences and other favors. "From whence are you; my son?" continued the Pontiff. "I am of Naples," was the reply. The Pope said in a sweet and gentle voice: "I bless you, your father and mother, and all the members of your family," at the same time according him several graces, with power to impart them to his friends.

CHAPTER XXXIV.

An abbot resigns his mitre to follow Father Liguori. — First general chapter. Liberality of the gentlemen of Pagani. — The jubilee at Sarno. — Missionary. Precious death of Father Sportelli. — A beautiful flower on a barren rock. "The Glories of Mary." — Other publications. — Sad events. — Letters.

THE approbation of the institute made a great sensation in Rome. Every one admired the fervor and charity that reigned among the Fathers, and, in consequence, men eminent for sanctity and learning applied for admission to their body. Among these was an abbot who had rendered great service to the Congregation at Rome. Though Alphonsus had resolved never to admit to his Congregation any one who had lived in another, yet, in consideration of the distinguished merit of this applicant, and the aid he had given the Fathers with regard to the approbation, he readily received him. Released by a brief from the Order of which he had been chosen Abbot, he took the habit of a Redemptorist, and departed for Ciorani.

In October, our saint held his first General Chapter. He invited all the members to accept the rules, and proceed to a formal election to the general offices. Though confirmed in perpetual rectorship by the Pope, he resigned his authority, humbling himself, and begging pardon for all he had done amiss in the exercise of it. He then suggested a retreat of three days, and insisted that the vocals should vote for those whom they deemed before God best qualified to fill the respective offices, doing all he could to rid himself of the burden of the generalship. All joyfully accepted the rules, and renewed their vows of poverty, chastity, and obedience, with the oath of perseverance till death.

Despite his precautions, our saint was unanimously elected Rector-Major. The other offices being filled, necessary regulations were established for the novitiate and house of studies; and the authors to be followed in *belles-lettres*, philosophy, and theology, were selected. The abbot was appointed professor of philosophy and theology, a post for which his vast erudition eminently qualified him.

During the session of the Chapter, the heart of the holy founder was gladdened by the liberality of some gentlemen of Pagani. From the modesty and general good conduct of the young students, they had formed a flattering opinion of the institute, and earnestly entreated him to transfer them to Pagani, promising to contribute to the expense. All, including the bishops and the dean already mentioned, subscribed annual stipends, and manifested the greatest interest in the education of the students.

Alphonsus opened the autumn mission, by preaching the jubilee at Sarno. Many professional brigands placed their daggers, pistols, and bayonets with the Fathers, and embraced a Christian life. For ten years after the taverns were quite deserted. The bishop, wishing to try Alphonsus, whose toilet was poor as usual, said laughing: "Notwithstanding our wish to be economical, we will undertake the expense of having you shaved." Alphonsus presented himself to the barber with perfect indifference, although for eighteen years a razor had not touched his chin. Four times he underwent this operation: first, at Rome, when he presented himself to Clement XIII for examination; second, at Naples, when he was invited to the table of King Ferdinand IV; third, when ordered by Mgr. Giannini; and fourth, as we have just related.

The clergy profited greatly by this mission, to the unbounded joy of the good bishop. Christian piety everywhere replaced idleness and licentiousness, and the frequentation of the sacraments became general among all classes. Accompanied by fourteen Fathers, he made a missionary tour through the whole diocese, and was everywhere blessed with the most signal success.

While at Malfi, our saint heard of the precious death of Father Sportelli, his first companion. Though partially prepared for this melancholy communication, as the good Father had recently been suffering from an attack of apoplexy, he was nevertheless extremely afflicted. Some months previous, Sportelli had foretold the day and hour of his death, adding (he addressed a

Father about to join Alphonsus): "Kiss the hand of our Rector for me, and tell him to recommend my soul to Jesus Christ, when he shall hear of my death." He died as he had lived a saint, and God glorified him by miracles. Years after his death, his body was found incorrupt, and blood was drawn from his veins. Alphonsus himself endeavored to procure the beatification of this dearly loved son, and it is piously hoped that God will yet glorify his faithful servant by raising him on the altars of the Church.

While laboring m the diocese of Malfi, Alphonsus gave a retreat to a convent of Carmelite nuns, whose piety and perfect regularity greatly edified him. He found it expedient to moderate their fervor, and to prescribe some relaxation of mind and body. The sanctity of these dear sisters filled him with admiration, and, poet as he was, he exclaimed with a burst of generous enthusiasm: "I did not expect to find so beautiful a flower on the barren rock of Ripacandida."

In the course of this year (1750), he published his useful and charming work, *The Glories of Mary*. It is incredible with what delight this beautiful book was received. It was speedily translated into every tongue of Europe, and has gone through numberless editions.

About the same time, he wrote his *Advice regarding a Religious Vocation*, in which he shows that when God calls, his creatures must obey, and expatiates with the unction characteristic of all his works, on the excellence and advantages of the religious state. His *Advice to Novices* is a sequel to the former. He presented these admirable little works to all the novitiates in Naples, and they were everywhere received with gratitude and delight. "If I could only contribute to the perfection of one of those called to the religious state," said he, "I should be abundantly recompensed for my pains."

As our saint was sometimes obliged to witness the spectacle of men who boasted their knowledge of philosophy and theology, yet were incapable of writing their mother tongue correctly, he compiled for them an abridgment of the most essential rules of *Italian Orthography*. He even applied his prolific genius to the troublesome task of composing an elementary arithmetic for the use of the lay-brothers. So true is it that charity, when ardent and sincere, finds a thousand ways of being useful to others.

Every thing had gone on wonderfully well, when a reverse came which changed the joy of the holy founder into bitterness. The abbot had gained the admiration of the students by his brilliant talents, and their affection by his edifying conduct. He had been sent with twelve of the most talented to Pagani, and their progress under his able superintendence exceeded all expectation. The fervor of the poor abbot, however, proved somewhat evanescent. Accustomed to command, he could not easily obey. The rule became too great a restraint on him, and he used his influence over the young men to inspire them with his disedifying sentiments. Father Mazzini gave him a friendly admonition which was received with a bad grace. Alphonsus treated him with the utmost gentleness and sweetness, and even removed Father Mazzini against whom the abbot was greatly embittered, though without any cause. Finally, the students resolved themselves into two parties, and matters grew so bad that it became necessary to withdraw immediately *the sower of discord* from among the brethren.

Yet the compassionate heart of the holy founder shrank from inflicting a public humiliation on the hapless abbot. He merely invited him to Ciorani to give a retreat to some clerics who were preparing for holy orders. But *belles-lettres* seemed preferable in the eyes of the distinguished scholar, and he showed such discontent that the saint was obliged to tell him that, in case he would not obey, he was free to leave the Order. Doubtless it was the heart of Alphonsus, rather than his judgment, that permitted the abbot to return to Nocera a little later and resume his lectures. Again, some were of Paul, and some of Apollo. The gentle saint was still unwilling to pain an aged man, and recalled him to Ciorani, but ostensibly for the purpose of establishing a house of the Congregation at Rome.

The abbot, suspecting the real motive of his recall, dissembled his displeasure, and meanwhile sought to involve the students in his ruin. He proposed to them to join him in founding altogether a different establishment, and four, the flower of the rest, determined to follow him. Next day Alphonsus learned the worst, when these poor deluded youths presented themselves before him, with staves in hand and mantles on their arms, demanding a dispensation from their vows. The affectionate Father could not bear up against this. Falling prostrate before them, the tears gushing from his eyes, he besought them to avoid the snare laid for their virtue by one who had so basely abused the confidence reposed in him. He proposed a retreat of eight days, but all was useless. These unfilial youths turned their backs upon the best of Fathers, and, without even waiting for a dispensation, set out on their ill-starred journey.

Circumstances now showed the protection a good God granted to his holy servant To justify himself, the abbot had drawn up a memorial signed by these unfortunate young men, and addressed to the Pope, in which was stated every calumny his malignity could invent. Alphonsus the same morning had sent an order to the rector of Nocera to inform the abbot that he no longer belonged to the Congregation. The abbot had gone to take leave of the bishop, and the rector followed to deliver his message. In his astonishment, the culprit had not presence of mind to return to his room and remove his papers. The memorial which fully unmasked him was found open upon his table.

At Naples, the unfortunate man was joined by the four students, and deceived a promising young priest, by saying that he had already established his Congregation at Rome, and that the Pope himself had signalized the four students as so many apostles destined to win the palm of martyrdom among the infidels. This done, the traitor abandoned his five victims, and proceeded alone to Rome.

These sad events made a painful impression everywhere. A most respectable Father of the Order to which the abbot had belonged, paid Alphonsus a visit of condolence, but the latter merely said: "The abbot has made us weep to-day, but later on he will make you weep." This prophecy was fulfilled when he disturbed the whole Order by separating the abbeys of the kingdom of Naples from those of the Pontifical States, and causing himself to be declared perpetual Abbot in Rome, and Commissary-General for life to the abbeys of the Papal States, and causing many annoyances to the convents in both kingdoms.

Alphonsus attributed the discovery of the plot to St. Teresa, for it happened between the first and second Vespers of her feast. His affliction was tempered by the return of two of the young men, whom he received as a tender father, and to whom he ever after showed a special affection.

"My dear children," said he, to the students on this occasion, "I earnestly recommend you never to keep your consciences closed, for, if these unfortunate youths who have gone out from us had manifested their temptations to their superiors, they would not be where they are now. Had they opened their hearts to those who hold the place of Christ in their regard and could not deceive them, this had not happened. During a temptation, never make a resolution, however praiseworthy it may seem, but go at once and discover all to your superior. When the temptation is upon us, we do not recognize that it comes from the devil. He conceals himself and puts upon our eyes treacherous spectacles, making us see things, not as they are, but as our passions represent them. The strongest temptations can never shake a soul that gives herself entirely to God."

The abbot had introduced among the students a forced application to study which afflicted our saint, because it was detrimental to piety. Yet he always recommended the closest application to science, both to students and priests. "A laborer without science," said he, "though he be a man of prayer, is like a soldier without arms." He would add: *Be wise, but be wise unto sobriety.*

These sad events caused a general discouragement throughout the Congregation. To reanimate his spiritual children, the saint addressed to all the houses the following circular:

"To my brethren of the Congregation of the Most Holy Redeemer. Blessed be Jesus, Mary, Joseph, and Teresa:

"My very dear brethren, you know I am not afflicted when God calls some among us to another life. As a creature of flesh and blood, I am touched by the loss of a dear son; but I am comforted because he has died in the Congregation, all the members of which I know will be saved.

"Neither am I afflicted when persons leave because of their faults; yea, I am consoled, seeing we are delivered from a sickly sheep that would have infected all the others. Far less am I grieved at persecutions; on the contrary, they inspire me with courage, because, if we serve God faithfully, we are certain God will not abandon us. What alarms me is to see among us persons who are negligent in obeying, and have little regard for the rule.

"My brethren, some who were with us are now out of the Congregation. What will their end be? I cannot tell. But of this I am certain — they will live in continual trouble, and die without peace, for they have renounced their vocation.

"They have left us that they may live more happily; but the thought that they have left God to follow their own caprices, will never leave them one day's rest. In prayer they will be torn by remorse, and God knows where they will end.

"I beseech you to avoid faults of deliberation, especially those for which you have been reprehended.

"If correction lead the sinner to amend, the fault will be nothing. But if he will not amend, the devil will employ every artifice to make him lose his vocation: thus he causes the loss of many.

"By the grace of God, wherever we go on a mission, we work wonders, and people say they never had such a mission before. Why? Because we go by obedience, we go in poverty, we preach Christ crucified; each acquits himself perfectly of the charge imposed upon him. I have been grieved to learn that some desire the more honorable employments, as preaching, instructing. But what fruit could he produce who preaches through pride? I have a horror of this. If ambition enter the Congregation, the missions will do little good, or, rather, none.

"Your most affectionate Brother,

"Alphonsus Maria.

"*Of the Most Holy Redeemer*"

CHAPTER XXXV.

Alphonsus resumes the missions. — A new sorrow. — Circular letter. — The saint's reception at Naples. — Illness. — Another annoyance. — Reaction. Extraordinary Conversions: — The saint pleads his cause before the king. Insults. — His sojourn in the capital. — Prophecy. — His moral theology. High opinion Pope Benedict XIV held of Alphonsus. — Offer of the king. Miracle. — Death of Father Cafaro.

TOWARDS the end of autumn, Alphonsus resumed the missions, and, as usual, with effects hardly short of miraculous; but his heart was pierced by a new sorrow, occasioned by the departure of a Father whom he tenderly loved and who was most useful on the missions.

Offended by a reasonable admonition of the Superior, he set off to join Alphonsus, believing he would give him satisfaction. On the road, reflection opened his eyes, and seeing that he was wrong, he had not courage to present himself to the saint, but directed his steps to his own house. All the efforts of Alphonsus and the rest to induce him to return, were unavailing. On this occasion Alphonsus again addressed a circular letter to his children, to make them still more fearful of the great disasters which pride is capable of producing in the souls of those who yield to its suggestions:

"To the Fathers and Brothers of the Congregation of the Most Holy Redeemer.

"Live Jesus, Mary, Joseph, and Teresa!

"My dearly beloved Fathers and Brothers in Christ:

"I beseech God to deliver us immediately from all haughty spirits who will not brook the least correction or humiliation. Whoever refuses to be as potter's clay under the feet of all, let him fly. Our Lord will be better pleased if there remain but two who

179

are humble and mortified, than if there were a thousand imperfect. What are we doing in the Congregation, if we will not suffer something for the love of our dear Lord? How dare we preach humility to the people, if we have a horror of humiliations? But as we are all so miserable, I command you, in prayer, in thanksgiving, to beg daily of Jesus Christ to be able to bear contempt without losing peace and interior joy. The fervent will even pray to be despised for the love of Jesus.

"I desire to impress this upon your hearts: never speak ill of your Superiors. Take account of your smallest faults, for these are the little foxes the devil uses to devastate our souls and render us careless about preserving our vocation. Let us recur continually to prayer, my dearest Brethren, otherwise we shall not succeed in any thing.

"Your most affectionate Brother,
"Alphonsus Maria
"*Of the Most Holy Redeemer.*"

After the mission of 1757, our saint passed through Naples on his return home. He alighted at a small hospice given him by his Brother Hercules; and the people, seeing his miserable dress, mistook him for a vagabond, and began to hoot and ridicule him. All this he was taking very good-humoredly, when a merchant, calling him by name, made the crowd understand that he was the brother of Don Hercules di Liguori. He had just lain down to rest when his brother came to visit him. Unwilling to disturb him, he withdrew and returned next morning; but, finding he had not yet risen, he forced the door, fearing some accident. He found him extended upon his bed in a fainting fit.

The nearest physicians were summoned, and they ordered that he should be immediately undressed. His body was found to be entirely covered with sackcloth. A copious bleeding restored his consciousness, and he complained bitterly to his brother for having permitted him to be undressed. Fatigued and exhausted as he was, he consented to preach to the students of the archiepiscopal seminary; nor did he refuse to visit any monastery which asked his aid.

This year a new annoyance disturbed Alphonsus. The king, while hunting in the territory of Illiceto, inquired concerning the house of the missionaries, which he perceived at some distance. "It is the convent of the new Fathers," replied the cavalier in waiting, "and they have done tolerably well here, being heirs to sixty thousand ducats." "Ah, then," rejoined the king, "they are like the rest; they have scarcely commenced when they endeavor to amass wealth." The chevalier had referred to the will of the late canon of Illiceto.

Deceived by what he had heard, the king speedily let the court see that he had changed his opinion of Father Liguori's missionaries, and every one spoke of their avarice and ambition. The Fathers were greatly alarmed, but the holy founder reassured them. Full of confidence in God, he exclaimed:

"The Lord will make our Congregation prosper, not by applause or the protection of princes, but by poverty, contempt, misery, and persecutions. When have we seen the works of God begin with applause?"

He had recourse as usual to our dear Lord, hoping to obtain mercy by prayer and penance, and exhorting the brethren to unite with him in these holy exercises. A reaction in his favor soon took place; and it being left to Alphonsus himself to state the amount of revenue his Congregation possessed, he did so with a candor that confirmed the king in the high opinion he had entertained of him. Nevertheless the ministers used their utmost endeavors to suppress the Congregation, saying, among other things, that, far from consenting to the establishment of new Orders, they would gladly abolish some of those already in existence. Alphonsus did not lose courage. He said that the souls would be blessed who should defend his Congregation; and he abandoned its interests to the protection of Providence and the piety of the king.

After Easter, 1752, he evangelized the territory of Gragnano, accompanied by twenty-two Fathers. Prodigies of grace occurred, especially among malefactors, many of whom deposited their daggers and pistols at the feet of the Blessed Virgin. One bandit, in the procession made for the purpose of erecting a Calvary, carried one of the crosses on his shoulders, weeping so as to cause the people to shed tears of joy.

Meanwhile, the Marquis Branconi invited our saint to proceed to Naples and plead his cause before the king. Accordingly, he presented himself at the palace, and informed his Majesty that for nineteen years he and his companions had been giving missions, chiefly in remote and abandoned villages, that thousands had been converted on his own royal domains, that they had given yearly over forty missions, that the archbishops of Conza and Salerno, and the bishops of Bovino and Nocera, seeing the good effected by the missionaries, had established houses of the institute in their respective dioceses, and that the Sovereign Pontiff had approved the Congregation for the whole Church.

As for acquiring riches, he showed the king how far he was from desiring the temporal aggrandizement of the Congregation: "I am persuaded," said he, "that whenever abundance reigns, the laborer will quit the axe and the spade, and take his ease. I seek only to procure a modest livelihood according to the intention of the Pope, and I beseech your Majesty to name a fixed revenue beyond which we may not go." He secured the influence of the queen, through the celebrated Jesuit, Father Pepi, and Mother Angela of Divine Love, who had once been his penitent. He visited the ministers, to urge upon them the importance of aiding to promote the salvation of the people. But on these occasions neither his well-known sanctity nor his illustrious birth always sufficed to protect him from insult. One minister listened to his passionate pleadings with marked incivility, and almost turned him out of doors, saying: "Do not talk nonsense to me; tell your stories to some old woman." The saint bowed his head and remained silent. On another occasion, he said to a minister: "My Lord, I recommend to you the cause of Jesus Christ." "Jesus Christ has no cause in the royal chambers," was the contemptuous rejoinder.

His sojourn in the capital was a continual mission. He gave a retreat during which many hardened in sin yielded to grace, and hundreds of infidels abjured their errors. The Chinese college and several convents profited by his labors. When the negotiations approached a close, he had many masses said, and multiplied his penances, to force, as it were, the blessing of heaven. To the souls in purgatory, to St. Joseph and St. Teresa, he made special vows; and he wrote to many monasteries, begging prayers and novenas for his intention.

Finally, the royal approbation was obtained, the king forbidding any increase of revenue, after allowing but the merest pittance for the support of each member. So many conditions and restrictions were placed in the decree, that it rather embarrassed the saint than helped him. Thus was partially fulfilled a prophecy he had made some years previous to Sister Mary Angela of Capua: "I believe that God will mortify my pride, and that this approbation will not be given until after my death." In reality the Congregation was not set on a proper footing till the next reign, and long after his soul had passed sweetly to heaven.

Notwithstanding his grave and multiplied embarrassments, Alphonsus published, in 1753, his justly appreciated *Moral Theology.* At the request of his spiritual children, he had, in 1748, enriched Busembaum with notes, which they wished to have printed, to be more easy of reference. At a later period, he enlarged this work, and dedicated it to Benedict XIV, who gave it his approbation.

This invaluable work, like every other that came from his pen, was the fruit of zeal for the glory of God and the salvation of souls. The images of Jesus and Mary were constantly before him, for he never handled his pen without invoking them. In short, it was seen even then, as the Pope himself prophesied, that Alphonsus was destined to be universally approved. Once when a celebrated Neapolitan ecclesiastic came to consult this learned Pope on a difficult cause, his Holiness would give no decision. "You have Father Liguori at Naples," said he; "consult him." Indeed this excellent Pontiff, whose tradition was a marvel, quoted our saint with approval, in his valuable work, *De Synodo Diocesana.*

The king, more and more pleased with the great missionary, offered to endow the Congregation with the estates of a once powerful body of monks, now dwindled away to the merest shadow of its former greatness, on conditions that seemed advantageous to all concerned. For grave reasons, the saint finally declined the flattering proposal, though deeply grateful for the favor his sovereign had shown him.

In July, 1753, he accepted an invitation to give the Novena of the Feast of Mount Carmel, at Saragnano. The missionaries lodged in the house of one Doctor Mari. Twelve Fathers arrived on a Thursday at dinner time, and as they had not been expected, no preparations had been made for so large a party. "Put what you have on the table," said Alphonsus to the embarrassed host, "and God will supply what is wanting." And lo! as the servants were carving in the kitchen, the meat became visibly larger, and when the whole party was served, a considerable quantity remained.

Mari attested that the meat had been increased at least sevenfold. In reply to his exclamations of astonishment, the saint said: "In all embarrassments, let us have recourse to God, and never doubt his Providence."

The autumn and winter of 1753 were fruitful in missions. Resina asked a mission, but Alphonsus refused, on account of its proximity to Naples. The people then applied to the king who commanded the saint to gratify them, and paid all expenses himself. The missionaries afterwards went to Persano, at the expense of his majesty, whose good heart delighted in affording means of grace to his subjects. The spiritual exercises were given in various religious houses, and were, as usual, signally blessed by God. Applications were sent from all quarters for the Fathers, and every diocese in the kingdom wished to have a Redemptorist convent. But the holy founder was slow in answering these applications, not having a sufficient number of subjects. The king proposed to suppress certain convents, and give Alphonsus the revenues to found new establishments; but he would never consent to any thing so detrimental to the ancient religious, whom such arrangements would affect.

This year, the tender heart of our saint was again rent by the decease of a companion, at once his father and his son, — Father Cafaro, his spiritual director. Prayer and mortification were the inseparable companions of this holy man. Untiring in his labors, he animated the other Fathers by his example to immolate themselves for God and for souls. How earnestly did not the sainted founder pray for the prolongation of his precious life! What prayers did he not procure for the same end, both in his own houses and in many monasteries of virgins! But the good God saw fit to grant him other blessings instead of this much-coveted boon, and he bowed profoundly beneath the divine hand that chastened him. His sentiments on this trying occasion found vent in a beautiful canticle on *Conformity to the Divine Will*, which he sovereignly loved and adored under the most distressing circumstance.

CHAPTER XXXVI.

Circular letter. — A foundation in the States of the Church. — Retreat at Ciorani.— Discussion.— Death of the Countess Liguori — Mission at Benevento. — Retreat to the Neapolitan students. — To the servants. — Other effects of the saint's zeal. — New publication.

YEARS and sorrows had already begun to tell upon the once vigorous frame of our saint. Though scarcely fifty-six, his frequent infirmities hindered him from visiting his absent children as often as his paternal heart desired. In 1754, August 8, he addressed to all the houses the following circular:

"Fathers and Brothers, it is not yet twenty-two years since our Congregation was formed, and but five have elapsed since its confirmation by the Holy See, therefore it ought not only to have preserved its first fervor, but also to have made progress. Many, I know, lead holy lives, but some are too easily discouraged. Yet God has called us into the Congregation to live as saints; and if remissness succeeds to fervor, where will our poor Congregation be fifty years hence?

"Poor Jesus Christ! if Thou art not loved in this Congregation which has received from thee so many special lights and graces, by whom wilt Thou be loved? Now that I am already old and sickly, the day is near on which I must render up my account. I wish to be as useful as possible to you, and God knows how I love each one of you as my mother and my brethren. But it is not the will of God that I should imperil my salvation by an immoderate love for any one of you. We all commit faults; but faults against obedience, poverty, humility, and brotherly charity,

185

must not be established among us. I adhere to the promise I have made to God, — never to yield to human respect, never to see my brethren fail in any important point, or in any manner hurtful to their neighbor, without reproving them.

"You know that my greatest fault is too much condescension; but I hope God will give me strength not to suffer those who will not amend — who even justify their imperfections. I beseech you, who now hold offices in the Congregation, never to excuse those who, after faults, justify, instead of humbling, themselves.

"I declare to you that I will accuse that superior at the tribunal of Jesus Christ, who, to avoid displeasing the imperfect, would wink at dangerous faults, and cause relaxation in the Congregation. I speak not of the past, but of the future; if any one has committed a fault, I do not mean to reproach him.

"I exhort you to value your vocation as the greatest favor God could bestow on you, after the benefit of creation and redemption. Thank God for it every day, and tremble lest you lose it. Do not allow the devil to deceive you — each of us knows that a priest, in the Congregation, will save more souls in one year, than he would during a whole lifetime out of it; and, as regards personal advantage, a subject will gain more in one year by practising obedience than he would in ten years, living according to his own caprice. By the grace of God, the Congregation is now well provided with subjects full of fervor and talent. Our fame is spread throughout the kingdom, and even beyond it. We are asked for missions on all sides. But should we not be able to do all we desire in this respect, it would always be better to preserve regular observances with a few, than to see the Congregation increased by relaxed subjects.

"Finally, my brethren, be persuaded that each of you is, after God, the single object of my love, and that for each of you I would willingly offer my blood and my life. Fear not to address yourselves to me in all your wants. Those who are at a distance can write. Do not fear to importune me; the thought that you can trouble me either by speaking or writing, can come only from the devil. Believe me, the more confidence you show towards me, the more closely you will bind me to you. I leave every thing when my children require my assistance. It is of more consequence to me to succor one of them, than to perform any other good work whatever. This is the good work God asks of me, especially while I am charged with the souls of others.

"To conclude: let us love Jesus Christ. We, above all others, owe him this. Let us love a God who has died for love of us. Let us become saints, offering ourselves to him to do with us what He pleases. I bless and embrace you all in the heart of Jesus. Lose not the beautiful crowns I see prepared for all who live according to our rules, and die in our Congregation."

Although approved by the Pope, the Congregation had no house in the States of the Church, till Mgr. Pacca, Archbishop of Benevento, applied, in 1753, for one. To arrange this business, Alphonsus despatched Father Villani, and Mgr. Borgia offered to accompany him.

The travellers experienced a special protection of divine Providence. Twice a thunderbolt fell at Mgr. Borgia's feet, without injuring him or his companion. The archbishop was so charmed with the results of the first labors of Villani, — a retreat given to the students, — that he went to Nocera to thank the holy founder; and during this visit, declared that it was to him, after God, he would confide the interests of his diocese.

During Passion-Week, our saint gave a retreat at Ciorani, on the invitation of Father Rossi. Priests and people crowded about the veteran missionary, till messengers had to be sent in different directions to warn them that there was no more room; but they passed the night in the air, rather than give up all hope of hearing his voice. About this time a discussion took place between Father Liguori and a Jansenist who had attacked his *Moral Theology*, and was not sparing of insulting personalities. But the sweetness and moderation with which Alphonsus met his adversary, drew upon him universal esteem.

On the road to Benevento, whither he repaired to give a mission at the request of the archbishop, he stopped at Naples to visit his beloved mother, then in a dying state. Having quieted her conscience on several points, and entirely cured her of some scruples that tormented her, he heard her last confession, and administered the holy sacraments of Viaticum and Extreme Unction. For three days, he was unable to tear himself from this revered and cherished mother, consoling and animating her; but, as he could delay the mission no longer, he begged her parting benediction, and, consoled by her sanctity, he set out for Benevento, happy to think she was about to die a death precious in the sight of the Lord, while she rejoiced that her son left her only to conquer souls for Jesus Christ, and bestow on others the blessings he had conferred on her.

He opened the Benevento mission with twenty Fathers. A prelate who attended, afterwards wrote: "It is long since we have seen men so truly apostolic. One can form no idea of the effects they have produced; but the arrival of Alphonsus awakened recollections that had long slumbered. The voice of the holy missionary was weakened by age and fatigue, but the sight of him was enough to soften and melt the hardest hearts. Benevento has been sanctified. The very malefactors have become models of piety. A general reformation of manners is the result of his labors."

The renown of this mission reached Rome, and Cardinal Orsini informed Alphonsus that the Pope had been so pleased with the good tidings, that he spoke to the Duke of Cerisan to obtain from the King of Naples an *exequatur* to the brief of approbation given to the Congregation.

After this mission, to render priests more skilful in hearing confessions, the saint published his *Moral Theology* in Italian, adding three interesting appendices. This work met with immense circulation. The demand became so great outside of Italy, that he re-wrote it in Latin under the title of *Homo Apostolicus.*

Business called him to Naples, February, 1756. Cardinal Sersales besought him to give the spiritual exercises to some students in a hall of the palace. But, instead of a few young men, the whole community assembled to hear him, and, with canons and other dignitaries, his audience swelled to a thousand. Even bishops attended, and pressed forward with the rest to kiss his hand, but he humbled himself interiorly, and endeavored to escape observation.

The cardinal, admiring the miraculous effects of this retreat, insisted that he should preach to the diocesan students, at least, once a week. Directors of seminaries in the city and its environs made the same request, so that he often preached several times in one day.

He did not forget the servants of the cardinal and of the seminaries, but, following the divine instinct which urged him to seek out the lowliest and most neglected, he assembled every one of them, and instructed them on the duties of their state. Henceforward, they were a comfort to their employers; and, besides performing all their duties well, found time to pray and to approach the Sacraments. The cardinal wept tears of joy over this reformation.

The convents, as usual, sought his assistance, and he never refused to instruct and console their cherished inmates, many of whom had once been his penitents. He greatly deplored the increase of vice consequent upon the reading of the infamous works of materialists and deists. To inspire the people with a horror of such productions, he condemned from the pulpit all who sold such books, or kept them in their homes, as guilty of grave sin. To neutralize as much as possible the evil effects of these devices of Satan, he published his erudite *Treatise in Defence of Religion and of the State*, a work which was found particularly useful against the sophists, who undertook to pervert the minds of the people and sap the foundations of their faith. This magnificent treatise is an enduring monument of our saint's elegant style and profound learning.

CHAPTER XXXVII.

The queen-mother consults our saint. — Stratagem. — Work on the confessional. — Criticisms. — The circus at Amalfi. — Earthquake. — Nola. The Seminary. — Bi-location. — The saint loses his dear son Rossi. Miracle. — Missions to Calabria.

ALPHONSUS returned to Nocera in Holy Week, 1756, but scarcely had he arrived, when he was summoned by the queen-mother, who desired to consult him on affairs of conscience. The court was then at Lauro. Here was also a monastery. The nuns, wishing to get a piece of his clothing, invited him to visit a beautiful reliquary in their church, and while he was giving it to them to kiss, one of the boarders cut off a large piece of his mantle. As it was cold in the evening, he spread his mantle on his bed; but finding it rather jagged, exclaimed to F. Galdieri who accompanied him: "This mantle is not mine; is it yours?" "It is yours," returned the Father, "but the nuns have been playing you a trick." "Yes," rejoined the saint, somewhat confused, "I see why that little girl was always so near me; but now it would require an old-clothes shop to mend it." Thefts of this nature were not infrequent wherever he went.

In July, he was again in Naples endeavoring to obtain the exequatur of the Apostolic brief. He had prayers and mortifications without number offered up for this intention. As usual, he had not a moment's rest. He published at this time his *Method for a Confessor to exercise his Ministry well*, in which he considers the Confessor as father, physician, teacher, and judge. Such was the admiration this work excited, that it was said his Guardian Angel had specially assisted him in its composition. In his *Dictionary of Illustrious Men*, Feller says of it: "It breathes a divine unction: all is moderation, gentleness, and that charity which seeks only the salvation of souls."

"What a precious book!" exclaims the learned Jesuit Zaccharia, in his *History of Literature*: "Father Liguori follows a just, a reasonable method which smooths the way for the poor penitent."

The name of Alphonsus was now celebrated. All the provinces of the kingdom, except Calabria, had been visited by the Congregation. An eminent physician offered to defray the expenses of the Fathers to this distant region. While the missionaries labored successfully there, our saint, with fourteen companions, repaired to Amalfi. During this mission, every woman of bad character in the place was converted. The evening before he left, Father Liguori said in a sermon: "We have been much fatigued in laboring for you, but as soon as we go, a devil will come from the mountain to destroy the fruit of this mission. Beware! otherwise God will punish your reprehensible curiosity by an earthquake."

Next day, a buffalo was let loose for the amusement of the people; but scarcely was the play begun when a violent shock frightened the whole town, and the terrified people ran from the ring to the church. The bishop received them, and as he recalled the prediction of the venerable Father Liguori, and the contempt they had shown for it, another shock was felt, so violent that the chandeliers were turned upside down. The prelate became alarmed, and ordered the priests to give absolution to all present.

From Amalfi he passed to Nola, whither he was invited by the bishop to aid in reforming the episcopal seminary. Many of the young people had given themselves up to all kinds of irregularities, discipline was unknown, and for several days he might as well have preached to the walls. The most awful truths of eternity became subjects of their ridicule, and not a few of the young wretches amused themselves by mimicking the tones and gestures of the preacher.

Though the bishop thought gentle means would do here, our saint knew that the case was a desperate one, and he warned the prelate that, by conniving at the evil by injudicious gentleness, he risked his eternal salvation — insinuating that bishops had been damned because of their seminaries. He continued to preach; but it was not till the exercises were nearly over, that any fruit appeared. Then all were seized with a sudden terror. Four of the most turbulent fled, and the remainder became truly contrite. This unexpected result was attributed wholly to the prayers and mortifications of the saint. During his long life, Alphonsus continued to take a deep interest in this institution, and every year, sent his missionaries to give the retreat, if he could not go in person.

When he had restored fervor in the seminary of Nola, he went to Cerreto. From the palace-gate, he was ushered into a hall which a servant was sweeping. "Please inform the bishop that I wish to have an audience," said the visitor. "Wait till I finish this," was the rough reply. As the broom whisked about the corner into which our saint had shrunk, the menial continued: "Don't you see me? Is there no possibility of making you rise?" Alphonsus rose, and when the sweeping was finished, repeated his request.

The bishop, on being informed that a poor ragged man awaited him, sent to learn his name and business. But, when the noble name of Liguori was announced, the prelate, who happened to be in his dressing-gown, called out to one servant for his soutane, to another for his wig, and to a third for his pectoral cross, that he might receive such a guest in a becoming manner. The servant speedily hid himself. When compelled to appear, he threw himself at the feet of our saint. The bishop having asked an explanation, the poor man told, with tears, of the rudeness with which he had treated the great servant of God, — Alphonsus laughing good-humoredly all the time.

While our saint was staying at Naples this season, the following example of bi-location took place. A woman whom he had reclaimed, used to come every Sunday for alms. Being told he had gone to the capital, she went to the Church and recommended herself to God. While praying, the saint called her to the sacristy and bestowed the usual dole, beseeching her to remain faithful to God. The woman then reproached the porter, saying, "How is it that people think you a saint, and yet you tell lies? Father Liguori is here; he called me just now and gave me money!"

The pastor informed the rector, who, upon inquiry, found that the saint had been laboring in Naples, and giving alms and good counsel in Nocera at the same time. A similar miracle happened at Amalfi, where he was preaching in the Church and hearing confessions in the house, simultaneously.

Other missions were asked for Calabria. Our saint supplied them, regretting that he could not go thither himself. On the 2d January, 1758, he went to Salerno with twenty companions. Of their mission, Mgr. Pinta wrote long after: "The conversions were innumerable and astonishing; the benefits conferred, great and lasting. The aspect of the whole town was changed; I myself owe the grace of being able to renounce the world, to the light I then received." It was everywhere said that, had the apostles themselves preached, greater effects could not have been produced.

The consolation derived from this mission by the apostolic man was not unalloyed. During its course, he had to bewail the loss of Father Xavier Rossi, the support of the house of Ciorani. But if he were afflicted by this premature death, he had sweet comfort in knowing that his old and cherished companion had died a saint. Despite his failing health, Rossi had always been a model of regularity. His obedience and humility were quite wonderful, and such was his devotion to Jesus, in the Blessed Sacrament, that it was said that there was no veil between him and his Savior. He had to combat against a temper extremely passionate. When almost overpowered by anger, he would struggle so violently against that passion that his face became yellow, and almost black. On several occasions, when it seemed impossible to resist it any longer, he ran into the stable and flung himself at the feet of the ass, humbling himself before the brute, until he could rise perfectly calm. He was singularly charitable; and Alphonsus, who knew the generous tendencies of his compassionate heart, set no limits to his liberality. The memory of Xavier Rossi will always be held in benediction by the Congregation of which he was so admirable an ornament.

During a visit made by Alphonsus to Naples, in Lent, the blood of the proto-martyr, St. Stephen, preserved in the monastery of St. Gaudioso, liquified in his presence, a miracle never before known to happen except on the feast of the martyr, or at the translation of his relics.

His companion, Father Galdieri, being about to embark for Calabria, the saint said: "I wish you would go by land. Wait a little: in a few days some one will arrive who has travelled by land, and you can return on his mule." Galdieri obeyed, and all happened as the founder had said. The vessel in which he was to have sailed was wrecked, and all on board perished.

The saint was considerably occupied with convents and monasteries, to which he always gave assistance when asked. One evening, having returned from the nuns, he had his office to recite and some proof-sheets to correct, when a duchess sent for him in the greatest haste. "Tell the duchess," said he to the messenger, "I cannot go now. The duchess will recover, and I shall see her grace to-morrow." The lady was perfectly cured.

His extraordinary gifts made our saint the object of universal veneration, but he ever humbled himself more and more. Invited by the Provincial of the Jesuits to dine at their house, — the Fathers, being very anxious to have something that had been worn by him, remarked that his belt was completely worn out, and offered him a new one. Guessing their design, our saint smilingly fastened on the new cincture without removing the old one.

Retreats and missions crowded upon our saint, as usual; miracles and extraordinary favors were wrought wherever he appeared. At Amalfi, his face glowed like a live coal, as it reflected the sunbeams that darted from our Lady's statue. Whilst thus favored, he published his beautiful *Preparation for Death*, a work that produced the effects of a gigantic mission throughout the whole kingdom.

In 1758, also, the cardinals of the Propaganda asked the saint for apostolic men, to labor among the Nestorians, who had declared to Clement XIII their desire to be united to the Roman Church. He instantly consented, and wrote to the Fathers to inform them of the circumstance, and inquire who among them were desirous of gaining the crown in a work of such great difficulty. Every one offered; all being eager to give their lives for Jesus Christ. Thirty novices wrote letters in their own blood to signify to him their desire of suffering martyrdom in the cause. Their zeal filled the glowing heart of their Father with ineffable consolation and delight.

In 1759, the Fathers, owing to a singular circumstance, were invited to Sicily. A swindling Neapolitan, knowing the veneration in which Father Liguori was held, wrote, in his name, to different dioceses, asking pecuniary aid. Large sums were sent him, — twenty ducats of which fell into the hands of our Saint, sent by

Mgr. Lucchese, bishop of Girgenti. Alphonsus wrote to thank him for his bounty, and thus the swindle was discovered, but the correspondence ended in the missionaries going to Sicily.

CHAPTER XXXVIII.

Reformation of the Royal Hospital of Gaeta. — New Publication. The Sicilian Mission. — The True Spouse of Christ. — The Fishermen. The Fathers Wrecked. — The Young Calabrian. — His tragic end a fulfilment of Father Liguori's Prophecy.

THERE was a royal hospital at Gaeta for female foundlings, which by mismanagement was reduced to a most miserable condition. The little ones, about four hundred in number, were consigned to the care of the more grown children, and as a necessary consequence of this unfortunate arrangement, every thing about the place breathed misery and sin. The king, knowing the zeal of Alphonsus, charged him with the reform of this place, which had already been unsuccessfully attempted by several clergymen.

Our saint shed tears of sorrow on hearing of the unnatural conduct of the mistresses of the institute, once founded by piety, and still liberally furnished with every thing necessary; yet, no better than a stable for the body and a hell for the soul. He sent thither Fathers Mazzini, Fiocchi, and Gajano as the best qualified for this difficult undertaking, and after working, not for months, but for years, they succeeded: with the aid of four Sisters of St. Vincent, this wretched asylum was converted into a little paradise, to the delight of our saint and the great satisfaction of the king.

Ever burning with zeal for souls, Alphonsus published (1759) *The Great Means of Prayer*, of which work he himself said, that, he wished to have means to place a copy in the hands of every human being; the neglect of prayer being the great cause of the ruin of those who are lost. This was quickly followed by a learned dissertation entitled *Of the Just Prohibition of Bad Books*. The Marquis Tanucci was displeased that such a work had been published, and immediately sent his emissaries to seize all the copies. But his opposition only served the good cause. The book, previously little known, was now so eagerly sought, that the booksellers raised the price, and, to supply the increasing demand, secretly printed many copies.

His next work was *The True Spouse of Christ*, published in Lent, 1760; an admirable book, full of sublime lessons on Christian virtues, by which all may profit, according to their respective states. This was soon followed by *Reflections and Affections on the Passion of Jesus Christ*, and that useful work known under the name of *Selva*, in which he treats of the sacerdotal dignity, gives directions regarding preaching, and the Sacrament of Penance, and lays down the principal rules of that popular eloquence of which he was so perfect a master. Meanwhile, the powers of hell seemed to have raised every possible storm that could keep the Redemptorist Fathers from Girgenti. They had embarked under a cloudless sky, and were soon in sight of Palermo, but a furious storm threw back their vessel to the Gulf of Naples. They set out again, but were driven from Palermo into the straits of Nocedo. A third voyage was met by a third tempest, and they were dashed between Sardinia and Corsica, — the vessel being so much damaged that the passengers were hopeless of ever landing.

All this war of elements was seen in spirit by the holy Founder, who was heard to cry out, raising his tearful eyes to heaven: "My poor children! my poor children!" The tempest lasted twenty-four hours. On the third day, the vessel, with great difficulty, reached Baja; their safety being an evident miracle wrought by the prayers of the saint.

Alphonsus, like an old soldier who desires to die sword in hand, went to wage war against the enemies of God at Amalfi. The town was ravaged by an epidemic which defied every kind of treatment. A canon having procured an old shirt of Alphonsus, lent it to several of the stricken, and every one whom it touched recovered. Going to and from the church, the canons were obliged to escort him, to save him from the pressure of the crowd that thronged about him.

The nuns of Conca entreated him to give them some instruction; and, as he proceeded to that place by sea, several fishermen complained that the sea no longer supported them, and besought him to bless it. Scarcely had he complied, when the fish appeared in myriads, and they quickly loaded their fishing-crafts.

At the Convent of St. Marcelina, he found one of the pupils, Catharine Spinelli, dangerously ill. "Catherine," said he, "do you wish to live, or die?" "To live!" said the girl. He made the sign of the cross over her, and said: "You will live, but you must become a saint." She was instantly cured, and afterwards became a nun of eminent sanctity.

Other retreats, missions, and miracles, were accomplished, and all the gifts of the apostles, "the first fruits of the Spirit," seemed revived in this great missionary. Inflamed with a desire of seeing priests perfect as to the fitting celebration of the holy mysteries, he published a work on the necessity of observing the holy rubrics, replete with salutary instruction on the dispositions with which the Holy Sacrifice should be celebrated.

He published also in the epistolary form, a dissertation, on the manner of preaching Jesus Christ. "Puffed-up orators," said he, "give out but wind; they think more of displaying their own eloquence than of glorifying Jesus Christ. If they escape hell, they will at least have to get rid of their inflation in purgatory."

His sermons, possessing as they did, genuine eloquence, continued as usual to people the cloisters, and cause every Christian virtue to bud and blossom in the hearts of his hearers. Once, whilst preaching in the Church of the Holy Ghost, he suddenly exclaimed in a transport: "O, thou who enterest here, and dost flatter thyself that thou canst be saved in the world as well as in a convent, — unhappy that thou art! — how far art thou wandering! — ere long thou shalt come to a deplorable end!" At that moment, a young Calabrian entered the church who had long struggled against the inestimable grace of a religious vocation. He naturally applied to himself the words of the venerable preacher, yet he dared to smile at the menace. Scarcely a month elapsed when he was killed by a musket-shot. When dying, he related to a friend the words, which Alphonsus, inspired by the Holy Spirit, had addressed him from the pulpit.

CHAPTER XXXIX.

Alphonsus as a Superior. — Humility. — Health.— Preaching. — Father de Meo's Sybils and Argonauts. — Confessors.— Example of a rigorist. — Father Rizzi obliged to apologize for an indiscretion. — Poverty and obedience. Instruction on various matter. — Rules for a Superior.

ALMOST seventy years had passed over the head of the greatest missionary of modern times, and he already believed himself close upon the end of his career. But it was the divine will to preserve him many years yet, that in a higher sphere, he should glorify God by giving to the world a perfect model of a fervent and zealous bishop, as he had successively been a model to laymen, ecclesiastics and missionaries. Before we follow him into this exalted station, we will speak of him in his quality of *Superior* and *Founder* of a religious congregation.

His first care was to inspire his brethren with his own burning zeal for the salvation of souls. "What have we to do in the world," he would often exclaim, "and why have we entered the Congregation, if not to sacrifice ourselves for the glory of God? We are His special children, and more than all others, we should be foremost in the ranks to fight His battles, since He gave His life for us. The love of Jesus Christ constrains us to love Him, — to draw all to His love. I am ready to die with grief when I see a priest indifferent about any thing that concerns God's honor. Our employment is the same as that exercised by Our Divine Redeemer and His Apostles. Whoever is destitute of the Spirit of Jesus Christ, and the zeal of the Apostles is not fit for this ministry."

The next virtue he required was humility: "Humility," said he, "makes us respected by the people; it attracts and gains sinners, however haughty and proud they may be." Having heard once that a missionary had shown a want of submission to a bishop, he sent him directly to make the fullest apology for his conduct. He exacted from the Fathers great humility towards each other, and especially towards Superiors.

Insubordination was a fault inexcusable in his eyes. He was willing that every difficulty the Superior might not have foreseen should be pointed out to him but simply, and without the least display of resistance. "If obedience be wanting," said he, "disorders and confusion will be the result." He cultivated in his brethren a spirit of mortification and a love of suffering, but he distinguished between effeminate delicacy and a reasonable care of health. "Health," said he, "is the capital of a missionary; if that fails he is bankrupt." But he charged the Superior to attend to the health of each, and would allow no discontent to be expressed with reference to food, clothing, or lodging.

He disliked undue familiarity with laymen, and considered idle discourses unworthy of the sacred ministry. He enjoined that in every sermon his Fathers should preach Christ Crucified, and required a simple, popular style, that every one could understand. "Jesus Christ," said he, "understood rhetoric better than we, yet, to be the more easily comprehended by the multitude, He chose ordinary comparisons." One Saturday, Father Alexander Meo, in preaching on the Blessed Virgin, introduced the Sybils and the Argonauts. "What!" he exclaimed, "is it thus they preach here?" He afterwards reproved the preacher severely, and condemned him to three day's silence, though he was a most exemplary man.

From confessors he exacted great prudence and profound skill, as from their judgment there was no appeal. He was rigid in examining confessors, and, when bishop, if he did not find the candidate fully competent, he refused him faculties. He inculcated the greatest charity and gentleness towards sinners. "Harshness," said he, "distinguishes the Jansenists, who do more harm than good, and certainly have not the spirit of Jesus Christ, or of the apostolic men whom we honor on our altars. An energetic word is sometimes useful, but it must not be repulsive, and before the penitent withdraws, he must be calmed by kind words, that he may be full of hatred for his sin, but at the same time full of confidence in his confessor." On another occasion he said:

"If it happen that you feel overpowered by bad humor, leave the confessional immediately, because your irritability would cause some penitents to commit more sacrileges than others would make good confessions."

He deemed it scandalous to show respect on persons at the confessional, "Charity," said he, "but not partiality. Ladies of quality will make way for themselves. It is not the confessor's business to take care of them. He ought to be equally at the service of all, and receive everybody with kindness and gentleness."

To encourage the timid, and inspire all with a great desire to train souls in the confessional, he said: "The preacher sows, but the confessor gathers the harvest. The confessional is the touchstone of the true laborer. Whoever does not love the confessional, disregards souls, to whom is applied therein the blood of Jesus Christ. In the sacred tribunal, we gather fruit for ourselves and our penitents; in the pulpit a breath of vanity may destroy the merit of our labors."

He insisted that his Father's should listen patiently to all, however wicked, and if they could not always give absolution, they would at least encourage the poor sinner, point out the means of amendment, and induce them to come back to God. He was especially delighted when he saw his young priests, zealous for abandoned souls. A learned and talented professor, fascinated by the doctrines of the rigorists, was deprived of the faculty of hearing confession by the saint, who had vainly employed every other means of correcting him. He haughtily demanded his dispensation. "My son," said Alphonsus, "if you abandon the Congregation because you persist in your erroneous opinions, you will suffer awful consequences." The words were verified. The poor man was attacked with a cancer in the face, after he left, and in an agony of despair, he ran about the streets uttering piteous cries. When near death, he begged with tears to be reinstated in the Congregation, and in consideration of his condition, his prayer was granted.

To inspire his sons with a true sense of humility, he would say: "Humility is necessary in the mission, in the house, at all times and in all places, if we would please God. I beseech God to destroy our Congregation the moment the spirit of pride predominates in it." One day, a Father chanced to say, "On my honor." This was a grave fault in the eyes of the saint. At the next conference, he continually repeated, "On my honor." "Our honor," said he, "is to be despised and vilified — to become like Jesus Christ, the reproach of men, and the outcast of the people. This is all the honor we can claim."

He never approved of indiscreet zeal. Father Ricci, having written to a bishop with whom the people were greatly dissatisfied, to remind him of his duty, the saint wrote to the superior: "Tell Father Ricci, he has done wrong. He acted through zeal, but he forgot that we are forbidden to meddle with things out of the confessional which may cause embarrassment to others. Let him say three *Ave Marias* as a penance, and when his Lordship comes to the house, he will go to him privately and throw himself at his feet, confessing his indiscretion and asking forgiveness."

Poverty and obedience he looked upon as the foundations of the Congregation. Yet, he did not wish to have poverty practised to such a degree as would be contrary to decency. One day, he noticed on a young cleric a pair of shoes greatly worn. He began to cast such looks from the shoes to the superior, that the latter readily understood his meaning. If he saw any superior negligent in procuring for the subjects what was necessary, urged by a holy zeal, he reprimanded and even chastised him for it. He was particularly displeased when he found superiors indulgent to themselves and stingy with others. "Oh," he exclaimed, "how many superiors will be damned for having violated the vow of poverty, and ruined charity and the common life."

Some of the Fathers thought common cloth not durable enough for mantellas, and that the houses would gain by purchasing a better material. "It is we," he answered, "and not the houses, that have made a vow of poverty; it is we, not the houses, that must take the consequences of the vow. Common cloth humbles and abases, and that is what is required by poverty."

To inspire his children with a high idea of their vocation, he used to say that vocation and predestination were the same thing, and that having been chosen by God to form part of a rising congregation was a grace, which of itself, required in us a great degree of holiness. "We must, therefore," he would add, "pray that the Almighty may cause us to understand the value of this grace, for should we fail to correspond to so holy a vocation, our eternal happiness would be risked. God has chosen us to be coadjutors of His Blessed Son, and to rescue souls from the grasp of the devil."

"We should be most grateful to God," said he, "for having taken us from the world into his own house, where the truths of faith are constantly put before our minds by meditation, spiritual reading, pious discourses and good example. All these things are great helps to us in difficult positions; whereas, those who are in the world, being constantly occupied with the things of the world, have few good ideas, and many depraved ones, which cause them to fall in slight temptations."

When God called any of his children to heaven, the saint felt mingled joy and sadness. If he wept for the loss of a fellow-laborer, he rejoiced at the translation of a saint. Therefore, he ordained, that whenever death visited his houses, general recreation should take the place of mourning.

He instructed all not to be satisfied with ordinary holiness. "If we do not aim very high," said he, "we shall not easily succeed in reaching the end God has appointed for us." If a reverse of fortune befel the parents of any of them, he sympathized with their distress, and did not fail to relieve them, despite his great poverty. Some of the fathers judged such charity excessive, but our saint replied: "Charity never falls into excess, and God repays all that is given in His name."

The heart of the most tender father could not feel greater love for his children than Alphonsus did for the students. "We are their Fathers," said he, "and the Congregation is their mother. They are the hope of the Congregation, because one day they will replace us. Since they have left their parents to give themselves to God, it is right they should be treated with the greatest charity."

He did not like to see them eager to study what is unnecessary. "True knowledge," said he, "consists in knowing Jesus Christ. Of what use is knowledge to us if its end is not to seek God? We must study, it is true, but our sole aim ought to be to please God, otherwise we may have to expiate the fault by a long purgatory." To inspire his students and novices with fidelity, he was wont to say: "Vocation and perseverance are two distinct graces; God may give us the former in the midst of our infidelities, but we must labor for the grace of perseverance." He required of the novices, humility, obedience and openness of heart;

and when he found these dispositions, he felt sure there was nothing to fear. With regard to the novices who became sick, his maxim was that if they were patient and pious, they drew innumerable graces on the Congregation. When a fervent novice was on the point of death, he was not distressed, but if a novice wished to leave on this account, he granted leave with pain. "If the doctors and remedies we have here," said he, "cannot restore their health, they will not recover in their parents' house. If God wills their death, it is better they should die in the Congregation than amid the snares of the world."

We will conclude this chapter by transcribing the wise rules Alphonsus laid down for superiors, and by which he guided himself, thereby becoming a perfect superior:

1. A superior ought to lead an exemplary life, for if he does not practice what he teaches, his government will be useless or dangerous.

2. The superior should constantly labor for God, and be persuaded that he will often meet with ingratitude from man.

3. A superior who is too severe, makes the subjects imperfect and deceitful, because they will act only through servile fear.

4. Pride makes a superior odious to all; it hinders his own sanctification and that of his subjects, as well as the preservation of order in the institute.

5. The superior should possess heroic patience. He must bear all kinds of labor, fatigue, and contradictions, and always appear calm, and be affable towards all.

6. The superior should give every one a reception full of charity and affection, and be all to all on every occasion.

7. The superior should show the same love for all, and assist all alike in their spiritual and temporal wants.

8. The superior who does not overcome his antipathies, is hasty in his judgments and commits many faults.

9. The superior ought not to be so presumptuous as to govern by his own light, only; he always needs prayer and counsel.

10. The superior should provide for the spiritual and temporal wants of his subjects, and relieve them with all the care of a father and a brother.

11. The superior ought to be vigilant as to observance of the rule; he must therefore, inquire into everything with great exactitude.

12. The superior must not judge things hastily, but weigh them well, and inquire and reflect, before giving any decision.

13. The superior should punish offences against the rule, but must first give repeated warnings, which should always be accompanied by charity.

14. The superior ought to be firm with the incorrigible, and take care to prevent the contagion of bad example.

15. The superior must be just, exemplary, prudent, affable and vigilant, if he would not undergo a terrible judgment at the tribunal of God.

CHAPTER XL.

The Congregation thirty years after its foundation. — Saintly members. The vacant See of St. Agatha. — Father Liguori selected to fill it. — He declines the honor. — His intense love for his Congregation. — A command from Rome. — "The voice of the Pope is the voice of God." — Terrible agitation of the Saint. — His heroic obedience. — He prophesies that he will return to die among his brethren. — Touching meeting of the Saint and F. Fatigati. — The episcopal ring and cross. — The Saint at Rome.

THE reputation which the Congregation had gained was a subject of consolation to the holy Founder, but its zeal and fervor filled up the measure of his joy. The rule was everywhere in full force; the love of holy poverty was universal; resistance and excuses were unknown; even the intentions of superiors were held in reverence.

The old were models for the young, and the young excited the emulation of the old. His children died saintly deaths; Father Sportelli and Brother Gerard are still invoked by devout clients with no small profit.[1]

Such was the Congregation thirty years after its foundation, when God saw fit to deprive it of its head.

The episcopal see of St. Agatha, had become vacant, and the succession to it was solicited by at least sixty candidates, among whom were bishops, and even archbishops. Clement XIII, embarrassed by the number of competitors, consulted the cardinals, and Cardinal Spinelli gave advice to choose a man whose merits surpassed those of all the rest, and proposed Father Liguori, who, from the lustre of his origin, science, and sanctity, enjoyed an esteem as general as it was well merited.

---

[1] Fr. Sportelli was declared Venerable in 1899. St. Gerard Majella was canonized in 1904.

The news of the Pontiff's decision was hailed with unqualified delight. Several distinguished persons who had known the saint in Naples, congratulated his Holiness on having raised a saint and a scholar to the mitre.

But little did our humble Father Liguori suspect what was going on in his regard. One day he remarked to Mgr. Borgia, that one of the greatest graces he had ever received, was that of having escaped the peril of being bishop; "a peril," he said, "he should have had some difficulty in avoiding had he remained with his family." Just then a courier arrived bearing letters which announced to him his election to the bishopric of St. Agatha.

Father Liguori was thunderstruck; he could not speak. His sons hastened to his room and found him silent, agitated, and bathed in tears. He, however, became calm, feeling sure that his refusal would end the matter, and that the election was a mere mark of esteem the Pope wished to confer upon him. He remembered how easily he had got rid of the crozier of Palerno.

He wrote to thank the Pope for his goodness, but enlarged on his own incapacity, his great age, his habitual infirmity, the vow he had made never to accept any dignity, and the scandal his acceptance would give the Congregation. When the courier was gone, Alphonsus said to Father Corsano: "This storm has cost me an hour and five ducats," alluding to the money he had given the messenger; he then added that he would not give the Congregation for all the kingdoms of the Grand Turk.

At the same time he wrote to every influential ecclesiastic he was acquainted with, insisting particularly on the vow that should retain him among his companions, and bringing forward every other reason that could be adduced by a man determined not to accept. Bishop Borgia in answer to one of these letters brought him a confidential communication from Cardinal Spinelli; stating that the Pope wished him to accept the bishopric immediately, to relieve him of his embarrassment, but that he should be at liberty to renounce it afterwards. The saint was in consternation at this. Persuaded that there was now no hope but in God, he made his brethren pray that the Lord would deign to exempt him from a punishment he deserved for his sins. He sought prayers on all sides, and redoubled his penances, neglecting no means of averting what he considered the heaviest of crosses.

He remained balancing between hope and fear, often repeating: "May the holy will of God be done." "If the courier comes," said he to the Fathers, "do not let me see him; he would seem to me like an executioner, axe in hand." At Rome, several distinguished persons interceded for him, dwelling particularly on his advanced age, and his enfeebled frame; and they had all but succeeded, when the Pope, without giving any reason, ordered the Cardinal-Auditor to expedite the letters of command, silencing all objections by simply saying: "*I will it.*"

Spinelli amazed at this sudden change, bowed his head saying: "God wills it. The voice of the Pope is the voice of God." Alphonsus awaited the result with extreme agitation of mind. When Fathers Ferrara and Mazzini after having made him recite an *Ave Maria*, made the worst known to him, he raised his eyes to heaven, bent his head in token of submission, and said with David; "*I was dumb, because Thou hast done it*; it is the will of God; God drives me out of the Congregation for my sins." Then turning towards the Fathers with an expression of unutterable tenderness, he said: "Do not forget me. Ah, must we separate, after having loved each other for thirty years!" The Fathers said, to console him, that there were friends at Rome who would make the motives of his renunciation prevail. "That is not possible," said the saint, "the Pope has declared his will in absolute terms, I must obey." At these words, he fell into convulsions, and for five hours remained speechless. When consciousness returned, he wrote to the Cardinal-Auditor and to the Nuncio, that he was ready to submit to the will of the Sovereign Pontiff.

All Rome admired the humility of the Saint in refusing the bishopric, but his prompt obedience gave still greater edification. When Don Hercules heard that his brother had accepted the mitre, he rejoiced, and immediately offered his services. "My dear brother," replied the bishop-elect, "I have been so stunned by the command of the Pope, that I have lost my senses. I thank you for your offer of advancing money. I was about to inform the Pope of my poverty, in the hope that my indigence should plead in my favor; but Cardinal Spinelli, who was to have done me this good office, has done just the contrary. You rejoice, I can only weep. Sleep and appetite have fled from me. A fever seized me this morning, and this evening it is not gone. I ask myself why is my old age to be afflicted by the painful labors of the episcopate, and why the Pope who never gives such commands, adopts a tone of such severity with me? To conclude, may the will of God be done; He desires the sacrifice of my life, I submit to His will."

It being customary in Naples, that bishops should possess in the city, houses suitable to their dignity, Alphonsus wrote to his brother: "As regards the house, I will not charge myself with much expense. One or two rooms on the first floor will be enough to receive the people who may wish to speak to me." To the lay brother who was to act as major-domo in this magnificent establishment, he wrote: "Four straw chairs will suffice. If I have accepted the bishopric out of obedience, I must follow the example of saintly bishops: do not speak to me about a carriage or livery. What good will it do me to act the great lord in Naples?" Bishops Borgia and Volpe, and his director Father Villani, having shown him the necessity of his having a carriage, he consented, and wrote to his brother: "Since I must have a carriage, I wish to learn first whether my predecessor has not left one, because I should get such a one much cheaper. I shall make such a short stay in Naples, that I shall not need to buy a carriage and mules at once; I can use the carriage of the Cordeliers during my visit."

The heroic effort Father Liguori made to obey the Holy Father, brought on a fever so violent that his life was despaired of. One thing alone consoled him: it was the hope of re-entering the Congregation. "I believe," he said, "that after the divine wrath is appeased, the Pope will compassionate my sorrows, and choose a more worthy successor for Mgr. Danza. Then he will send me back, to die within these very walls which I am now compelled to leave."

The illness of the saint afflicted the Holy Father, who was obliged in consequence to defer his journey. Don Hercules, hearing of his dangerous condition, hastened to Nocera, bringing one of the first physicians of Naples. When interrogated as to his state, the holy invalid replied: "I am under the hand of God." Several of his religious hastened to visit him. On seeing them, he wept and said: "You have come to expel me from the Congregation." When Don Hercules endeavored to console him, he cut him short saying: "I must accomplish the divine will."

The submission of Father Liguori to the will of the Pope caused great joy at St. Agatha, but the news of his serious illness spread consternation among the inhabitants. In union with their clergy, they offered up prayers for his restoration. Public supplications were also offered to God in all the houses of the Congregation, that God would spare him who had been so long their cherished Father.

As his mind became calm, his body regained its strength. On Easter day he resolved to go to his bishopric. He set out for Naples in a miserable conveyance, accompanied by Father Villani. On the Saturday before his departure, he had preached, according to his custom, in honor of Holy Mary. On leaving Nocera, he begged all present not to forget him in their prayers, that the Lord Jesus and His Blessed Mother might aid him to bear his heavy burden. "Do not grieve, my brethren," he added, "because I am going away; I promise to return here to end my days."

He stopped a few moments at the house of the Garganas, a family greatly devoted to him. "I go to Rome," said he, "feeling sure that representations which were powerless at a distance, will be favorably heard when I am on the spot. The Holy Father will let me die among my brethren when he sees this miserable carcase of mine."

At Naples, being obliged to pay his respects to the ministers and magistrates, and beset at home by crowds who came to compliment him, he was literally miserable. "Recommend me very particularly to Jesus Christ, and tell the rest to join you," he wrote to Father Mazzini, "for if I do not lose my senses now I shall never lose them. Unhappy that I am! I left the world in my youth, and in my old age I am obliged to return to it."

Very touching was the meeting between our saint and F. Fatigati. Some years before, having heard that this friend was going to be elected bishop, he said to him impressingly: "Father, do not accept the episcopate; if you do, you will be damned." When they met, they were mutually silent; they wept together, the features of Alphonsus showing the bitterness of his heart, while those of Fatigati were eloquent of the compassion he felt for his friend.

In Father Liguori, the poor religious was more conspicuous than the bishop. His episcopal ring cost a few carlins; it was adorned with a bit of glass; the brilliants in his pectoral cross were false. "Oh, what a heavy cross you bring me!" he cried out to the jeweller, "so heavy alas, that I know nothing more overwhelming."

He set out for Rome, accompanied by Father Villani, April 19. At Cisterna, he visited Cardinal Spinelli. "My lord," said he, "you have not acted fairly towards me." His eminence related all that had passed at Rome, and urged him to take up his cross courageously, adding: "My lord, be of good courage, for God has certainty called you to this bishopric."

His first visit, on arriving at Rome, was to the Tomb of St. Peter. For over an hour, he remained before the altar in an ecstasy of devotion. All Rome seemed preposessed in his favor. The pious workers wished him to make their house his home, and the Prince of Piombino placed his palace and carriage at his disposal. The latter was accepted on account of his age and infirmities. "I have no quality which in the least fits me for a bishop," said he, to the Abbé Bruni who visited him, "I submit because the Pope commands, and God wills that I should obey His Holiness." "I have come to Rome," said he, to Abbé Troppi, "to let the Pope see that I am but a machine out of order."

He excused himself courteously from most of the invitations he received. The Fathers of the Mission having invited him to dinner, he said: "Please give my dinner to the poor of Jesus Christ for me, that he may show me his holy will distinctly while I am in Rome."

Cardinal Orsini who had invited several distinguished persons to meet him, would take no excuse. He was told he must put on a courtdress, but he presented himself in the habit of his Order, saying: "I have come as I was, your Eminence, and I know you are ashamed of me." "Well," returned the cardinal, smiling, "my wish is that you should shame me," and heartily embracing him, he led him to his cabinet.

Receiving and returning mere visits of ceremony was irksome work to our saint. "My sojourn in Rome," wrote he to Count Hercules, "seems like a thousand years. O how I long to be free from all their tiresome ceremonials." As the Pope was at Civita Vecchia, he resolved to visit the holy House at Loretto. Father Villani tried to dissuade him from this additional fatigue. "My good mother Mary will strengthen me," he replied. "Nothing will hurt me if I have the satisfaction of visiting the house in which the Eternal Word became man for me."

This journey was a real pilgrimage. He commenced before daybreak a long meditation. This was followed by the canonical hours, a visit to the Blessed Sacrament and the Blessed Virgin, the Rosary and Litany. He then made his servants recite the Rosary with uncovered heads. He said many prayers for the souls in purgatory, and filled up the remaining time in singing pious hymns and in holy converse with his companions.

Every day he celebrated Mass, making a long preparation and a still longer thanksgiving. Other spiritual exercises he undertook during the evening, and, on arriving at the inn, he said Matins and Lauds for the next day. His attendants were humility and poverty. He ate at the same table with the drivers and servants, as if he were one of them.

During the three weeks of his stay at Loretto, he experienced ineffable consolation. It is here he would rapturously exclaim, *that the Word was made flesh! Here Mary held Him in her arms!* During the twenty-one nights he never went to bed, as was testified by his servant who watched him through the crevices of his door.

The pilgrims crowded around the saintly man, and he relieved them spiritually and corporally, as their respective necessities required. The days he passed at this holy place were days of intense spiritual joy; and it may be said that, when he withdrew, he left his heart behind him.

A heavy rain fell the night after his departure, and next morning, leaving Marino in a boat, the saint fell into the swollen Tami, and disappeared in the midst of its waters. The servant threw himself into the stream and succeeded in saving him, almost miraculously. Mgr. Acqua, Bishop of Spoleto, being informed of the approach of his saintly colleague, sent his carriage to meet him. This prelate was then confined to bed, and in great mental anguish regarding the state of his diocese. He opened his heart to one whose writings he admired so much, telling him of all his trials. Our saint consoled the holy bishop who passed most of the night with him, blessing God for being permitted to converse with a man so filled with the divine spirit.

Alphonsus reached Rome just as his Holiness had returned from Civita Vecchia. He immediately went to do homage to Christ's Vicar; as he bent to his feet, the Pope raised him up, and, embracing him, made him sit beside him. A second time the holy man prostrated himself before him, begging with tears to be exempted from a charge for which his age, his infirmities, and his incapacity, rendered him unfit.

"Obedience," answered the Pope, "enables one to work miracles. Trust in God, and He will assist you." He then questioned him upon the state of Naples, both in its political and its spiritual relations, and for an hour and a half they continued to converse.

When visiting the Cardinal-Secretary, he would have remained in the ante-chamber till all who had asked audiences were satisfied. But a bishop who happened to know him came in, and immediately informed the gentleman-usher who had taken him for a beggar.

The Pope conferred with him on many affairs of importance to the Church, and spoke of him with the greatest admiration, so that it was rumored he would be made cardinal. In one of these interviews, the conversation turned on frequent communion; and Alphonsus mentioned that he had been opposed at Naples on that subject by several ecclesiastics more rigorous than devout. The Pope charged him to refute his adversaries. Our saint therefore published a treatise on the subject, which the Holy Father received with great satisfaction.

When he was asked what treatise he would be examined on, he left it to their own choice; but as the examiners insisted that he should name some, he named *De Mutuo* and *De Legibus*. On the eve of the examination, the thought of the burden about to be imposed on him brought on a sick headache which deprived him of rest and appetite. One of the questions proposed was: "Is it lawful to wish for the episcopate?" Alphonsus begged the questioner to raise his voice a little, whereupon Cardinal Gallo provoked a smile from the Pontiff and the assistants, by remarking: "Holy Father, he does not hear because he does not want to hear."

When, at the conclusion, a cardinal suggested that he should return thanks to the Pope, he feigned not to understand him. The suggestion being repeated, he said: "Most Holy Father, since you have deigned to elevate me to the episcopate, pray God that I may not lose my soul."

On the 20th of June, he was consecrated in the Minerva by Cardinal Rossi, assisted by two bishops. That was the saddest day he ever saw. He confessed that he had had two great battles in life: one when he had to struggle against the tenderness of a father who clasped him tightly in his arms; the other, when he

216

was forced to be consecrated bishop. "Then," said he, "I was terrified to think of the burden to be imposed on me, and the account I was one day to give of it to God."

Some one hinting that if he wished to wear a calotte at the altar, he must obtain a brief: "A fine proposition truly," he exclaimed, "so I must apply for the privilege of showing less respect to Jesus Christ!"

The Fathers, fearing for the Congregation after his departure, besought the Pope to allow him to remain Rector-Major of the institute. This favor the Holy Father, after some demur, granted with great kindness, saying to Father Villani: "I desire that your Congregation should prosper, and be supplied with subjects; nor do I intend it should suffer any harm from the elevation of its founder, for the good it has effected in the Church and in the kingdom of Naples is a great consolation to me." This helped to alleviate the sorrow of Alphonsus who had believed himself cast out of the Congregation for his sins.

The Holy Father desired the new bishop to come to a private audience on six or seven occasions. At his last visit, he loaded him with kindness and seemed unable to separate from him. He recommended himself and the Church to his prayers, and in his turn Alphonsus besought him not to forget before God the poor bishop of St. Agatha and his diocese. The good Clement XIII gave him his bulls gratuitously, and the Secretary of the Consistory defrayed all his other expenses.

Before leaving the Eternal City, the bishop went to Frascati to take leave of the Prince of Piombino who had testified the greatest respect and veneration for his person. He always dressed in the habit of the Congregation, wearing the rosary at his girdle, and a broad-brimmed hat. A person of high rank once said to him: "In retaining the habit of your institute, you have given a most edifying example here." In short, such was his life at Rome, that the Pope, with supernatural discernment and the spirit of prophecy, exclaimed: "On the death of Bishop Liguori we shall have to honor another saint in the Church."

CHAPTER XLI.

Bishop Liguori leaves Rome. — In Naples again. — The priest of Arienzo. The equipage of the saint. — His shoe-buckles. — At Nocera. — His intense grief. — His entrance into his diocese. — Green pears. — The new Bishop will not give sumptuous repasts. — His Rule of Life. — His circumspectness regarding women of ill repute. — Meals.

ON the 21st of June, after celebrating Mass at the altar of St. Aloysius at the *Gesu*, Bishop Liguori left Rome. Poverty continued to be his inseparable companion. Though a bishop, he ate with the drivers, and would allow no distinction to be made in his favor. He reached Naples on the 25th. The first nobility of the capital hastened to compliment him. He visited the regents of the young King Ferdinand, and was invited to the royal table. To a minister, the Marquis of Marco, he said: "I go into a diocese somewhat in disorder, and each one will wish to justify his conduct. I pray God they may be really able to do so; but I entreat you to regard the honor of God and the welfare of souls." "Do not be distressed," rejoined the minister, "and if you require the king's support, be assured you will obtain it." In drives through the city, he ordered the coachmen never to seek precedence, but to give way on all occasions, even to a groom. The religious of the principal convents invited him to their churches, but he was able to gratify only a few of them. With the concurrence of the cardinal, he gave the sacrament of Confirmation to a daughter of his cousin, Francisco Cavaliere, in the chapel of the Cavaliere palace.

Among other visitors came a priest of Arienzo, all curled and perfumed, whose buckles covered his shoes. "My son," said the bishop, "these buckles are not becoming to a priest, and that head-dress does not at all suit you. If you act thus, who should be an example to the people, what will men of the world do?" This correction was taken in good part and produced amendment.

Cardinal Sersale received our saint with the tenderest proofs of friendship, and said, smiling: "You are caught at last." "Obedience has so willed it," returned the bishop. "But you have assumed the livery of a cardinal?" continued his Eminence, looking at his equipage. "It was not I who ordered it, but Hercules," was the reply. He wished it to be of a dingy ash-color, but the count had it made crimson on a blue ground! Looking on his shoe-buckles, the cardinal proceeded: "These buckles are superb; you have no doubt bought them at Rome at a dear rate?" The mean little iron buckles had not cost five cents.

He arrived at Nocera on a Saturday, and preached, according to custom, on the Blessed Virgin. His audience melted into tears. The Fathers, knowing that many visitors would crowd around him, gave him a commodious room with a cell adjoining. One evening, passing before his old sleeping-place, he exclaimed: "O my cell! formerly it was my consolation to see thee, now it is my affliction!" He was so overcome that he could not refrain from weeping.

"My brethren," said he with the utmost tenderness, as he took leave of the Fathers, "do not forget me. I go into exile far from my dear Congregation." — He could say no more, for sobs choked his utterance — his emotion was extreme.

As the burning heats of summer still continued, the doctors of Nocera advised him to defer his journey; but considering that a good shepherd gives his life for his sheep, he set out immediately, saying: "A bishop should never think of his own life, but should sacrifice himself for the souls confided to him." They also counselled him to reside some time at Arienzo, on account of the comfortable house and salubrious air he would have found there; but he would rest only at St. Agatha, the place where God had fixed his abode.

Crowds lined the roads as he entered his diocese, on Sunday, July 11, eager to receive his first benediction, and he was welcomed with such demonstrations of affection that he wept with emotion. His entry into his episcopal city was a complete ovation. The peals of cannon and the acclamations of a joyous people rent the air, and the streets were so thronged as to be almost impassable. Affected by the pious eagerness of his new children to participate in his first benediction, he descended from his carriage, entered the parish church, and after a short act of adoration of the Blessed Sacrament, comforted them by a simple pathetic discourse.

He was received by the regular and secular clergy, and a number of distinguished inhabitants of the town and diocese. The canons, discovering that he had no hat or green cap, presented that which was placed on the tomb of the late bishop. After the Blessed Sacrament had been exposed, he prostrated himself for a long time with his face on the ground which he bathed with tears. When the *Te Deum* was chanted he descended from the throne, and delivered an exhortation in which his love and zeal were equally shown forth. The assistants shed tears of joy, and thanked God for having given them such a pastor. "We have a saintly bishop— we have a saint among us," was repeated on all sides by his flock as they left the church; so wonderful was the impression made by the sight of his poverty and humility, and the words of his burning zeal.

During his first sermon he had been attacked by an obstinate fit of coughing, upon which one of the canons jocosely remarked that it would soon be necessary to elect a new vicar-capitular, as Monsignore would not be able to stand another similar attack. This speech being related to Alphonsus, he jestingly retorted: "The canon does not know that green pears fall more easily than ripe ones." Shortly after, this ecclesiastic, then in the prime of life and in vigorous health, died suddenly.

This evening (Sunday July 11) he returned quantities of provisions sent him by the wealthier people of the town; giving money to the servants, and expressing gratitude for their kindness. Later in the week, the Provincial of the Dominicans sent him several choice dishes, but he declined all. The Conventual Fathers sent him a basket of little cheeses, with a quantity of sweetmeats and wax tapers. He took one of the cheeses and sent back all the rest. The secretary in consideration of Count Hercules and several distinguished guests, having provided an elegant repast, "God forgive you," said the holy prelate, "what have you done? I have not come here to give sumptuous suppers; I do not wish to treat you harshly, but let me have no more of this extravagance. When poor people are starving, it does not become us to make such good cheer."

His austerities, far from abating, became more severe than ever. He chose the plainest and most inconvenient room for himself, and even the very first night of his arrival did not retire to his empty paillasse on boards, till he had severely disciplined himself.

Finding the kitchen garden destitute of trees and vegetables, he ordered a brother to plant a number, as if it were spring. The brother obeyed cheerfully, though not without representing that it was not the proper season. Every one was surprised to see that all throve wonderfully well.

His rule of life was this: As soon as he arose, he took a severe discipline. Then followed half an hour's meditation with the household, the grand vicar alone being free to absent himself. The canonical hours recited, he prepared for mass, which being over, he heard a mass of thanksgiving. He next gave audience to all who desired it, and to relieve them of the tedium of the ante-chamber, he desired his servant to usher in immediately every person, however poor. Pastors, vicars, and confessors could always enter unannounced. "These are my privileged ones," said he, "they must not suffer any restraint." Should no audience be asked, he began to compose or dictate, for, so avaricious was he of his time, that he could not bear to lose a moment.

The furniture of his room was plain and scanty, the chief decorations being the crucifix and a picture of Our Lady of Good Counsel. People soon learned that he was unwilling to waste time. If after hearing what they had to say and giving counsel, they did not retire, he would say: "Now then, let us not lose time," or, "Recommend me to Jesus and Mary." If dealing with people whom he could not with propriety dismiss, the constraint he suffered was sometimes depicted on his countenance.

If ever he had to reprimand women of loose behavior, he wished to have some member of his household present. When he went to the Church, he wrapped his right hand in his handkerchief, and held the left in the opening of his cassock. Should a women offer to kiss his hand, he would say: "Kiss the habit, that will suffice, my child."

As bishop, our saint presided at high mass, vespers and the canonical hours — no indisposition hindered him; he was known to officiate when seized by fever, and when from the effects of the painful remedies applied to his distempers, he trembled from head to foot.

During meals, each of his household read in turn, generally from the life of St. Charles Borromeo. The time he passed at dinner and recreation did not exceed an hour and a half. At dessert, he conversed with the grand-vicar on the affairs of the diocese, or on some point of devotion, or received those who had not been able to speak to him in the morning, especially if they were poor, or messengers. After dinner he took some rest; twenty minutes or half an hour sufficed for him. He never neglected to say before lying down the Five Psalms in honor of the Name of Mary, a devotion he had practised from his youth. He was so particular in turning his time to good account, that he often studied, instead of taking this little siesta, which he needed so much.

CHAPTER XLII.

OUR holy bishop attached great importance to the reading of the Lives of the Saints. "The example of the saints," said he, "encourages us and excites us to do good." He never omitted to employ half an hour each day in this exercise, as he had done in the Congregation. He liked above all to study the lives of sainted prelates, among others, the Lives of the Venerable Bartholomew of the martyrs, of St. Francis de Sales, and of Mgr. Cavalieri, Bishop of Troia, his maternal uncle.

On feast days, and especially in Lent, he instructed the children and taught them the catechism. He was too ardent a lover of God and man to be unmindful of the works of mercy. He visited the poor and sick every evening. He was particularly attentive to ecclesiastics who might be unwell, regarding it as an indispensable duty to comfort them.

At half-past five, the bell rang for the visit to the Blessed Sacrament, and he daily discoursed to the people for half an hour, to inspire them with sentiments of faith and love towards Jesus in this mystery. On these occasions, he introduced hymns full of piety and unction, giving out the tone himself and singing with the people. A doctor warned him that this weakened his chest but he replied: "I must make the people like these hymns to disgust them with dangerous songs."

In the evening he gave audience again, and distributed alms, then said matins and lauds, followed by half an hour's meditation with the lay-brother. In winter he worked till nine or ten, but in summer he assembled his household early, for rosary, litany, examen, acts of faith hope and charity. All who happened to be in his house had to assist at these devotions; even prelates, princes, and great lords were not exempt. Supper was next served, after which the bishop conversed a while with the grand-vicar and others, on affairs of his diocese. When all had retired, the saint resumed his literary occupations or continued in prayer. For a long time he took no supper but a glass of water, and Father Buonapane attested that he regularly employed sixteen hours a day in prayer, study, and work.

The family of the prelate included a priest who filled the offices of secretary, steward, and almoner, one servant, a watchman who did the work of groom and cook, besides the vicar-general and Brother Antony.

The servants were obliged to assist at Mass daily, and to approach the sacrament every fortnight. Gaming was forbidden them, public houses still more strictly; in a word, he desired that the members of his household should be irreproachable. Regarding their moral conduct, he was extremely exact. He made it a rule never to receive a servant who was not married, and who had not his wife at St. Agatha. He incessantly reflected on that maxim of the Apostle: "He who knows not how to govern his own house, is not fit to rule the church of God."

Alphonsus found the diocese in a lamentable condition. On the Sunday after his arrival, he began the spiritual exercises for the clergy, and on the evening of the same day, he opened a mission for the people. This sanctified St. Agatha: the sacraments were frequented, the Blessed Sacrament and the Holy Virgin became objects of great devotion, and every evening saw the church filled with fervent worshippers.

Every one was surprised to see a man laden with years and infirmities subject himself to such incessant labor. "We prayed God to send us a good bishop," said a dean, "and he has heard us, but Monsignore will kill himself." The grand-vicar was reproached for allowing a bishop who had cost his flock so many prayers and tears, to shorten his days by excess of work. And his confessor was appealed to, to moderate the zeal of this saintly penitent, whose love allowed him no repose.

As often happened to him before, he began to suffer such violent pain from toothache that he could take no rest. Some suggested that a Neapolitan dentist should be sent for, but he would not hear of it: "Have we not a barber?" he asked. "Let us be patient; God wills that I should employ the people of my own diocese." The barber having been drinking all night was unable to present himself till morning. The secretary advancing to hold him, he pressed his crucifix to his lips saying: "What better support can I have than He who suffered such pain for me?" He bore the extraction without the least word of complaint. He had now only one tooth, and as that troubled him considerably, he determined to relinquish it, but it was removed only with the greatest difficulty. "Oh," he exclaimed, "how firmly it was fixed in!" Then turning to the barber, he said, gaily: "Signor, for the future you will have no more of my custom."

Mgr. Liguori celebrated pontifically at St. Agatha for the first time, on the Feast of the Annunciation, the title of his cathedral. He obtained of the Pope a plenary indulgence for all who should be present, or visit the cathedral on that day, on the usual conditions. From morning till night, the cathedral was thronged. He attained the same favor for his episcopal visitations. He was greatly consoled by the success of his first labors, yet there was a gloomy side to the picture: "I am well," he wrote to the Fathers of Nocera, "and thanks to God, our labors are fruitful." But he wrote to Father Villani: "I am full of anxiety for my church, the spouse which God has given me."

The saint had not yet been able to convert all. To a canon who for many years had given scandal, he showed unalterable meekness. Throwing himself at his feet, he presented the crucifix, and said with tears: "My son, if you will not obey me as your bishop, be converted for the sake of Jesus Christ, who died for you and for me."

But the unhappy man was insensible to everything except the gratification of his sinful passions. Alphonsus sent several good people to reason with him, but without the least success. Seeing that meekness and gentleness only hardened him in sin, the saint threatened to recur to the royal authority. This so exasperated the culprit that he almost used personal violence towards the bishop.

Mildness was equally unsuccessful with a beneficiary at Majano. Hearing that the mother of the object of his passion had appealed to Alphonsus, he fired against the door of the house, killing her, and wounding a little child. Alphonsus then applied to the king, and the two culprits were imprisoned. The relations of this person used all their influence to conciliate the bishop, who, in consequence, sought for some one to inform them of the impossibility of yielding to their unreasonable demands. Happening to call a chaplain who was vested in choir-dress, he said in an excited tone: "Take off these things." At these words the chaplain fainted and fell at his feet. Our saint quickly understood the cause of his terror. Being engaged in evil courses, he thought himself arrested like the other: "Two pigeons are taken with one snare," remarked Alphonsus; "the finger of God is here let us pray Him to perfect what he has begun." This poor man became so sincere a penitent, that some years after, the bishop restored his faculties. One day, Alphonsus sent for the other delinquent, and said: "My dear canon, it is not you I punish but your sin. I love your soul, and cannot consent that it should be lost. Remember that you have a soul, and that there is a God." The excessive sweetness, and tender paternal admonition of the saint, were unexpectedly rewarded. By degrees, the hard heart softened. He often sent him books of devotion and pictures of Jesus Christ and His Blessed Mother. Finally this poor sinner also became a sincere penitent.

There was in the diocese a monastery of four religious whose conduct was any thing but regular. They laughed at the saint when cited before his episcopal court, and when he complained to the provincial, the latter defended them. The saint was sterness itself on this occasion: "Your Reverence," said he, "must then order your subjects out of my diocese, otherwise I shall call in the secular power." This menace had the desired effect.

In the first mission, a woman whose life was openly scandalous was so touched by contrition that she publicly confessed her sins in church, and begged pardon of the people for the scandal she had given them. To the inexpressible sorrow of the bishop, she again fell into sin, and the accomplice being admonished by the saint, openly threatened him. The king was informed of it, which so provoked the wretch that he hired a troop of brigands and would have proceeded to extremity had not a gentleman dissuaded him. When the bishop heard of this, he said calmly: "He can assassinate me, if he likes; well! he will only give me the crown of martyrdom." The woman was finally banished from the diocese. The gentleman being obliged to fly, afterwards stealthily returned, and remained concealed in his own house. Our saint feigned ignorance of the matter, and in the end had the satisfaction of seeing his meekness and clemency triumph, for a day came when the wretched man cast himself at his bishop's feet, and consoled his loving heart by the sincerity of his repentance as much as he had formerly grieved him by his scandalous conduct.

The sentiments inspired by these occurences were productive of salutary effects. A still more deplorable event cast a gloom over the people and their zealous bishop. A young liberated galley-slave was living in crime at St. Agatha, and being frequently reprimanded, despised all charitable warnings. At last the bishop referred the case to the magistrate. The hapless creature was seized in the house of his accomplice, and resisting the officers of justice, was killed on the spot. His corpse was placed on a mule, between four lighted torches, and carried out of the town to be thrown into a ditch.

The blessing of heaven followed all the acts of the saint. Only God could have enabled him to change this field full of weeds into a flourishing garden of the church.

CHAPTER XLIII.

Episcopal visitation. — The Seminary. — Judicious Regulations made by the saint. — His rigid discipline. — Examples. — His severe but just censures of Genovesi. — He prohibits the use of his work in the Seminary.

ALPHONSUS began his episcopal visitation in the town and adjacent districts, "Why put off till to-morrow," said he, "that which can be corrected to-day?" when some persons would dissuade him, "it is wrong to temporize with abuses." He convoked several distinguished ecclesiastics to advise with him regarding the interests of his diocese. The seminary was the principal object of the first visitation: "All my hope of sanctifying my diocese rests on the seminary," said he, "if that does not second me, all my trouble will be of no avail."

He found it populous enough in scholars, but all were not according to his heart. He therefore ordered a general examination at which he assisted in person, and then gave vacation earlier than usual.

Vacation over, he wrote to all the pupils telling them that if they wished to reenter the seminary, they should each address him a letter to that effect. Thus he was able to make his choice: the pupils were decimated, so to say; a proceeding painful enough to the rejected subjects, though they soon appreciated the wisdom of their bishop, and were consoled more speedily than were their friends and relations. The seminary buildings wore rather the aspect of a prison, being confined, unhealthy, and subject to a very plague of troublesome insects in summer. He summoned architects from Naples to repair them, but instead of wasting much funds in repairing, he judged it best to have them pulled down, and replaced by the present spacious buildings.

For the government of the seminary, he established new rules, so full of wisdom and prudence that other bishops adopted them. Don Lucas who had been head of the institute for years was more than an octogenarian, and for that, and other reasons, little suited to so arduous an undertaking; but, unwilling to hurt the feelings of the poor old priest, he confirmed him as president for life, and gave him a coadjutor in the person of Father Caputo, a Dominican, and master in theology. Nothing was spared to procure good teachers. He abolished the custom of giving the office of prefect to a student, thinking that such an office required rather an exemplary priest. For porter he chose a diligent man, full of the fear of God. "If death enters us by the windows," said he, "it enters seminaries by doors." Alphonsus dismissed a porter for no other fault than having gone out without leave from the president.

The autumn vacations were shortened, and replaced by innocent recreations and feasts. "A month of vacation," said he, "is enough to destroy all that has been gained with much labor during the year." He found the terms reasonable, but he would not allow the scholars to be charged if they happened to be removed through sickness or any other cause; and it was with difficulty that he consented to the seminary's receiving money for the month of vacation, though the custom was universal.

He did not wish to see any distinction as to food, between the rector, the professors, and the young men, but ordained that all should fare equally well, and he himself frequently went to the college to examine whether good, nutritious food was served up, whether all was clean and neat, and he was very particular as to the quality of the bread and wine. On one of these occasions, he found that the bread was not good. He immediately reprimanded the superior and housekeeper, and ordered that all the bread in the house should be given away. Whenever he officiated pontifically, he provided sweetmeats for the seminarists. Indeed he sometimes sent his own cook to see that all was right in the kitchen department, but if the converse of "practise makes perfect" be true, the visit of Mgr. Liguori's cook could not much advance the benevolent object his master had in view in sending him to superintend.

232

He ordained that printed books should be used, instead of dictating the lessons — Italian poetry and romances were prohibited. Greek he did not deem necessary: "It is very good in the East," said he, "but for us in the West, Latin is what we want. My diocese requires good confessors, who may aid me in saving the souls of the poor country people." However, he wished as much Greek to be studied as would enable the pupils to understand certain passages that occur in the philosophical and theological course.

He did not admit day scholars, saying: "They serve as messengers for the seminarists, which is dangerous to the morals of both parties." He delighted to listen to the rehearsals, and took part in debates and discussions. Once a month, theses were publicly maintained in theology and philosophy, and so anxious was he to be present at these exercises that when confined to bed by illness, he desired that the meetings should take place in his room.

He interdicted the celebrated work of Genovesi, because it contains this passage: "Preserve the religion of your country, and combat for it." To a priest who endeavored to explain this in a good sense, he wrote: "How can you put a good construction on 'the religion of your country' when it is followed immediately by this blasphemy, *even though it be false.* According to this sophistry, we should become heathens if we went to China, and defend the Koran in order to obtain citizenship in Constantinople! It is true the author elsewhere has put *the Christian religion,* but that is precisely what proves his bad faith, for why not say THE CATHOLIC RELIGION? And even with this change, we should still be in doubt, since he adds, *even though that religion should be false.*" Genovesi was wounded by this prohibition, but Alphonsus severely called him to task, instead of withdrawing his censures.

CHAPTER XLIV.

Spiritual exercises of the Seminarists. — Mortifications. — Vigilance of the saint. — The Seminary becomes a model. — Liberality to poor students. Solicitude of the saint with reference to penance and the Holy Eucharist. The elaborately-curled wig straightened out by the saint. — Minute regulations. — Neatness of the churches. — Dangerous illness of the Bishop. Cases of conscience. -- Confraternities. — Mental prayer. — New Books.

ALPHONSUS was not less zealous for the sanctification of the seminarists than for their instruction and comfort. He established a half hour's meditation daily after mass, and prescribed examen in common, thrice a day, besides a visit to the Blessed Sacrament and the Blessed Virgin, and the recital of the Rosary. Spiritual reading was made at two meals daily. On Saturday before going to the church, he would preach to them on the beauty of virtue. He introduced the practice of novenas before the principal feasts, with some mortifications occasionally, recommending them to forego something at table, to eat kneeling, or sitting on the floor, bidding all the young people to fly effeminacy. He exhorted them strongly to cultivate humility, obedience, and fraternal charity. One day in each month was devoted to retreat, and an eight day's retreat preceded the opening of the classes after vacation. He composed hymns for them, set them to music, and employed a professor to teach them chanting. Nothing delighted him more than to see these young sons of his joyous and contented.

Under this judicious surveillance, the seminary became a model. Charity dwelt amongst the pupils, and their proficiency soon became a marvel. The bishop was wont to call it the apple of his eye, and the jewel of his diocese. To preserve it in this flourishing state, he watched diligently to keep out every seed of corruption. Secret inspectors did duty here, and the rooms were frequently visited. No one was spared: a very orderly young man was surprised reading a Neapolitan poet. Alphonsus made him come down from rhetoric to the grammar class, in which he had to remain until a new course began.

Several instances of his severity are recorded. He once dismissed the nephew of a professor, who asked the youth's pardon with tears, and because it was not granted, sent in his resignation. But it was only to the vicious that he was inflexible. "What charity! What! Charity!" he would exclaim to those who interceded for the culprits, "to ruin all the rest through pity for one; that is not charity, but cruelty."

Such of the students as were poor he generously aided, and when he found promising boys among the peasantry, he would receive them free, if they gave any signs of vocation. To those who objected to this most useful charity, he said, "The seminaries were founded for the help of the churches; pious persons who endowed these establishments could have no other intention than the good of the people, especially the poor." The saint made rules even for vacations, and sent copies of them to the respective pastors. No one was readmitted to the seminary who had not a certificate of good conduct from his priest.

During the visitation, his principal care referred to the Sacraments of penance and the Holy Eucharist. He instructed the priests in the rubrics, and when he found them very ignorant on this subject, he sometimes suspended them for months. This necessary rigor caused the rubrics to be studied diligently. He examined several priests with regard to the confessional to see if he could with propriety continue their faculties, and when he found them incompetent, he withdrew the faculties, but in such a manner as to save their reputation. With regard to pastors who found pretexts for non-residence, he compelled them to resign their benefices or reside at their parishes.

Seeing an elaborately-curled wig on a priest, he asked leave to examine it, and quickly straightened out the curls by plunging it into boiling water; curls, perfumes and colored mantles he would not tolerate in ecclesiastics of any grade. In this matter he was particularly exact with the younger clergy. It was his greatest grief to find priests whose lives did not fully exemplify the holiness of their vocation.

He made stringent regulations against precipitation[1] in celebrating the holy mysteries. He ordered that, throughout his diocese, the children should be catechised on Sundays and Feasts, as in Lent. To remedy the gross ignorance of many, he made an abridgment of the Christian doctrine, and had it printed on a sheet for their convenience; besides, he ordained that these short instructions should be read from the altar every feast day at the first mass, which most of the poor were in the habit of attending. Nor would he have any one admitted to absolution at Paschal-tide without being examined on the principal points of Christian doctrine. Fearing that private baptism was not properly administered in dangerous cases, he examined the nurses himself, and instructed them if necessary. He caused all women of loose lives to be brought to him, and thus addressed them: "If you reform, you will find in me a father full of compassion and charity; but if you remain obdurate, then shall I be to you a severe judge, who will never leave you at rest." A great many of this unfortunate class experienced his love and clemency, but with the incorrigible he kept his word, though his worst severity was always tempered with mercy.

This Saint of the Blessed Sacrament was not less zealous even for the material churches, in regard to which he descended to the minutest particulars, such as careful dusting and cleansing of the holy-water stoops, and he insisted on their being kept with neatness and in good repair. Cleanliness and decency become God's house," said he; "too much pains cannot be lavished on a place so worthy of respect; and besides, how can people pray when their sight is painfully affected by what they see!"

He desired that images should not be kept which had become disfigured by time. "An image is useless," said he, "when it fails to inspire devotion." On his visitations, he insisted that things capable of being repaired should be put in order, and rejected many albs, copes, chalices and missals, as unfit for use. Perfect cleanliness he required in all details, and as much magnificence as possible. When altar linens, canopies, &c., were wanting, he procured them, and he would have all tabernacles lined with silk. So exact, and even severe, was he with persons inclined to

---

[1] Meaning to say Mass hastily.

carelessness in this respect, that he declared that wherever these items were neglected he would stop the revenues.

As he continued his visitations everywhere, stirring the good spirit in the hearts of his clergy, and inspiring them with his own intense devotion to the Blessed Sacrament and Holy Mary, God proved him by various infirmities. At Airola he became so ill, that some clergy and other gentlemen proposed to send to Naples for a physician. "The doctors of Airola will suffice for me," said the saint; "have they not the same books as the Neapolitan doctors? besides, my life is of no great value." During this illness, he communicated daily at a mass said in his own room, and never failed to make his customary meditations. On the ninth day, he inquired if there were any real danger, to which the physician, knowing his firmness, replied in the affirmative. The saint then sent for his secretary and begged him to administer Extreme Unction which he received with sublime devotion. Far from fearing death, he invoked it as the friend that was to deliver him from his exile and restore him to his true country.

When visitors called, they never delayed very long; for they always found the illustrious patient meditating, or listening to the reading of some pious book. To the doctor, who feared he would injure himself by excessive application, he replied: "It is that which relieves me: without it, my illness would be too painful." After the fifteenth day, his health began to improve, and he was scarcely convalescent when he resumed his labors for the good of his diocese.

In all populous parishes he instituted "Cases of Morals" for the clergy, and in order that the same "case" should be discussed on the same day throughout the diocese, he had the list of cases for each week published in the calendar of the diocese. Notes for future reference were taken at all the conferences. He founded, besides, a school of moral theology attached to the cathedral which assembled every week in his palace, he himself presiding over each session as often as possible. This academy was a source of sweet consolation to the bishop, and among its members he generally sought out pastors. He founded societies for aiding to educate young men of ability too poor to maintain themselves in colleges; also a society of priests at St. Agatha destined to give missions; confraternities for gentlemen, for the old as well as the young, boys and girls, rich and poor, in which all were instructed in their duties, and encouraged each other in virtue and goodness. One day, as he preached to the gentlemen's confraternity, he suddenly fell into an ecstasy, in which his countenance appeared so radiant with celestial glory as to illuminate the whole church.

He introduced the practice of mental prayer in common in all the parishes. To facilitate this holy exercise, at the first mass a priest read at intervals sentiments on the passion of Christ, the enormity of sin, and the joys of heaven.

To remedy several disorders he had perceived in the course of his visitation, he composed his little book on the Mass, with acts of preparation and thanksgiving; also, another practical book containing an easy and devout method of assisting the sick and dying; of both of these he distributed copies to all his priests. Finally, he summed up in one small volume all that is essential for the right administration of the Sacrament of Penance: this invaluable treatise was written in the vernacular, and entitled by the author, *The Guide for the Confessors of Country People.* "The words of this admirable book," said the celebrated Dominican, Sacco, "should be weighed, not counted; for the author has included enormous treasures in few words." Many bishops testified their gratitude for this treatise, and it was speedily to be found in the hands of every ecclesiastic throughout the kingdom.

As long as our saint was bishop, he made a through visitation of his diocese every two years, each year doing half. He never once failed in this important point.

CHAPTER XLV.

The saint's mode of progress through his diocese. — Apt rejoinder. He refuses a carriage. — Compares himself to a vender of fowls. — Kindness to a servant — Accident. — Miraculous cure. — Magnificent hospitality of the Prince of Riccia. — "The saint that smooths our way to heaven." — The little monk. — The saint's kindness to children and young people. — His vigilance. His charity to the poor.

HUMILITY and charity were the companions of the bishop of St. Agatha, on his visitations as well as everywhere else. His suite consisted of himself, his vicar-general, his secretary, a canon of his cathedral, and a servant. Being very aged and infirm, a servant had to support him in the saddle, while the servant's son, a lad of twelve held the bridle of the ass upon which the great dignitary rode. As he never omitted his ordinary devotions, and never let any poor person pass by without consoling him, the burning heats of noon commonly overtook him, for which reason the grand-vicar excused himself from starting, and was satisfied to catch up with the cortége towards night.

"Why do you travel on an ass, my lord?" said a distinguished gentleman of Frasso, who coveted the honor of the saint's presence in his house. "Some in chariots, and some on horses, but we in the name of the Lord," was the apt rejoinder of the smiling prelate.

A gentlemen at Mignano once offered him his carriage. "I am really so comfortable on this poor beast," said he, "that it is wonderful." On another occasion of this kind he pointed to a vender of fowls who was passing, and asked: "Which of us is the more comfortable – this man tramping on foot with his basket on his head, or I seated on this ass?" One day he could not procure beasts enough for all his followers; unwilling to inconvenience any one, he set out on foot, accompanied by his servant. As it was during the heats of August, the young man perspired profusely, and the saint, compassionating him, made him remove part of his clothes, and insisted on carrying them himself, to the confusion of the poor servant. Once in going from Durasano to Frasso, being indisposed, he used a vehicle, to please the vicar. The coachman upset them twice. The second time, Alphonsus fell over the vicar and dislocated his wrist, but though in great pain he showed no sign of dissatisfaction, but continued his journey on a mule. Arrived at Frasso, he repaired to the church as if nothing had happened. He opened the visitation, and consoled and instructed the assembly with his usual gentleness and sweetness.

A merchant who had forced him to alight that the surgeon might set his wrist, was rewarded for his charity by the miraculous cure of his son, who had been despaired of by all the physicians in that part of the country.

At Airola, the prince of Riccia placed his palace at the disposal of the holy bishop, and he accepted the generous hospitality, only that he might not displease a nobleman who had so powerfully protected him. The steward had prepared him a magnificent bed in the apartment the prince usually occupied. Alphonsus praised the elegant apartments, but he chose to sleep in the room destined for his valet, saying: "I shall be best off here, because my chest suffers in large apartments where there is too much air." At Frasso, the grand vicar was much dissatisfied with the room prepared for him. While he was at church, Alphonsus had his own straw pallet moved into it, and made that dignitary sleep in the airy room destined for his own use.

At Real-Vale, the room in which the good bishop slept had been for many years infested with beetles; but, after his departure, it was entirely freed from these annoying insects. It was during his visitations especially, that he won the love, confidence and reverence of his people. His incessant labors in their behalf, the unvarying kindness and gentleness with which he received them, no less than the affecting spectacle of his heroic sanctity, were well calculated to inspire these sentiments in the breasts of a people naturally religious. Already was *the voice of the people*, in his regard, *the voice of God*: "Let us go," they would exclaim, as he entered their hamlets, "let us go to hear the saint that smoothes our way to heaven." Glorious testimony! glorious indeed from the mouths of infants and sucklings, from the mouths of the people, of the poor. Glorious testimony! and gloriously confirmed by the universal church: for the upright of heart have ever recognized in this sweet saint, THE SAINT WHO SMOOTHES THE WAY TO HEAVEN. Which of us has he not consoled, soothed, re-animated, in the weary pilgrimage from our exile to our *home*, our *patria*? Who, since his day, has led a life of holiness without the aid of the great doctor, strong and sweet in his teachings? But well does Faber ask: *Would that sweet spirit, St. Alphonsus, have been half as lax had he been but half as holy?* Verily, to posterity as well as to contemporaries, will the admirable Founder of the Congregation of the Most Holy Redeemer be sweetly known as THE SAINT WHO SMOOTHES THE WAY TO HEAVEN.

This sweet and childlike spirit loved to be surrounded with guileless little ones. He was wont to assemble the children after vespers, and teach them to love Jesus and Mary. He deemed it a privilege to prepare them himself for the holy sacrament of confirmation. Once a mother of Durazzano presented him a little cherub of five, already arrayed in the religious habit, beads, and cincture — by reason of a vow she had made before his birth — and besought the holy prelate to confirm him. But the saint though charmed with the precocious piety of the infant, declined to admit him to this sacrament. Next day the mother again presented him, but in the ordinary garb of a child. Among hundreds of children the dear saint recognized the babe and smiling upon him, saying: "Ah, there is my little monk." The pastor besought him to gratify the pious mother, whose eloquent pleadings had already touched the tender heart of him who could never bear to refuse what it was at all in his power to grant. Eager to have her boy confirmed by a saint, she feared Alphonsus would not live long enough to impose hands on her "little monk," if his confirmation was delayed; hence her gentle pleadings backed by the intercession of the good pastor, and hence her innocent *ruse* to deceive the holy bishop, upon whose tender heart the guileless face of her angel-child had made such an indelible impression.

When he learned that young people and children were in danger of death, he would visit them, and, if necessary, administer to them the sacrament of confirmation, lest otherwise they should be too long deprived of this powerful means of grace. Once when he went to confirm a sick youth named Pascal, he said: "Be glad and rejoice, my dear Pascal, for in three days you will go to paradise." The prophecy was fulfilled, contrary to all expectation, and Alphonsus was consoled, because he had "smoothed" for this poor boy, as for so many others, the strait and rough "paths that lead to heaven."

He was extremely watchful over every ecclesiastic in his diocese. His priests found him indeed the tenderest of fathers. For any irregularity, his usual remedy was to send the erring party to make a retreat of eight days in a house of his own Congregation or in the Congregation of the Mission. If he found good priests not well instructed in the rubrics, he would remedy the defect, but without reproaching them for it. He was, if possible, still more strict with religious priests, and, in case of their not correcting any serious defect he pointed out to them, he would appeal to their provincial, and even request their removal.

The poor were the constant objects of his solicitude; he inquired into their condition, and if he found such evil effects arising from poverty as might lead to crime, he would go to any expense to obviate them. He was particularly exact in seeing that the houses of the poor were supplied with a sufficient number of beds for each family. Widows and young women in danger, the sick, and especially the sick poor, shared his solicitude; and food and medicines were daily furnished to the needy, all at his expense.

In this respect his charity knew nothing of worldly prudence; he invariably returned from his rounds wholly destitute of money, and not lightly burdened with debts, which it was not always easy for him to meet, as he had reduced the visitation fees to almost nothing. He would never allow his servants to importune people for their perquisites, according to the custom of the time and place, recommending them to be guided by that maxim of St. Francis de Sales: "Ask nothing, refuse nothing."

Such charity and disinterestedness won him, everywhere, admiration, love and esteem, so that people revered him as a saint, and deemed themselves happy if they could procure a shred of his garments. Whatever had been sanctified by his use, they preserved as relics; and God blessed their simple faith, for miraculous cures have been operated in favor of the sick, to whom these relics were applied.

CHAPTER XLVI.

Count Hercules Liguori marries a second time desiring to have heirs. Letters. — The saint's present to the bride. — The bridegroom's indignation. Preaching. — Sermons. — Ecstasy. — Periodical missions. — Rigor more hurtful than indulgence. — Style. — Extraordinary meekness of the saint. "Poor Jesus Christ" — The Famine. — Heroic Charity.

I N 1763, Don Hercules Liguori, who had lost his first wife Donna Rachel Liguori some time previous, informed his brother of his determination to choose a second, asking his prayers and the celebration of many masses, that God might bless his second marriage with an heir, the late countess having brought him no children. The following is the reply of our saint: "I have this morning again celebrated mass for the lady Rachel, at the privileged altar. To-morrow and after, I hope to celebrate for your intention. I pray you to be very careful as to the person upon whom you fix your choice. She should be of the purest morals, without haughtiness and without vanity, and not too young, lest she should take advantage of your advanced age. It would be better that your wife should be of humbler birth and less fortune, than that you should run the risk of some vexatious embarrassments. Declare your intention from the first to the object of your choice and to her parents. When the wedding is over, take your bride to Marinella and keep her there as long as possible, that she may have good habits from the first."

In a subsequent letter, dated November 12, he says: "I rejoice that such good alliances are offered you. Use all possible diligence to make a choice which you will not have reason to regret. I wish to give you another caution: now that you are alone, dismiss all your young female servants. You can promise to take them again when you set up your establishment."

Don Hercules espoused Lady Mariana Orsini, of the illustrious house of Nilo, a lady of exemplary conduct and extraordinary piety, whom Alphonsus was proud to have as a sister. "I promise myself all sorts of felicity," wrote the count, "as a consequence of your prayers and those of your congregation, as well as the excellent qualities I perceive in Donna Mariana. She has always been pious, but her goodness at present quite astonishes me." The enraptured bridegroom was not many years younger than his episcopal brother.

The solicitude of our saint for the count, proceeded from an intense zeal for the happiness and salvation of his dear brother. He never showed the least curiosity regarding the temporal interests of his kindred. During the thirty years he lived in the Congregation, he never set foot in his own house but once, and that was to aid and console his pious mother in the illness that carried her to the tomb. Though Don Hercules lived in the palace in which the saint had a hospice for his brethren, he never once entered his brother's apartments. On the count's marriage, the saint being invited to officiate, politely declined. His wedding present to the bride was a paper print of the Blessed Virgin, inclosed in a little wooden frame, which Don Hercules indignantly sent back. "My brother is offended, " said the saint, "though I have more cause; what did he expect to receive? I have poor here dying of hunger, and yet people want me to make presents!"

Alphonsus held preaching to be among the first duties of a bishop. "This ministration is almost the only one that Jesus Christ seems to have imposed on his apostles; it is the one which he exacts of bishops, and to fail in it is to neglect an express command." He accomplished in this article the advice he gave to Cardinal Sersale when the latter was raised to the See of Naples, in 1754: "I hope our Lord has sent your Eminence to remedy all defects, and I feel that I shall see you renew the days of St. Charles Borromeo, who preached with such fruit to the people of Milan. O how much more efficacious are the words of the chief shepherd than those of others! Pardon my boldness; it is only for the glory of Jesus Christ that I speak. How much good you may do by preaching, especially in the first year! I desire equally that you would give the spiritual exercises to all the clergy. All the disasters that the Church deplores come from this: that men are admitted to the altar who were not called by God. It imports much then, that those you select give proofs of their divine calling, not merely as to doctrine, but chiefly as to morals and the ecclesiastical spirit: this is the most indispensable point."

Our saint was remarkable for his assiduity in preaching. Every Sunday he preached after vespers, and on all feast days which fell during the week he preached in the parish churches. Every Sunday before the sermon he catechised the children, giving them rosaries, pictures, and even money to attract them; and he preached later in the day to the congregation of nobles, and to the sodality of young girls which he had founded. When he was at Arienzo, as the people could not easily come to the collegiate church, he preached alternately in one of the seven parishes, and, as his sermon was always accompanied by exposition, he provided the candles for these occasions himself, saying: "I desire God's glory, but I am unwilling to burden you with expenses." Every Saturday he fulfilled his vow to publish the praises of Mary. The protestation for a good death, he made for the people at least once a month, with sermon and exposition. It is impossible to calculate the good effects of this practice alone.

During the last three days of the carnival, the holy prelate endeavored to hinder the people from going to the public shows, by making the ceremonies of the Church as attractive as possible throughout the diocese. Sometimes he preached in convent churches, and upon these occasions he ordered the sums set aside by the nuns for this purpose to be given to the ordinary clergy. During Lent, he always assembled the secular and regular clergy, for the spiritual exercises either at St. Agatha or at Arienzo. He continued to lay the greatest stress on preaching, and with reason: "We have lost much of our trade since Monsignore's arrival," said a Neapolitan magistrate; "for his sermons and those he caused to be preached have made the people so peaceable that there is no longer any disorder to be found."

He sought workmen of learning and piety to aid him in the gigantic task of reforming his diocese. Jesuits, Dominicans, Priests of the Mission, Pious Workers — all were pressed into the service by this untiring laborer, whose zeal literally gave him no moment of rest. Once, when speaking of Mary, at a mission at Arienzo, his countenance glowed and sparkled till the whole church was illumined by its rays of supernatural splendor. "See," he cried out in ecstasy, "the Blessed Virgin is coming to scatter blessings among us; ask her, she will grant you everything." This was but one of many similar occasions when his soul exhaled its divine ardors and his face beamed with heavenly fire. He ordained that a mission should be given in every parish in his diocese at least every two years, besides the novenas and triduos with which he strove to confirm the good and awaken the sinful. At first he would not invite missionaries of his own order, lest he might be suspected of some sinister intention; but when the people knew him, this was not to be feared, and he freely employed Redemptorists towards the close of his episcopate. Charity towards sinners, and a popular style of preaching, were what he chiefly desired of the missionaries. To one who leaned towards rigorism, he said: "My father, too much indulgence may be hurtful to souls, but too much rigor is still more so....With sinners, mildness and charity are necessary. This was the method of Jesus Christ, and if we would save souls we must not imitate Jansenius, but Jesus Christ, the Chief of missionaries."

As to preaching, the saint was wont to say: "When Jesus Christ preached, he did not use obscure but elegantly turned periods, words of learned length or rhetorical exaggerations; all his words were on a level with the people's comprehension. His proofs were natural and never abstract. He used parables and comparisons which triumphed over the will by striking the mind and heart. The apostles followed their Divine Master in this respect, and if we fail to imitate them, journeys, expense and fatigue will be useless."

The expenses of these incessant missions were entirely defrayed by himself. He even furnished oil and candles for the churches, and enabled the missionaries to give much relief to the poor, charging them to take particular care of all necessitous families, converted women, and young girls in danger. Still, he sometimes found priests who were unwilling to have missions: one excused himself saying, he had no house for the fathers. Alphonsus, who divined his real feelings, said: "Well, purchase one at any cost. The expense will be defrayed for you." The priest replied in such terms, that the grand vicar and other dignitaries said he ought to be imprisoned. But our saint blamed their imprudent zeal, and pitied the weakness of the poor priest, who was so won by his sweetness that he himself asked for the mission. The holy bishop even apologized to him. "I do not say," he wrote to him, "that your reverence has put any impediment in the way, but I thought you did not show the anxiety I would have wished; if I have been wrong in this, I hope you will excuse me, and now let us love each other as before. Blessed be God who has permitted this unpleasantness to arise to you as well as to me."

During Lent, he wished the confessors mutually to exchange parishes, and by this means the Lenten exercises produced general advantage. When preachers and confessors presented themselves for his benediction, he liked to keep them for some days with him that by conversing with them he might form some idea of their capability and knowledge. He could not bear those preachers whose high flown oratory rendered them unintelligible to the people. "Poor Jesus Christ!" he would murmur as he listened to them. To one of this genus, he indignantly said: "Is it not to betray Jesus Christ and the people, to preach in that way? If I did not order you out of the pulpit, it was through respect for the habit you wear. What fruit have the people gathered from all the tropes and metaphors and pompous phrases with which you entertained them? For yourself, this was mere vanity, to be expiated in purgatory. Your end should be to move hearts, and cause tears of contrition to flow; but no one was touched, the people understood nothing."

In 1763, Italy was ravaged by a fearful famine, which our saint had predicted previous to his elevation to the episcopate, and on several occasions after that event. During the harvest of the fatal year, like another Joseph, he ordered his secretary to buy up an enormous quantity of the cheaper kinds of provisions. Every body laughed at this, but ere the end of November the scarcity had spread from one extremity of the kingdom to the other. The starving poor had recourse to their common father; by hundreds at a time they thronged his halls and besieged his residence, craving a morsel of bread. Alphonsus was affected to tears by this misery, and commanded his servants to relieve them all, saying: "They only ask for what belongs to them." He sent in every direction to procure corn, and applied to Count Hercules, then governor of Naples, who liberally supplied St. Agatha, though corn was already sold at famine prices. He appealed to his rich patrons and friends, and they were not slow to respond to the pleadings of his charity. Our dear old saint was overjoyed at being able to assist his suffering children. In the great hall of his palace all the necessitous were registered alphabetically, and they received relief as they presented themselves.

But this did not satisfy the all-reaching charity of his paternal heart. He could not sit down in comfort while a single human being in his diocese wanted bread. He sought out those who were ashamed to beg, and those who, through infirmity, were unable to leave their cold and dreary homes. Love, and even reverence, for the poor! Beautiful Catholic charity! — what is like unto thee? Political economy! A plague upon the hateful thing that would stamp the divine image from out the lineaments of the poor, the sorrowstricken and the lowly! Accursed progress! Vile civilization! whereby man calls his brother a *pauper*! Yet triumphant charity, all-pervading *Spirit of Jesus*! Triumphant indeed, since it is Catholic charity, in fact, and in tradition, as well as in heroic example, that compels even the infidel governments of to-day to dole out a niggard stipend to the poor, having first robbed them of their revenues, and rendered powerless the arm that was wont to sustain them. The heroic, the ever-living charity of the church has *shamed the heretic and the unbeliever*; for Alphonsus is neither the first nor the last saint, who not only relieved all who presented themselves, but made it a *duty* and a *study*, to seek out the bashful and infirm poor, and relieve their bodily wants without paining their over sensitive hearts. Beautiful spirit of Jesus! Glorious characteristic of His Church! The poor we have always with us, and He who deigns to be styled the Father of the Poor can never be far from those who love His dearest children.

Despite the excessive tenderness of our saint, the frenzied people often reproached him, and even accused him of having sold the corn his own brother had sent him for their relief. "My poor people deserve compassion," said this good pastor, "it is not they who speak, but the famine within them; their hearts are good." And, verily the saint meant what he said; for, a furious woman having violently assailed him, and the Sacristan having scolded and pushed her away by the shoulder, the good Bishop was so indignant at the officious and censurable zeal of that rough official, that he actually sent him to prison for four days.

The scourge increased to such a pitch, that, as our saint had predicted, human beings were seen devouring the grass of the hedges, and roving through the county like spectres. Alphonsus was almost heartbroken. He sought assistance from the wealthy, and commanded priests and superiors of convents to retrench their ordinary expenditures in behalf of the poor. Nothing but the cheapest and coarsest food was served on the episcopal table: "We must do without something," said the saint, "when our people are dying of hunger." Hearing that the superior of a wealthy convent was stingy towards the poor, he reproached him severely for his hardheartedness. "I am obliged to maintain my family," said the superior, "what is over and above, I give to the poor." The saint burning with indignation, rose from his chair and exclaimed with vehemence: "Do you know what maintain means now? Eat enough to preserve life, and give the surplus to the poor. You became a religious to lead a life of poverty and penance. Do you believe in the Gospel or are you a Turk?"

This reproof doubly terrible in the mouth of the meekest of bishops, had a powerful effect on him to whom it was addressed. The poor of his quarter were ever afterwards bountifully, and even tenderly, cared for.

Rest was unknown to Alphonsus during this terrific season. Not a single room in his palace but was open to the poor, and not an hour of the day when they did not throng around him. One evening after all had been relieved, a man was found stretched in the hall, motionless and apparently expiring. The holy prelate hearing this, came quickly with the ordinary restoratives, but it was only after repeated efforts that he had the happiness of seeing the poor creature restored to consciousness.

The famine continued to madden the unfortunate people. One day they rushed upon the dwelling of Dominic Carvo, the superintendent of provisions, whom they threatened to assassinate. The hapless official succeeded in escaping to the episcopal residence, but the mutinous crowd followed shouting; "Life for life!" The saint offered himself as a victim to appease their rage: he went into the midst of them, wept over them, pressed them to his heart, and when this spectacle had somewhat calmed, or rather stunned them, he distributed all the bread and meat in the palace, seminary, and public stores, among his dear children, the poor rioters.

When our saint had exhausted his own resources and the fruits of the bounty of his friends, he obtained leave of the Holy Father to mortgage all his income for the poor. He would have sold the plate of his predecessors, the pectoral cross, ewer and candlestick, heirlooms of the See, had not his canons refused to allow this episcopal property to be alienated. However he sold the ring which had been presented to him at his consecration by his friend and penitent Jane Versale, as well as that which he had received from Bishop Giannini. His own pectoral cross quickly followed; a plain gilt one served in future for pontifical ceremonies. He ordered his secretary to sell what little plate he owned, and was about to dispose of his very rochet, until he was assured that it was all but worthless. When his grand Vicar urged him not to sell his carriage, he said: "St. Peter was Pope and he owned no carriage, I am not greater than St. Peter, and therefore can do without one." To the count Hercules who also objected to this measure, he wrote; "Pretexts to induce me to keep my carriage, I regard as temptations of the devil…I cannot bear to see mules in my stable nearly all the year with nothing to do; the coachman wasting his time the while, and the poor asking for bread." His brother Cajetan purchased the episcopal carriage and mules at an exorbitant price, to prevent their passing into the hands of strangers.

It struck the saint that though the canons would not allow him to sell the episcopal regalia pertaining to the See, they would at least agree that he might pledge them. But they negatived this proposal also. The poor dear bishop wept and wrung his hands in anguish, and here we have a singular spectacle — Alphonsus, the saint of holy poverty, envies rich prelates who need place no bounds to their benevolence. Nay, he even desires supernatural power, but not separated from sanctity. "O that I merited as much before God as St. Thomas of Villa Nova," he exclaimed with holy envy. "I might find my granaries filled with corn as he did!" Covetous saint; but covetous only for the poor of Jesus Christ whom he carried in his heart as his best beloved children.

Regarding sin as the cause of the terrible scourge that desolated the diocese, he redoubled his austerities to appease the divine wrath, or turn its darts from his children upon himself. He daily addressed heaven in their behalf, and besought the sinful among them to be converted to their heavenly Father, and to weep over the sins that had brought upon the country so dire a calamity. At last God was propitious to the prayers of his servant; the famine gradually abated, and returning spring brought with it new resources. But the disorders and abuses consequent upon this awful visitation were neither few nor slight. Creditors tortured their debtors, usury was extensively practised; nor could a broken-down people resist the unjust and the hard-hearted. The father of the people inveighed against these abuses with his usual fervid eloquence, and the merchants and financiers, to their credit be it recorded, could not withstand the sweet pleadings of this great heart. He enjoined upon the parish priests the relief of the sick, the convalescing, and the necessituous, and secured their co-operation, and that of the most influential people of the diocese, in endeavoring to do away with the miserable effects of the famine as speedily as possible. So powerful is heroic sanctity.

Greetings, shouts of joy, ovations improvised by the hearts of a grateful people, awaited Alphonsus at every stage of his next progress through his diocese. His mere presence among them, caused his people to exult with the most rapturous delight. He was now not merely, "the saint who smoothes our way to heaven," but the saint who carried them in his bosom, who bewailed their trials as his own, who suffered in his soul, and even in his body, the physical evils which, but for him, would have tried them beyond endurance, and which he had more than beggared himself to alleviate, if he could not wholly remove.

CHAPTER XLVII.

Alphonsus presides at a General Chapter of his Congregation — His old opponent Patuzzi again attacks him. — Alphonsus dedicates his Defence to the reigning Pontiff. — Want of courtesy in Patuzzi. — Apology. — Proposed Synod. — Decrees issued. — New arrangement of parishes.

I N JULY 1764, our saint accepted an invitation to preside at a general chapter of his Congregation to be held at Nocera, whither he repaired towards the close of September. In passing through Nola, he stopped at the Seminary, and being asked to address the seminarians, he spoke to them for over an hour on the subject with which his heart was ever filled, the love of Jesus. Here he saw bishop Caracioli, a kindred spirit; they met with mutual delight, and conversed a long time on the affairs of the Church in general, and of their respective dioceses. The bishop among other things remarked that a colleague had lately addressed him as "Excellency," but that he did not return the compliment. "You did well," rejoined Alphonsus, "I cannot understand how this title came to be used. The Council of Trent deigned to grant us the title of 'Right Reverend,' now some wish to add, 'Most Illustrious.' If we had coveted 'Excellency,' we should have remained at home."

When the saint entered the church to adore the Blessed Sacrament, he was conducted to the episcopal seat, but, with that elegant politeness and keen sense of propriety which always distinguished his intercourse with his brother clergymen of every order, he rested on a simple bench, declining to usurp any mark of distinction in the cathedral of another prelate.

During the chapter which lasted a month, the rules and customs already in use were revised and confirmed. As the saint was the soul of the assembly, everything was done in a manner most satisfactory to all concerned. Eager to rejoin his flock, he set out for St. Agatha on the termination of the chapter, and was then obliged to combat a new enemy.

Father Vincent Patuzzi, who had formerly criticized very severely the Moral Theology of the saintly Doctor, now renewed his attacks. "I am rejoiced that he attacks me," said the saint, "for the truth will be displayed all the more clearly, which is solely what I seek. If he proves me wrong, I am ready to retract."

The holy bishop replied to his adversary in a learned and moderate address, in which he sustained his doctrine by the authority of the canons, the holy Fathers, the most celebrated theologians, especially the great Dominican Divine St. Thomas Aquinas, and which he dedicated to Pope Clement XIII, with this declaration.

"I protest that in all I have written, I have had no desire, save to make the truth evident in so grave a matter, on which depends the good or evil direction of consciences; and as I had the honor of dedicating my Moral Theology to the sovereign Pontiff, Benedict XIV, I venture to submit to your Holiness, this treatise, which is an appendix to its sense; that your Holiness may deign to correct, modify or cancel, whatever may be opposed to the maxims of the Gospel and the rules of Christian prudence."

It is not pleasant to describe the spirit in which Patuzzi continued the controversy, and we do not find it easy to excuse the opponent who could use towards a prelate of undoubted sanctity and extraordinary learning the following phraseology: "It is impossible to imagine how you could have so far mistaken the doctrine of St. Thomas...Study these questions better, that you may not expose yourself to the raillery of intelligent men...You have no just ideas on these matters...You ought to blush for your statements." ...

It is singular that Patuzzi should regard as calumny our saint's eloquent but temperate refutation of his ill-judged attacks. " If you think I have calumniated you," the bishop wrote, "pardon me, I can only offer my excuses." But he facetiously adds: "Unhappy that I am, I am abused, and then accused of being the culprit!"

Alphonsus sent his "Apology"[1] to the archbishops and bishops as well as to other theological doctors, who all united in praising his wonderful learning, and still more the extraordinary humility and moderation he displayed towards so virulent an adversary. The numerous letters of approbation he received on that occasion, were afterwards appended to the Moral Theology of the saint, where they may still be seen by those who desire to examine them.

The discussion or rather dispute, was briskly kept up, on one side at least. "I have received," wrote Alphonsus, "your well-meant letter of mingled praises and reproaches, admonitions, menaces and counsels. You say you are astonished that, while leading an edifying life, (it were more correct to say that I deceive the public), I profess erroneous doctrine. My dear Father, I judge precisely the contrary. I see that my life, far from being exemplary, is full of faults, while I regard my system as wise, and even incontestable."

Elsewhere the saint writes: "As your reverence counsels me to reflect whether I am not guilty before God for having maintained too indulgent an opinion; I would suggest that you, who are constantly administering the sacrament of penance, would examine whether you may not have a stricter account to render than I, for having followed rigorous opinions, by which you have embarassed consciences, and forced your penitents to hold as sinful that which is not sinful; in consequence of which you may have caused many formal sins to be committed which were not such before God, and occasioned the damnation of many souls." As it was now evident to all the world that Patuzzi acted through mere party spirit, several prelates advised the saint to take no farther trouble to refute his sophisms, an advice he willingly followed, convinced that having once clearly stated the truth, his time could be more profitably employed than in refuting an opponent with whom it was no honor to grapple. Posterity as well as contemporaries have abundantly vindicated the great saint, on whose brow our Infallible Pontiff has but lately placed

---

[1] The writer is obliged to Mr. Justin McCarthy for instructing Mr. Disraeli that the word "Apology" bears more meanings than one. In the "Apologies" put forth by Doctors and martyrs, from the "Apology" of Tertullian in the second century, to that of Dr. Newman in the nineteenth, Catholic Doctrine, &c., has rather been explained and defended than apologized for. (Editor's original note)

the crown of Doctor of the Church, a dignity as rare as it is illustrious.

When the bishop had made himself thoroughly conversant with the state of his diocese, he informed the Pope of the necessity of holding a synod, but as this proposal was not well received by his brother-prelates whom he had consulted, — though the approbation of His Holiness was freely given — the saint gave up his design, saying: "I will accomplish by simple decrees what I wished to regulate in a synod." After advising with the most eminent and learned among his clergy, and others celebrated for wisdom and moderation, the articles prepared for the synodical assembly were replaced by six ordinances, which he promulgated in due form and caused to be rigorously observed.

The first decree referred to canons and chaplains, priests of the cathedral, the rubrics, the discipline of the choir and other similar matters.

The second referred to the duties of archpriests, vicars and rectors. He renewed the order he had previously issued regarding the instruction of people and children in the Christian doctrine, and added several minute directions as to preparation for paschal and first communion; he gave particular directions that all who desired to enter the married state should be examined in the Christian doctrine, and if necessary instructed. He inculcated the duty of preaching every Sunday, and reminded the parish priests that they sinned grievously if they did not administer Extreme Unction till the dying person had lost his reason. To prevent sin, which may be said to have been the great aim of his life, he ordered the parochial clergy to require that all betrothments should be followed speedily by marriage. Besides the Easter Communion he appointed two general communions for the young of both sexes. It was prohibited to accept of any legacy without first informing the bishops, who had to decide whether the conditions imposed by the testator could be fulfilled. Various other regulations increased the usefulness of this ordinance.

The third reminded all confessors of the absolute necessity of studying moral theology, and added some valuable instruction as to the duty of the confessor in the confessional. He called their attention to the Bull of Pius V which imposes on physicians the duty of sending for the priest after their third visit to a patient in danger. He advised the confessors to exhort their penitents to pray often, especially in times of danger and temptation, to invoke incessantly the names of Jesus and Mary, to recite the rosary, and three *Aves* morning and evening in honor of the Mother of Purity and Perseverance, and to teach a brief method of mental prayer to those most inclined to piety.

The fourth decreed suspension to any priest who should celebrate mass with such indecent haste as to finish in less than a quarter of an hour. Under the same penalty games of chance were prohibited. He forbade hunting with a gun or with nets, without the written permission of the bishop, which never extends to days of obligation, and he exhorted all clerics to aid their parish priests in instructing the people in the Christian doctrine.

The fifth related to candidates for holy orders.

The sixth to the dress of the clergy, and affords a curious illustration of the age and country. The hair was not to be curled, perfumed, studiously arranged, or worn so long as to cover the neck or ears; colored cloaks, shirt ruffles and plaited lace were severely interdicted. The holy bishop enforced these regulations so as to punish rigorously all infractions, "Any contempt shown to myself does not affect me at all," he said "or rather, I thank God for it; but I cannot suffer my ordinances to be disregarded."

During his pastoral visitations the saint found that thousands of his people were so situated as to be left in great spiritual abandonment. The population of his episcopal city and its suburbs exceeded twenty four thousand. Some of these people were four or five miles from their parish church, a great distance for the poorer classes who had no conveyance, and who found walking painful in the summer heats, and nearly impossible in the snows and rains of winter, which rendered the bad roads almost impassable. The very old and the very young rarely saw their pastor. The instruction of the people was neglected, and many died without Extreme Unction and Viaticum.

To remedy these evils as much as possible, the saint made a new division of parishes, and with the surplus benefices of the richer parishes was able to supply several rural chapels. When this was not practicable, he established a chaplain, to celebrate mass on Sundays and festivals, and added to his salary from his own income to induce him to preach and to catechise the children. This, as will be readily perceived, was a work of extraordinary difficulty, as it required all the energy as well as all the meekness of the saint to encounter the opposition manifested by interested parties. But his persuasive eloquence, supported by his all-powerful example, overcame all obstacles, for who could resist one that did a thousand times more than he exacted of the most fervent?

CHAPTER XLVIII.

Dangerous Illness of the saint. — 'Non recuso laborem.' — Miracle. — The saint refuses to play on the harpsichord. — At Nocera. — Impatient to return to St. Agatha. — Letter. — Bad books. — The saint's measures against their circulation. — His Prophecy regarding the Free Masons. — Papal Infallibility. The assembly. — Society of Jesus. — Circular Letter. — He endeavors to resign.

EXCESSIVE austerities and perpetual labors laid our saint in a bed of sickness towards the close of 1764. His life being despaired of, Extreme Unction and Holy Viaticum were administered; and the saint besought the priests who stood near his straw pallet to suggest some sentiments of love. Tears choked the utterance of the Dominican Father Caputo, but a deacon who was present, said: "My Lord, when St. Martin was near death he addressed to God this prayer: 'If I am still necessary to Thy people, O Lord, I refuse not to labor.' Our saint who scarcely breathed, faintly echoed: "*Non recuso laborem.*" I refuse not to labor.

Bitter was the grief of the inhabitants of St. Agatha at the dismal prospect of losing their bishop and their Father. The poor especially bewailed their best benefactor, and their tears and prayers were incessantly poured forth for his restoration, and heaven was not deaf to their supplications. While yet oscillating as it were between life and death, a miracle attested his sanctity. One day, the canon Charles Bruno, brought him a present of fig-peckers. He was accompanied by his nephew a boy of four, who had never yet uttered a syllable. The saint with his customary sweetness towards children, desired a lay-brother who was present to bring the little innocent some bonbons, and asked the canon his name. "He is called Thomas," was the reply, " but," added the uncle, sadly, "he is quite dumb, he has never articulated

261

a single word." This intelligence grieved the saint. He made the sign of the cross on the child's upturned forehead, and giving him a picture of our Lady to kiss, said: "Do you know, my little one, how this Lady is called?" The child kissed the picture, and without the least hesitation, replied, "The Madonna!" From that moment the child spoke perfectly well. Alphonsus, to conceal the miracle, said to the canon: "The child is not dumb, there is an impediment in his speech, but that will gradually disappear." Nevertheless, the miracle became noised abroad, and added to the high idea already entertained of the venerable prelate by all who knew him.

The doctors ordered him to Nocera, but he refused to leave his See, and it required a command from Father Villani, his director, to induce him to obey them. When he was with his dear Congregation once more, he never failed to be present at all the common exercises, and when he had any leisure, he would resume his literary labors. One day a priest asked him to play the harpsichord, an instrument on which he greatly excelled. "What!" he exclaimed, "ought it be said of a bishop that he passes his time playing on an idle instrument instead of thinking of his diocese? It is my duty, and the duty of every bishop, to give audience to all, to pray, to study, but not to play the harpsichord."

The rector caused him to be treated with some distinction, because of his dignity, and infirmities, but this well-meant politeness was a martyrdom to him. One day, he asked for a glass of water, and the brother who was waiting on him handed him in mistake a vase of water in which flowers had been kept some days previous. The saint drank it as if it had been just drawn from the purest spring.

God continued ever and anon to favor him with graces that seem to belong to a brighter world than ours. One day as he was beginning Mass, he fell into an ecstasy as he cast his eyes on the picture of our Lady of Sorrows. It was not until the Father who served his Mass had shaken him several times that he was able to proceed. He could not rest while away from his diocese, and was perpetually tormented with scruples. Hearing that a person whom he had banished from St. Agatha on account of her ill-conduct, had returned, he would delay no longer. Mgr. Volpi one day said to him: "My Lord, why are you so unquiet?" "Because I am a bishop," was the reply. "My Lord," said he to the same prelate, on another occasion, "I have a spouse. God wills me to be with my spouse at St. Agatha, not at Nocera." When his strength was somewhat restored, he continued his visitation, and would have resumed all his ordinary austerities, had not his director, Father Villani, prohibited them. When he judged that his health was quite restored, he wrote to Father Villani, October 28, as follows:

"The milk diet has quite cured me, and if you permit, I will resume the straw bed again. I have begun to wear the chains on the part where the old blister was. I ask your blessing for this...Father Majone has desired me to partake of a second dish at dinner; but I ask your Reverence as my principal director to allow me to eat the bouilli only; if you do not approve of this, I will submit to your decision."

The mind of our holy prelate was continually on the rack at this epoch. Bad books which issued from the press by thousands, especially in France, were clandestinely circulated through Naples to the great detriment of faith and morals. His age and still more the heavy burden of the episcopate left him no leisure to refute the errors now breathed everywhere, but he besought the king and his ministers to hinder the introduction of this silent but powerful emissary of evil. He desired Father de Meo to undertake the refutation of the pernicious works of Basnage, whom he ironically styles our friend, and whose works he considered particularly injurious. His Moral Theology was again attacked by Father Patuzzi, who was now joined by Father Gonzales. "Let them do as they please," wrote the saint, "I did not write to gain honor, but to make the truth known. If my writings bring conviction to my readers, it is well; if not, I do not wish to be victorious by obstinacy...Meanwhile souls go to ruin; let us pray God to put a stop to this."

The proceedings of the Jansenists almost broke his heart. "Their intention," says he, "as unveiled by themselves is to overthrow the Church." Arnauld's book on Frequent Communion, flippantly quoted at the time as La Fréquente, particularly annoyed him. "He speaks only of the purity and perfection with which one should approach the Holy Eucharist, but his sole object is to keep the faithful from this Sacrament, the only support of human weakness."

His words with regard to the sect of Free-masons were prophetic: "This sect," said he with tears, "will cause evil not only to the Church, but also to kingdoms and sovereigns. Kings will recognize their fatal significance when too late. The Free-masons act against God now, but they will soon attack kings." Must not the saint have seen in spirit the shattered thrones of the nineteenth century! But he held the Jansenists in especial aversion. "They are more dangerous," said he, "than Luther and Calvin, because they are hidden, and one does not avoid them."

About this time he wrote Father Saprio of the Oratory:

"I am engaged in writing a complete refutation of the errors of modern deists and materialists. Recommend me to God that He may aid me to write, so as to undeceive poor young people who, in such numbers, imbibe these errors, principally from bad books. We must weep and pray over the poor church, but let us have confidence, *the gates of hell shall not prevail against her.*"

His greatest sorrow was to hear the Papal Infallibility questioned. In his "Reflections on the Declaration of the Assembly of France, &c" he proved the Pope's Infallibility as a matter of faith, by the authority of the holy fathers and Ecumenical Councils; and showed how little value was to be attached to this Assembly, which, so far from being a general Council, consisted only of forty-four bishops, convened by the command of Louis XIV, who, in retaliation for the Pope's having refused him the revenues of the vacant bishoprics, forbid the Sorbonne to make any opposition, and commanded the adhering bishops to teach this doctrine in their dioceses.[1]

The saint was deeply grieved at the dangers which threatened the Society of Jesus. He wrote to J. Mattei, Provincial, as follows: "I have not received any tidings about your Society, and I feel almost as uneasy as if the disasters threatened our own little Congregation. A Society is threatened, which has, so to say, sanctified the world, and which continues unceasingly to sanctify it." When Clement XIII. issued a Bull to confirm the Society anew, the saint was so rejoiced that he wrote to the Sovereign Pontiff to thank him from the depths of his heart.

Weighed down, as it were, by his solicitude for all the churches, he did not by any means neglect his own Congregation. This was the dearest of his works, and he cherished it as his own

---

[1] The forty-four bishops themselves assured the Pope in a protest that they did not condemn the contrary opinion, i.e. Papal Infallibility. (Editor original note)

soul. The smallest defect, the least stain, grieved him to the heart, and in this respect, trifles were considerable in his eyes. Love and grief made him speak of the little faults and weakness of his sons in a true exaggeration, for he would not have spot or wrinkle in a work he so tenderly cherished. "I perceive with sorrow," he writes, "that fervor begins to decay among the members of the Congregation. I beg of each to watch carefully over himself for the future, because I cannot suffer any relaxation in the rule. I am told there is very little inclination for poverty and mortification. Alas, have we entered religion to enjoy ease and escape pain? I hear also that obedience is less strictly observed; if obedience ceases, the Congregation will not survive it.

"I have told Father Villani to punish public faults by public mortifications, and to expel the incorrigible. We have no need of subjects, we covet only those who are resolved to become saints. If ten who really love God remain, it is enough. It is too ungrateful to repay God by failings, for the love he bears towards the Congregation. Do we wish to become like those who cause scandal rather than edification to the Church? I have told Father Villani that his government is too weak and mild, and that I wish to be better informed of everything of consequence that occurs for the future...Let none of the young Fathers ever fail to have his sermons revised by some of the seniors who understand the matter, and let each before preaching or giving an instruction, read over what he has to say, that all may bear the impress of order and solidity, without studied terms or highflown language...Above all we must mortify ourselves to please God, otherwise God will not aid us, and we shall preach in vain."

In the year 1764, our saint thought of resigning his bishopric, as he had been promised when he accepted it that he could afterwards renounce it. But the Pope refused to accept his resignation. The saint, however, was not discouraged by this refusal. Later on he wrote some letters on the subject from which we give the following extracts:

"The principal reason for my resignation must not be the desire for retirement (this not being a sufficient one) but my advanced age and ever increasing infirmities. Besides my usual affliction of the chest, I was ill almost constantly last winter. I may say I am so still, having been confined to bed for upwards of a month. It is true, for I must tell all to prevent scruples — that I attend to business, and that everything is done as usual; but as long as winter lasts I am unable to go on the visitation, or to assist in choir. In summer I can go through my diocese during three or four months. I am forced to ask my demission, for I am overwhelmed with scruples at seeing scandals which I should not tolerate. I tremble too, lest I may seek my own ease in this resignation, and not God's glory: hence I wish to be sure as to what will really conduce to the divine honor.

"I meet with much to disgust me, but I have the words: *If you love me, feed my sheep,* and it matters little whether I live or succumb. The uncertainty as to whether or not I do God's will in giving in my resignation, is my greatest anxiety."

All this our saint represented still more strongly to the Pope, though with entire submission. Cardinals and prelates took sides with the holy old man, but to no purpose. *"His shadow alone would suffice to govern the whole diocese,"* was the energetic reply of the Pope. Among other mediators, the saint had employed Mgr. Pallaviano, the Nuncio at Naples, but the Pope informed him also, that he positively wished that Bishop Liguori should continue to bear the burden of his high charge. "The same will of God which made you a bishop," said the Nuncio to him, "will know how to aid you in ruling your church."

Mgr. Borgia, who had also interceded for him, now soothed him saying: "Do not be distressed: it is indeed the will of God." And the thought that it *was* the divine will enabled the saint to endure, even if he had to sink beneath the burden. Singular to relate, from the first of June 1765, he and those about him, heard a great number of little blows from his pectoral cross every time he said the rosary. They examined whether there was an insect in it, but found none. But as soon as he had received the Pope's negative, they were heard no more.

He concluded that God willed him, for the present, to continue to bear the cross with which he had been invested by apostolic authority.

CHAPTER XLIX.

Nuns of the Most Holy Redeemer. — Remarks of Archdeacon Rainone. The Church of St. Nobody. — Sister Mary Raphael of Charity. — Additions. Grand Reception. — Our Saint's Attention to the Wants of the Sisters. Success of the new foundation.— Alphonsus conducts the retreat of the novices. — Liberality of the Saint — His Kindness to the Sisters. — His way with them.

ONE OF the most important works undertaken by our saint was the establishment of the nuns of the Most Holy Redeemer. It is singular that so ancient and distinguished a city as St. Agatha, had no convent for the education of young ladies of high family. The absence of such an institution was regretted, on account of the expense and inconvenience consequent upon sending to a distance, the daughters of noble houses, to receive their education, and often to take the veil. To supply this deficiency, our saint exerted all his ingenuity, and he succeeded, despite obstacles that seemed insuperable.

"The establishment of the convent of the Most Holy Redeemer," wrote Archdeacon Rainone to Father Tannoia, (who may be called the Boswell of the great Bishop), "is undoubtedly a work most worthy to promote the glory of God, most honorable to his Lordship, and most useful to our town. The Lord has reserved for our saintly Prelate, the honor of making this foundation; his zeal, his constancy, and his great solicitude were necessary for its success."

Two centuries ago this work had been attempted, but failed. In 1610, the Lords of Mazzi had begun something similar, but this patrician family became extinct before the building was finished, and the church, partially raised, was styled by the people, St. Nobody's Church. During the episcopate of Mgr. Danza, who was raised to the see in 1681, Canon Talia established in this church without a patron, a pious confraternity, which became the edification of the whole town, but this did not long survive the death of its worthy originator. A community of Franciscan nuns replaced the scattered brethren, and did much good during half a century, but discord penetrated into this holy spot, and it was finally abandoned. The Duke of Costa thought of establishing a convent of cloistered nuns there, but his death prevented the realization of his pious wishes. Finally the edifice became a sort of temporary barracks for superfluous troops.

When it became known that Alphonsus designed to change these unlucky quarters into a nest for doves, he was assailed by a storm of opposition. Some wanted a cloistered monastery, some an asylum for men, and others, nothing of the kind. "Explain your meaning," said the saint to the more influential, "if you intend to found a convent of servants of God, I will co-operate, but if you want a mere assemblage of women, you better say no more about it." At last, the people wisely agreed to leave the affair entirely to him, and he decided on inviting a little colony from the convent of the Most Holy Redeemer at Scala. There was no sufficient revenue for this purpose, but the holy prelate redoubled his confidence in God, and ere long an income of over six hundred ducats was forthcoming, which, with the dowries, was quite sufficient for his designs.

The work seemed to go forward as if by magic. The saint was on the spot every day, to encourage and quicken the workmen. He was greatly aided by Don Francis Mastillo, agent of the Duke of Maddalon. When the approbation of the Pope and the consent of the King had been obtained, Alphonsus presented his request to the monastery of Scala. Sister Mary Raphael of Charity was chosen superioress, Sister Mary Felicia of the Holy Nails, Sister Mary Celestine of Divine Love, and a lay-sister, Mary Joseph of Jesus and Mary, completed the foundation. All four were models of piety. They reached Nocera June 27, 1766, and St. Agatha next day. They were accompanied by two ladies, who had gone to meet them, the treasurer, a canon of the cathedral and Fathers Villani and Ferara. Two young ladies of quality were so taken with the virtues of Mother Raphael during her stay at Nola, that they immediately joined her.

The saint was so rejoiced at the arrival of the sisters, that he persuaded the people to adorn the gates of the town with unusual magnificence, and to ornament the streets with wreaths of myrtle, rosemary and evergreens. He advanced to meet them in his pontifical vestments at the head of his chapter and all his clergy. The firing of cannon and the ringing of bells were in unison with the joy of the people. After visiting the Blessed Sacrament, the religious went in procession to the new convent, preceded by the conventual fathers, the seminarists, the clergy, and the chapter, after whom went the bishop followed by all the nobles. The Blessed Sacrament was exposed in the convent chapel and the *Te Deum* chanted. The ladies of the city had the privilege of visiting the sisters until Wednesday, the Feast of the Visitation of Our Blessed Lady, on which day the grand Vicar went in the bishop's name to establish inclosure with the usual ceremonies.

The saint provided every thing for these his dear children. Corn, wine, cooking utensils, table-linen, furniture — nothing was wanting. For the first eight days, he sent their repasts already cooked, and would have continued this liberality for a month, but the nuns declined, wishing to live in the poverty prescribed by their rule. When it became known that Bishop Liguori had made a foundation, the convent was speedily filled with pupils, and the good odor of Jesus Christ was spread abroad by the regularity of the house and the holiness of its foundresses.

The two accessions already mentioned, were speedily increased to four, and all about to take the habit. The Bishop gave them the spiritual exercises himself, and their fervor filled him with joy. But there was one postulant so tormented with melancholy, that she wept and sighed unceasingly for her father's house. One evening, our saint called her, and having succeeded in restoring her serenity, gave her a crucifix to kiss, and made her promise to take Jesus Christ for her Spouse. The poor child felt within her a complete change, she returned joyfully to the novitiate and was never again troubled by such temptations.

Alphonsus acted differently towards another postulant, who repented of the step she had taken and lived in such a manner as to injure herself and do no good to others. "We must distinguish between temptation and obstinacy," said he, and though the lady was Archdeacon Rainone's niece, he silenced human respect, and sent her home to her parents.

The young ladies who had joined Mother Raphael at Nola, were objects of the saint's peculiar kindness. Their brothers, dissatisfied with the step they had taken, for several years refused to pay their pension. The holy bishop knowing their sensitiveness on this point, paid it for them, but their brothers refunded their portions previous to their profession.

This convent was to Alphonsus as the apple of his eye; it successfully rivalled the seminary in his affections. He never ceased to be its most liberal benefactor, never failing to send present's of oil, wine and corn at stated times, besides frequent donations of from ten to thirty ducats, the stipulated allowance he sent the Sisters once in a week, or at the farthest, once a month, and he promised to maintain the four foundresses while he lived. On feast days, he always sent presents of some kind, and whatever sweetmeats etc. were sent him from Naples by his relations or others, found their way, for the most part, to his dear monastery.

The third Sunday in July was chosen for the solemn feast of the Most Holy Redeemer, and the saint caused it to be preceded by a *triduo*, and celebrated with extraordinary pomp. These good religious called *Redemptoristines*, have spread into Austria, Belgium, Holland and Ireland, and "every where," says Cardinal Villecourt, "The daughters of Alphonsus have shed the sweet odor of their virtues."

The saint, as will be readily conjectured, always took the greatest interest in convents. He wished to revive every where ancient monastic discipline, and nothing calculated to compass this end escaped his incessant vigilance. On his first arrival at St. Agatha, he sent Father Villani and other Fathers to give spiritual exercises in all the monasteries, and this was repeated at least once a year. "A retreat," said he, "is a fire in which the most rusty iron ought to become purified." He frequently visited the convent himself, and would preach on religious duties at the grate, exciting in the sisters, his most dear children, an ardent love for Jesus Christ, and special confidence in His Holy Mother. He particularly advised them to practise frequent communion, and by this means caused them to love prayer, and mortification, and led them into paths of the sublimest perfection.

Virgins consecrated to God he considered the most precious portion of the flock entrusted to him. When he preached to them, he often spoke quite strongly about trivial faults, so that they remarked he went too far. "What shall I do?" said he smiling. "Ought I to have told the sisters they were saints? When one preaches, one may suppose things which do not yet exist." He enjoined abbesses and confessors to watch over the intercourse which took place at the grate, and wished to be informed of all disorders, however small, that he might remedy them immediately, and as the nuns were strictly cloistered, he did not wish them to be visited, except by relations of the first and second degrees.

Alphonsus was extremely cautious in selecting confessors for convents. He weighed the gestures, the words, and searched into the very opinions of the candidate. He allowed the confessor to receive some tokens of gratitude from the nuns on certain feast days, but would not tolerate the frequent giving of presents, and required all to be offered in the name of the community. Nothing gave him more delight than to see young virgins consecrate themselves to God. He aided them in every way, and left the most important business to assist at the ceremony. He accepted every invitation to a profession, whether of a choir or lay-sister, and never omitted to preach. "It is my privilege and my duty," said he, "to consecrate to God these victims of divine love." To stimulate their fervor, he gave his religious every possible advantage, introducing into their churches exercises calculated to increase in their hearts the love of God, as benediction, exposition, novenas, and a sermon in honor of the Blessed Virgin on Saturday evening. He often preached this sermon himself in the convent chapel.

He arranged that the nuns should have an extraordinary confessor whenever they asked for one, and he sent such confessors to all the convents every three months, whether asked for or not. In short, with regard to conscience, he insisted that religious should enjoy perfect liberty. "When a religious asks for a new confessor," said he, "it is a sign she has not courage to open her heart to the usual confessor, and if there is a sin on her conscience, she may be led to commit a thousand sacrileges." He was deeply grieved on learning that a neighboring bishop was too cautious in granting these privileges, and that nuns absented themselves from the holy tribunal in consequence. Hearing that a regulation allowed the religious of a certain convent to write only to the ordinary confessor, he sent for the superior, and ordered, that this rule should be relaxed whenever any of the religious wished to apply to any confessor of well known probity.

Although several instances of apparent severity, regarding the dismissal of subjects, are recorded in the memoirs of the saint, yet perhaps no founder of an order was ever more lenient in this respect. When urged by Father Tannoia, novice-master for twenty-four years, to consent to the dismissal of a lay-brother, he wrote the following reply, which undoubtedly explains his own practice in this respect.

"When once a subject is admitted to the noviciate, he should not be sent away without grave reason; and when he has been admitted to profession, the reasons should be still more grave, and the subject incorrigible; otherwise a superior sins mortally in expelling a subject." This deserves to be generally known.

He endeavored to restore monastic discipline everywhere. Among the Franciscans of Ariola, the rules were so difficult that the nuns could not fully observe them. "He curtailed all that was too rigorous," said Sister Mary di Lucca, "and what he reformed was fully observed." In the new edition of the rules which he had printed, one recognizes the spirit of St. Francis de Sales, for he condescends to every want, yet avoids effeminate indulgence.

In connexion with this convent, he learned that the religious suffered great annoyances, because their revenues were collected and administered by strangers, and purchases made in such a manner, that, with ample rent, the poor sisters were often without food or clothing. The saint appealed to the Prince of Riccia, and backed by this powerful noble, deprived the stewards of the convent money, and placed it in the hands of the abbess. He endeavored to establish community life everywhere, but when his designs were violently opposed, he temporized. "Calm yourselves," said he to the nuns on one of those occasions, "I proposed this measure for your good, but as you judge others wise, forget all I have said about it." So far from being offended with these religious, he paid them a fatherly visit the very next day, and made no allusion whatever to it.

It was customary in a certain convent that when a young lady was clothed or professed, she should remain seated at the door during the rest of the day to receive the congratulations of her friends and relations. Seeing in this senseless custom an occasion of general dissipation, he ordered that neither the grate nor the door should be opened after dinner, and allowed exposition of the Blessed Sacrament, that the new bride of Christ might obtain of her Spouse abundant blessings.

Again: when a candidate made the vows or took the habit, it was permitted her to dine in the parlor with the guests. This the saint entirely abolished when two noble ladies, daughters of Lady Catherine di Lucca, made their profession. The guests he allowed to be entertained but the newly professed dined in the refectory with her sisters.

The ritual of a convent in Arienzo stated that the novice should make her profession between the hands of the bishop, and, ridiculously enough, this was interpreted, literally: at a profession, the master of ceremonies explained it to the bewildered saint. "O Jesus!" he exclaimed with unwonted impetuosity, "what has that to do with the vows? Let her keep her hands to herself and I will keep mine." He afterwards explained the true meaning of the phrase, and suppressed forever this foolish ceremony.

He next undertook to reform the music of the convents, and help to restore the grand and solemn Gregorian chant, by forbidding the flimsy music, with which bad taste had replaced it. "The church," said he, "is not a theatre, and religious are not opera singers." Besides, he did not wish the nuns to sing solos. The musicians, however, were not over scrupulous in carrying out his views. One evening, while a nun was singing the Litany of the Blessed Virgin to figured music, the bishop suddenly presented himself, and it was to no purpose that the *artiste* with much presence of mind, continued the words to a Gregorian air, for Alphonsus himself was an accomplished musician, and possessed even in old age a voice of such refined culture and marvellous sweetness, that, when he sang, his auditors melted into tears. After a while, he approached the grate, and said, laughing: "You have been trying to deceive me, and that was not right, I forbade light music, because I thought it might attract young libertines to your church, which would be a source of numerous irregularities."

A daughter of a choir-conductor who was an excellent musician, applied for admission, and the saint not liking to refuse the nuns, consented, but prophesied that the musical novice would not persevere. The nuns soliciting the admission of another, also a musician, the saint consented, saying: "This one will not persevere any better." Both returned to their homes after a few months, and the nuns resolved to be satisfied with the plain chant in future.

On one occasion when it was thought he would command two windows of a certain monastery, which looked into a house belonging to seculars, to be closed, one of the religious openly resisted him, and threatened to appeal to the king. To this unexpected insult, the saint mildly replied: "Be tranquil, I do not wish to cause you any pain;" after which, he dexterously changed the subject, and the conversation went on peaceably.

The Rochettines of Arienzo wishing to obtain purer air, asked leave to open a little belvidere above their church door. The bishop sent the Vicar General and two architects from Naples, to examine the place. When he heard that the proposed belvidere would look into the premises of the Augustinian Fathers, he immediately refused. The good religious were not at all offended at this, for, on reflection, they themselves saw the impropriety of their request.

From time to time, the Pope had granted cloistered nuns permission to absent themselves from the convent. Some nuns were about to seek a similar dispensation, but Alphonsus warned them to abstain: "The Pope refers it to the ordinary," he said, "and I will never grant it. I know what a bad reputation these goings out have. The least evil which results from them is great dissipation of mind." To the lady Catharine di Lucca who had leave from the Pope to spend one day in the year with her bedridden daughter in a cloistered convent, he sent the following message: "Tell Donna Catherine that I suspend the permission for the present. The Pope can do what he pleases, but if he refers it to me, I cannot grant it, as others would seek the same privilege to the injury of enclosure." Some nuns complained that they never got anything they asked from him, and that they had met with three refusals consecutively. "Let them ask what is light," said he, "and I will be sure not to refuse them, but to unreasonable requests, I must give a decided refusal."

Whenever any of the nuns wanted one of his fathers as extraordinary confessor, the favor was granted. Those at a distance from the father they wished to consult, could do so by letter, and it was the saint's wish that the father thus consulted should be allowed to respond. Father Villani, when rector, having refused a permission of this nature, the saint wrote to him immediately telling him to comply. So desirous was Alphonsus that these doves, whose office it is to hover about their heavenly spouse and sing his praises, should never know a moment's uneasiness which it was in his power to prevent.

No saint ever did more for virgins consecrated to God, and for the religious state in general, than this great doctor. It is indeed doubtful if any other saint did so much. His writings reanimate and reform religious, console and fortify them, in every clime. *The Nun sanctified, Exhortation to Religious to advance in the perfection of their State, Advice to Novices, Consideration on the Religious State, Advice regarding Religious Vocation,* various admonitions to superiors, subordinates, lay-brothers, scattered through his rules, his circulars, his private letters, form a complete epitome of all that is necessary or useful for those concerned.

In his sermons and instructions, he was ever urging the religious under his charge to heroic perfection. Frequent communion, even daily communion, became customary among them. He rigorously examined the confessors he sent them, lest the Jansenistic tendencies, then too common, should enter this cherished fold, and he knew well what Jansenist confessors had done with all the convents in France to which they had gained access. The nuns under his jurisdiction never knew the want of any spiritual advantage. He himself was ever ready to console and encourage the lowliest among them in moments of desolation or temptation. He received them, he professed them, he instructed them, he gave them retreats, he heard their confessions, in short, he wished that in all their necessities, spiritual and temporal, they should know they had in him a *Father*, whose greatest happiness was to assist his cherished children, but in proportion as he loved to see these dear spouses of Christ fervent and devoted to Jesus, he dreaded relaxation, and was wont to say, that it was easier for a soul to be saved amid the gayeties of the world than in a relaxed religious house. Severe judgment from the most enthusiastic advocate of convents that ever lived; but, as Faber remarks, "few men have had such experience of these matters as good St. Alphonsus."

CHAPTER L.

A SAINT so intensely devoted to the most Blessed
Sacrament must naturally have interested himself in
the material temples wherein Jesus reposed, veiled in
the great mystery of his love. He rebuilt or repaired every church
in his diocese that needed renovation, and spared no expense in
decorating them. Several of the churches of the diocese, from
being little better in appearance than ruinous barns, became,
under his fostering care, basilicas worthy to rank with those
which have gained the world's admiration in Rome and Naples.

Paintings by the first masters, and statuary whose beauty
could not fail to elevate the minds of the worshipers, became quite
common in the days of our saint, who wished that the priceless
gems of the great masters, of whom Italy has been so prolific,
should be gathered in at any cost to beautify the house of God.
Ornamented pillars, door-dressings, stuccoing, elegant ornaments
of every kind supplied employment to architects and artists
during the saint's episcopate and for many years after. Nor did he
give less attention to the interior embellishments of the house of
God. He required that the churches should be kept scrupulously
clean, and the altars decorated with magnificence, or at least,
becomingly. He was extremely particular about the altar linens,
and insisted that they should be changed at stated intervals, and
removed as soon as they began to wear out. "I have never seen a

priest allow soiled or worn linen at his table," he said, "everything they use for themselves is neat; it is only for Jesus Christ that dirty things are allowed." He desired to see the altars profusely ornamented with flowers, and from his day it has been customary in his congregation to cultivate the rarest flowers to bloom and fade before the tabernacle. So accomplished a musician could not fail to make stringent regulations regarding the singing of high mass and the chanting of the office, but he never favored what he called theatrical music. He loved the grave, dignified music of the Church, of which a true musician never wearies, and which fully answers the end of church music, to inspire or aid devotion.

It was not the divine will that our saint should sanctify himself in prosperity and peace. Persecutions thickened around him towards the close, and his last years were dragged wearily out, in misery and sorrow, but the joy of the Holy Ghost sustained him, and now "he remembereth his anguish no more." His congregation was flourishing; its name and fame had reached distant lands, but hell instigated a new persecution against it. Some three years back, a difficulty occurred between the house at Illiceto, and Don Maffei, a proud, turbulent noble, about a certain fief then in litigation. The fathers remained neutral for peace sake, but Maffei was so incensed at their not taking sides with him that he swore to destroy the whole congregation, saying: "He that is not with me is against me." Baron Sarnelli also cherished a secret resentment against them, because of the property bequeathed to Alphonsus by his brother, Father Sarnelli, of holy memory. Some mark of attention having been accidentally omitted in church towards his wife, the baroness, this was as the last drop which caused the vials of his wrath to overflow. Between Maffei and the baron, the Fathers were vilified in every part of the kingdom. "If Don Maffei is offended," said the old bishop sadly, "I grieve for the poor house! I know his dispositions, and what he caused the venerable Mgr. Lucci to suffer. May the good God deign to be our protector."

He ordered fasts and prayers throughout the congregation, and recommended that discretion and charity should be exercised towards their adversaries, against whom no arms were to be used but prayer and observance of rule. "Behold my dear brothers," he wrote, "how the Lord has visited us in these tribulations — He chastises our negligence in regular observance but let us hope in

His mercy; He will not permit the congregation to be destroyed. Let us appease the divine wrath by prayer, and by avoiding all voluntary transgressions, especially such as result from disobedience or nonobservance."

Calumnies of the strangest description were everywhere circulated against the Fathers, and the rage of Maffei went so far that he appealed to the Supreme Court to deprive them of their rights of citizenship, as men who habitually plotted against state and sovereign and led scandalous lives! The saint, besides urging his own spiritual sons to penance, solicited the prayers of several monasteries and holy persons at Naples. He also sent a great quantity of wax candles to the hermitages of Camaldoli, that they might expose the Blessed Sacrament and intercede for his congregation, and he sent several large alms to the Capuchin nuns entreating them to make novenas and other pious exercises for his intention.

It was while this infamous persecution was going on, that the holy doctor published his great work in defence of the Church. "The Truths of Faith," which was received with universal applause. A canon of Naples in a report on this work addressed to Cardinal Sersale, wrote as follows:

"Nothing can hinder or slacken the zeal of this apostolic man. In his devotion to the salvation of souls, he enters into the lists with indefatigable courage to maintain a generous combat for truth, despite the double burden of the episcopate and old age. In this book he has re-established the integrity of faith and morals among the faithful, to avenge the calumnies of the wicked, and to scatter the darkness of error. He completely overthrows all the dreams of materialists, deists and other impious men."

Pope Clement XIII was extremely gratified on reading this great work and acknowledged the dedication (to himself) by a brief, testifying in flattering terms his high esteem for the extraordinary learning of the great doctor.

At the same time he published his useful "Instructions on the Decalogue, &c," which was and is highly prized by all who have at heart the instruction of the people.

The disturbances regarding the houses of Illiceto and Ciorani increased to such a pitch that the fathers besought Alphonsus to go to Naples and confer with the minister Tanucci.

He refused to leave his see, thinking that the business would be done as well by letter, and by friends in the capital, but Father Villani and some other father came to St. Agatha and with tears described the imminent danger of the Congregation, adding that if he wished to save it from utter destruction, his presence in Naples was essential. Moved by their entreaties, and still more by their affliction, he borrowed a carriage and set out for the capital which he reached July 16.

His first visit was to the Cardinal Archbishop who having greeted him with utmost cordiality, inquired the cause of his unexpected presence in Naples. "My Congregation is passing through a crisis, your eminence," answered the saint, "our enemies wish to destroy it, but I rely on the omnipotent arm of God to sustain it." As he took leave, the Cardinal said: "Monsignor, you are Archbishop of Naples, you have all the power that I can confer, use it as you please."

Prelates, canons, nobles, thronged the room of a man whom they regarded as an honor and an ornament to their country. He was unable to acknowledge their profuse courtesies as he desired, and with that elegant urbanity which has always marked the dealings of the saints with their friends and benefactors, he begged them to excuse him, if, having come to Naples on urgent business, he reluctantly failed in any of the duties of politeness or civility. He accepted of his brothers' hospitality, but declined the magnificent state apartment that had been prepared for him, and took refuge in a lumber-room. He wore the habit of his Congregation, now so old and patched that it gave him the appearance of one of his townsmen, the lazzaroni. His shoes and hat were quite in keeping with the habit. Count Hercules was particularly annoyed at the hat, as the like had not been seen in Naples for years; he abstracted it and put one of the current fashion in its place. This made matters worse, as the saint had nothing to match this elegant addition to his scanty wardrobe. However, he sold it, and having bought four common hats with the proceeds, gave three away and kept one for himself. As he had no cloak he used an old mantilla, but being told that it was unsuitable, he sent it to a pawnbroker and got an old cloak in exchange. It particularly annoyed him to be styled Excellency. "Come now," said he to a servant one day, "drop this word, I will not have it." "But you are a nobleman by birth," returned the servant, "it is only your hereditary title." "That is enough," said the saint shortly, "never let me hear it from you again," and he was obeyed. To a gentleman who observed that he carried humility too far, he replied: "Humility has never injured any one."

The saint's mode of defending his beloved Congregation was such as to increase the esteem and veneration in which he was already held. He managed to justify the Fathers without injuring those who had calumniated them. But his very appearance in Naples had ruined the cause of his adversaries. They wished to suspend the business indefinitely, but through the influence of Alphonsus, the eleventh of September was fixed for the discussion of the cause of Sarnelli. About this time the saint's carriage came into colision with another carriage. The windows were broken, the coachman wounded, our saint and his companion hurt severely but not dangerously. The Duchess of Pirelli, whose palace was at hand, sent for them, and after they had rested awhile, lent her own equipage to take them home. When this accident occurred, the poor bishop had the misfortune to lose his splendid new hat, and the wooden stick he used as a cane — to his infinite regret, for they were not easily replaced.

The royal court of St. Clare was in session, Sep. 11, but no plaintiff appeared. One of the advocates alone came, but only to declare that he had not courage to speak against a bishop whose sanctity was proclaimed by the whole kingdom. The saint was displeased that an opportunity had not been offered him of disproving one by one all the calumnies his enemies had been circulating, and which they were expected to produce in open court; but his triumph was all the greater, his very presence confounded his enemies.

During his stay in Naples, the saint as usual occupied himself in waging war against sin, and planting virtues in the hearts of all with whom he came in contact. Among other good works, he thoroughly reformed the convent of the "Religious of the Wood." He put an end to all dissensions, restored perfect peace and harmony, and reestablished prayer, the frequent use of the holy Sacraments, and perfect observance.

The superior of the Propaganda was desirous that the saint should preach the novena of the Assumption, but feared to ask this on account of his other great labors. A canon suggested that by his authority as superior he could obtain what he desired, the holy bishop being still a member of the Congregation of the Propaganda. When the order reached him, he bent his head and said: "Pray that the Blessed Virgin may give me strength, for I have not time to prepare any thing; you must be satisfied with what God and Our Lady will deign to suggest to me." And never had an audience been better satisfied.

One evening the saint's servant was obliged to use the carriage of Don Hercules for his master, but lest the latter would persist in going on foot rather than ascend such an elegant vehicle, old harness was put on the horses and old covering on the seats, which caused the bishop and his equipage to present a singular if not ridiculous appearance. The novena was wonderfully blessed. Every day the cardinal assisted, and could not refrain from weeping at the touching spectacle of a whole congregation in contrition. It was said that ten missions would not have effected so many conversions. Already was the man of God revered as a saint. Pieces were cut off from his garments, and Mgr. Bergamo deemed himself fortunate in being able to exchange his hat for another. He attempted also to take his rosary, but Alphonsus missed it and asked for it, on account of the indulgences attached to it.

On the eve of the Assumption he went to visit the Blessed Sacrament in the church of the convent Regina Coeli. It happened that three abbots were officiating pontifically while the nuns were chanting vespers, and when one of them recognized Monsignor Liguori. "Just look at that bishop," said he, "does he not disgrace his character." But the prince of Monte Miletto was not of the same opinion. Despite the shabby garments of the saint, he approached, knelt to kiss his hand with every demonstration of reverence. The Duke of Andria and other noblemen present offered the same homage, having more correct discernment than the Abbots. When the Carmelites commenced the devotions of the Wednesdays in honor of St. Teresa, Alphonsus attended, but sat on an humble bench among the people. The Fathers presented him with an easy-chair and a velvet cushion, but the saint declined all marks of distinction, as was his wont.

The gifts of knowledge, counsel and prophecy were often made evident in our saint. A daughter of the Duchess of Bovino was about to marry, and sent her mother to ask his prayers: "No, no," said he, "she will not marry. God will detach her from the world and draw her to himself." The duchess no sooner returned home than a note was handed her from her daughter stating that it was her intention to enter a convent.

During our saint's stay in Naples, his sister-in-law gave birth to a son, whom he was asked to baptize. While the ceremony progressed, an attendant priest continually addressed Alphonsus as "Excellency." At last his annoyance found vent in this mild rebuke: "Reverend sir, if you wish to style me most illustrious, you can do so, but you would oblige me very much by using the simplest language in addressing me."

The indefatigable bishop preached for the confraternity of coachmen, footmen and other domestics. His dear brethren of the chapels, among whom was his old penitent Barbarese, had the intense gratification of hearing him once more. He also preached, at the request of the worthy men at the head of the guild of saddlers, to an immense concourse of the lowest classes. They besought him to preach the novena of our Lady's Nativity, and he refused no request of these humble disciples and fervent admirers. He preached to three hundred orphans by special request, but this did not end his labors. The people not only crowded about the church in which he officiated, but thronged his house, though for want of enough chairs, most of them had to sit on the floor; and his loving kindness to these poor people won him the admiration of all Naples. He visited almost every convent in Naples, preached to the nuns, and heard the confessions of any who wished to come to him. But here he practised his customary humility, for when the first religious asked him to hear her, he applied to the cardinal for faculties, although his Eminence had already given him the fullest power to preach, confirm, officiate, and in fact, do what he pleased.

Shortly after this, our saint had an affliction in connection with his sister, Lady Mariana Liguori, a nun in the convent of St. Jerome, which did not grieve him the less because it happened to be a realization of his own prophecy. This lady suffered much from scruples, and as she would not submit to her director, the only cure for one in her condition, the saint predicted that she would die crazy, which happened soon after. Of the Princess Zurlo, who wished to become a nun, he said: "No, she will return to the world and lead a saintly life there." Of another young lady, he said to an over-zealous relative: "Leave her alone, the convent is not for her; she is not fit for it, nor does she want to go there."

Alphonsus was totally free from human respect. He acted in the same manner towards convents for the rustic and the penitent, and visited them as frequently as convents for women of noble birth, or rather he gave the former the preference. He was accustomed to visit the sick and infirm in all monasteries, especially such nuns as had once been his penitents. Indeed he preached for all religious societies whenever he was asked, and, faithful to his own instructions, he preached Jesus Christ in such a manner as to cause an audience of priests to exclaim: "A true apostle! Thanks to God for having given us a bishop of the primitive age!" In his sermons, heart spoke to heart, both preacher and auditors were so absorbed as to be utterly unconscious of the extraordinary eloquence that renewed upon the earth the marvels of conversion and contrition which were as "the first fruits of the spirit" in the days of the apostles.

Although the saint, like his Divine Master, went about doing good, and heaven visibly blessed his unceasing labors, yet he counted the moments until he could return to his diocese, the spouse, as he said, that God had given him to cherish. "Were it not for the interests of my persecuted Congregation," said he, "which labors so successfully for God's glory and the salvation of souls, I should believe that I sinned mortally in remaining so long in Naples." Not a day passed on which he did not receive a courier from his diocese, and regulated from afar its now prosperous affairs. The business that brought him had no sooner reached a successful issue than he replied to those who would have urged him to remain a little longer that he might preach other sermons and novenas, "Jesus Christ no longer wishes me at Naples: St. Agatha is my place."

On one occasion he went to the Prince della Riccia to procure through his influence the admission of a woman who had been in his service, into the refuge of St. Raphael; but the valet said the prince was absent, attending on the king. A soldier of the Italian guard seeing the neglected appearance of the saint, who, except as regarded personal cleanliness, took little pains to keep up his dignity in externals, remarked to a comrade: "Look at that shabby lord; he has not a penny to get himself shaved." Alphonsus smiled and said: "I thank Thee, oh Lord, for allowing me to be censured even by soldiers." A second time also, he was unable to see the prince. On a third visit the secretary suspecting the real cause of these refusals, slipped some money into the valet's hands and lo, the prince was at home. He was very angry when he learned that he had been denied to the saint, and immediately did all that was requisite for the penitent woman, so that the saint had the consolation of seeing yet another of his straying sheep in a place of safety.

CHAPTER LI.

The saint leaves Naples.— His Emotion.— Letter. — Unreasonable complaints. — Calumnies. — Letter to Father Villani. — Fault finding. The meekest of bishops accused of rigor. — Incident. — Murmurs against his works. — His reply. — Illness. — He makes his will. — Sufferings. — His tedious convalescence. — The most zealous doctor. — New literary labors. Treatise for men. — He again appeals to the Pope to ease him of the burden of the episcopate.

O UR SAINT left Naples, after a busy sojourn of two months and three days, with a firm conviction that he would never again return to that dear city, in which he had so often tasted the ecstacy of joy as well as the anguish of grief. When he visited for the last time his beloved church of Our Lady of Mercy, where he had received so many graces, — graces that had been the turning points in his life, — recollections of his early struggles and successes, of the joys and sorrows of his marvellous vocation, rushed upon his mind and for the moment completely, overwhelmed him. Raising his tearful eyes towards Mary, *his Mother*, towards that dear image of Our Lady of Mercy through which miracles had been wrought in his favor, his emotion became incontrollable: "O my Queen!" he exclaimed, in broken accents, "we shall meet no more in Naples, but we shall see each other again in Paradise!"

He reached Arienzo September 19, 1767, his mission to the capital having been entirely successful. He was now firmly resolved to leave his diocese no more, unless, indeed, the Sovereign Pontiff, in consideration of his years and infirmities might allow him to retire to the bosom of his beloved Congregation, and prepare to render to the Chief Pastor of Souls, an account of his stewardship; — a hope he fondly cherished. "Tell my brother, Count Hercules," he wrote from St. Agatha, to his man of business in Naples, "that he may freely dispose of the apartments which he reserves for me, because I shall return thither no more."

The extraordinary vigilance of our saint in the government of his diocese gained universal approbation, the Pope himself was accustomed to cite him as a model bishop. The people regarding him less as a man than an angel, were sometimes unreasonable enough to fancy that he was capable of annihilating sin in his diocese, and hence they loudly criticised the least disorder. The murmurs reached Naples, and a certain respectable religious of that city condemned several regulations made by Alphonsus, of which he had heard. Being asked to justify himself, the saint replied: "There is no need of my doing so; St. Francis de Sales, Father Torres and so many others have declined to defend themselves...Tell me where is there a diocese to which nothing is wanting?...I cannot avoid these reproaches; besides, they are useful for my spiritual welfare, by humbling me through the contempt and disfavor I meet with. I should be delighted if Father N. _____ would come to see me; then he could see the real state of things." The religious really did visit the saint, and not only was undeceived, but from that period became his warmest panegyrist.

The saint liked to hear whatever was said in dispraise of him, and Father Villani who tenderly loved him, was always careful to let him know of every complaint he heard, that he might be always on his guard, for open enemies and deceitful friends were never wanting. A priest on one occasion having informed him of an injurious report circulated against him, he wrote in reply: "I thank you for the information your letter conveyed. These things serve to maintain me the more in humility and vigilance."

It was next affirmed that his reputation had become so low in Rome that the Pope was by no means proud of having made him a bishop. This report pained the Congregation deeply, and no doubt touched the heart of the saint at his most sensitive point. "I do not know," he wrote to Father Villani, "how I could have been more careful. I always note down in writing all that has to be done for the present day and the following, and when any business connected with the diocese is in question, I leave everything else to attend to it. Every one who knows me knows this, God will do the rest, but after all, this will only enable me to get my resignation accepted the more easily."

Again, our saint, the great model of episcopal meekness was accused of exercising too much rigor in his government. But he kept the even tenor of his way, whether he was accused of superfluous meekness or superfluous severity. "Human respect," said one who knew him well, "could never succeed in influencing Monsignor Liguori." One day, several gentlemen were discussing the case of a priest whom they alleged to have been unjustly banished. Yet the offences of this priest were of a grave character, but our saint had thrown the cloak of charity over them for the love of God. When he heard that he had been censured for his action in this matter as he had never particularized the offences for which he banished the delinquent, he smiled, but not a word escaped him. That he might taste the bitterness of the cross in every form, some, and even those of his own Congregation, carped at the publication of the wonderful works which in our day have gained him the title of Doctor, as though he neglected the care of his diocese to compose them. Being informed of this, the saint wrote thus to Father Villani:

"In reply to those who regard my labors of the pen as a crime, I could remind them that the bishops most celebrated for zeal, published works while ruling their diocese, as St. John Chrysostom, St. Augustine, St. Ambrose, St. Francis de Sales, and many others. In winter I am forced to keep my room, and I see no society. I make meditation three times a day, I make an hour's thanksgiving after mass, as well as a spiritual lecture, at least when not hindered by some urgent duty. Afterwards I endeavor to turn to profit my few moments of leisure by laboring at things which I consider useful."

Even the expenses which his works were supposed to entail — works worth a million times more than their weight in gold, or rather immeasurably beyond all earthly price, — excited the disaffected and called forth their murmurs. It is superfluous to say that the holy doctor did not write to make money, yet he brought out his works without any pecuniary loss. His own letters to his publishers prove this. But when we consider the utility of his hundred volumes, not a line of which is without its use, — works written for the most part to supply the wants which he himself discovered, in those whose ignorance would become the ruin of their flock, or to defend the doctrine and discipline of the Church of Christ against powerful and numerous adversaries — we can well imagine the anguish which these censures must have caused his sensitive heart. It was a consolation to him, as it is pleasant to us to recall, that Clement XIII, far from sharing the sentiments of these ignoble murmurers, encouraged the saint in his literary labors, by assuring him that his works were useful not only to his diocese but to the whole Church. But the saint was not to be deterred by the grumblings of these petty, we had almost said, contemptible, spirits. He wrote solely for the glory of God and the good of the Church, and *his works remain to praise him in the gate* . Could these narrow-minded murmurers but have foreseen the day when in consideration of these very works, the delight, the edification and the glory of the Church, over eight hundred prelates of Christendom would petition the Holy See to place the name of Alphonsus de Liguori, in the short but illustrious category of DOCTORS OF THE CHURCH!

The year 1768 had other troubles in store for our saint; for God overwhelms with sufferings those whom He designs to elevate to high sanctity, and this is the explanation of the chain of spiritual and corporal sufferings which traversed his long career. He was almost seventy-two years old when he was attacked by a violent fever, which, after three days, suddenly disappeared to give place to a sciatica arising from rheumatic tendencies, of which he gives the following account in his letter to Rev. Father Villani, his director:

"I am continually tormented with internal pains, so that I am only half alive; the pain seems to fix itself in the hip-bone. Blessed be God who has sent me this suffering! It will be difficult for me to make the visitation this year. The physicians no longer know what to think of my case. I place myself in the hands of God to bear my cross as long as it shall please Him."

He strove, however, to preach the novena of the Assumption, and, despite his suffering, he succeeded in crawling to the pulpit. But on the sixth day, the pain became so intolerable as to render it impossible for him to go on. He had to go to his bed once more, but even here it was only the body that rested. He administered the affairs of his diocese, dictated his works, and continued to direct the ordinary exercises of his household.

As no relief could be obtained, it was proposed to him to send to Naples for a physician, but, as usual, he would employ only those of his own diocese, and when those who loved him disobeyed him in this matter, his countenance plainly showed how much he suffered.

Every one was affected by the tender piety of the saint, which found vent in the most touching ejaculations to Jesus and Mary. But he seemed quite confounded that he had not, as he affirmed, corresponded to their goodness. To a Father of his Congregation, who was about to say mass, he said with profound humility: "Pray that God may be merciful towards me." His confidence being chastened by a holy fear which made him tremble at the thought of the judgments of God, he repeated from time to time: "Enter not into judgment with Thy servant, O Lord, but deal with him according to Thy mercy." Having received the last Sacraments, he made his will on the 26th of August. He would not have had anything to bequeath had not two farmers of the episcopal demense just paid his steward four hundred and twenty-three ducats. He ordained that this sum should be deposited with the archpriest Romano, who was to devote a certain portion to have masses celebrated for his soul, another to the poor, and the rest to be distributed to his servants, in token of his gratitude for their services, two hours after his death. He wished that his body should repose in his cathedral.

As the fever abated, his pains increased until they became so violent, that being unable to remain in bed, he was obliged to get into an arm-chair, but he was unable to rest anywhere. As he could not help himself in the least, and was at times unable even to move, his sufferings, though they elicited no groan from himself caused his attendants to shed tears of compassion. "Lord," he would exclaim, "I thank thee for having given me some share in the sufferings Thou didst endure in Thy nerves when Thou wast nailed to the Cross. I wish to suffer, dear Jesus, as Thou pleasest, and as much as Thou pleasest, only give me patience. Here burn, here cut, but spare me for eternity. Poor damned souls, how can you suffer without merit! My Jesus Thou art my only hope, the sole remedy for all my ills!"

As death seemed to approach, he would cry out joyfully: "O how good it is to die fastened to the cross! The poor who love God die more content than the rich of this world." As he was tormented by want of sleep, he said: "I should like to have a little repose, but God does not will it; well, I am glad to dispense with this comfort." And casting his eyes on his poor bed, he exclaimed: "O my paliasse,[1] thou art worth more than all the thrones in the world!"

Terrible were his sufferings when the rheumatic or neuralgic affections to which he was a martyr settled in the vertebrae of the neck. His head bent over his chest to such an extent that, viewed from behind, he seemed almost headless. The beard pressed into the skin by the weight resting upon the chin, made a painful wound in the breast, and when the surgeons endeavored to raise the head, they were obliged to desist lest they might break his neck. By stretching him on a sofa, however, they were able to examine the wound but as it almost bared the bone, they had considerable difficulty in preventing mortification. During the remaining seventeen years of the saint's life, his head continued to rest on his chest, in which position his later pictures always represent him.

During this cruel malady his patience was superhuman: "Through a mass of pains," said Father Raphael, Provincial of the Alcantarins, "he never uttered the slightest complaint. A look towards heaven, a fervent aspiration — such were the signs of unusual suffering; but through all, he expressed himself so calmly that all present were confounded." A surgeon from Naples could not conceive how he suffered these terrific pains with unalterable serenity.

"Had I to endure such tortures," said he, "I should become frantic."

At last the saintly invalid was removed from the sofa to his poor bed. For nearly fifty days he remained almost immovable in the only position he could adopt, a position at once painful and uneasy. Through all this anguish, he verified the words of St. Augustine, that he who loves does not suffer. His obedience to the orders of physicians was remarkable. "Let us obey them," said he, "and then resign ourselves to die." He never showed the slightest repugnance to any remedy, however painful or disagreeable. One day he said to a doctor. "At my advanced age what can I hope for? I obey you that I may do God's will in doing yours."

---

[1] A thin mattress made of straw.

Our saint was not only serene but joyous, in his sufferings. A priest having asked how he passed the night, he laughingly replied: "I chase flies by day, and I catch spiders all night." To a canon he once pleasantly remarked: "People have called me a cripple so often that I am caught at last." "There," he exclaimed on another occasion, slightly raising his head, "that is the *ne plus ultra*, my head can do no more."

Despite his agonizing sufferings, he neglected none of his customary exercises. It was in his room that his household assembled every night to recite the rosary, the litany and other prayers. During a great part of the day, the Lives of the Saints were read to him by a priest or by Brother Anthony. The affairs of his diocese he administered with his ordinary diligence. He desired that every parish in it should receive the benefit of a mission this year, and entreated Father Villani and several heads of Congregations in Naples to send an extraordinary reinforcement of laborers into his vineyard.

"What astonished me most," said a canon, "was that he not only never ceased to watch and labor for the good of souls, but even extended his zeal beyond the limits of his own diocese." Having learned that a bishop had done something detrimental to the glory of God and the salvation of souls, he sent him a letter by an express to draw his attention to the error. "It is thus, my dear Benedict," he remarked to me, "that we are obliged to aid each other."

Amid these pains and labors, he prepared for the press that admirable work entitled THE PRACTICE OF THE LOVE OF JESUS CHRIST, in which he but lays bare the sentiments that inflamed his own great heart. Knowledge, piety, and ardent zeal and the special characteristics of this beautiful book, every page of which tells us to avoid sin, to love our dearest Lord, to refer all our actions to Him, with the superhuman eloquence and peculiar unction characteristic of the devotional works of our *Most Zealous Doctor.*

His convalescence was painful and tedious. He was obliged to walk about on crutches, supported by two persons, but reaped no particular benefit from this clumsy mode of taking exercise. On the 2nd of November 1768, he tells Father Villani, that he is still incapable of moving, but he adds: "However, my head is clear, and by God's grace, I am cheerful and resigned." He composed at this time a work against a writer in Naples who had attacked the authority of the Church and her immunities, but never published it, as Father Villani, on account of several circumstances, advised him not to have it printed. He published an excellent treatise ON THE CEREMONIES OF THE MASS, in which he clearly expounds all the rubrics to be observed, enlarges upon the defects most commonly committed in this respect, and urges upon all priests the absolute necessity of making the preparation and thanksgiving so august a mystery demands.

As his sufferings every day became more and more acute, he wrote a touching letter to the Sovereign Pontiff, begging to be released from the burden of the episcopate, yet as before, protesting that he would regard the will of the Pope as the will of God. This letter was forwarded in December 1768, but it is probable it never reached the hands of Clement XIII, who passed to a better life early in 1769.

CHAPTER LII.

The new Pope, Cardinal Ganganelli. — The Congregation persecuted in Sicily. Interesting Letter of the Saint. — His Moral Theology again attacked. Increased alarm of the saint regarding his houses in Sicily. — Incident. Letters. — The saint refuses to moderate his zeal. — Remarkable cure. Accidents. — "An old carriage, an old coachman, old horses, and an old Bishop." — Recreations. — He resumes the daily celebration of mass. Regularity and austerity of his life.

PENDING the election of a pope, the saint ordered all his priests to say daily the prayer *Pro eligendo summo Pontifice*, and he recommended all the persons who visited him to pray that God would grant a worthy pastor to his church. "After God," said he, "is the Pope. Without him, in what confusion should we not be! It is the Pope who makes known to us the will of God, and puts our consciences in peace."

When he heard that Cardinal Ganganelli was elected, he wrote him a congratulatory letter, in which he extols his learning, his piety and his zeal for our holy religion. He dedicated to the new Pope his great work on dogmatics, a compliment which Clement XIV appreciated so highly that he thanked the aged author in a special brief. It is a proverb that troubles never come singly. While our saint was nailed to his bed of pain, a violent persecution arose against his Fathers in Sicily, where they had been previously so much valued and honored that he had written more than once to the Superior: "This universal applause makes me tremble." But the Sicilian Missionaries could no longer complain of having no share of the cross. Their revenues were sequestered, their acts calumniated, their doctrines branded as heretical. "I have received the sad tidings you sent me," wrote the saint to Father Blasucci, "but no, nothing can be sad God wills. He wishes to mortify us, may His name be blessed forever! What I beg above all is, that you do not lose confidence in Jesus Christ. If turned out of your house, rent another. You must not yield too soon; on the contrary you must persevere until God shows you that he no longer wills you to be at Girgenti. At the worst, there will be fewer missions, but you will never want a morsel of bread. Wait and see what the deputies will do, what steps the new bishop will take; and, above all, what God's will may be. I am crippled from head to foot, but I bless God, and thank Him for having given me peace and patience."

As Alphonsus learned that his Moral Theology was attacked on this occasion, he wrote to all the bishops of Sicily in justification of his doctrine. He also represented the true state of things to the Marquis of Fogliani, Viceroy of Palermo, who in reply eulogized the virtues and learning of the great prelate.

This wound was not healed when a new misfortune increased his alarm regarding his children in Sicily. In the seminary of Mgr. Lanza, the new bishop, there was a wolf in sheep's clothing, whose blasphemous doctrines, secretly disseminated, compelled the good prelate to withdraw his faculties as confessor, and dismiss him. As Father Blasucci had been chosen by the bishop as his confessor and theologian, the degraded priest blamed him for his dismissal and vowed vengeance against the Congregation. Having gained several influential persons to his side, he presented himself at the royal junta of the viceroy and the president, declaring that he had been persecuted by the missionaries, because he had deemed it a duty to oppose the heresies they were promulgating, to the prejudice of souls.

Although Mgr. Lanza immediately undertook the defence of the Fathers, and gave the true character of their infamous calumniator, yet many who had heard the accusations, knew nothing of the refutation, and their dismissal from the island was confidently spoken of, to the dismay of many pious persons, who fasted, prayed, caused masses to be said, and gave abundant alms, that God might avert so great a calamity. Alphonsus urged the members of his Congregation to be humble and respectful towards all, to be patient and silent, and if the truth must be made known, to declare it, without injuring those who had shown such perfidy towards them. "I put all my confidence in God," he wrote, "He will protect us as He has always protected His Holy Church, persecuted throughout all ages. Let us act towards God as we ought, and He will comfort us." An "apology," written by Father Blasucci with spirit and energy, undeceived the royal ministers, and helped to produce a calm, but a treacherous calm, as we shall subsequently see. Our saint testified the most lively gratitude towards God, and wrote to his children; "We see that Jesus Christ has lovingly defended us against the efforts of hell. Thank Him, and thank Mary who has protected us in a special manner...I recommend to all the perfect observance of the rules. Remember that we are surrounded by enemies who wish to work our utter ruin — they will speedily succeed if our conduct is not what it ought to be. I pray God to protect with His omnipotent arm this mission so advantageous to souls."

" The prayers of Monsignore Liguori," said Father Drago, an eminent Oratorian, to the missionaries, "will protect the house at Girgenti. Have confidence. God will change your confusion into glory, and after these reverses, your Congregation will be more honored than ever in the Island of Sicily."

The saint meanwhile continued to work and pray as heretofore. "If it has been said of St. Jerome," remarked a venerable ecclesiastic who visited him, "that he triumphed over his maladies by reading and writing incessantly; if there is reason to marvel at the voluminous writings of St. Gregory who never enjoyed good health, the holy bishop of St. Agatha may well excite admiration in the highest degree, because of the numberless works he accomplished when in a worse state than even St. Jerome or St. Gregory endured."

Friends and admirers of the heroic old man besought Father Villani as his director to moderate his labors, but he mildly replied: "I do not think I ought to remain idle. I could employ myself in reading instead of dictating, but my head would gain nothing by that. When I have read for twenty minutes or half an hour, I can do no more. Besides I do not neglect my devotions. But there are many days which are entirely taken up with the affairs of my diocese, and while the visitation goes on I leave my writings to slumber. I enter into all these details with your reverence, that I may obtain your blessing."

On account of the unnatural curvature of the saint's neck, it was a martyrdom for him to eat, and nearly impossible to drink. It was only by means of a quill or pipe that he could imbibe liquid nourishment. One of the lay-brothers made him a wooden pipe, but it was found that silver alone — as a still more precious metal was not to be thought of, — could transmit hot drinks without splitting or rusting. A silversmith made him a silver pipe, but was obliged to pretend that it was of some less precious metal, as the saint would be horrified at the idea of using anything so costly. It pained him to be unable to visit his dear sick, though he procured zealous priests to supply his place, and sent them everything needful. Hearing that a poor cloistered nun had met with an accident that rendered her unable to leave her room, though she was still able to knit and sew, he assigned her a pension of five carlins a month. When Father Morgillo of the Pious Workmen broke his leg and endured dreadful sufferings for ten days from the unskilful manner in which the bone was reset, Alphonsus sent a servant to him with a little picture of the Blessed Virgin, telling him to have confidence, for Mary would obtain his cure. The sick man placed the picture on his face saying: "My Queen! by the merits of Bishop Liguori deliver me from this torture," and he was cured from that instant. Father Morgillo ever after honored the picture as a relic of the saintly prelate from whom he had received it.

The doctors seeing the body of the saint almost entirely paralyzed and his mind devoted to study, ordered that he should drive out daily. But this prescription did not please him. "The money a carriage and horses would cost me," said he, "ought to be employed in relieving the poor." Yet a poor carriage was procured which he was informed was a present from Don Hercules. The horses and harness were quite in keeping with the carriage; so that the wits of Arienzo sometimes amused themselves at his expense. "An old bishop," said they, "on old coachman, an old carriage, and old horses." His drives afforded him but little pleasure. If the wheels came in contact with a stone, it was torture to the invalid, whose head was, so to say, dislocated by every jolt.

Once the carriage was upset, and it seemed miraculous that the fall did not kill him. Brother Antony and the servant lifted him up, and some poor woman who perceived him, moved with compassion, lent him a chair. Frequently a shaft or something else broke, and he had to wait in the middle of the street till the damage was repaired. One of the horses had singular habits: after various contortions of his stubborn head, he would suddenly lie down, and refuse to get up again till he had been pulled by the ears for a long time. The incapacity of the poor coachman multiplied the accidents; either he did not see what was in the way, or else, did not know how to avoid obstructions, so he was sure to dash against something at almost every step. But the bishop, to whom these drives must have been anything but pleasure trips, never thought of changing coachman, carriage or horses.

Not to lose a moment, at the beginning of these charming recreations he would recite certain prayers, and then have a spiritual book read to him. He most frequently went to St. Mary de Vico, where he visited the Blessed Sacrament, and excited the people to devotion by a fervid exhortation. When helped back to the carriage, the reading was resumed, and the book was not closed till he reentered the palace court. Even in his bed, the watch was always before him, and he often prolonged his studies till midnight, especially in summer.

After some time he became scrupulous about the expenses of this elegant equipage, and wished all to be sold for the benefit of the poor; and this would certainly have been done despite the representations of the grand vicar and the doctors, had not Father Villani commanded him to desist.

For more than two years the saint was unable to celebrate mass, and this without doubt was the greatest privation he ever experienced. He was however daily present at mass and received Holy Communion from the officiating priest. One day, Father Marcorio an Augustinian came to invite him to preach in the church of St. Augustine, and the saint after having accepted the invitation, exclaimed: "Oh, if I could only celebrate mass in your church as well as preach, what a consolation it would be for me!" The Augustinian pitying his intense affliction, told him that necessity dispensed him from the less essential rubrics, and that by placing himself on a chair, he could easily partake of the sacred contents of the chalice. These words caused him the greatest joy, and he could not cease thanking the priest who had suggested such a happy expedient. From this time he said mass every day, and obtained permission from Rome to say the mass of the Blessed Virgin at all times.

As he was exact in observing the rubrics, he used to bend his knee until it touched the platform, which rendered his genuflections very painful, for he could not raise the knee again without aid, and when mass was over he was quite exhausted. But his devotion was so great that the seraphic ardors of his soul gleamed on his countenance. In thanksgiving he would hear the mass of his chaplain, and at the *Et incarnatus est* he always fell to the ground in humble adoration, as he did also at the consecration.

Such was the condition of our saint during the remainder of his episcopate. "His life was so austere and so regulated," says one of his Fathers, "that I suffered when sharing it with him at Arienzo, though I was then but thirty three years old. As for the bishop, notwithstanding his great infirmities, he never appeared to be fatigued."

CHAPTER LIII.

Ever increasing zeal of the saint. — The Seminary. — The Visitation of 1769. The saint does more than a hundred ordinary bishops. — He defends his Grand Vicar. — He is accused to the King. — Letter. — The saint defends his conduct. — Reply of the King. — The saint's conduct towards his calumniator. Absurdity of the charges preferred against the bishops.

W HILE overwhelmed with physical sufferings the saint never neglected the concerns of his diocese. He caused his bed to be placed in a room where all could come to him, and the door was open to every one, the only priveleged class being his priests and the poor. Every day he seemed to increase in solicitude; if he heard of any disorder, he knew no rest until he had concerted measures for its removal. "You see the state in which I am," he would say to his priests, "if you fail to inform me of disorders, you will be responsible for their evil results, and I myself will accuse you before the tribunal of God." "He took neither food nor rest," says his grand vicar, "until he saw the evil which was reported to him cut down to the roots, and when anything of this kind was in question, the only meal he took was supper."

His interest in his seminary rather increased than diminished. Several times a week he inquired concerning all that was done there, and when he received information detrimental to any Seminarian, he caused him to be reproved, and if this was not followed by amendment, the delinquent was expelled; so that the young men were more afraid of displeasing their bishop when he was a paralytic, unable to move from his bed than when he was up and well. He spared nothing that could conduce to the health, comfort and happiness of the pupils, but his vigilance over their morals and his severity towards candidates for ordination and for the faculties of confessors, redoubled in his latter years, because, as he said, he did not wish to give his successors occasion to weep over sin.

He opened in person the Visitation, on the 2nd of July 1769, in the collegiate church of Arienzo, being helped thither and supported by the servants. The audience were affected to tears on seeing and hearing him once more. He always manifested the greatest interest in these pastoral visitations, and considered them of paramount importance. As he was now unable to go to distant places, he delegated his grand vicar to act for him, to whom he especially recommended poor widows, and young girls whose indigence exposes them to danger.

He watched particularly over the regulations he had made for what may be called the externals of divine worship. When a church needed repairs, or had bad furniture, or soiled vestments, or was not kept with that neatness and regularity becoming to the house of God, he sometimes caused the money necessary for these purposes to be deducted from the revenue of the incumbent, but more frequently paid for all himself. As he was no longer able to conduct the spiritual exercises for priests and religious, he frequently assembled them in his palace, and for two or three days together instructed them on the duties of their state. Zeal was more than ever, if possible, his distinguished characteristic; he neglected nothing calculated to promote the spiritual advancement of his people. "A hundred bishops together," said Archdeacon Rainone, "would not have done what Mgr. Liguori did alone, notwithstanding all his infirmities."

It was rumored that if no one could reproach the invalid saint with anything, it was not the same with the grand vicar. Referring to this, in an animated manner, Alphonsus one day said smiling: "The Marquis Tanucci has said that I am a saint, and that my grand vicar is unjust: two fine lies! I am not a saint, and my grand Vicar is not unjust; he does nothing but by my orders."

But saint and wonderful saint as Alphonsus was — and wonderful especially in his sleepless zeal for the spiritual and temporal welfare of his flock, — he was never long without accusers and calumniators. A lawyer whose unjust pretensions he was unable to gratify, accused him to the king of despising his episcopal city and residing elsewhere, and of committing or countenancing several other grievous abuses. His Majesty transmitted to the saint the heads of the charges lodged against him, and this being a tacit command to justify or explain his conduct, the saint forwarded to the king a letter of which the following is a condensed translation:

"Sire,

"I have received with respect the dispatch sent by your Majesty, in which two causes of complaint are alleged against me: first, that I do not reside at St. Agatha; and secondly, that I confer prebends on strangers in preference to inhabitants of the town. I lived at St. Agatha for about five years from my entrance into the episcopate; but that city is very damp on account of the mountains that surround it, and I was compelled at last to seek a drier air because of the asthma to which I am subject, but I acted according to the physician's order. Arienzo is a portion of my diocese. My health has been benefited by the change, and I remain without scruple, as Pope Benedict XIV declares in his bull, 'Ubi primum,' that it is enough if bishops reside in their diocese."

The learned prelate proceeds to show at some length that in conferring benefices, and especially prebends, on the most worthy, he has acted in accordance with the fathers and the canons, and kept in view the will of the founders, the bishop being not the master but the distributor: having explained the office of the canons of a cathedral, he adds with energy:

"Such being the case, if the citizens of a cathedral town should always have the preference, over our more worthy diocesans, a common and a double injury will result to the whole diocese; for the diocesans will take less pains to advance in their studies, knowing that citizens will always be preferred to them; and the citizens will take little pains to become meritorious, knowing that they will always be preferred to more worthy diocesans; the chapters will be filled with ignorant men, and bishops must recur to strangers for advice.

"I have thus represented what I could touching this matter, conformably to your majesty's orders; I have now only to prostrate myself before your royal throne in expectation of your decision."

This erudite and reasonable letter fully satisfied the king, and the saint received a private as well as the official letter, in which he was told to continue to bestow benefices with perfect freedom, as he judged right before God.

The saint, as usual, showed great affection to his calumniator, and did him substantial service, to the great indignation of the citizens who ill-naturedly, if not ill-humoredly, remarked that in order to get into Mgr. Liguori's good graces, it was necessary to win his favor by loading him with injuries and ill-treatment.

But what complaints! The king must be appealed to, because a bishop gives offices to the most worthy; and because Alphonsus, a poor, bedridden invalid, resides at Arienzo by order of his physicians and directors! And Arienzo is but a pleasant walk — scarcely eight miles from St Agatha! The second charge is even more absurd than the first.

CHAPTER LIV.

The Count and Countess Liguori visit Alphonsus. — Prophecy.— The saint and his god-children. — Death of one of his nephews.— The bishop comforts the afflicted father. — Advice regarding the surviving children. — Their mother Lady Marianna loses her senses. — Circular Letter. — Tanucci. New Troubles in Sicily. — Apology of Alphonsus. — Maffei's expedient for regaining Popularity. — The Fathers leave Sicily. — Request of the people.

COUNT Hercules and the Lady Marianna came to Arienzo to visit the bishop just before the birth of their first child, which they earnestly hoped would be a boy. The saint gave his sister-in-law a little picture of the Blessed Virgin, saying: "You will give birth not to a boy but to a girl, and I should like you to call her Mary Teresa." A year or two later the parents of the little Mary Teresa followed the saint to Airola, to entreat him to pray God to give them a son. Alphonsus told his sister that God would grant the prayers, and presented her with two little pictures of St. Louis. Two pictures of the same saint seemed one too many, but the pious lady understood the mystery when shortly after God blessed her with twin sons. In the course of the following year, a third son was given her. The saintly uncle became sponsor to each of these children, and this office made him exact in seeing that they received a thorough Catholic education.

He frequently wrote to urge his brother to attend to the education of his children. He even composed a rule of life for them, and desired to be informed as to their progress in virtue and learning. "For the love of God," he wrote to his brother, "often call to mind the business of your eternal salvation, as I have frequently begged you to do. I am pleased to hear that my little god-children practice the devotions I have recommended for them; I hope they will be inclined to become saints."

Don Hercules was rejoiced at obtaining three sons from God in his old age, and as he thought he owed this favor to the prayers of his brother, he took the three to Arienzo to present them to their illustrious kinsman. "See, Alfonso," cried the infatuated father, "how beautiful they are! This is Alfonsino, and here are the twins, see how well they behave." His lordship looked at the twins earnestly, and said: "Would you not be very sad to lose one of these little ones?" "O heavens!" cried the old noble, "do you tell me that!" The saint had prophesied. Some months after, one of the twin-brothers died. The afflicted father came to the bishop for consolation. "Ah! my brother," said he, "say no more of the future of any children; your prophecies are too inauspicious." "Fear not," returned Alphonsus, "your boys, Joseph and Alfonsino, will live to grow old." The saint took great interest in the progress of these children. He explained to them their duties towards God and their parents, the hideousness of sin, how greatly bad conduct dishonors a Christian and a gentleman: above all he endeavored to inspire them with a tender devotion to Jesus and Mary. It was he himself who confirmed them, after having diligently instructed them. One of these nephews, then a venerable gray-haired man, supported the pendant of St. Alphonsus Liguori's banner, in the magnificent procession which commemorated our holy bishop's canonization by Pope Gregory XVI, 1839.

Count Hercules wishing to place his sons in the college for the young nobility, communicated his design to his brother, who wrote: "I cannot approve of your placing your sons in that college, because I have not a good opinion of it; besides, boys should not enter a college until they are at least ten or twelve; lest they should imbibe vice in their childhood, keep them with you. Later on, we shall see God's will regarding them. I should like them to be where they may become virtuous as well as learned."

In a subsequent letter he wrote: "Keep them under your own eyes. The malice of one pupil is enough to ruin a hundred. Have their spiritual good at heart, and Providence will take care to supply their temporal wants without detriment to their souls." The old father now became anxious to present his beautiful and idolized boys to the king, but their unworldly uncle would not hear of it. "If the king were to tell you he wished your sons to become cadets in the brigade or some other regiment, you would be obliged to make them cadets or soldiers, thereby risking their souls as well as their bodies." He goes on to express his fears that they will not be brought up properly and adds: "It is the love I bear towards you and your dear children which forces me to write in this manner."

The mother of these beautiful children became such a prey to scruples in 1768, that she partially lost her senses. This was a grievous affliction to her aged husband, and was deeply shared by our saint, who wrote to his poor brother in the tenderest strain, and endeavored to console him. He also wrote to Father Villani to have prayers offered in all the houses of the Congregation for the hapless wife and the bereaved husband. In view of the great age of Hercules, and the still greater age of his brothers Cajetan and Alphonsus, the latter prevailed on him to make his will and select suitable guardians for his children.

About this time he addressed to his Congregation a beautiful circular, in which he admonishes his brothers and sons of their faults, expatiates on the virtues they should strive to acquire, and insists on the perfect observance of the rules. However slight external faults might be, he would have them followed by penance. "Uncorrected faults," said he, "become established evils." Hearing that some clerics had relaxed in the observance of the rules, he sent them back to the novitiate to regain their fervor, nor would he ordain them till he was assured of their amendment. He had severe trials from some of his own Congregation. Two went so far as to answer his gentle remonstrances by defying him to his face, and saying they would remain in the house in spite of him. The old bishop was deeply grieved, but yet would not expel them, remarking that God would do it for him, which accordingly happened. Both asked their dispensation within the ensuing year. "I know," he wrote to the superior of Frossinone, "that the patience of a saint is necessary with some…but we must fulfil our duty, happen what may." And to Father Cajone, he wrote: "I beg your reverence to govern with all possible mildness, but be firm against attacks on the rules, for they do us more harm than all our persecutions. When you must correct, do it privately in the first place, and with charity, and treat every one with affability and kindness."

The enemies of his Congregation were active indeed. No sooner had he left Naples, than with a bravery common to calumniators, they again attacked his sons, and rather increased than diminished the former slanders. So violent were these opponents and so artfully did they gain the ear of the influential, that it was commonly thought that the Congregation of the Most Holy Redeemer would be suppressed, and the most sanguine did not expect that it would survive its founder. He strove to re-animate his desponding children. "This Congregation does not come from me," said he, "it is in no sense dependant on my existence. God, whose work it is, and who has preserved it for two and forty years, will continue to maintain it...Our stability depends first on Him, and next on our own good conduct. Let us then be careful to unite ourselves to God, to observe our rules, and be charitable towards all; above all let us be humble, for pride can destroy us, as it has destroyed other societies."

But the Fathers did not share his confidence. Villani and other Fathers besought him with tears to repair again to Naples. Perceiving by the earnestness of their supplications that they looked forward with fear and trembling to the speedy death of their founder, he bade them not be alarmed, for that he was not to die yet.

Maffei now applied to the Prime Minister Tanucci, who certainly had proved himself no great friend to the Congregation. New slanders varied the old ones, and affairs began to assume a worse aspect than ever. It was no great feat to gain Tanucci to the wrong side, for he was rarely on the right in religious matters. This worthy prototype of the robber ministers, who act for the robber kings of to-day, was of obscure birth; he governed the two Sicilies for nearly half a century, hated by the people and despised by the nobility, during which period, besides innumerable other acts equally edifying, he suppressed seventy eight monasteries, and showed himself on all occasions the implacable enemy of the Sovereign Pontiff, and indeed of every worthy and zealous prelate and priest with whom he came in contact. He pursued the Jesuits with unrelenting hatred, and when he had annihilated the Society of Jesus in the Neapolitan dominions, he endeavored to persuade the king that the Redemptorists were but a reproduction of the Society of Jesus, and deserved a like fate. But the saintliness of Alphonsus had gained him friends and protectors in the highest circles, and the upstart minister was happily over-matched by the saint. The holy founder never wavered in his trust in God. "Let us act as we ought towards God," said he, "and He will aid us, for

God can do more than man. Let us recur to prayer; innocence and prayer are all powerful with God."

To his children in Sicily he addressed a consoling letter, bidding them however, prepare for new trials. He was suffering so much with his limbs when he wrote it, that he signed it "Brother Alphonsus Mary, the cripple." His forebodings were prophecies. Their adversaries in that island renewed their attacks daily with ever increasing malignity. Their settlement in Girgenti, their doctrine, their morality, — all were grossly misrepresented. Alphonsus was obliged to justify himself and his sons in an eloquent apology; Father Peter Blasucci made similar representations to the supreme junta at Palermo, protesting, with the energy of truth, that both he and his Fathers followed, whether in morals or in dogma, the system most conformable to the spirit of the Gospel and the teachings of the Catholic Church.

The minister sent a kind reply to the aged bishop, and the slanders of their arch enemy, Canella, were crushed for the time. But Maffei had prepared another snare. All Illiceto, except the poor, aided him in endeavoring to compass his ends. This proud, turbulent noble was always at war with the populace, and he now hit upon the bright expedient of making friends with the Fathers, that they might become mediators between him and the common people, with whom, he found it rather inconvenient to be at variance. The friends of the Congregation approved greatly of this project, but Alphonsus saw deeper than the lawyers who undertook to befriend him. When Father Villani informed him of the proposal, he gave a decided negative. "It would only," said he with his usual acuteness, "it would only alienate the people from us, without effecting our reconciliation with Maffei, — If our Father Fiocchi spoke in favor of Maffei, they would believe we spoke not because he is right, but to win his friendship. Now everything leads me to believe that right is not on the side of Maffei, but on the side of the poor people whom he oppresses. It would therefore be difficult for Father Fiocchi to say anything in favor of that man without wounding justice...I am therefore decidedly of opinion, that no member of the Congregation should accept the office of mediator, on any terms whatever." This decision greatly disconcerted the turbulent baron, who now explained his difficulties with the people, by representing the missionaries as the instigators of the disaffection they showed towards him.

Meanwhile the situation of the missionaries in Sicily became so precarious that the holy founder recalled them. "If God wishes us to be there," said he, "He will know how to procure our return, and then we can go back blessing God and the king." This was a source of the most lively anguish to the pious Monsignor Lanza: "You shall return here again," said he, "in spite of hell. Were it necessary to sell my mitre and cross for this end, I would not hesitate to sell them, for God, for you, and for your work." The chevaliers, magistrates, nobles and ladies of high rank sharing the sentiments of their worthy bishop, petitioned the king to obtain the return of the Fathers. Although they departed secretly in the night, multitudes accompanied them to the shore, bewailing the loss they were about to sustain. The clergy and religious orders, without exception, addressed the king and the holy founder, imploring the return of their dear Fathers. Alphonsus was deeply affected at this touching testimony of the love and esteem his sons had inspired, and promised to yield to their wishes, as soon as the storm then raging should have passed away; a promise which he religiously fulfilled a little later.

CHAPTER LV.

Clement XIV refuses to accept the saint's resignation. — Prophecy. — Circular letter. — New literary labors. — Foundations. — Gratitude of the saints. Letters. — Work on the Psalms. — Criticisms. — Persecutions. — Revolution. His grief at the suppression of the Jesuits. — He regards it as temporary. His sympathy for the Pope. — He assists at his death bed. — Bilocation proved. The saint requested to write the qualifications necessary in the future Pope. He complies.

T HE SAINT imagining that his infirmities rendered him all but useless to his Church, and hoping, that though unfit for episcopal functions, he could still aid his Congregation, again petitioned to be released from the burden of the episcopate, at the same time resigning his will entirely to that of his holiness. Clement XIV, aware of the good he still effected, encouraged him to continue the administration; and when Cardinal Castelli solicited him to consider the great age of the saintly prelate and release him, his holiness replied: "It suffices that he governs his diocese from his bed." "But he is not able to make his visitations," objected the cardinal. "One prayer addressed to God from his bed of sickness is worth more than a hundred visitations," was the reply of the Pope. "The voice of the Pope is the voice of God," said Alphonsus, "I am now content to die under my cross." Several bishops and missionaries counselled him to give in a formal resignation; seeing him crippled with rheumatism, suffering the most excruciating tortures in every joint, his head so bowed upon his breast, that viewed from behind he seemed headless, they thought that mercy itself demanded his release. These venerable men laughed heartily when the paralytic cheerfully replied: "This Pope is firm; if I gave him my resignation he would not accept it, let us have patience and wait for his successor." Ganganelli was not then sixty, and was of a robust constitution and vigorous frame. He was seventeen years younger than Alphonsus; yet the words of the saint were prophetic; this celebrated Pope died two years after, 1774, and the bishop lingered thirteen years longer (1787), not however without obtaining his demission from the next pontiff, Pius VI.

Our saint being entirely incapacitated from visiting his dear children of the Congregation now addressed them a beautiful circular, in which, having as usual exhorted them to a more fervent observance of rule in order to merit the favor and assistance of God, he adds pathetically: "I can do no more; I, who am decrepit, bedridden and paralyzed. It is you, my beloved children, who must sustain the Congregation, and be assured that if we only act as we ought, God will always assist us, and the more poor and despised and persecuted we are, the more good we shall do, and the greater will be the reward which Jesus Christ will reserve for us in heaven."

But our saint could do much more than he admitted. Within a short interval, he published three valuable works called forth by the exigencies of the times; viz, "Reflections on Divers Spiritual Subjects," his book "On the Truth of Faith," and his long and learned dissertation entitled "Reflections on the Truth of divine Revelation, against the Deists." "If the enemies of our religion," said he, "are never satisfied, although they publish thousands of books against it, why should the friends of religion grow weary of defending it?"

Close upon the above works followed his "Triumph of the Church" in which he warmly defends the infallibility of the pope and his preeminence in the Church; and his "Sermons." In the appendix to the latter we find his most useful "Letter to a student deliberating as to choosing a state in life;" also a second and a third letter, in which respectively he treats of the great utility of missions, and of the manner of preaching with apostolic simplicity.

His next was that precious little book "On the True Happiness of Man, and on His Submission to the Will of God." This was said to have been inspired rather than composed. A pious person was so moved by the benefit he derived from it, that, in gratitude to God, and desirous that others should participate in this favor, he caused it to be gratuitously distributed every where.

Amid all these labors and troubles, God willed that Alphonsus should have the comfort of seeing his Congregation make two new foundations in the States of the Church. The first occasioned the second. In the course of their missions, Father Francis de Paul, superior of the new house, and another Father, visited the celebrated Trappist Abbey of Casamari. The virtues of these Fathers gained the affection and esteem of their hosts, and a plan was concerted between both parties for establishing a Redemptorist Convent in the neighborhood. A priest of Avignon had recently built a church for the peasants of the neglected hamlets of Scifelli, Candi, and St. Francis, and had just added a commodious dwelling for such priests as he hoped would join him. However, the bishop of Veroli coveted the services of this holy man, and named him his grand vicar.

When Alphonsus heard of the spiritual destitution of the poor laborers who formed the population of these villages, he shed tears of compassion, and instantly resolved to send his missionaries among them. "I have consented to let this foundation be made," he wrote to Father Francis de Paul, May 28th. 1773. "I have written to thank the Abbé Arnaud for it; it is to him we are indebted for all concerning it." Abbé Arnaud, the priest above alluded to, willingly bestowed on the missionaries the spacious house he had built, and Alphonsus was anxious that so particular a benefactor should be most graciously treated by his missionaries. Nothing is more remarkable in the Lives of the Saints, than the gratitude they evince towards benefactors. "Take care," wrote he to the new rector, "not to displease him in things not absolutely contrary to the good order of the house, for we owe him every thing. Divers things must be yielded for the sake of peace and conscience.

"Let him see that you esteem him, and listen to his opinions as far as possible...Nevertheless I advise you to keep up the observance of rule from the beginning, and this I beg of you for the love of God and your neighbor." In another letter he says: "I trust to your prudence not to do anything to pain Mr. Arnaud, and that all the fathers and brothers will maintain strict observance of rule."

The new house was extremely poor. Alphonsus did not fail to assist it; not however, with the revenues of his diocese, but with the pension he received from the College of Doctors in Naples.

"Tell the subjects in my name," he wrote to the superior, "to remember that this foundation is new, and in another kingdom. In all new foundations there is much to be suffered, both on account of poverty, and also because one has to deal with people whom one does not know." But hearing that the superior had purchased some books while his subjects suffered for want of neccessaries, he was much distressed and wrote to him: "Is this a time to buy books when your children have not enough to eat? Really, I can hardly believe it. See if those books cannot be sent back, even at some loss."

Father Francis was very much displeased that the missions should be interrupted, because the Bishop of Veroli wished to have the missionaries with him in his pastoral visitations, but Alphonsus wrote to him as follows: "By making the visitation with the bishop you may do much good, for you can remain long enough in each place to give at least a *triduo*, and also some little mission where there has not yet been one. Arrange these matters with the bishop, whom we are bound to obey next to the rule."

God blessed the labors of the Fathers in these parts most abundantly. " I cannot help giving thanks to God," wrote the saint to Father Francis de Paul, "for having given me so many consolations in my old age. Praised forever be Jesus and Mary."

Early in 1774, Alphonsus made a translation or rather a paraphrase of the psalms into the vernacular, which he dedicated to the reigning pontiff; Clement XIV. This work was so highly esteemed that Benedict Cervone who subsequently became bishop of Aquila said: "Had the saintly bishop of St. Agatha written nothing else in support of religion and the Church, this work alone would suffice to render him worthy of immortality." The learned Canon Massa, passed a high eulogium on Alphonsus for having given to the faithful this greatly needed work. He extols his piety, wisdom and indefatigable zeal, which neither infirmities, nor age, nor the labors of his administration could slacken. "He explains the meaning of the psalms," says he, "and the obscure passages in them so skilfully, that, without detracting from the purity of the inspired word, he aids the minds and hearts of those who read it." In the same year, he published his "Triumphs of the Martyrs," the object of which was to kindle in all hearts a greater love for Jesus Christ and a greater zeal for that faith for which the martyrs so cheerfully gave their lives. By this, as Cervone said, he showed himself "full of solicitude for the grand affair of salvation, omitting nothing that could open or facilitate the road to the celestial country."

Meanwhile Baron Sarnelli and Don Maffei renewed with ever increasing venom their malignant attacks. Broken down by years, labors and infirmities, as the old bishop was, the spirit of the lawyer rose up within him, and he himself arranged a plan of defence and placed it in the hands of the advocate Celano. However he was very uneasy as to the result. "I have caused prayers to be said everywhere," he wrote, "and masses to be celebrated...Get the people to say an Ave *before* the sermon, and procure prayers in as many monasteries as you can." To Father Majone, he wrote: "When the ministers are spoken to, the Congregation must not be named; I only should be spoken of, since I am the person principally aimed at in this affair." He addressed all the prominent ministers and lawyers, and in an eloquent memorial to the king, he represented the innocence of his missionaries, the labors they daily underwent for the welfare of the kingdom, and their respectful submission to all the royal decisions. In a lengthy circular to all his houses, he exhorts his beloved brothers and children to increased fervor in virtue and regular observance, as the best means of securing the divine protection to the congregation. "I am sure," he added, "that God loves our little Congregation as the apple of His eye; for we see that He never ceases to protect us amid so many persecutions, and to render us more worthy of laboring for His glory in divers countries, by the assistance of His manifest graces. I shall not see it for my death is at hand, but I know that our little flock will increase more and more, and that, through our labors, Jesus Christ will be better known and loved. We shall one day meet again; we shall be re-united in our heavenly home never more to be separated. We shall meet there, in the enjoyment of eternal happiness, hundreds of thousands who once lived without the love of God, but who, through us, recovered His grace, and will form our glory and our joy for all eternity. Should not this thought alone stimulate our fervor and make us love Jesus Christ and draw others to love him?"

His biographer regards as certain that the saint had been favored with some special revelation on this subject which his humility made him conceal, for the same year he wrote to Father

Majone: "I am full of joy, for it seems to me that the Blessed Virgin will bring us safe and sound out of this tempest. Therefore let us abandon ourselves into the hands of Jesus Christ; let us pray to Him, and He will turn all to His greater glory."

Our great bishop who may be said to have carried the whole Church in his bosom, could not see scandal or disorder anywhere, without being, as the apostle said of himself, on fire. During the stormy pontificate of Clement XIV, his heart was torn by the troubles that disquieted the Church, and he continually offered up prayers to God for the hapless pontiff and his persecuted flock. What particularly distressed him was that most of the crowned heads of Europe, to their eternal shame be it recorded, incited by Jansenist or infidel influence, insisted on the suppression of the world-renowned Society of Jesus. "No one," says his friend and biographer Tannoia, "can imagine how he sorrowed over the storm that raged against the Jesuits; he never spoke of it without feelings of the deepest distress."

"It is nothing but intrigue on the part of the Jansenists and the unbelieving," said the saint; "if they succeed in overthrowing the company, their wishes will be accomplished, but if this bulwark falls, what convulsions will there not be in Church and State! The loss of the Jesuits will place the Pope and the Church in a most disastrous situation; the Jansenists aim at them, because through them they will be the more certain of striking at Church and State."

Such were the fears and sentiments of St. Alphonsus, but the judgments of God are impenetrable! Clement XIV suppressed the Society of Jesus, by a brief dated July 22, 1773. When the aged bishop heard this, he felt as though a thunderbolt had been hurled against him. It may well be believed that of the thousands of Jesuits which this brief disbanded, not one felt the blow more keenly than Alphonsus. Respect for the pontifical judgment closed his mouth, but the unspeakable anguish of his heart was plainly depicted on his venerable countenance. When he received the brief, he adored in silence the judgments of God, and then said: "The will of the Pope is the will of God." One day the grand vicar and other persons of distinction appeared to cast blame on the dispositions of the Pope: "Poor Pope," he exclaimed, "what could he have done in such delicate circumstances, when so many monarchs demanded their suppression. As for us, we have only to adore the secret judgment of God, and remain in peace." Yet he seems to have regarded the suppression as merely temporary: "I assert," said he with unusual energy, "that if but a single Jesuit be left in the world, he alone will be sufficient to re-establish the Society."

After this sad concession, made to worthless sovereigns, on the principle that the peace of the Universal Church required the sacrifice, troubles accumulated upon the unfortunate pontiff. "Pray for the Pope," wrote Alphonsus, "he is overwhelmed with sadness, and not causelessly, for there seems not to be a shadow of peace for the Church. Pray for the Pope; God alone knows how I feel his afflictions. I have heard that he wishes for death, so great is his distress at the trials which afflict the Church. I pray that God may come to his aid." In another letter we find this passage: "I hear from various quarters that the Pope is in sorrow, that he is shut up and does no business. Let us beseech God to deliver him from this profound melancholy."

On the morning of September 21. 1774 Alphonsus immediately after mass threw himself into his arm-chair, in which he remained all that day and all the following night perfectly motionless, and without articulating a single word. The servants not knowing what this portended, remained all night at the door without daring to enter. Later in the day, he appeared to awake, and rang the bell to announce that he was about to celebrate mass. At this signal, his whole household surrounded him, and Alphonsus with an air of surprise asked what was the matter. "You have neither eaten nor spoken for two days," they replied, "and you ceased to give any signs of life." "That is true," said he, "but you do not know that I have been with the Pope who has just died." Tidings soon reached the town that Clement XIV had passed to a better life, September 22, at eight in the morning, the very moment in which Alphonsus had come to himself. The advocate of the cause of our saint has ably demonstrated that this prolonged repose, or apparent stupor, was a continual ecstacy, "an admirable favor which God accorded to our saint and to the dying pontiff."

Cardinal Castelli aware of the high reputation of Alphonsus for sanctity and the veneration with which the sacred college regarded him, asked him to write a long letter on the abuses which ought to be rectified in the various orders of the ecclesiastical hierarchy. The cardinal wished this memorial to be presented to the Conclave; hoping that it would be of use in causing a pope to be elected capable of remedying all the ills of the Church. Such a request covered the humble prelate with confusion, but, urged by the friends who were commissioned to use their influence with him, he invoked the light of the Holy Ghost, and complied, in the following form:

"MOST REVEREND CARDINAL: — You ask my sentiments on the present state of the Church and the election of a pope, but what sentiments can a miserable creature such as I am express? All I can say is that it is necessary to pray, and to pray much; for in order to raise the Church from the remissness and confusion which, alas! are but too prevalent, prudence and human wisdom are insufficient; nothing short of the powerful arm of God will suffice. Few bishops have true zeal for the salvation of souls. Most religious communities are relaxed; observances are neglected and rules despised.

"The situation of the secular clergy is still worse; therefore an absolute reform is necessary among ecclesiastics that they may afterwards be able to reform the conduct of the laity; we must then pray to Jesus Christ to give His Church a head containing something more than knowledge and human prudence; to give her, in short, a pontiff who through the spirit of God may be filled with zeal for His glory, and totally detached from all parties so as to be able to resist the suggestions of human respect. If we have the misfortune to have a pope who has not God's glory in view, we shall receive but little aid from heaven, and things will become worse.

"Prayer is the sole remedy for such great misfortunes. Hence I have not only enjoined on my little congregation to pray with more than ordinary fervor for the election of a Supreme Pontiff, I have also ordered all the regular and secular clergy of my diocese to say during mass the Collect, *Pro eligendo Summo Pontifice.* I pray frequently during the day about this election, but what can my poor prayers avail? Nevertheless, I put all my trust in the merits of Jesus Christ and of the Blessed Virgin, and I hope that God will comfort me, by permitting me to see the Church relieved before my death, which my age and infirmities admonish me cannot be far distant.

318

"I desire also to see all reigning disorders reformed, and a thousand ideas on this subject come into my head, which I should ardently wish to communicate to you, if the knowledge of what I am did not take away all boldness, by convincing me that it is not for me to pretend to reform the world. I desire that the future pope, when he has vacancies to supply in the Sacred College, would select only the best informed and most zealous among those proposed, and that he would request all princes not to present any but men of well known learning and piety as candidates for the cardinalate.

"I wish also that he should exercise unalterable firmness in refusing livings to those who are already sufficiently provided for, repress luxury in prelates, and fix the number of their servants. This would help to put a stop to the slander and detraction of our enemies. He should also endeavor never to confer benefices on any but those who have merited well by their labors for the Church.

"I should wish him to be very strict in choosing bishops, and to obtain information at all hands about those proposed for this high and important office, and be certain as to the goodness of their character and doctrine, which are indispensable qualities in ruling over a diocese. It is on these chief pastors that the good of religion and the salvation of souls chiefly depend. I should like him to require metropolitans and others to inform him in secret as to any bishops who are careless about the welfare of their flocks; also to threaten with suspension or the supervision of a vicar apostolic, both negligent bishops and those who are non-resident, as well as those who scandalize the world by the luxury of their attendants and the excessive expense of their equipage, festivities, &c. In some cases it does not do to be afraid of putting these threats into execution; corrections purify the Church from the corruptions that sully her, and restrain other bishops through fear of public blame, which admonishes them of their back-slidings, and causes them to return to a sense of their duty, to the great advantage of their flocks.

"In fine, why should the future pope be too lenient in granting favors injurious to the maintainance of discipline, such for instance, as permitting nuns to leave their enclosure without any real necessity? He should not readily consent to the secularization of religious, on account of the evils which result from it; and above all he should recall all religious to the primitive observance of the rules of their institute, at least on all important points.

"I will not try your patience any longer; I can do nothing further, save to beseech God to give us a pontiff full of His own spirit. Accept the sentiments of profound respect with which I have the honor to remain," &c., &c.

CHAPTER LVI.

Calumnies against Alphonsus. — His Moral Theology censured and defended. Violent persecutions. — He refuses to go to Naples. — He prescribes means of obtaining the Divine Mercy. — He refuses to seek the mediation of a lady. Some gleams of sunshine. — Good Bishop Lanza. — The saint's administration. — Examples. — Testimony of Tannoia. — Extraordinary sweetness of the saint. — His zeal to prevent the slightest faults in priests. His surveillance extends beyond his own diocese. — The regulars.— Vigilance over the laity. — Anecdote.

U P TO THIS time the enemies of the Congregation had spared its head; the veneration inspired by his name caused them to leave him in peace even while they persecuted his cherished children. But seeing that they could not injure the members while they evinced respect for their head, they now turned their weapons against him. As his private life was not only blameless but saintly, they attacked his doctrine, and published every where that his *Moral Theology* was not only too indulgent, but contained all the lax principles attributed to the Jesuits, the mere word *Jesuit* being sufficient, then as now, to rouse the worst passions of the impious.

The book was no sooner denounced than the Congregation shared its fate. But God caused it to be approved at the very time its adversaries expected its condemnation. Some copies were sent from Naples and had reached the custom house, when they were stopped by the king's procurator-general who was prejudiced against the work, and wished it to be examined with utmost strictness by Father Majone, a Conventualist. This learned religious assured him that the doctrine was perfectly sound, and that there was no proposition in the book deserving of censure — a judgment since repeated by the highest earthly tribunal. "Well," exclaimed the officer, "what atrocious calumnies have been spread! I am delighted and rejoiced at this news, for I should grieve to be obliged to pain this saintly old man." Thus did heaven frustrate the plots of the wicked and turn them to the glory of the servant of God.

But the enemies of the Congregation were still active. The suppression of the Jesuits caused ancient and distinguished orders to tremble; how much more those which as yet had scarcely taken root. Maffei and Samelli were as powerful and as inveterate as heretofore; they redoubled their attacks, leaving nothing undone to compass the ruin of missionaries who had done them all manner of good, and never, even under extraordinary provocation, done them the slightest injury. Even Alphonsus, who heretofore was full of courage, now trembled, as though God had withdrawn the powerful grace that had hitherto sustained him. The Fathers themselves considered matters all but desperate. All, especially Father Villani, besought him to go to Naples and cast himself at the feet of the king. The old man thought of his shrunken figure, his paralyzed limbs, his bowed head, his wasted frame, and said smiling: "What a figure I should cut before the king as I now am! Would he not mistake me for a phantom, and order me out of his presence? My brothers, let us place ourselves in God's hands, and distrust human means; for the Congregation is a divine work, not the work of man, nor is man capable of upholding it."

Alphonsus did not neglect any means of obtaining the divine mercy. Besides the customary penances and mortifications, masses and prayers were obtained, and the Blessed Sacrament exposed in all the houses. The psalm *Qui habitat* was recited in common, followed by an *Ave* for the persecutors.

Other causes of anxiety arose, too tedious to dwell upon. As the Congregation was in imminent danger of ruin, Alphonsus was advised to gain the patronage of a lady who was very influential in a certain high quarter, but with his usual dread of sin or its occasions, he would not entertain such a proposal. "Never," wrote he to Father Majone; "let the Congregation be destroyed rather than become the occasion of even the shadow of sin or scandal to any one."

Amid these incessant tempests, the aged prelate enjoyed some gleams of sunshine. In April 1775, the house at Girgenti was resumed in a manner honorable to the missionaries and their sainted Founder. The clergy and people testified the most lively joy at seeing them once more. The good Bishop Lanza was so deeply affected that he could not forbear exclaiming with holy Simeon: "Now dost Thou dismiss thy servant, O Lord, according to Thy word in peace; for mine eyes have seen Thy salvation." And indeed he might well have adopted these beautiful words, for he fell asleep in our Lord, in the arms of his tenderly loved missionaries, but a few weeks after their return. His successor Cardinal Branciforti was equally devoted to the Congregation.

As we have now almost reached the term of our saint's glorious episcopate, we shall here add some details of his mode of administration, which will serve to magnify our ideas of his wonderful zeal as chief pastor.

Alphonsus had so high a standard for the ecclesiastical state that he wished sanctity to shine brightly in all who embraced it. The clergy were the dearest and most valued portion of his flock. What did he not do to banish vice from among them, employing for their amendment, now sweetness, again severity, but always with the most admirable prudence! Father Caputo thus describes the methods used by the holy bishop to draw them to God: "His lordship's first reproof was full of sweetness and humility, if no improvement followed, he gave a second reprimand of mingled sweetness and severity. If he found that the delinquent was incorrigible, chastisement followed," irrespective of the rank, talent, or position of the culprit.

Drunkenness and incontinence were the vices he specially abhorred. He said that we can expect more from a brute than from a drunkard; as to the other vice, homicide in his eyes was no worse. When he saw ecclesiastics in danger, or who through weakness had made a false step, his principal remedy was a retreat; but if things went farther, he used the strongest method for eradicating the evil. One day, having placed a large crucifix across the doorway, he sent for a person who had grievously offended. Having arrived, the wretched man seized with sudden terror drew back: "Enter," said the holy bishop, "trample the crucifix under foot; perhaps it will not be the first time." He then gave free vent to his zeal, and with burning words set forth the enormity of the crimes, which he held in such abhorrence. The culprit wept bitterly, and solemnly promised to change his life. He not only kept his word, but for the rest of his days was a model of edification.

Mild measures were not always successful, and when they were exhausted, the zealous bishop imposed exile to remove the sinner from the occasion of sin, and suspension to avenge the dignity of the sacred ministry. He even had recourse to the king and the pope, in short he left no method untried to root out vice of every kind. One day he said to Don Nicholas Rannucci of Naples: "If a priest falls from grace, I must render an account of it;" and as this good priest tried to tranquillize him, he repeated in an agitated tone: "It is I, my dear Nicholas, and no one else, who must account for it to God."

Sometimes the saint exiled culprits for six, or even ten years, sometimes he imprisoned them. There was one who, after many paternal warnings and remonstrances, relapsed into sin. He was shut up in the prison of St. Agatha, but did not amend: "Let him alone," said the saint to his vicar, "God's justice will reach him;" and in fact, he shortly after died suddenly. Sometimes he merely sent such persons to some religious house; mercy always tempered his justice, and however degraded the erring man might be, he invariably allowed him from his own poor resources, sufficient for his maintainance. In one instance, as the sin had been public he determined to inflict such a punishment as would strike terror into all evil doers. "Who can keep the keeper?" he exclaimed with holy indignation. The miserable culprit became alarmed, and knowing the goodness of the old saint's heart, went to him, like another prodigal son, and obtained the forgiveness he so earnestly implored. The example of this true penitent, was such in after life, as to produce the most salutary effects upon all with whom he came in contact.

While giving a mission at Arienzo, he was informed that an ecclesiastic had entered a dangerous house. He immediately had him seized and brought into his presence. Indeed his severity or rather his unsleeping vigilance was so well known throughout the diocese, that there was no chance of rest for a dissolute man, but to give clear proofs of amendment. Yet for one whose angelic soul so utterly abhorred the shadow of vice, who had never sullied, even by the least wilful thought, the delicate lily of his purity, his mercy to these unhappy people was surprising. A priest who had been summoned to St. Agatha was sentenced by the chapter to pay a fine of four ducats. His lordship no sooner understood that he was poor than he gave him twenty carlins, merely telling him to give the balance in charity. To a priest who disapproved of his lenity on this occasion, he said: "We must punish the guilty, but they should be dismissed with mildness the better to correct them." If he found it necessary to remove a priest for a time from his missions, he would always support him at his own expense.

When he had evidence of certain faults in priests, he not only suspended them as confessors, but forbade them to celebrate the holy sacrifice. His severity, however, was only for the incorrigible. To one who complained of the rigor with which he was treated, the saint said with touching sweetness: "My son, do you think I have acted through anger? Have not you yourself constrained me? Amend, and I will gladly give my life blood for you." "He had," says Tannoia, "a most admirable charity for those who really amended; he received them to his heart with all the tenderness of a father, and forgetting their misconduct, never again alluded to the sorrow they had caused him.

An ecclesiastic, belonging to a noble and distinguished family, who lived in a most disedifying manner, was sent for by the saint three times but never deigned a reply. The prelate told his vicar to make out a cause against the nobleman, and left orders that if he called he was to be sent to the vicar. The delinquent hearing this and fearing lest his name might figure in the public records, hastened to the palace. Being refused admittance to the saint's room, he created a great disturbance in the ante-chamber, so that the invalid was obliged to send for his secretary to learn the cause of the commotion. The "cause" followed the official, and Alphonsus seeing him enter, immediately referred him to the vicar. But the poor man fell on his knees at the foot of the bed, saying: "I do not know the Vicar Rubini, but I acknowledge Monsignor Liguori for my father." At these words, the servant of God became deeply affected: "My son," he said, "I sent for you and you would not come; I was obliged to place you in the arms of justice; you know the scandal you have given." Ashamed and confused, the delinquent now truly contrite, confessed his sin with bitter tears upon the spot, adding: "This is my confession; now do with me what you will." "Since you acknowledge your fault," said the man of God, with the greatest sweetness, "and confess the truth to me, I leave you to choose your penance." So much goodness completely unmanned the penitent; he answered with sobs: "I choose the house of San

Angelo for my place of retirement, and never will I depart from it till God tells me he has forgiven me." Seeing that his repentance was sincere, his lordship took the papers which had been prepared against him whether as indictment or proof, and tearing them in pieces, said: "My son, may God do the same in heaven." Fathers Caputo, Ferrara and Crisci who were present, were filled with admiration at such excessive charity. It is pleasant to add that the priest who was the object of it became a model of edification in the diocese.

In his eyes the slightest fault was a considerable sin when there was question of a priest. Thus he severely reprimanded an ecclesiastic who went into a public square dressed in a slovenly manner. Another who had taken part in a play, relying on the protection of the prince in whose palace the play was performed, was suspended for fifteen days and ordered during that period to refrain from saying mass, and remain in the strictest retirement. His surveillance extended over those portions of other dioceses that touched his own; as soon as anything disedifying happened, Monsignor Liguori knew all about it; sometimes he knew all without any visible means of finding things out, so that certain culprits once exclaimed: "It is either an angel or a devil that betrays us, and tells him everything." By this constant vigilance, and his extraordinary prudence and charity, Bishop Liguori worked the complete reformation of his diocese.

With the regulars, he was still more severe. "Edifying religious," said he, "are a consolation to bishops and priests, but if religious are imperfect, they are a burden to their bishops and a misfortune to the people." He spared no pains to convert irregular subjects: "For," he remarked, "if they are not cured, their malady will be communicated to others; it is with them as with fruits — the bad spoil the good by contact, and to avoid the loss of all, the bad must be thrown away." Besides private reprehensions, he called in the aid of their superiors and provincials, and if speedy amendment did not follow, he insisted on their being sent elsewhere. To one who neglected the poor, to visit families of rank, he said, after withdrawing his faculties for hearing confessions, "How can you feed the flocks of others, who allow your own to be ravaged with impunity?" If application to the superiors or provincial failed to succeed, he appealed, and never in vain, to the general of the order. In one year alone (1768) he compelled as many as fifty two to leave his diocese, "I can truly say, that during his lordship's time the monasteries of the diocese were so many gardens where all breathed forth the sweet odors of innocence and virtue." Such is the testimony of his grand vicar, Rubini, witness, and sometimes minister, of his zeal.

But the servant of God held in particular esteem and affection religious who walked worthy of their high calling. He appointed them examiners, confided to them the care of many convents; often sent them to preach the lenten sermons, consulted them on knotty questions, and liberally rewarded their merit. He took particular pleasure in assisting and befriending these worthy priests in every possible way.

The laity were almost as strictly watched over as the clergy, especially if their irregularities were of a nature injurious to public morality. "I am not merely the shepherd of priests and religious," said the saint, "a bishop's flock includes all classes; God has confided all these souls to us and we must render Him an account of them." "Never was there a bishop," says one who knew our saint well, "who employed himself in stopping offences against God and procuring the good of the faithful with more ardor than Monsignor di Liguori." He held sin in such abomination that he was implacable in hunting it out, even from its most hidden intrenchments. He appealed to magistrates and syndics, and with tears besought them to use the strong arm of the law against such scandalous sinners as lived in open crime. He even, if the expression may be applied to *his* dealings, bribed the officials; a large fraction of his revenue was spent in making presents to those among them who could inform him of existing scandals and aid him in rooting them out. But before calling on the secular power, he tried every gentle method that his fatherly heart could devise. He would send for the offender whether noble or plebeian, reprove, entreat, command him — and not till he was convinced of the inutility of such measures, would he adopt more rigorous ones.

A gentleman of high rank seeing that the vigilant pastor thwarted all his infamous plans, repaired to the palace and angrily reproached him for not leaving him alone. The saint calmly told him he was about to inform the king of his ill conduct, which gratuitous information excited the wretched man to fury. "Ill-treat me," said the courageous old man, "abuse me if you will, I do only my duty; I did not accept the episcopate to be damned. Would to God that I might have the honor to die a martyr in His cause! My dear child, I pity you! return from your evil ways, otherwise I shall never let you rest in your sins."

CHAPTER LVII.

The saint's zeal to convert women of irregular lives.— He establishes prisons for the incorrigible. — He exiles some. — An objection answered. Examples. — He reproves his secretary's remissness. — He replenishes the wardrobe of one of his proteges. — One of the ninety-nine just reproaches him. Marriages. — His care to preserve the innocence of his lambs. — The gold necklace. — The Most Zealous Doctor. — The office of a bishop. — The saint and the amateur actors. — He will not allow women to be instructed in the priest's house. — Letter to the king against duelling. — Burthen of the episcopate — Brother Welcome. — The saint's strictness regarding the Paschal precept.

O UR SAINT was indefatigable in laboring to convert or punish women of irregular lives. He entreated them, he warned them, he pictured in the burning words of his extraordinary eloquence the enormity of their crime, and hell yawning beneath their feet; then in order to deprive them of all excuse, he offered to maintain them. When his Fathers went on missions, he recommended them especially to look after these unfortunate creatures. "The conversion of one of these," said he, " is no small gain. Grant them whatever they wish, regardless of expense, provided they sincerely renounce their shameful course." As some of them unhappily would not be converted, and as the prisons already in existence were in a miserable condition, he got a prison for women built in each place; and when imprisonment did not produce the desire effect, he would have them exiled. The authorities did not always relish this mode of dealing with them. "I have just given an order for the banishment you desire," wrote a commissioner, "and wish nothing worse may result. But these culprits will go, where, being free from your paternal admonitions, and deprived of your alms, they will abandon themselves to their worst passions." "Let each bishop protect his own sheep," replied the saint, "and when these miserable people find that they are chastised wherever they go, left without refuge and covered with infamy, they may open their eyes and renounce their sins."

One of these women had become quite notorious for her evil behaviour. The saint ordered that she should be brought before him. When the secretary saw her exceedingly repulsive countenance, he hastened to tell his lordship that, being as ugly as famine, she was incapable of doing harm. "Well, but in time of famine, even hemlock is eaten," was the episcopal comment. Being severely reproved, she made protestations of future good conduct, and explained the misery from which her ill life resulted. The saint touched by her sorrowful story, forgave her, and dismissed her with a considerable alms and a paternal admonition.

The grand vicar, Rubini, used to often relate that when the bishop received tidings of the arrival of some intriguer in the town, he would not sit down to table till he had put it out of the power of the miscreant to do any harm. "Things of this description," said he, "do not admit of any delay; offences against God are in question, and if there were but one single sin involved we are bound to prevent its commission." "Don Felix," said he one day to his secretary, who had shown a little remissness in taking steps to stop a scandal, "when an offence against God is in question, we should leave every thing to put a stop to it."

He spent enormous sums of money in procuring the arrest of the incorrigible, and aiding true penitents, especially those whose indigence had been the occasion of their ruin. Even the soldiers could not refrain from extolling his extraordinary zeal in this respect. "It is incredible," said one of them, "how many sins Monsignor Liguori prevented, and how many scandals he extirpated." But the joy he experienced when he succeeded in converting one of these hapless creatures fully repaid his toil. There was no sacrifice which he was not ready to make to rescue them from sin and misery. A wicked girl, who had ruined soul and body by her vices, was at last obliged to seek refuge in the hospital of incurables. Our saint sent several priests to aid her to save her soul, but it was long before the poor creature yielded to the inspirations of grace. When he heard that she was beginning to show some good dispositions, he shed tears of joy. As her mother was a good poor woman, he agreed to her taking out the girl, and promised that they should not want The following contains a list of the articles which he considered necessary for her simple wardrobe. It is taken from a letter addressed to the priest Tramontana:

"I hear this girl is in the greatest destitution; she must then be clothed from head to foot...Procure for her two new chemises, a kerchief for the head, and another for the neck, a serge petticoat, an under-dress of canvas, a mantle, white stockings, and a pair of shoes...I should not trouble you with all these commissions but that I know your great charity...Inform me how much money I must send you, because as soon as she is clothed I shall make her mother take her back."

His liberality towards these poor penitents did not always please the "ninety-nine just." One evening, as he was leaving the church, a woman thus bitterly reproached him: "Monsignor, it is only wicked women that get into your good graces; would to God you had never come here. Those who lead virtuous lives need not hope for any thing from your lordship." The indignant secretary who accompanied him would have scolded this woman, but the saint interfered: "Be quiet," he commanded, "perhaps the poor woman has some want which I can satisfy." Then turning to her he said: "I should like to assist every body, but I must begin with those who are in sin; it is of urgent importance to free them from it." Even some priests thought he was too liberal to these persons, and told him plainly that not a few of his supposed penitents were impostors: "It matters little if I am deceived," he used to reply, "provided I thwart the plans of the devil. It is no slight gain if one can prevent sin, were it but for a quarter of an hour. Besides several of them are really converted and do persevere in virtue." To Archdeacon Rainone who suggested that he should withdraw the allowance from some whose perseverance was doubtful, he said: "If I abandon them they may yield to despair; besides, if they commit but one sin less, is not that a great thing for God's glory?" On another occasion he said: "I am ready to give my blood and my life for these poor penitents; if they act sincerely, I will not fail to assist them, were I obliged to go without food for that purpose."

Alphonsus, if he could not induce the persons to enter some refuge attached to a religious house, endeavored to get them married, and if possible to those who had led them astray. He was always willing to dower these poor brides with a sum that was quite a fortune for an Italian girl of the humbler class. In these cases he dispensed with all fees, and procured the necessary license at his own expense. It was universally remarked that these marriages turned out happy ones, although our saint himself said that he did not approve of forced unions, "but," he added, "of two evils one must choose the less."

Though the saint loved to rescue his wandering sheep, he took, if possible, greater pains to save the lambs confided to his care. Poor girls beyond number owed the preservation of their honor to his timely alms. He even went so far as to procure them innocent adornments to take away from them all temptation to envy or sin. A poor woman of Cava called to see him one day accompanied by her daughter, whose neck was graced by that hideous appendage, a goitre. The mother took the bishop entirely into her confidence, and, among other things, informed him that the girl had had an offer of marriage, but that she could not procure the indispensable *tonnino*. The puzzled saint, upon further inquiry, learned from the lady that this precious article was a collar of small gold beads to adorn the neck; upon which the secretary burst into a fit of laughter, and volunteered the ungallant remark that all the *tonnini* in the world would not be enough to ornament a neck like that. His lordship could not help smiling, but moved with compassion, he ordered that the bride elect should be given a sum more than sufficient to purchase the coveted trinket. No doubt the necklace gratified the heart of the poor maiden, besides helping her to make a more imposing appearance, even if it had the undesirable effect of making her deformity appear more conspicuous.

Were we to mention but half of the instances recorded of the extraordinary and unflagging zeal of the saint, our work would necessarily appear in many volumes. To prevent sin, to destroy the effects of sin, to draw souls to the love of Jesus Christ — here was the sole aim of his life. Verily, we have had a golden-mouthed doctor, a seraphic doctor, an angelic doctor, a honey-tongued doctor, a subtle doctor, and even a monarch of the doctors, but it was not a less happy inspiration which styled our great Neapolitan saint, the MOST ZEALOUS DOCTOR.

There was nothing too high or too low to escape the notice of the bishop when there was sin, or danger of sin. He was a peace-maker among his flock; enemies were reconciled by his gentleness, who had resisted the strongest entreaties from other sources. He promoted and maintained a good understanding among his clergy, regular and secular, and did all in his power to make them holy and happy. To bind up wounds, to heal dissensions, to unite all, clergy and laity, in God, in charity, — such he regarded as the chief function of a bishop. Whatever seemed an occasion of sin, that he strenuously set his face against, using mildness or force, meekness or rigor, persuasion or threats, irrespective of persons, as occasion seemed to require.

Upon arriving at St. Agatha, he learned that the principal gentlemen of the place were casting a play for the carnival: entitled, "La Contessa Sperciasépé." He gave them the spiritual exercises, and immediately after administering to them the holy communion, he said to them: "Will you not be good enough to do me the kindness of adding to the promises you have already made to Jesus Christ, that of not acting the comedy?" The gentlemen did as he wished, and the play was cast in vain. It may be here added that actors and strolling players, found little favor with a bishop so sternly bent on removing the occasions of sin; though he himself had once been a play-goer, and escaped unscathed, he bewailed to the last day of his life the moments lost at this diversion.

Hearing that women were instructed in the houses of some pastors, he strictly forbade it, and commanded that children and others, requiring instructions, should be instructed in the church. The barbarous custom of duelling caused him much anxiety. He addressed to the king, a learned and elegantly worded memorial on this subject, which concluded as follows:

"Sire,

"Your Majesty will greatly enhance your glory if you extirpate from the kingdom this accursed plague spot, which kills life both in soul and body. The undersigned, therefore, humbly entreats your Majesty, to renew the laws published by your predecessors against duellists, and cause them to be strictly observed by enforcing the penalties against all, but especially against the military, among whom duels are so frequent; and also to declare that those who do not accept a challenge, will preserve their office and their honor, but that duellists shall always be branded with infamy, as transgressors of the law.

"This declaration will be especially useful to your Majesty at present, as you have established the new royal brigade composed of valiant men in the flower of their age, whose effervescing passions might easily lead them to challenge each other in their disputes. Your Majesty's soldiers should not lose their blood or their lives for a false point of honor, but only for the defence of their faith, and the preservation of their prince and country."

Upon receipt of this admirable letter, the king promulgated another very severe law against duelling.

Though our saint's zeal never flagged, though his efforts to destroy sin and promote virtue were unceasing, yet he often trembled at the bare thought of the account he must on the judgment day, render to God for the souls committed to his care.

One day, Monsignor Albertini, whose guest he was at the time, asked him the number of the souls in the diocese of St. Agatha. "Forty thousand," replied the saint. "There are as many in mine," observed Monsignor Albertini; whereupon Alphonsus bent his head, and said: "My lord, we have each of us a burden of forty thousand hundred weight upon our shoulders, woe to us if one of these souls be lost through our negligence!"

Among other vices, he urged a determined war against blasphemy. As the law that compelled a blasphemer to stand in the public square had been abolished, he enjoined the magistrates to punish this execrable sin by imprisonment. There was a public crier nicknamed Brother Welcome, from having once been a novice with the Capuchins, who was greatly given to this vice. The saint commissioned his servant Alexis to bring him to the palace, but this was effected only on the servant's pretence of wishing to learn the price of corn. When the culprit appeared, the bishop plainly told him what he wanted with him; "I hear," he added, "that there is not a saint in heaven that you do not blaspheme." He threatened to have him arrested and condemned to the galleys, and this menace completely cured him. In future whenever Alexis chanced to meet Brother Welcome, the latter would pleasantly ask him if he wanted to know the price of corn. The poor brother became a true penitent, and made a happy end.

The saint was very particular in enforcing the observance of the paschal precept, and in this matter as well as others, he showed how entirely devoid of human respect he was. In case of failure to comply with it, the first gentlemen in the land had to submit to the mortification of seeing their names affixed to the church door. He ordered priests to refuse the sacraments to those who had given public scandal, or neglected their duties, however rich and noble they might be. A notorious sinner had the boldness to present himself, unshrived, to receive Holy Communion on Maunday-Thursday; the bishop stopped short before him, and said: "What! do you not blush to approach the altar? We do not cast pearls before swine. Unhappy man, change your life." The saint passed on, communicating the rest, and the wretched man withdrew from the communion rail in great confusion, but whether he was converted or not, the archives do not say.

CHAPTER LVIII.

Supernatural lights of the saint — Example. — Testimony of one of his officials. — Incident — Persecutions. — The saint's goodness towards his enemies. — His Patience. — His exquisite tenderness of heart — The Doctor. Trouble in the episcopal kitchen. — The saint a hero to his valet. — His extraordinary meekness and humility. — Instances. — The saint a thorough gentleman. — His deference and politeness towards his priests. — He refuses his likeness to his publisher. — Alexis obtains it — The device of the Congregation. — Episcopal immunities not claimed by the saint's household. His deference to members of his own Congregation.— Father Majone refuses to live at St Agatha.

AMONG other rewards which the Great Pastor bestowed on the vigilant bishop, may be reckoned those particular lights with which he was favored, and by which he frequently discovered, in a supernatural manner, the evil intentions of several members of his flock, and hindered their being perpetrated in outward actions. One night his own cook and his coachman agreed to commit a grievous crime, but being suddenly seized with fear, they happily desisted. At daybreak our saint summoned them to his presence, and having reproached them with his accustomed fervor, exhorted them to prepare for confession.

"It was marvellous," said one of his priests, "that many things of which we were ignorant came to his lordship's knowledge. Iniquity committed at dead of night, or in a distant village was made known to him instantaneously, and he would caution us to take immediate measures against it." There was a notary in the diocese whose misconduct was a source of grief to the aged prelate. Having reprimanded him several times without any good result, he warned him with tears that the life he was leading would bring him to a miserable end. When this unhappy man was waiting in the prison chapel to be conducted to the scaffold in January 1800 — he had just been condemned to lose his head for participating in the conspiracy of the Jacobins — he said weeping: "This death was foretold me in my youth by Monsignor Liguori."

Although up to that moment, he had remained hardened in his guilt, the remembrance of the gentle but fervid admonitions of the saint, who had so often vainly claimed him as a son, caused him to reflect then, to repent sincerely, and fortified by the sacraments of the Church he died full of hope and peace, invoking the saint in heaven who had wept over his follies on earth.

Those who were the objects of the saint's zeal were not, very naturally, always pleased with his efforts to reclaim them, and it sometimes happened that the excitable people, among whom his lot was cast, loaded him with injuries, and not only threatened his life, but almost attempted to take it. The saint made ample allowance for the effervescing character common among his countrymen, and bore their insults as well as their weakness with incomparable meekness and charity. "When charity is patient," said he, "it is also kind; if we are really anxious to win to Jesus Christ those who do us harm, we must do them good." Upon this principle he used to shower all possible kindness on those who ill-treated him.

A priest who was exasperated, because the saint had inflicted some punishment on his brother, came into his presence and bitterly reviled him: "Do you not see," said he "you are unfit for your office? How much better had you remained at Ciorani to weep over your sins, rather than come here to play the role of bishop?" The saint smiled sweetly on his adversary, but the grand vicar requested that the delinquent should be deprived of his post. Alphonsus not only did not accede to this request, but promoted him to the next vacancy.

A gentleman whose evil plans had been thwarted by the bishop, came to the palace in a rage and asked to see him. Volleys of abuse burst from the lips of this poor crazy sinner, and as his insolence was speedily made known to the governor, the latter hastened to imprison him. When this news reached the ears of Alphonsus, he was greatly distressed, and sending for the magistrate begged the release of the prisoner, nor would he desist till he procured his liberty, that very day.

In the case of another who had grievously injured him, the saint acted in a similar manner. The grand vicar, Rubini, was greatly displeased, and earnestly entreated him to allow the culprit to be left in prison, as the governor had just incarcerated him. Rubini expatiated particularly on the dignity of Don

Alphonsus Liguori and on that of the bishop of St. Agatha. "What position, what dignity," exclaimed the prelate, "if people must be put in prison on my account!" He would not rest until the offender had been released.

To a priest who threatened to injure him and his Congregation with their enemy, the procurator-general at Naples, Alphonsus turned a deaf ear. The grand vicar who could not bear to see the saint insulted, wanted to interfere, but he prevented him. Some time after the priest fell ill. The saint immediately visited him and showed him every possible kindness. He continued to assist him until his death which occurred soon after.

Instances of the extraordinary meekness of our saint are as numerous as those of his wonderful zeal. One day, an ecclesiastic from the country insulted him grossly. Archdeacon Rainone, who was present, was not pleased by the gentleness which knew not how to take offence: "My lord," said he, "the manner in which you act is degrading to your character and encourages the wicked." "Oh, my dear canon," returned the saint, "I have been laboring for forty years to gain a little patience and you want me to lose it all in a moment." "Our saint," said the Dominican Father Caputo, "acquired such complete control over himself, that he no longer seemed human, but rather an angelic being in the form of a man." "I know not," said Rainone, "whether he bore insults more like an incarnate angel or a perfect man."

Neither years nor sorrows abated the exquisite tenderness of heart which our saint habitually displayed. "You cannot imagine," he wrote to a penitent at Naples, "how much it costs me to use severity towards certain persons; I think one succeeds better by gentleness." He would weep if obliged to reprimand sternly, and his tears more than once touched the hardened hearts of some whom his eloquence had failed to move. If he only spoke a little too strongly, he was sure to do some kindness to the person to whom his words had been addressed. Once having spoken authoritatively to his physician, he presently sent for him to feel his pulse. "But," said the doctor afterwards, "he was very well, and only made use of this harmless stratagem to show that he harbored no ill will towards me."

The troubles of the episcopal kitchen not unfrequently ascended to the audience-room. One day the cook and the scullion became so animated in a dispute, that the latter brandished a knife which caused his adversary to beat an ignominious retreat. The ruler of the kitchen rushed into the saint's room, and held the door firmly closed, but the scullion who seemed resolved on killing him, pushed it violently from outside; Alphonsus ordered the door to be opened, and with a look and a gentle word calmed the infuriated menial. The officials of the palace wanted to have the hero of the knife dismissed and imprisoned, but the saint preferred to reconcile enemies, and from that day these two servants were the best of friends.

Tannoia testifies that Bishop Liguori's meekness was perfect. Brother Francis Anthony who lived with him fifty years, declared that whether with his brethren of the Congregation or with strangers, he always evinced unalterable sweetness and equanimity; Father Tannoia who was in close communication with him for forty years attests the same; and the venerable priest Arcieri invariably described him as the Francis de Sales of the age. The saint himself said with unwonted energy: "There is nothing more unseemly in a bishop than anger. A bishop who gives way to this passion is no longer the father of his flock; he is an intractable tyrant who draws upon himself universal hatred."

The humility of the saint was not less admirable than his meekness. Entirely detached from the world, which he regarded as vanity and dross, he gloried not in the nobility of his origin, and would not allow the great achievements of his ancestors to be mentioned in his presence. When one of his guests happened to mention the honors and dignity which his deceased cousin the Count Cavalieri enjoyed while governor of Mantua, the saint exclaimed: "How much more should I rejoice if I heard him praised for his virtue! How much more proud of him would I be if his death had been the death of a saint!"

In his palace the saint was more like a servant than a master. He made his bed, cleaned out his room, dressed the issue which annoyed him for years, and never allowed a valet to assist him in dressing or undressing. "By God's grace," said he one day, "I have never yielded to vain glory. Yet once, while I was being incensed on my throne, I experienced a sort of pleasing sensation. Now see how the devil tried to tempt me."

The holy bishop as far as possible dispensed with all the state and attendants which were considered, in his age and country, as essential to the episcopal dignity. He went out alone, especially to his devotions in the church. If he found the door closed, he would patiently await the coming of the sacristan. The slightest mark of deference was more annoying than pleasing to him. He would give the *pas* to any one that happened to come across him, and when walking or driving with any of his clergy, he declined the post of honor, and made another take it. Nothing grieved him more than to be made the object of any special attention. The officials in his house who were kept partly for state, soon found their office the merest sinecure.

So far was Alphonsus from domineering over his clergy that, in things lawful and indifferent, he was submissive even to his servants. Judging from the copious details left by his biographers, his manners in private life were those of a perfect gentleman. The saints as a class have been distinguished for their exquisite urbanity, and Alphonsus is remarkable for this, even among the saints. No word ever escaped him which denoted arrogance or a domineering spirit. Even to the lowest among his servants, he never spoke but in such terms as these: "Do me the kindness — Have the goodness to — I beg you to do such a thing — &c.," — But towards his priests, his conduct ever displayed the most extraordinary deference. He would never, during the whole time he was paralyzed, allow a priest to wait on him; nor would he ask a priest to do him the slightest service; if, while one priest or more, were in his room, he wanted his pen or a book or anything else, not being able to reach his half paralyzed arm for it, he would ring for the lay-brother who waited on him in his illness.

Nor would he give an order to a priest but by way of a request. When he wanted Don Bartolini to continue the spiritual exercises in a convent a few days beyond the ordinary time, instead of commanding, he said: "Don Pascal, the nuns would like to have you a little longer." "Your lordship can dispose of me," returned the priest: "You have but to command." "True," said the polite bishop, "but a superior ought to be discreet." If a request sufficed, he would deem it wrong to command.

He used to say that a tone of superiority can only diminish the authority of a bishop; yet if he were resisted in a thing he had a right to demand, he would let it be seen that he was a bishop, though, however great his firmness, he always spoke politely and never said anything offensive. When he wrote to his vicars and priests, he always gave them the title of Most Illustrious, though he declined it for himself. In dealing with the superiors of religious houses, he almost put himself in the position of a subject. Happening to go to the Capuchin Church on St. Anthony's day, and seeing that it was quite crowded, he turned to the superior and said in the humblest manner: "Father Guardian, if you permit it, I should like to say a few words to these people." He acted in a similar manner towards all ecclesiastics, especially those in office, nor would he officiate in their churches at any unusual time without asking permission.

He would not allow the simplest cleric to remain standing in his presence. Whoever called to see him, whether priest or layman, was invited to his table, for he was the soul of hospitality, and for admission to his humble board no pompous invitation was necessary. He loved to converse with the rude and illiterate and to inquire into their affairs, hence they were always kindly received in his palace. Father Fatigati, the great friend of Alphonsus, made the following observation to Father Tannoia: "During my life I have known two bishops who were thorough gentlemen, and who took pleasure in being with the poorest people and treating them with familiarity; these were Monsignor Liguori and Monsignor Borgia."

Our saint's publisher, Remondini, wishing to give greater value to his *Morals*, besought him to have his portrait taken, for a frontispiece. The aged author laughed at what he considered the absurdity of such a request, and on being urged by his secretary to consent, said: "Do not speak to me of such a thing; my work would only be depreciated in value if the head of such a mummy were put in it. The publisher was not to be daunted, however. He gained his cause with Alexis, the servant, who secretly made a hole in the door of the episcopal dining room, and thus a painter was able to trace his venerable features while he took his repast.

The arms of the noble house of Liguori were not to be seen in the vicinity of Alphonsus, he preferred the device he had chosen for his Congregation, and this consisted of the instruments of the Passion, with the appropriate verse. *Copiosa apud Eum redemption, With Him there is plentiful redemption.* When the arms of his predecessor were removed from some episcopal vestments, lest the sight might prove offensive to the saint, he ordered them to be replaced, asking whether the ceremonies, during which these vestments were to be worn, would be of less value on that account. His brother, Count Hercules, once made him a present of a magnificent piece of cloth, which the saint had made into vestments. When the canon spoke of having them adorned with the arms of his house, he rejected the proposition on the plea that what he had expended for the making of them had not come from his personal income, but from the episcopal revenues, of which he did not consider himself the owner.

Nor would the holy bishop allow any of his household to avail themselves of the immunities which custom seemed to authorize. "Formerly," said the agent of the Duke of Maddalon, "no one dared to bring before the courts of justice, any of those who were attached to the bishop's establishment, such as farmers, &c., but in Monsignor's time, the horror he had for all sorts of unjust pre-eminence caused him to abolish these privileges."

When he required anything unusual of his own subjects, he entreated it as a personal favor. As founder and superior-general of the Congregation, he had a right to claim the services of any member of it, but he did not do so. Desiring to have Father Majone to assist him at St Agatha, he had the mortification to learn that this Father did not wish to go. "This gives me great pain," he wrote to Father Villani, "I want an able subject, who can assist me in difficult cases; for I am surrounded by a thousand difficulties...Try to induce him to aid me willingly; me, a poor old man weighed down by cares and crosses. Tell him he will thereby be sure of doing God's will, and that he will do me a great charity...I say *willingly*, for otherwise he would be more burdensome than useful."

CHAPTER LIX.

Wonderful charity towards the poor. — The saint's present to his sister-in-law. He does not wish her to remain too long at his palace. — His preference for the poor. — The fair at Maddalon. — Alphonsus' care of the bashful poor. Instances. — The poor noble. — How a bishop should act with regard to giving charity — How the saint acted when poverty was an occasion of sin. His privileged poor. — His charity to pilgrims and strangers — To members of his household. — Testimony of an eye-witness. — Prisoners. — St. Misery. Mario. — All misfortune appeals to the saint. — Letters. — Indignation of the saint at the imprisonment of one of his servants. — The smuggler. — The Albanian soldiers.

THE SAINT'S charity to the poor has already been alluded to, but it would not be possible to describe it fully. His palace was open to all, and he never sent away any one till he had relieved his wants. Rubini affirms that he gave all his income, subtracting officials' salaries and the expenses of his table, to the poor. On Wednesdays and Fridays, there was a general distribution of alms, but the needy came on all days, some asking for sugar, some for salt, some for lard, some for money. They applied to him also for medicines, and he continually kept a stock of quinine and other simple remedies for their use. According to the united testimony of his biographers, he not only deprived himself of necessaries for the poor, but contracted heavy debts to relieve them.

When Count Hercules and his second wife, the Countess Marianna, came to visit him, the grand vicar suggested that he ought to make the bride a present. He immediately sent her a garland of flowers which had been presented to himself. When the trifling nature of the gift was represented to him, he replied: "Do you want me to rob the poor, in order to make presents to my sister-in-law?" The countess took pleasure in prolonging her stay at St. Agatha, but the saint did not like the expense of entertaining her retinue and he plainly but very politely intimated the same to Don Hercules. "It would be pleasant to me to keep your retinue a longtime," said he, "but how could I meet the expense it entails? What one takes from the Church, one takes from the poor."

When candidates for offices in his household presented themselves, he always chose the poorest, if they were as fit as the others. When he read of anything in particular done by some saint for the poor, he presently endeavored to imitate it. Once a recently elected prior of the Dominicans sent him a present of excellent fish. The same day the brother read a spiritual lecture for him out of the life of the Venerable Bartholomew, and, coming to a passage where it says, that the Archbishops of Prague were in the habit of sending a certain fish to the king every year on a particular solemnity, and that Bartholomew in consideration of the expense of this, resolved to employ the money in the service of the poor, his Lordship thus interrupted the reading: "To-morrow there will be a fair at Maddalon; take care to sell the fish and give the money to the poor." It being objected that it was too trifling a thing, and that the payment of the man for selling it would amount to more than the fish was worth, he replied: "I know nothing about that; do as I tell you."

The good bishop charged himself with anticipating the wants of the bashful poor, and always ordered the priests to make them known to him. He secretly supplied whole families with food and clothing, and gave several others a monthly allowance of from five to six or more ducats. Hearing that a young orphan of rank lived in great misery, he immediately charged himself with her maintainance, and amply supplied her necessities through the medium of her parish priest. To a lady, mother of a numerous family, who was in great distress, her husband being a gambler, he sent a supply of corn every month; but the gambler got some one to go for the alms in his wife's name, and he no sooner laid hold of it than he sold it and gambled the proceeds. Alphonsus then sent the allowance in the absence of the gambler, but hearing that he again got hold of it, he secretly sent the poor woman a monthly stipend by a priest.

Though our saint, on the whole, disliked visits, he took pleasure in receiving certain reduced noblemen, and one in particular who had a very large family. In relieving the poverty of this family, the saint exercised the most refined delicacy in deceiving the excusable pride of the indigent nobleman. One of the king's officers whose family was too large for his income, informed the bishop of his position, and while his regiment remained at St. Agatha, a monthly allowance was given him from the episcopal revenues.

"Whoever is raised to the episcopacy," said the saint, "ought to think a great deal about the poor, whose tears no one thinks of drying; it is they who are chiefly recommended to us by Jesus Christ." One day when he was with the bishops of Gaeta and Fondi, who were both his penitents, the conversation turned upon almsgiving. "As to that," remarked his lordship of Gaeta, "I do not believe I am much in fault; thanks be to God, I give largely to all who ask me." "It strikes me that you act as a priest rather than as a bishop," returned the saint; "you do not understand the meaning of these words of the Gospel: 'Let not thy left hand know what thy right hand giveth.' I advise you to think, in giving alms in secret, of widows, of families in trouble and of the poor who hide themselves."

When poverty became an occasion of sin, the saint was even prodigal in relieving it. Hearing that the six children of a poor woman shared the same bed, he instantly sent thither all that was necessary to remedy this; he was always particular in this regard with the poor, and desired to be informed where families were too poor to procure as many beds for their children as decency and modesty require. Not only did he keep a well stocked storeroom for his poor, but he bought a great quantity of stuffs of various kinds to help to clothe them. He called the nuns of the Holy Redeemer his privileged poor, and he extended the same epithet to those of St. Philip, and the Capuchinesses. Besides alms in money, he every year supplied them with stores of oil, corn and wine. The money he received on his pastoral visitations he remitted to his vicars, to be distributed among poor families. His charity embraced the poor of his whole diocese. If he found among his letters a petition from a poor person, he would joyously exclaim: "Ah, this pleases me: it is a request for charity."

Though the saint considered it his chief duty to aid the poor of his own diocese, yet he was liberal even towards strangers and pilgrims. One of these who was of noble birth had a regular weekly allowance from him, and as this did not at times cover his expenses, he would come to the palace and insist upon having more. On one of these occasions the saint said with ineffable gentleness: "My son I am overburdened with poor, and I know not what more I can sell to aid them, be satisfied for the present, and God will provide the rest." But as the man went off grumbling, he sent after him, and gave him twenty carlins. He was particularly kind to the sick of his own household, and never failed to visit them daily. When his servant Alexis became ill, he allowed his wife a sum sufficient to meet her expenses, and promised in case of her husband's death to allow her his wages as long as she lived.

The following testimony of a priest, who knew our saint well, may fittingly conclude this subject:

"I was filled with admiration at the acts of charity this saintly old man practised, especially towards the sick.

"Infirm, paralytic, bending under the weight of seventy-seven years, he still continued to go about the neighborhood to visit the sick. To see an old man almost wasted away, so weak as to require the aid of myself and his attendant in getting in and out of the carriage, to see such a one enter houses in search of the suffering was a sight which I could not contemplate without tears. I asked him one day how he, who received daily the visits of two medical men, could continue to visit the sick, he said with vivacity: "What sort of charity should I have, were I not able to suffer something for my children? O how much greater are the obligations of a bishop than those of any other Christian! I will even say, of any other ecclesiastic! The shepherd who watches over his flock properly must not forget his sick sheep, but should take care of them according to their requirements."

His presence among the sick and afflicted was as the presence of an angel. He exhorted them to patience, he encouraged them to receive all trials as punishments sent by God; he disposed them to receive the sacraments, he inspired them with love and confidence towards the Blessed Virgin, whose picture he always gave them. He inquired into their wants and had them supplied immediately.

The saint loved to visit prisoners, and in case of those incarcerated for debt, he usually freed them himself, by defraying the claims of their creditors, or at least interceding for them. At the opening of one of his pastoral visitations, he told the people how ardently his heart desired to relieve all their miseries and assuage all their sorrows, and expressed regret that his poverty would not allow him to do all his love wished. At this, a wit, named Mario, turned to the priest and said jestingly, "We have at last found our prefect," in allusion to a confraternity, called in derision, *of St. Misery.* When this was repeated to his lordship he only laughed, but hearing soon after that Mario was in prison for debt and his family starving, he remembered the witticism and said laughing: "We must assist him since he is our fellow-member." He then paid the debt, and as Mario was in debt elsewhere, he settled on him a monthly allowance.

Every description of misfortune appealed to Alphonsus as to the refuge of all; smugglers, criminals of every shade, conscious guilt and oppressed innocence — all recurred to the mercy of the tender-hearted bishop. His letters to persons in authority and to his personal friends teem with requests like the following:

"Take pity on this unfortunate man and do not have the cruelty to allow him to die in prison. My dear Don Carlo, do me this kindness and I will not fail to recommend you to God...I hope you will kindly give me this consolation, and spare me the sorrow of hearing that he has died in his mournful prison, and perhaps destitute of spiritual aid."

Hearing that one Mark Berjamo was about to be ejected from his farm, and the said Mark having appealed to him, he wrote to Don Pavone, the landlord, as follows:

"I assure you that this farmer is an honest man, and if he has not satisfied you it is not his fault. I therefore earnestly entreat you to leave him in his farm, and to treat him with all the charity with which your good heart is filled: I shall never cease to be grateful to you for what you shall do in his favor."

This compassion our saint had sometimes to exercise at his own expense. One of his servants who had been robbing the episcopal storerooms for a long time was found out at last, and lodged in jail by his indignant companions. When the saint heard this he reproved them severely. "What!" he cried, "imprison a poor creature for a few apples! Go to the magistrate directly and get him set at liberty."

Among the saint's correspondence we find numerous letters regarding the relief and release of prisoners. Indeed the great and the powerful who were friendly to him had often to show their friendship, with regard to the unfortunate, for it was impossible to resist the pleadings of his paternal heart. As privilege of sanctuary was then allowed, he was greatly pained to hear that a poor man who had smuggled some tobacco, and, on being discovered, taking refuge in a church, had been dragged from that holy place and cast into prison. "Our immunities are in question," said he, "and I would sell my mitre to obtain justice." He immediately demanded the release of the delinquent, and would not rest till he had obtained it.

Five Albanian soldiers having deserted, were rash enough to turn their arms against the officers who were sent in pursuit of them. Two were killed, and the survivors being captured, application was made to the bishop to know if, under the circumstances, they could enjoy the privilege of sanctuary. They unfortunately could not, but as he abhorred the thought of imbruing his hands in their blood, he would give no decision. "My Lord," said one official to him, "your pity injures the culprits, for now that the mixed court must decide their case, they will surely be condemned to death." These words so alarmed the saint that he immediately sent for the commanding officer and asked what could be done for these unfortunate men. "Nothing but your intercession can save them," was the reply; whereupon the saint immediately despatched couriers to Prince Jaci, to the Marquises of Tanucci and Marco, and to the secretary of war, to ask the pardon of these criminals, saying that, if he were not assured of their safety, his own life would be endangered; for, paralytic as he was, he would go in person and throw himself at the feet of the king. To the amazement of every one, they received a complete pardon, and soon after came, accompanied by an officer of justice, to thank their deliverer. He received them with the greatest joy, remonstrated with them as a tender father, and labored to save their souls as he had already saved their bodies.

CHAPTER LX.

The saint's hospitality. — The Archpriest and his companions. — The bishop's coachman. — The saint's disinterestedness. — Instances. — His advice to Bishop Rossi. — His care of the episcopal property.— His dislike of lawsuits. Letter. — His elegant courtesy towards the Duke of Maddalon. — His efforts to improve his lands, &c. — His interest in the culture of olives, mulberry trees, &c. — The raising of silk-worms. — He beautifies the episcopal gardens.

W<small>E SHALL</small> here allude, once more, to the hospitality and other virtues which Alphonsus invariably practised. All priests, students, and even agents of priests, who came to St. Agatha were invited to stay at the palace. Priests who came to give the spiritual exercises, or act as extraordinary confessors, had the same general invitation. The archpriest of Durazzano who did not know of this universal hospitality, asked Alphonsus on one occasion, whether he might remain at the palace during his stay at St. Agatha. "By all means," said Alphonsus, and perceiving that two gentlemen who accompanied him were about to start for the hotel, he would not allow it, but commanded them also to stay, saying that the house of a bishop is at the service of all, especially ecclesiastics. On these occasions, which indeed were frequent, often daily, the episcopal table was better supplied than when there was no company, which made one of his guests laughingly ask: "How does this sumptuousness agree with the poverty of your lordship?" "Hospitality," exclaimed the saint, "is the daughter of charity not of poverty."

The palace was frequently turned into a public hospital. If his guests or their servants took ill, he would not allow them to leave, but had them carefully nursed and supplied with medical attendance at his own expense. When Bishop Borgia's coachman fell ill, while his master was conferring with the saint, he was immediately placed in a comfortable room, and as his illness became serious, the last sacraments were administered, and his host frequently came to assist and console him. The son of the coachman came from Naples to see his father, and he too was received with the greatest kindness, and made remain until the invalid was perfectly recovered; for a month, Alphonsus watched over the convalescence of this humble servant, saw that light and nutritious food was served to him, and treated him with the greatest consideration. According to the testimony of the saint himself, his palace was almost always full, and he was sometimes obliged even to borrow beds.

Our saint's disinterestedness lessened the revenues of his diocese at least one half. "I have retrenched many of the sums I formerly received," he wrote, "for I felt scrupulous about them, and I think with reason...I consider it a very good kind of alms to decline marriage fees, especially if there is poverty or danger in question...I often remit considerable sums, and those who serve me know what a horror I should feel in violently exacting what is due to me." He refused to receive anything for ordinations, saying: "What has come to me gratuitously ought to be given away for nothing." Nor would he accept of the ordinary offerings made at the reception or profession of nuns. "I cannot ask anything for these ceremonies," said he, "since nothing has been fixed by Pope Innocent III."

There were sixty-four very rich chapels in the diocese, the administrators of which were obliged to pay the bishop a considerable sum at the patronal feast of each, but he generally left this in their hands for the poor of the place. The people of this diocese were noted for being very generous to their pastors, but the saint would never receive a present from the poor, knowing that his duty was to nourish rather than impoverish them. When he elevated priests to canonries or other offices, he declined to accept any present on the occasion, saying: "One ought not to receive any present for doing one's duty."

With regard to the episcopal farms, he was most careful that the farmers should not make bargains injurious to their own interests. In a word, says his grand vicar, Rubini, he made so many deductions that he never had a tenant who paid him the full amount.

Alphonsus ejected from a house of his a woman against whom several false reports had been made him. The poor woman began a novena to St. Joseph, and then appealed to him in person. Having asked to what saint she was most devoted, she replied, "St. Joseph." "Ah, well," he continued, for he had already been undeceived, "St. Joseph has been gracious to you, and has ordered me not to turn you out." This was not enough; the petitioner complained the rent was high. "How much do you wish to pay?" he asked. "Twenty-one ducats," said the tenant who had previously been paying twenty-seven. The saint agreed to this, but after his resignation she was obliged to pay thirty-one.

On one occasion the bishop found that a steward had a deficit, amounting to about one fifth of the episcopal revenues, but, as he confessed his fault with tears, the easy master sent him away in peace. Several people said such a culprit should be brought to justice. "What do you say about justice?" exclaimed the saint with emotion: "This man has satisfied justice by confessing his fault, what a sight it would be — a bishop bringing an unfortunate man to the courts to ruin him outright, for sake of his own interests?" We may add here that the saint was particularly exact in paying the wages of his servants and workmen; he often even forced payment on them for mere trifles. "I am an old man of ninety," said Father Raphael de Ruvo, "and yet I never saw a prelate so charitable and disinterested as Monsignor Liguori. His purse was always open to give, and closed only against receiving." Everything was gratis for others, but he paid doubly what he himself owed. "When the saint's successor visited him, he gave him this advice: My Lord, if you wish to do good and to succeed at St. Agatha, dispose of your own purse, but never of that of others."

The saint, however, knew how to distinguish between his own personal interests and those of the episcopal revenue. One day a priest said to him with reference to a yearly tribute due the bishop: "I cannot see what gave rise to this custom, would it not be better to give this tribute to the poor?" "It is I who have to give the alms," said Alphonsus quietly, and he declared he would not do anything calculated to injure the rights of his successor. On hearing that the syndic (mayor) of Arienzo had hindered a priest from sending his dues to the cathedral, he wrote to all his priests advising them to state the matter to the royal council, adding that if the syndic or any other official prevented justice being done, he himself would undertake to defend the canon law. Yet he hated lawsuits of every kind, and was accustomed to say that a bad accommodation is better than a good lawsuit. He endeavored to settle by arbitration some difficulty he had with a certain priest, and sent for him several times without even receiving an answer. At last he wrote in the following humble strain: "If I had a carriage, I would have sent it for you long ago; come, I entreat you."

In a dispute which arose between the saint and his friend, the Duke of Maddalon, regarding the right of pasturage over a fief belonging to the episcopal revenue, he wrote to the ducal agent: "I am obliged to defend the property of the see, which possesses the double right of pasturage and lordship...If I be pushed to extremities I will apply directly to the Regency...Could I reconcile it to my conscience, I would yield up my rights, and say no more of this affair. God knows how I detest lawsuits, the very name makes me tremble; yet how can I yield after having taken an oath to defend the rights of my church?...This weighs upon my conscience, otherwise I would yield directly." Nevertheless the saint, with that elegant courtesy which always distinguished him, placed the whole business in the hands of one of the defendant's lawyers — a delicacy of politeness which so disarmed the generous nobleman that he ordered his agent to leave things as they had formerly been, and pay up all the arrears which the bishop could claim. Indeed every one who knew Alphonsus, believed, with the Neapolitan lawyers, that, "what is taken from Monsignor Liguori is taken from the poor."

A poor gentleman whose family was very large had great difficulty in paying for one of the episcopal farms which he rented, and got the Lady Catherine di Lucca to intercede for him. The saint not only remitted the debt, but gave him a monthly allowance of corn. Yet to prevent injury to the episcopal property, the debtor was obliged to appear every year with the rent, which the saint accepted and then gave back to him as an alms. In consequence of the saint's judicious administration, the property greatly increased in value. He was careful to have dead trees removed and new ones planted, especially olive trees, so useful in Italy. He would not leave the episcopal gardens so bare and unsightly as he found them, but had them profusely planted with lemon and orange trees, flowers of every hue and variety for the altar, and the plants and vegetables most useful for the kitchen and for medicinal purposes; thus giving employment to many hands, and spreading among the humble classes knowledge of the most useful kind. We may well believe that the aspect of the episcopal city was greatly beautified under a bishop who was an elegant amateur in horticulture and architecture, as well as in music and painting. But he did not confine himself to the beautiful; he was still more anxious to promote the useful; and as the raising of silk was the great industry of the people of his diocese, he paid particular attention to the cultivation of mulberry trees, carefully informing himself as to whether the white or black mulberry yielded the most profitable leaves, and propagating only the best species.

CHAPTER LXI.

How the saint practised holy poverty. — He wears out the old clothes of Bishop Danza. — He replenishes his wardrobe from an old clothes shop. Putting in new sleeves. — "Old things suit an old bishop." — Letter of Don Spota. — Why the saint practised economy. — Details. — Opinion of the bishop of Caserto. — The saint's episcopal ring. — He will use only the produce of his own diocese. — His mortification. — Incident. — He takes vinegar for wine. — Fruit sent to him does not stop at its destination. Why he did not keep caged birds. — The harpsichord. — Rubini's testimony.

A S OUR saint was a member, or rather the founder of a religious congregation, he was eminent also in the virtues which may be regarded as peculiar to the religious life, and especially holy poverty. By this virtue, made obligatory by vow, the religious not only renounces all property in earthly things, but detaches his heart from them, and endeavors to assimilate himself to the poor in spirit, to whom belongs the kingdom of heaven. On his elevation to the episcopate, Alphonsus could not avoid procuring one violet suit, but when this — and it was of the plainest description — was worn out, he was satisfied with the old robes of his predecessor, and used no others during the thirteen years he governed the See of St. Agatha. The habit of his congregation was his ordinary dress, because nothing plainer could be devised. He had but one, and while that was mending, he was obliged to have recourse to Bishop Danza's old wardrobe, or remain in his room. One day as he was passing by the Dominican monastery in a cassock pretty well patched, but out at the elbows, one of the fathers could not forbear compassionating such poverty. The saint pleasantly accounted for it by saying that he had sent to an old clothes shop in Naples for four articles of clothing, but that they had not yet reached him.

On one occasion, a brother adroitly substituted a new habit for the old one. "Ah," said the saint next morning, "you have been putting in new sleeves." "Yes, monsignor, the others were too much worn," was the reply. But later in the day finding the whole garment was new, he said in a tone of authority which he rarely assumed: "I am the master here, and I think this cassock is quite new." "Well," said the brother, apologetically, "the other was no longer decent." "Never mind that," said his lordship, "bring it hither." The excuse for its non-appearance was that it had been given to a beggar. "You will always act of your own accord," was the bishop's indignant comment. Hempen shirts and a habit of common cloth, dyed black, composed his wardrobe; his rosary was of wood, and his garments were such that the beggars used to refuse them. The laundress having complained that his shirts fell to pieces in her hands, Father Telesca told him he ought to get new ones. "Old things suit an old bishop," observed the saint; "besides I ought to think of clothing the poor."

Don Dominic Spota, grand chanter of the cathedral of Girgenti, after a prolonged visit to the bishop of St. Agatha, wrote the following details to Father Blasucci:

"I have admired Naples, I have been overawed by the magnificence of Rome, but the life of Monsignor Liguori has made a greater impression on me than either...I have seen a saintly bishop of the primitive ages; he is confined to bed by the most painful infirmities, but his serene countenance betokens the tranquillity of his soul. The glory of God and the government of his diocese occupy him unceasingly; I have noticed his extreme moderation in sleep and food, and such is his poverty that the only blanket on his straw bed is his cassock; his pastoral ring would not excite the envy of a beggar — a false stone is its only ornament; and his pectoral cross is in perfect keeping."

One of our saint's principles was that whatever was wasted or superfluous in a bishop's household, was so much taken from the poor, he practised the strictest economy as regarded himself. His table was of unpolished wood, and so old, that it could not be sold except as firewood, or valued except as a relic. His inkstand was of bone, his snuff-box of wood, for his compositions, he used the cheapest paper that could be procured, and the envelopes of letters. "If we were to act as he does," exclaimed the bishop of Caserta, after making the saint a visit, "we should continually breathe forth the odor of sanctity. Everything about Monsignor Liguori commands respect, veneration, and homage." Besides his books, the only ornaments in his room were the crucifix, which he had always before him, and a little picture of Our Lady of Good Counsel, which was on his table.

One morning as the bishop was going to officiate, his ring could not be found. A gentleman who happened to be present was distressed at its disappearance: "If it is the loss of the gem which makes you uneasy," said his lordship, smiling, "never mind; it is only a bit of glass. My uncle's[1] ring which was given me, was sold for the relief of the poor." Once when the members of the household were joking about the value of his ring, he said pleasantly: "Such as my ring is, it has figured at Rome, and every one regarded it as a precious article; 'but you do not know,' said I to myself, 'that I broke my best decanter to adorn it'."

It was culpable in the saint's eyes to send to a distance for meat, wine or fish. He would not allow this even in his worst illness. "I ought to eat the produce of my own diocese," said he, "I cannot waste money that belongs to the poor. I am their father and their steward, not the destroyer of their possessions."

The spirit of penance and mortification was equally conspicuous in our saint; he unceasingly offered himself to God as an expiatory victim for the sins of his people. Every day he disciplined himself to blood. A Dominican prior who had come to his house on account of the examinations, occupied a room near the bishop's, and as he was leaving, the very day they were over, being entreated to remain longer, he said, "I would return home were it midnight, for I have not the heart to listen any longer to the flagellations of this poor old man."

For several years, the saint ate but once a day, and during another period of his life he ate only abstinence food. Even this he was accustomed to season with bitter herbs. During the whole time he was bishop, he never once complained of any dish being badly cooked, though accidents of this nature were of frequent occurence in his house. One day at dinner the servant served vinegar instead of wine. His lordship drank it, but the grand vicar no sooner tasted it than he angrily reproached the servant. The saint excused him and laughed at the accident. On another occasion the same thing occurred, but he drank it without making a remark. Next day however, he said pleasantly to the servant:

---

[1] Monsignor Cavaliere, the saintly bishop of Troia. (Editor's original note)

"Do not give me the same wine I had yesterday; I really took it for vinegar."

The saint liked fresh fruit, and it was very beneficial to his health; for this reason his brother used to supply him with the best fruit to be procured at Naples. But Alphonsus usually sent it to the nuns of the Holy Redeemer; he disposed in a similar manner of rare fish, bonbons and other delicacies which his relations frequently sent him.

He would not allow caged birds in his palace. "A bishop's house," said he, "is not a place of pleasure but of penance." One day when he was offered a present of canaries, he refused them saying: "No, no, a little later and we should weep over them." "These things" he remarked to his secretary, are so easily destroyed, and when one loses them one feels sorry for weeks after." Before he became a bishop, he used often play on the harpsichord or piano at the community recreation, especially when the young students were present, to amuse them and teach them to sing his hymns; and of these instruments he was a perfect master; but while he governed St. Agatha he entirely denied himself that innocent pleasure.

Even in his sufferings, the saint rarely sought any alleviation beyond that prescribed by physicians. One day as he was oppressed with a violent headache, Father Caputo suggested that he should have recourse to St. Vincent Ferrer, "For such a little thing!" he exclaimed. "Ah, let us rather ask him for the salvation of souls, and for a good passage to eternity."

We will conclude this chapter with the testimony of the grand vicar, Rubini:

"His lordship was as cruel to himself as he was kind to others. I should make you shudder were I to relate all the particulars of his macerations, his abstinence from food, his daily scourgings to blood – of the hair-shirts and iron chains which kept his body in continual mortification, his watchings – in short everything that can afflict the flesh was made use of unceasingly by Monsignor Liguori."

CHAPTER LXII.

Doubts and fears of the saint as to his resignation of the bishopric. — Regret of the people. — A general mission. — Wonderful vigilance of the saint. — His resignation accepted. — Letter. — Grief of the clergy. — Sentiments of the retiring bishop. — Of the citizens of Naples. — The weight of Mount Taburno removed from the saint's shoulders. — The Vacant See. — Monsignor Rossi. The pension. — Characteristic disinterestedness.

WE SHALL ere long have to follow our saint into retreat, for no sooner had he assisted at the deathbed of Clement XIV, than he resolved to resign his bishopric, knowing as he had already prophesied, that the successor of Ganganelli would accept his resignation. But as usual he was full of doubts and fears, and he would be glad if the new Pope would, of his own accord, release him. "Show me that I do God's will in leaving my diocese," he wrote to Father Villani, "that I may leave it in peace." Though this Father had not heretofore approved of his resigning the bishopric, he now gave full consent, and the holy bishops, whom he had consulted for the saint, were also of opinion that, in consequence of the accumulation of maladies, which rendered him unable to make the least movement without assistance, he need have no scruples in resigning his office. Father Villani doubted whether the resignation would be accepted; "but," wrote Alphonsus, "there is no reason to doubt; the Pope will accept it, I am certain that I ought to die in the Congregation, and you will even see that I shall die as a subject."

No sooner was it known at Arienzo that the saint had sent his resignation to the Pope, than the news spread throughout the diocese and caused general regret. The superiors of religious houses wept for the loss of a protector who was no less powerful than zealous; the nuns for a Father and a consoler; while the clergy felt as if, in losing him, they lost the very soul of the ecclesiastical state. The people bewailed the most tender and vigilant of fathers; all classes united in supplicating heaven for the preservation of their saintly bishop, consoling themselves with the hope that, as Clement XIV had decided that he could govern the diocese from his sick bed, Pius VI would refuse to accept his resignation.

Pending the decision of the Holy See, the saint redoubled his exertions for the welfare of his diocese. To the last moment of his stay, he was zealous in rewarding the most virtuous, chastising the tepid, and expelling the incorrigible. He designed that, previous to his leaving, the whole diocese should be thoroughly evangelized, and he applied to the heads of Congregations for the necessary workmen. His zeal was so fully seconded by all to whom he appealed, that not a hamlet, town, village or estate throughout his diocese was left without a mission. From his bed or his arm-chair, he arranged the smallest details of this great work. He bespoke the hospitality of the nobles or princes of each district for the zealous missionaries, who had so generously responded to his call; and it was freely accorded. Meanwhile, but little of what was done throughout the diocese escaped him, "You must be watchful of N___," he wrote to one of his missionaries, by his secretary; "You know where he lives, and you must see whether he continues to visit the house of N___, to the scandal of the neighborhood. I want to be informed about this as soon as possible. Come this morning that I may consult with you about this matter."

That the Passion of Jesus Christ might be engraven on all hearts, he caused a large picture to be painted, in which the more striking scenes of it were depicted in the most natural manner, and had it carried in procession through the church on the last evening of the mission. To excite the faithful to compassionate the Sorrows of Mary he also caused the statue of Our Lady of Dolors to be exposed and carried processionally. Besides, he indicated to the Fathers in a circular letter, all that should be done in order to excite the people to compunction. "Let the preachers," said he, "inculcate what a grievous crime it is to conceal a sin in confession through shame; in their sermons let them dwell much on the necessity of recommending oneself to God, especially when assailed by temptation, let them always make mention of love towards Jesus Christ crucified, and devotion to the Blessed Virgin. And when any habitual vice exists in a place, frequent reference must be made to it...If the people are made to say an *Ave Maria* it should be said before the sermon, not after, for fear they may get cold, and complain when they return home."

When Cardinal Castelli presented to the Pope our saint's resignation, his Holiness was not in the least disposed to receive it, though the cardinal represented his great age and incessant illness; for he knew too well the wonders the saint was effecting who "ruled his diocese from his bed." About this time, two Fathers of the Congregation presented themselves to pay their homage to the Holy Father, who at once inquired about Monsignor Liguori. Thinking to do something pleasing to their holy Founder, and eager to have him once more in their midst, they did not fail to confirm what the Pope had already heard concerning his infirmities, and even exaggerated them. "If this be the case," said the pontiff, "we must not distress him further." He therefore commissioned a cardinal, May 9, 1775, to write to the saintly bishop of St. Agatha, as follows:

"His Holiness felt sincere sorrow on learning, through the letter forwarded to him by Cardinal Castelli, of the sad state of your health, which has urged you to tender your resignation. This causes the Holy Father to feel great regret knowing as he does, how to appreciate your merits and your pastoral vigilance; but being aware of the full justice of the motives which impelled you to this step, he declines to prolong your mental anxieties, and accepts your resignation, which must be made according to legal formalities. With sentiments of the highest esteem, I heartily kiss your hand, and am &c."

This letter filled the saint with joy, but among his poor children lamentations resounded every where. "It is a chastisement from God," said Archdeacon Rainone announcing it to the chapter, "we have not known how to appreciate him." There was not a canon or priest in the whole diocese who did not go to Arienzo to complain with tearful eyes of the step he had taken.

The gentlemen of the diocese came in a body to express their sorrow, and those who had experienced his severity were among the first to express their grief for the irreparable loss their district was about to sustain. Canon Francis Petti, whose indignation the saint had aroused by causing the arrest and imprisonment of his brother, repaired to his bedside weeping, and exclaimed: "What are you about, my lord? may God forgive you! The harm you are doing our diocese can never be repaired."

"Which of us can now fulfil his duty?" cried out the disconsolate clergy. "With Monsignor Liguori disorders were remedied by merely telling him of them, for he could do anything both for priests and seculars, with the barons and the king. Where shall we now find the purse always open to relieve suffering or prevent sin?" Even the archpriest of Frasso, who had given him so much trouble, when told that Alphonsus, sinking under the double weight of years and infirmities, felt unable to govern the diocese any longer, said: "That is not true. Monsignor Liguori is capable of governing our diocese by his name alone," and he expressed the bitterest regret for the approaching departure of the saintly prelate.

"Do you think I am not sad at leaving you?" said the loving saint to his weeping clergy. "In truth I am but too sad, for I shall leave my children. I go, only because God wills it. The state to which I am reduced compelled me to inform the Holy Father of my sufferings, but I declared to his Holiness that if my diocese would suffer the least injury from my departure, I was ready to toil on here until my death. If I go away in body I leave my heart in the midst of you."

The poor felt the loss most keenly of all. Indigent and penitent women, distressed families who had relied on his assistance, the bashful poor, even among the nobles, whom he secretly relieved, bewailed it as the greatest of earthly calamities. The peasants were inconsolable. It is not generally known that the holy bishop kept a *crèche* in his establishment, but such was the case. When these poor people went to work they dropped their babes at the palace door, knowing that their good Father would have them nursed and fed. "Alas," said a poor villager to Father Gaudinot, "who will now receive our poor little ones? When we used to go to the mountain, we left our children at his lordship's palace, and we felt sure that they would be fed and cared for; but now that he is going away, to whom can we have recourse?"

The sick and the prisoners wept with the rest. "Alas," said the latter, "who will now comfort us, who will send kind friends to console us, intercede for us with the magistrate, or plead for us with our creditors? Monsignor was a saint, every one honored him as such, and he was all-powerful." This universal outpouring of filial love grieved the affectionate heart of the saint, and if it had cost him much to be united with this dear spouse, it cost him still more to separate from her when he had learned to love her.

At Naples the people entirely sympathized with the bereaved flock of St. Agatha. "His presence was enough of itself to govern his diocese, and make every official in it do his duty," said the Marquis of Avena, a member of the royal council, and he severely censured Monsignor Liguori for having taken this step.

The saint's resignation being formally accepted, some one jestingly remarked to him that he appeared to hold his head more erect since he heard the news: "Yes," he replied, "and that is not surprising, since the weight of Mount Taburno[1] has been taken off my shoulders." From the depths of his grateful heart, the ex-bishop thanked his holiness for the great favor of releasing him from an office, the responsibilities of which weighed so heavily on his over-sensitive conscience. He then entreated to be permitted to preserve the privileges annexed to the episcopate, especially the portable altar. The Holy Father having granted his request, expressed an opinion that he ought to enjoy a pension from his church, and Alphonsus, not wishing to be burdensome to his dear city of St. Agatha, named four hundred ducats as sufficient; the Pope was so edified at this moderation that he assigned him double that amount, and released him from a debt of one hundred and five ducats which he owed to the apostolic chamber. The College of Doctors at Naples, of which he was so bright an ornament, agreed, without a dissentient voice, to give him his whole pension, and not enforce the ordinary condition, residence at Naples.

The saint was not oblivious of the interests of his own institute. He prevailed on his brother, Hercules, to settle on the Fathers of the Congregation the apartments which they were

---

[1] Taburno is a mountain which overtops St. Agatha. -Ed.

accustomed to occupy in his palace, as sons of the great Founder, Don Alphonsus Liguori. Mgr. Rossi, Bishop of Ischia, was nominated to the vacant see of St. Agatha. When the saint heard of this appointment he exclaimed, with unusual earnestness: "My God! my God! I will at once write to Rome to obtain leave to reside here till the arrival of the new bishop. My poor church," he continued, with unwonted animation, "how long thou wilt have to remain a widow!" This was a prophecy, for the clergy of Ischia incited the Neapolitan government, or the government incited the clergy – to oppose the translation of their bishop, and St. Agatha remained without a bishop for over four years. Alphonsus would have resided there till the arrival of his successor, but, according to present discipline, a bishop, whose resignation was accepted, had to leave his diocese immediately. At the request of the saint, Monsignor Rossi visited him at Nocera, and learned from his own lips the real state of that dear church, in which the greatest of its bishops had left his heart, as he himself had declared to his loving children.

CHAPTER LXIII.

The saint's last visitation. — Touching scene. — The art of arts — Anecdote.
He visits his religious communities. — His present — Mother Raphael. — An
alms. — The church. — Miracle. — The saint's departure from St. Agatha.
His constant residence during his administration. — A melancholy ovation.
Reception in Nola. — Miracle. — Enthusiastic reception in Nocera. — Eased of
one burden to assume another. — Touching letter. — New persecutions.
Discipline relaxed. — The saint endeavors to restore perfect observance.
His labors among the people. — The carminello. — His apartments.

U NDETERRED by his infirmities, the saint once more
visited his dear children in person, to testify the
warmth of the affection they had inspired in him, and
to leave them his blessing. In this last visitation of the parishes, he
inculcated perseverance in well doing, the avoiding of sin, the
frequentation of the sacraments, and above all, love of Jesus
Christ and devotion to Mary. He then humbly asked pardon for
his numerous failings and the scandal he had given, according to
his own account of his administration, and besought them to pray
earnestly for his soul, especially when they should hear of his
death. He protested that he had loved them all without exception,
and indeed of this there could be no doubt, since those towards
whom he had acted with the greatest severity, regarded his
chastisements as gentle strokes of a fatherly hand and were
inconsolable at the prospect of his departure. Indeed the intense
affection manifested for Alphonsus, both within his congregation
and outside of it, would lead us to suppose that the few instances
recorded of his severity are greatly exaggerated.

He appears to have been a perfect master of that art which
the saints themselves agree to be the most difficult of all arts, as it
certainly is the most disagreeable of all duties, that of correcting
others: that the saint sometimes corrected severely is manifest
from his own letters, but in scarcely one instance was the reproof
badly received; some, indeed, were carried away by anger, but it

was only for the moment. Even those who were not at once converted, afterwards acknowledged the justice of the admonition, and the saint's zeal invariably bore fruit in time. "Now," said he to a wicked surgeon whom he had imprisoned, "that I am going to leave my diocese, do you leave off vice." The poor sinner was so moved by the tender entreaties of the saint that he mingled his tears with those of his benefactor. He afterwards made a public confession of his crimes, and died in sentiments of sincere repentance, blessing the name of Alphonsus di Liguori.

The saint visited all his religious communities, humbling himself wherever he went, and beseeching the religious to pardon the perhaps too-great severity with which he had endeavored to maintain them in perfect discipline, assuring them that it was inspired by the great and singular love he bore them, and that he had always sought to have them honored as the most precious portion of the flock of Christ, and conciliated the esteem of the people in their regard. He exhorted them once more to perfect observance of rules, and advised superiors especially to have no human respect where the glory of Jesus Christ and the good of souls were concerned. "Remember me before the tabernacle, and forget not my poor soul when you shall hear of my death," were the touching words with which he concluded every exhortation made to his beloved children.

The nuns of the Annunciata having asked him for a keepsake, he sent them the little picture of Our Lady of Good Counsel which he used to keep upon his table. He gracefully added that he left them his heart, and begged them to say a *Hail Holy Queen* for him every Saturday before that picture, and recite the litany for his soul, for three days, when they should hear of his death, all which they faithfully accomplished.

Mother Raphael, not being able to see him, wrote him a most affectionate letter, and, among other things, said she hoped that he would bequeath his heart to his daughters of Our Most Holy Redeemer at his death. This request did not by any means edify the saint: "I have always considered Mother Raphael a sensible woman," said he, "but now I cease to have a high opinion of her." The only memento he sent them besides a letter of good advice, was a simple wooden cross with the emblems of the passion, which had adorned his dining-room, and which he used to kiss whenever he entered or left the room.

To the canons he left the large wooden cross that stood on the first landing of the staircase of his palace; to the Capuchins some flowers which adorned the altar of the Blessed Sacrament in his chapel, to the seminarists several books which belonged to him as bishop, not having been procured for him by the Congregation, and copies of all his own works. His old mattress and arm-chair he begged as an alms from the chapter of the cathedral, who, while granting his request, shed tears of devotion at the poverty of their beloved bishop. Everything about his room was carried off; already those who knew him felt certain he would one day be raised on the altars of the Church. The barber of the palace not being able to find anything better, asked for his crutch. "Take it," said the saint, "it may one day be serviceable to you." Some years after, it was used by the barber to affect a miracle on his daughter-in-law, when all had despaired of her recovery.

It was on the 27th of July, 1775, that Alphonsus bade a last adieu to his dearly loved diocese. Amid the tears and groans of his clergy and people, especially the poor, he was helped into his carriage. The affliction of his cherished children pierced his paternal heart like a sword, and his eyes were suffused with tears. He had governed the Church of St. Agatha for thirteen years and fifteen days, during which period he had so scrupulously observed the law of residence, that he was absent only three times, and on each occasion but for a very short period. The first was in 1764, to assist at a general chapter of the Congregation: the second in 1765, when, by order of his physicians, he went to Pagani for the benefit of his health after a severe illness; and the third, in 1767, when he repaired to Naples to avert the threatened destruction of the Congregation.

An immense concourse of people impeded the progress of the episcopal cortege, eager to receive the last blessing of the saint. But when the object of this melancholy ovation perceived that the priests, canons and other gentlemen intended to convey him to his destination, he tried to dissuade them, yet graciously thanked them all, and assured them of his abiding gratitude for this last token of their affection. Some, unwilling to yield to his entreaties, accompanied him to Nocera. On the way he continued his devotions, and said the rosary and the canonical hours with Father Villani, who sat by him in the carriage.

It was dinner time when they reached Nola. The retired prelate was received there as an angel from heaven. Owing to the intense emotion he felt at parting with his beloved flock, he had not said mass in the morning; he therefore went to the seminary and offered the holy Sacrifice in presence of the faculty and the students, who were extremely edified at his extraordinary devotion. He made his thanksgiving during Father Villani's mass, which followed his own and, at the request of the superior, addressed a few simple but burning words of superhuman eloquence to the pupils, and gave them his blessing. As he re-entered the carriage he wrought a miracle on a nobleman who had become blind, by making the sign of the cross on his eyes.

When they reached Nocera the bishop, Monsignor Sanfelice, who had the greatest esteem and veneration for his holy colleague, ordered that all the bells should ring out to welcome him. The people testified the most lively joy at seeing once more the great doctor, whose learning and sanctity had shed such lustre on their little city, but they were grieved to find him in so helpless a condition, and wept as they called to mind his ancient promise to come to Nocera to end his days among them. All the clergy and several of the nobles approached to kiss his hand and beg his blessing as he descended from the carriage. When on the threshold of the convent he paused, and exclaimed, with transport, "*Gloria Patri et Filio et Spiritui Sancto!*" On reaching the choir he prostrated before the Blessed Sacrament, saying: "My God, I thank Thee for having released me from so heavy a burden. My Jesus, I could bear it no longer." The community assembled in choir to receive him and sang the *Te Deum* in thanksgiving to God for having restored to them their beloved Father.

The grand vicar of Nocera visited him that evening to pay his respects, being deputed by the bishop. In the course of conversation, that dignitary observed that the people of St Agatha were very much displeased at his departure, "And why?" asked the saint, innocently. "Because they have lost a pastor who did so much good," was the natural reply. "Jesus and Mary!" exclaimed the holy bishop, greatly disturbed, "what does the grand vicar say of me, who have done no good at all, *none, none, none!* If any good has been, done, it was God alone who did it." Monsignor Sanfelice came himself next morning, and courteously conferred full powers on him to exercise all authority in the diocese. The bishops, nobles, superiors of monasteries and people of rank of the neighboring cities were continually pouring in, so that several days elapsed before he could obtain any rest.

The saint was filled with joy at being once more among his beloved sons. "By God's grace I am at Nocera," he wrote, "and I feel as if I were in paradise," but he soon found that he had been eased of one burden only to assume another. All had recourse to him for advice and consolation, "I had hoped," he wrote, "to find relief at Nocera, but I have met with a thousand cares which deprive me of rest. My head is exhausted. I am obliged to keep a wet cloth constantly beside me, to prevent giddiness or fainting, so great is the number of letters I have to write…I feel scrupulous if I neglect writing the inspirations God sends for He gives to superiors knowledge which he does not communicate to others, and it is this thought that makes me write so often." Serious dangers again threatened his beloved Congregation, and its adversaries never ceased to beset the royal courts, but the saint while using all the precautions prudence suggested, felt a holy confidence, or rather certainty, that his great work would survive him. "I experience a sweet security," he wrote to the Fathers, "because I know for certain that Mary will help us to weather this storm." The following paragraph forms the conclusion of the circular letter he addressed to his sons at this time:

"I bless you all one by one. Pray about the persecution we endure, now more intense than ever. I trust in Jesus and Mary, who will not abandon us. Pray daily for me that I may have a happy death. For my part, I do nothing but pray for you, you know well that I love you far more than I ever loved my own relations. May you be blessed, and blessed also be all the labors you perform, both in the houses and on the missions."

Meanwhile the holy Pope Pius VI testified in every possible manner the affection he felt for the veteran missionary. "One cannot do enough for Monsignor Liguori," said his holiness. Indeed Pius VI had so high an opinion of Alphonsus that he sought occasions of doing him favors, and loved to exhibit the esteem and veneration which his virtues inspired.

The perpetual and ever-increasing persecutions the Congregation had to endure disheartened some of the weaker brethren, and notably affected religious discipline. The fear of being dispersed any day by the secular power made some even think of leaving, without waiting to be turned out. All this pained the holy Founder intensely. He endeavored to remedy all deficiencies by laboring to restore perfect regularity and primitive fervor. "Persecutions," said he, "are to the work of God what frosts are to plants in winter; far from being hurtful, they make them take deeper root, and become more fruitful. It is chiefly worms that injure plants. The worms we should fear are voluntary faults; let us root out these and God will infallibly protect us...One violation of rule gives me more pain than a hundred persecutions. Let us kiss the very walls of our cells, and the more we are persecuted the more closely let us be united to Jesus Christ."

Every Saturday, however weak or ill he might be, he never failed to drag himself to the chapel to assist at the chapter of faults, and to animate his dear religious to perfection. "What are we doing in the Congregation," he cried out one day, "unless we become saints? This is the end our dear Lord had in view in calling us from the world. Had He not willed our sanctification He would have left us in the midst of its dangers." He inculcated zeal for souls as the great end of the institute. As he had made a vow to preach every Saturday on the glories of Mary, he would ascend the pulpit, aided by a lay-brother and his servant, and preach as if he were quite well; but the people, on seeing his emaciated countenance and broken frame, would weep tears of compassion. His burning words, spoken from the abundance of a heart on fire with divine love, excited the faithful to love Jesus in the Blessed Sacrament, and Mary, His ever blessed Mother. Priests and lay-men, nobles and plebeians, crowded his poor room that they might profit by his advice. The confessors of the royal family, and the ministers of the kingdom, sought to be enlightened on their duties by the words of wisdom which dropped from his lips; and many ladies of the highest rank learned from him to be docile children of the Holy Church, without neglecting an iota of the onerous obligations of their state in life.

A zealous congregation of priests at Nocera admired the saint so much, that they wished to have him among them as often as possible, to renew their fervor, through his touching exhortations. One day, as he was conversing with them on holy purity, he used the following remarkable words: "Old as I am, even in coming here, I must come with downcast eyes, to prevent temptations against this delicate virtue. Some people use no control over their eyes, and then wonder that they are tempted." He visited the nuns of the city from time to time, to gratify their pious eagerness to learn from his lips the love of Jesus and Mary. His mere presence effected in the asylum, called the *Carminello*, what several confessors had vainly attempted, the reconciliation of two of its members who had lived in a state of scandalous enmity. Upon seeing him, one of them humbled herself and cast herself on her knees before her enemy, and they mutually asked pardon and embraced each other in charity.

The superior of this establishment one day begged him to remember her in his prayers, that she might obtain the cure of a cancer in her left breast, which the doctors declared incurable. He encouraged her to bear it patiently: "Even should it reduce you to the last extremity," said he, "do not distress yourself; place yourself in the hands of God, and embrace your cross; you will thereby please Jesus Christ, and your sufferings will be more easy to bear." Still the saint's heart was touched with compassion for the poor invalid, and he could not refrain from exercising the gift by which he had cured and comforted so many. On his return, he sent her a bottle of water with directions to bathe the diseased part, and when she had done so, she was entirely cured, to the great consolation of herself and her sisters.

The suite of apartments devoted to the use of the retired prelate consisted of two little rooms, one of which served as his oratory. Then might he be found during the greater part of the day praying, reading, or composing. The crucifix and a few pious pictures, were its only ornaments. The poor were still his friends and favorites, and on them was expended the greater part of the annuities he enjoyed as bishop and doctor.

CHAPTER LXIV.

New work. — Opinion of Bishop Cervone. — Other works. — Letters from Pius VI. — Persecutions. — Prophecy. — Gratuitous counsels.— Tanucci retires from office. — De Leon's animosity. — His ironical prediction fulfilled. "Time is a courteous gentleman." — Honor done to the missionaries. Letters. — Circular. — Untimely death of two of the saint's persecutors. The Baron of Ciorani ceases to afflict God's servants. — Alphonsus victorious over all his enemies.

THIS YEAR the saint finished his celebrated book on *Divine Providence*. To this work he added a treatise on the love of God and the methods of acquiring it, and another, containing advice to a soul in desolation. This book eloquently proved that neither age nor suffering had abated the zeal of the saint who was one day to be known as the Most Zealous Doctor. When Monsignore Cervone, the royal censor, examined the work, he wrote a critique on it for the king, in which the following passage occurs:

"The writings of the most Religious Don Alphonsus di Liguori, late Bishop of St. Agatha, are far above the average of ordinary spiritual writings, being as superior to them as he himself is to our other writers in personal holiness."

The saint next undertook to refute an eccentric priest of Calabria, who had endeavored to throw discredit on certain approved practices of devotion to our dear Lady, "practices which," says the devout client of Mary, "are most salutary, and have been dear to me from my earliest infancy." In token of gratitude to Pope Pius, for many favors received from his Holiness, he dedicated to him his work on *Divine Providence*, which he sent him, together with all his later writings, begging him to correct whatever was amiss, and bless whatever might be useful to the faithful. The Pope was much gratified at hearing once more from the venerable bishop, and testified his satisfaction in a brief, of which the following is the tenor:

"We have received with particular pleasure, your works, in which shine forth the admirable zeal for virtue which your piety inspires, no less than your wonderful learning. These are fresh motives to cause an increase of our paternal love for you, founded on your virtues and merits. Be persuaded that all we have hitherto done in your favor is only an earnest of the good will which we shall evince towards you on every occasion, to the utmost of our power."

Alphonsus, overwhelmed by so much goodness, hastened to offer his most humble thanks to the Holy Father, but Pius VI, who would not permit himself to be outdone in courtesy, responded by a new brief, dated November 16, 1776, from which we make the following extract:

"You could not have bestowed upon us anything more acceptable than your late works, for which we are as grateful as if you had sent us a gift far more valuable in the eyes of the world. We have glanced rapidly over them, and will read them attentively as soon as we are at leisure. To us they are a fresh and conclusive proof of your indefatigable zeal in feeding the flock of Jesus Christ as far as lies in your power. Though you have resigned your bishopric, you have not therefore renounced the solicitude and duties of a bishop. As to the Congregation of the Most Holy Redeemer, which you recommend to the protection of the Holy See, be persuaded that there is nothing which we would not cheerfully do for you and for it, because of the eminent piety which animates you and which we delight to honor."

The Dogmatical Dissertations (1776), and the *Victories of the Martyrs* (1777), were composed by our saint, with several minor works, after his resignation of his bishopric. While he continued to turn to account every moment of his precious time, according to the terms of his vow, the enemies of order and religion persecuted his Congregation with a persevering malevolence which ended only with their lives. These wretches were among the miscreants who had persecuted the society of Jesus, and all but compelled its temporary suppression; already their diseased imagination saw the Church, the real object of their bitter hatred, deprived of the devoted Congregation of the Most Holy

Redeemer, and gloried in its destruction, which, nevertheless, was not to take place.

"We shall now see," said some, "what this Liguori is, and what kind of disciples he has mustered together." "The tribe of relaxed casuists and their adherents will be extirpated," said others. Alphonsus himself acknowledged that, humanly speaking, no redress was to be hoped for. The chief of the commissioners entrusted by Tanucci with the examination of the affair had already declared that the Congregation was useless. "My God!" wrote the saint, "we have been of use for upwards of forty-four years, aiding the souls of so many poor shepherds and villagers in the mountains of Calabria, in the Abruzzi, in La Pouille, and now we have become useless and even hurtful!" The Fathers were anxious that he should go to Naples, but he was unable to undertake the journey. His health was so much impaired at this period that his adversaries proclaimed that if their efforts failed to destroy the Congregation, the death of its Founder would ultimately extinguish it. "They say," he wrote, "that when I die the Congregation will become extinct, but I affirm that this Congregation is not my work but the work of God, and that He will sustain it after my death as he has hitherto done." To some of the Fathers he remarked: "Do not be afraid, I shall not die just yet. God wills that I shall die a subject, and not chief superior." Several years previous, the saint made a similar observation, and the event showed that he prophesied.

When people imagined that the society of the Redemptorists was about to be dissolved, many undertook to give the holy Founder, enlightened as he was by the Eternal Son of Justice, the benefit of their flickering lights. "Make each house independent," said one; "open seminaries for the education of youth," quoth another, "preach Latin sermons" was the advice volunteered by a third. But the saint, who knew well that in his regard, the light that was given by officious friends was darkness, declined to be guided by it, confiding in God, who would infallibly preserve the Congregation so long as it remained faithful to its special vocation, as it had heretofore done, to the immense benefit of souls in every grade of life.

An old calumny, the enemies again affirming that they hoarded money in their houses in the Papal States – and a hardly less mischievous one, which was far from being new – that the doctrines of Alphonsus contained laxity, error, malice – caused Tanucci to withdraw the cause from the royal council and refer it to the Junta of Abuses. Their adversaries had recourse to bribery in order to obtain false testimony against them, and according to all human calculations, the Congregation of the Most Holy Redeemer was close upon its end. The saint prayed and procured prayers; he wrote to the great and powerful; he interested, in behalf of his cause, every influential person at court with whom he was at all acquainted – no lawful means, natural or supernatural, was left untried, to promote the preservation and well-being of the community. It was considered providential, and an answer to the united prayers of so many fervent servants of God, that, in the midst of these troubles, October, 16, 1776, the prime minister, Marquis Tanucci, retired from office, and was succeeded by the Marquis of Sambuco, a great friend of our saint and his institute. This event, so favorable to the hopes of the persecuted Congregation, did not in the least disconcert the persecutors.

The report of the procurator, Leon, was at length presented to the king, February 13, 1777. In this the hapless members of the Congregation were styled *rising Jesuits*, than which, in the eyes of the world, a more injurious and opprobrious epithet could not well be devised, even by the implacable enmity of Leon, at that particular epoch. Numerically small as the Congregation then was, its archives show that during the first five months of the year 1778, thirty-five missions were given, eight retreats were conducted for priests, seven for seminaries, and nineteen for convents; besides many triduos and other devotions by its members. Therefore Alphonsus had some reason for saying: "Redeemed souls ought to be the advocates of our cause;" and by expatiating on the success, that almost invariably crowned their labors, he sought to inspire them with ever increasing zeal for the glory of God and the salvation of souls.

The bishops and clergy did not show themselves ungrateful for the wonders of grace which the missionaries had been instrumental in effecting in their respective districts. Numerous petitions reached the king, which bore grateful testimony to the probity and disinterestedness of their lives, their submission to authority, and the good which was invariably effected by their labors; and in consequence it was finally decided that the cause, after having been examined by the minister, should be sent back to the royal council. Alphonsus, overjoyed at this arrangement, wrote to Father de Paul: "I can do nothing, but thank Jesus and Mary for the many blessings they shower on me in these latter days of my life...Matters have now assumed an altered appearance. Blessed forever be Jesus and Mary. Amen."

The following curious passage forms a fitting conclusion to the infamous document which Leon had the audacity to lay before his king:

"Let not your majesty imagine that you can arrest the progress of this new institute without using powerful remedies. Other orders have arisen amid contradictions; nor will contradictions suffice to destroy this. They will wait for a more propitious time; and ultimately the controversy of to-day will be numbered among the glories of the institute; and my name, which otherwise deserves obscurity, will be famous in the Life of Don Alfonso di Liguori, *wherein it will be related that the devil stirred me up against the Congregation, as he always raises up enemies against every good work.*"

Verily, out of his own mouth we may judge this new Caiaphas. His candor is admirable when he truly avers that his name deserves to be consigned to oblivion; but who would expect to find him playing the role of prophet, and not proving a false one? Undoubtedly, the name of the procurator has become immortal only as the bitterest among the opponents of the saint, "*stirred up*" to use his own remarkable words, "*by the devil, to destroy the Congregation of the Most Holy Redeemer.*"

In defence of his *Moral Theology*, also attacked by Leon, the saint wrote an able pamphlet, in which he proved himself, despite his advanced age and unceasing infirmities, a master canonist and theologian. While he defended his doctrine and disciples, he was so courteous and gentlemanly towards his enemies, that they were constrained to acknowledge his moderation, and in future they ceased to attack him save through his missionaries.

Though the saint wrote to every influential friend he possessed, he did not wish the cause to be immediately discussed in the council. "Time," said he, "is a very courteous gentleman; he is of wonderful assistance to the persecuted." His adversaries also would willingly temporize, but they feared that delay would be dangerous to their cause. It was, nevertheless, deferred till August, 1779, when the Marquis of Marco wrote to the saint as follows:

"I stated to the king the representations of your lordship touching the accusations so injurious to the Congregation you direct. His majesty has commanded me to reply that, as the Catholic king, his august father permitted the missionaries, of whom your lordship is the head, to give missions, and to reside in the houses of Ciorani, Nocera, Caposele and Illiceto; and prescribed the conditions under which this great undertaking was to be maintained, his majesty also consents to there being a superior in each of the above named houses, to watch over internal order, and see that the other offices be properly distributed; and as it was the intention of the Catholic king[1] that this salutary work should never cease to exist, his majesty also approves of young men being received, and taught such things as are needful to enable them to supply the places of those who may become incapacitated through advanced age or any other cause."

In proportion to our saint's gratification on learning the contents of this letter, was the chagrin of Leon: "If the Grand Duke of Tuscany had come here in person," said he, "he would not have obtained from the court the favors which this handful of upstarts have got."

Nor did the king's favor stop here. The Pope having granted leave on Nov. 21, 1777, to have a jubilee celebrated in the kingdom of Naples, the king selected the Redemptorist Fathers to announce it to the people, and, about a year later, the Marquis of Sambuco wrote to the holy Founder:

"In consideration of the constant labors of the missionaries of the Most Holy Redeemer, which tend to instruct the people and lead them to true piety, and of the solicitude with which they disseminate those good principles which are calculated to form

---

[1] "It was the intention of the Catholic king that this salutary work should never cease to exist." Did the king then mean to live forever to protect it? We trust God has rewarded his good intentions; but, though the Congregation of the Most Holy Redeemer is little more than a century old, it has already seen the end of his dynasty. - Ed.

pious Christians and loyal subjects, his majesty has determined to make use of your Congregation to publish a jubilee, the sole object of which is the salvation of the faithful and the good of the state. Therefore the king has commanded me to inform your lordship that, in return for the happy success which will bless your labors in this undertaking, he will not fail to give you proofs of his royal gratitude."

Many circumstances rendered this mark of the royal confidence invaluable to the Congregation. Our saint seconding the zeal of the pious sovereign, addressed to his sons, on the 8th of November, a short circular in which he sets forth the excellence of the missions, and exhorts them to further, by every possible means, this great work for the glory of God and the good of souls, reminding them that what the king counseled and commanded was nothing more than the accomplishment of the end of their institute. Full of gratitude for the blessings which Providence continued to bestow, his first thought was to thank Him for them. He wrote to all the houses, directing that every evening the following prayers should be recited in common three times: "What have I in heaven, and besides Thee what do I desire on earth? Thou art the God of my heart and my portion forever. My Jesus, I devote myself entirely to Thee, I wish for nothing but Thee," adding each time a *Pater, Ave,* and *Gloria Patri.* He incessantly inculcated that prayer is all-powerful with God, and that He is to be perpetually thanked for his benefits.

The honorable distinction conferred by the king on the Congregation was a real pain to its enemies, especially the procurator. "Strange fancy!" he exclaimed; "it would seem as if scandal is to be made lawful, though it should ruin Church and State." The decree by which his majesty sanctioned the mode of government established among the missionaries tried his patience still more severely; but had he been able to draw aside for a moment the dark veil of futurity, he would have seen how little he need be concerned about sublunary things. He was prematurely cited before Him who will judge with justice, dying as he came out of a bath, without having time to receive the last sacraments. His companion, the commissioner, quickly followed him: this unprincipled official was found dead in his bed a little later. One by one the other supporters of the Baron of Ciorani disappeared, and all in a tragic manner, so that, recognizing the hand of God in these unlooked-for occurrences, the stubborn noble no longer had the heart to persecute God's servants. Thus it was that sooner or later, God rendered his servant victorious over his enemies, prolonged his life, blessed him on earth, and delivered him not to their impious will.

CHAPTER LXV.

The saint's zeal for the houses outside the kingdom. — He insists upon each religious having a cell to himself. — Letter. — Favors granted by Pius VI. The saint's solicitude for the health of his sons. — His great love for them. His endeavors to promote perfect charity. — He wished superiors to show great gentleness towards them. — His work on Fidelity of Subjects to their King. — Extract. — His zeal for the great. — He destroys letters received from sovereigns. — He stirs up the zeal of his literary friends. Correspondence with Abbé Nonnote. — Voltaire. — Conversion of Metastasio.

MEANWHILE Alphonsus considering the continual dangers and persecutions to which his Congregation was exposed in the kingdom of the Two Sicilies, left nothing undone to consolidate his establishments in the States of the Church, regarding them as a secure refuge in the event of a temporary suppression in the kingdom. "The house of Frosinone," he wrote to Father de Paul, July 7, 1772, "interests me more than that of Girgenti, because it is independent of the kingdom. I attach the greatest importance to maintaining that foundation, for which we are indebted to the Pope...If it be God's pleasure, I should like to live until I can succeed, through my pension, in finishing the building, now commenced I hope to receive some money from St. Agatha soon, and be sure I will send you as much as I can."

The saint was very particular in seeing that the subjects had each his own room, and always planned his convents so as to make that luxury universal, instead of permitting the members of his institute to sleep in dormitories. "Without a cell of his own," he wrote, "a religious is a most miserable creature; he can have no privacy, spiritually or temporally." His opinion on this point has had considerable influence, and has caused, and will yet cause, many a recluse to bless his name.

The poverty of the houses in the States was extreme. The saint's letters at this period show that he not only grieved over it, but sent his dear sons almost all the money that came into his hands — his pension, his allowances — in short all that he could claim, beg or borrow. He desired to be informed of everything that occurred in these distant foundations, and so great was his solicitude for their welfare, that it pained him to be left in ignorance of the smallest matter that involved their interest. "I have never dispensed you," he wrote to Father de Paul, "from communicating to me what you do. Thank God, I am not dead yet, nor have I lost my senses. I have been a lawyer and a bishop, and have had to transact such business frequently. I am still superior general, what reason can there be then for not informing me? In charity, tell me what is done. I have given a thousand opinions as bishop and as advocate, but you do everything of your own accord and look on me as quite useless. Perhaps no house has caused me more trouble than Frosinone. God be praised!"

He knew little how much it was yet to give him. The solicitude of the saint extended to everything, especially the missions. "I wish," he wrote, "that missions, should be conducted with all possible prudence and edification, and in an apostolic spirit." To increase the good produced by them, he entreated Pope Pius VI to communicate to the Congregation the graces, privileges and indulgences lately granted to the Passionist Fathers,[1] a favor which His Holiness readily granted. He did not wish his missionaries to undertake Lenten sermons, panegyrics, or any species of oratory which might attract the public attention from the matter to the manner, and excite admiration without changing the heart. He was displeased when Fathers accepted engagements of this nature, and wrote very decidedly on the subject to Father de Paul. He continually urged upon all the rectors of the States, the necessity of keeping and enforcing the rules. "You know," he wrote, "I keep up those houses in the Romagna, that the rule may be rigorously observed. Manage so

[1] The Passionist Fathers had already begun to evangelize Northern Italy when St Alphonsus founded the Congregation of the Most Holy Redeemer in the South. It is worthy of remark that our saint's learned and most pious uncle, Monsignor Cavalieri, Bishop of Troia, was the great friend and protector of St. Paul of the Cross and his companions, who used to say that the labors and austerities of this holy prelate, even in old age, made them ashamed. – Ed.

that the Fathers can make the accustomed retreat, or, if they are ill, at least part of it." He was ever scrupulously careful of the health of his sons:

"You tell me," he wrote to Father de Paul, "that the house might very well be inhabited, but the doctor thinks it should not be used before October, and I will not suffer remorse for causing the death of any of my brethren." The following letter addressed to the same Father, when made superior of Frosinone, shows how ardently he desired that those who govern in the Congregation should rather be Fathers than superiors:

"I entreat your Reverence to be humble towards your companions, and affable towards all, especially in mission times, and to treat your brethren with all possible consideration, remembering that they are far from their country and their family, and therefore have the right to claim that charity should be redoubled in their behalf."

He was accustomed to say that, when health is lost, a subject can no longer be of use to himself or his neighbor, and he was, as his letters show, extremely particular on this point. But though nothing escaped his affectionate vigilance, he always dwelt most emphatically on the importance of preserving perfect union and charity. "If we had the riches of Croesus," said he, "all would be useless without charity. When the bond of love is wanting, everything is wanting. He was especially displeased if the superiors manifested the slightest want of charity with regard to their subjects, or assumed imperious airs when treating with them. His own exceeding gentleness and considerateness made him inexpressibly dear to such of his subjects as had personal intercourse with him.

About this time he composed a most useful and opportune work entitled, *The Fidelity of Subjects towards God is a sure pledge of their Fidelity towards their King*. "Monarchs will never have peace," said he, "if they do not aim at the prevention of immorality. Where religion does not reign, perfidy is rife; admit sin, and all is in danger; but if kings only make their subjects faithful towards God, they will be equally faithful towards them." Though the saint's zeal was chiefly for the destitute and abandoned, he at all periods of his career endeavored to lead to sanctity nobles, magistrates, and persons in power, hoping, through them, to influence the masses, and hence we find him ready to repair to court whenever he was summoned thither for the spiritual direction of any member of the royal family. In this way he was able to effect much good for his diocese, and for many who sought his mediation, even in temporal matters.

When he wrote the above work, he said to one of the fathers, in a transport of holy zeal: "Have as many missions as you please, but if I gain one sovereign, I shall regard the conquest as worth more than a thousand missions; for the good a monarch can effect who is touched by the grace of God, could not be effected by a thousand missions." He transmitted copies of this work through Cardinal Castelli to all the foreign ambassadors, and directly to the august empress, Maria Teresa, to the electoral princes of Cologne and Tréves, and to the Prince-bishops of the German Empire; also to Prince Charles, governor of the Netherlands, the kings of Spain and Portugal, the grand Duke of Tuscany, the Duke of Parma, and all the other Catholic sovereigns. These august personages courteously acknowledged his gift by autograph letters expressive of admiration for his vast and wonderful erudition, and reverence for his undoubted sanctity, but with his characteristic humility, he destroyed every one of these flattering epistles. The book was immediately translated into French. "This work," says the translator, "is the voice of a soul which thirsts only for the glory of religion, the spread of morality, and the welfare of rulers and their subjects, and which has no ambition but to make men virtuous and happy."

When age and infirmity no longer left our Most Zealous Doctor able to wield his most prolific pen in the cause which was dearer to him than life, he encouraged his literary friends in Naples and elsewhere, to refute the errors of the infidel writers of the day, especially Rousseau and Voltaire, over whose libertinism he often wept bitterly. The writings of these renegades were already handed about in Naples, and even formed one of the pastimes of several Neapolitan ladies, to the great detriment of religion and morality. Happening to see a French work by the Abbé Nonnote, in which the errors of these murderers of morality were ably combated, he was filled with joy, and thanked God for having raised up a man who braved the spirit of the world and devoted himself courageously to the cause of God. In an elegantly-worded letter, he congratulated the zealous abbé on his useful achievement, and encouraged him to persevere in directing his able pen against the impious.

This letter, from the most distinguished prelate of the age, afforded inexpressible pleasure to the worthy priest, as he testifies in a lengthy epistle which contains the following passages:

"I am accustomed to appreciate nothing except in conformity to the spirit of God; and it is an unspeakable pleasure to me to meet with men who entertain similar sentiments. Your letter informs me, that there is at least one such man in the kingdom of Naples — one who appreciates only the things of God, and who being in himself greater than great dignities could make him, forces one to doubt which should be the more admired, your genius or your virtue...All who have read your excellent and justly celebrated work on *Moral Theology*, congratulate me on having received such a flattering letter from so eminent a prelate, and I congratulate myself for having deserved the approbation of so distinguished a man."

The correspondence between the bishop and the abbé did not cease with the occasion that called it forth. In a subsequent letter, Nonnote gives a gloomy picture of the state of religion in his native country, and informs his illustrious friend that, for over twenty years, he has been fighting against the errors of the sophists, and far from getting help from any one, he was loaded with invectives by the impious. "O God," exclaimed the saint on reading this sad letter, "is their no one else at Paris, which abounds with Christian orators, to oppose this monster Voltaire?" The abbé had informed him, that he could not publish at Paris a book he had written in defence of religion, because of the great fear inspired by this sarcastic man. "Miserable beings that we are," proceeds the saint; "this is the authority of the Church at Paris! She cannot face an infidel and reprove his audacity! A book in defence of religion, must be transported to Geneva for publication! Poor France, I pity thee and the many innocent people who will be involved in thy ruin!" Remarkable words! Or rather prophetic words, when we consider that they were uttered only ten years before the revolution which deluged the county with innocent blood.

A rumor of the conversion of Voltaire was a gleam of consolation to the holy prelate, and he wrote to the prodigal to congratulate him on his return to grace, and the great good his conversion would effect. To encourage him to a public retraction of the ruinous errors he had spent his base and wretched life in promulgating, the saint addressed him an affectionate and most eloquent letter, felicitating him on his supposed conversion, and encouraging him to perform the little that lay in his power to undo the mischief he had already done, and even to attack Jean Jacques Rousseau, a name almost as vile as his own. But the saint had the affliction to learn that it was merely a hypocritical simulation of conversion in an impious man, who had once corresponded with the great Benedict XIV, that now for the hundredth time or more, deceived the people. "Alas!" cried the saint, "such conversions are not common; they are effects of the divine mercy, but not in its ordinary degrees. God grants blessings of this kind only to those whose errors have not arisen from a bad intention, like St. Paul. But in Voltaire all has been excessively bad." Already this wretch was almost blind, and the saint had encouraged him to dictate some refutation of his blasphemies, if he could not write. But God did not will his cause to be aided by the vile pen of Arouet de Voltaire.

On the thirtieth of May this year (1778) the infamous philosopher of Femey passed from his miserable death-bed to eternity, vainly coveting the favors conferred on the dying, through the ministry of that blessed Mother-Church which he had spent his life in reviling. Suicide rid the earth of his colleague Rousseau a little later. "Thanks be to God," exclaimed our saint, "for having in so short a time delivered the Church from two of her greatest enemies."

Our saint had, however, one consolation of this nature in the thorough conversion of the celebrated Metastasio, for whom he had always entertained esteem and admiration. This elegant poet and complete master of the Italian language, entirely gained the heart of his most zealous contemporary by the sorrow he eloquently expressed for having written the beautiful but dangerous poetry which had gained him a European reputation. "May I be permitted to manifest," wrote the saint,[2] (*Spiritual Reflections*), "the great joy that filled my heart on learning that the

---

[2] It is hardly necessary to observe that, though the saint was at the head of the literary men of his country for some two thirds of a century, his genius never emitted a spark of literary jealousy. (Editor original note)

celebrated Peter Metastasio, whose poetry received so much praise throughout the continent — poetry which is all the more dangerous because of its exceeding beauty — is going to protest his profound repentance, and his wish, if possible, to withdraw his profane poems from the hands of the public at any expense, even that of his blood...I have learned too, that he leads a retired life, quite devoted to prayer and spiritual exercises. This has given me unspeakable consolation, because this public declaration and the great and good example he gives, will cause many misguided young people to think seriously, who have tried to gain applause by amorous poems written in imitation of his. It is certain that Metastasio gains more praise by this, than if he had published a thousand brilliant poems...Therefore while I detest the vanity which made him glory in being the author of such compositions, I cannot now cease to praise him, and were it possible I would gladly kiss his feet, seeing that he has become the censor of his own works, and desires to stop their circulation, even though it should cost his life, as he declares."

Alphonsus abhorred all amorous poetry, however great the genius it displayed, to such an extent as to inspire a natural aversion for its authors. On the contrary, his delight in sacred poetry was so great, that when any well written poems came under his observation, he became the most ardent panegyrist of their authors. He was particularly pleased with the style of Xavier Maffei who translated the Psalms into elegant Italian verse. "If all poets," said he, "consecrated their talents in this way to the giver of all good, we should soon see lascivious poetry banished from the lips of youth." Maffei, grateful for the praises lavished on him by Alphonsus — who, besides being a saint, was universally regarded as the most elegant scholar of the day, and had early distinguished himself in poetry and music — publicly thanked him in the preface to his next work,[3] and, at the same time, forwarded him a private letter, expressive of his intense gratification at having won the approbation of the most distinguished *savant*, and the holiest man in Naples. Alphonsus wishing to encourage his brother-poet to pursue his literary labors, wrote to him in a highly appreciative strain Nov. 30, 1774:

---

[3] Find this book – interesting historical detail

"Your dear letter overwhelmed me with delight. When I made my little translation of the Psalms, I kept your excellent work constantly before my eyes. You have written for the learned and the ignorant, and your charming poetry is as instructive as it is enchanting. It has been applauded by literary men throughout Italy, and, I may say throughout Europe; while my prose is only for the ignorant, and will scarcely please a small number of the devout. I am pleased at the renown you gain as a lawyer, but what joy it will give me if you continue to use your great talents and science for the advantage of the Church. But, even in your present position, you can do a great deal for religion, since in our days every one undertakes to discuss theology and the Holy Scripture, and puts forth whatever propositions suit his fancy."

CHAPTER LXVI.

The greatest evils done the Congregation. — Efforts of the founder. — "Edify or go." — Family matters. — Little Joseph. — Interesting letter. — Death of Count Hercules Liguori. — Resignation of the saint. — Cure of Don Gavotti. The Lady Teresa Liguori. — Letter. — The lady Antonia Liguori. — His anxiety about his niece's vocation. — His usual advice to noble spinsters. Teresa becomes a nun. — Her visit to her uncle. — Her profession. — The young Count Joseph.

T HE GREATEST evil done the Congregation by its enemies, was the interior derangement and relaxation that resulted from the perpetual uneasiness in which the members were kept, as to whether it would not ultimately be entirely destroyed.

Some took advantage of these troubles to insist on having their own way, others even pretended to brave the rule and yet wear the habit, and a few went to the lengths of supplying the adversaries of the institute with weapons against it. But these last, God did not suffer to remain long in his house.

After the defeat of the enemies of the Congregation, the holy Founder, who now enjoyed the good graces of the sovereign, endeavored to remedy the injuries which regular observance had sustained. "Edify or go," was the alternative he proposed to such as were remiss. "I require," he wrote to the local rectors, "that each be compelled to the most exact observance of rule. All have embraced it of their own free choice, and besides, we do not keep any one by force. If any repent of having come amongst us, let them settle the question with God; I am ready to dispense them; better be few but good; those who are not edifying are always a burden, injurious to themselves and to others."

While the saint was thus endeavoring to reestablish perfect discipline, he heard of an event in his own family that caused him great pain. His nephews, Joseph and Alfonsino were still at the College of Nobles, when Count Hercules entered into a matrimonial negotiation for the elder, then a boy of thirteen. "Ah," exclaimed the saint on learning this, "my little Joseph is going to lose the grace of God." Father Villani having observed that the affair would remain a secret, between Don Hercules and the father of the intended bride, he remarked: "It suffices that it be known to one servant. It is by valets and coachmen that the children of the nobles are led astray. The domestics will begin by saying: 'good news, little Joseph! Your papa has found you a pretty wife.' This is accompanied by other light words and unseemly gestures; and thus young hearts are corrupted." He wrote a most severe letter to Don Hercules, who was prompt enough in excusing this premature engagement. But he could not satisfy the saint, who would allow of no necessity for seeking a bride for a boy of thirteen; and indeed Count Hercules had no excuse to allege for his indecent haste, save that of his own advanced age.

That our saint took great interest in the education of his nephews may be gathered from the following letter, which he wrote them, April 4, 1780:

My Very Dear Nephews,

"I would gladly have you with me in order to bestow upon you my last benediction and my last advice; for it is by a miracle of his goodness, that God prolongs my life to give me leisure to weep over my sins. I bless him though he does not give me the consolation of seeing you; I do not deserve it. From the depths of my heart I bless you, and I pray God to send you his benediction from the heights of heaven, to fill your young hearts with his fear and his love, and thereby to conduct you to a happy eternity, where I will await you if he shows me mercy. Always fear God as your sovereign master, but love him as your tender *father*. Every day you call him by that sweet name of father, when you say OUR FATHER in the Lord's prayer. Since he is your Father, love him tenderly. He is a father, good, sweet, loving, beneficent and merciful — these titles should inspire you to love him with a cordial, tender, and grateful affection. Happy, if from your infancy you love him sincerely! The yoke of the Lord would then never be burdensome to you. You would find it as sweet as his holy law is amiable.

"Learn to correct all that is disorderly in you, and to triumph over the enemies of your soul. Habit will make virtue easy; you will find sweetness in what is very difficult to those who have not learned to serve the Lord betimes.[1]

"Love God, my children; I call you my children because I love you as a father, and because I wish to inspire a holy love in your hearts. O my dear sons! love the Lord God and his son, Jesus Christ; love him much; preserve this love jealously in your hearts, fearing to lose it. It is a great loss to lose God, his grace, and his friendship. Yes, it is a frightful calamity to incur his indignation, and expose oneself to his vengeance.

"I recommend you to be humble: he who is humble avoids danger; and if temptation comes in spite of him, he has recourse to God with confidence, and thus preserves divine love. The proud easily fall into disgrace with God. Without humility you would never do good, your virtue would be neither sincere nor solid, and you would easily lose it. God resists the proud, and shows mercy to the humble; he looks on the humble with an eye of goodness, they are his friends. If you reflect well on yourselves, you will not be proud, because you can always find enough to humble you. Your birth is a gift of God to which you have not contributed. You are in a college which is directed by professors, full of zeal and science, whose nobility of blood is enhanced by their rare virtues; your education is conducted by prudent, wise and regular men; this is another benefit from the Lord.

"You are now, I trust, in the grace of God; this also is an effect of his goodness. Whatever is good in you is a gift of God, for which you are indebted to his tenderness, and should use only for his glory. If you look on your failings — and such things are truly and properly yours — you will undoubtedly find matter enough to keep you humble. If you be humble, you will always obey, with sentiments of gratitude and love, your superiors, who take such pains to instruct you. Whether they treat you mildly, or correct you, they always give proofs of their affection. It is true that their corrections may pain you, but, nevertheless, they are effects of the love these good religious bear you. Obey them as

---

[1] "Betimes" means early or before the expected time.

your father, for it is your father who has confided you to their care; you should then obey, love, and respect them as your own father. I hope you will show these dispositions to please God, your father and myself.

"I learned with disappointment, that you had but little application to study. O my children, how you would weep could you see the consequences of this! Ignorance and idleness are the two great sources of sin. Study, then, attentively, diligently, and ardently, to know God, his benefits, his rewards; to be able to contemplate and love him much. An ignorant man has little knowledge of God, of the duties he imposes, and hence, he leads an evil life. Study well then, and before I die let me have the satisfaction of seeing that my advice has not been fruitless. I approach the term of my career, and know not if you shall ever see me more; let my last words then be engraven on your young hearts, and produce in you the effects desired. Read this long letter, get some one to explain whatever you do not understand in it, and imprint my counsels on your memory that you may put them in practice.

"Have a great love for God, study to know and love this amiable master, and to love him always more and more preserve in your hearts this holy love with humility, obey your superiors and your father with docility and affection. Observe exactly the rules of the college, in order to please God. Be devout to the Blessed Virgin; I leave you under her protection, and I recommend you to her with affectionate tenderness. I bless you in Jesus Christ, that you may be devoted to him as I desire and hope, in time and in eternity."

Five months after the young scions of the illustrious house of Liguori received the above beautiful letter, their aged father, Count Hercules, who Had always enjoyed the most robust health, was suddenly snatched away by a violent illness. God had given our saint a presentiment of this, some three months previous to its occurrence; "Hercules will cause me sorrow this year," said he to Father Costanzo; and when this afflicting news arrived, the Father asked: "Is not this the sorrow which you said Don Hercules would cause you?" But the saint replied only by his silence. On learning that his brother was no more, he bowed his hoary head[2] in submission to the divine will, and exclaimed, "Blessed be God!" He was much consoled on learning that the deceased had given the tutorship of his children to the lawyer Peter Gavotti, but subject to his own authority, and that of Don Nicholas Vespoli, a relation of the family. In reply to a letter written by the saint, urging the tutor to attend to the religious education, not less than the temporal interests, of his wards, Gavotti wrote: "I am quite at your service, and will devote myself as much as possible to the interests of these children, but your lordship must beseech God to deliver me from headache, which continually torments me." "Take care of these little children," replied Alphonsus, "and be sure that God will relieve you." Gavotti has attested that when he received this letter, he was instantly cured and never after suffered from headache.

Our saint took particular interest in his niece, Donna Teresa, who was now about sixteen, and still a boarder in the Convent of St. Marcellinus at Naples. This young lady was a precious pearl in the eyes of her aged uncle, who eagerly desired to see her consecrated to God. "Being now eighty-five years old," he wrote to her, "I feel that I am no longer good for much, yet whenever you need anything let me know, and I will see that nothing is wanting to you. Meanwhile, recommend me to Jesus Christ. If any one advise you to leave the convent and throw yourself over a precipice, (marry), listen to no such counsel, for you would repent of it the second day. Think only of saving your soul; it is the most important of all affairs. Ask advice of your confessor, and of some exemplary religious. I recommend you to Jesus Christ, that He may inspire you to take the true road to heaven. Pray to our Lady for me, because the hour of my death is near."

Writing to his cousin, Antonia Liguori, a nun, he says: "Salute Teresa, my niece, on my part; tell her not to be duped by the world which would persuade her to renounce Jesus Christ. This would be a sure way to create for herself a miserable life, and a still more miserable death. Nowadays, ladies in the world are hardly saved. See that she does not neglect prayer and communion, and that she reads pious books. I am afraid that some servant of the monastery puts the world in her head. I am very grateful to you for the care you take of this dear child. I know she

[2] Meaning, showing signs of age with grey or white hair

wishes to become a religious, but I fear lest she should change these pious sentiments for worldly views."

As the young lady ceased for a while to open her mind to her saintly uncle on this subject, he wrote to her guardian: "I will not dissemble the pain I feel regarding my niece, Mary Teresa, who had once a great desire to enter religion, but now no longer speaks of it. I fear some marriage may be arranged for her, and this would endanger her eternal salvation. Married women are saved only with great difficulty, because the greater portion of them live in sin, in consequence of the dangers to which they are exposed. I have prayed her confessor to nourish her religious vocation. I ask the same favor of you, for, if she marries in this corrupt age, I shall look upon her as lost."

He repeats the same sentiment in a letter dated April 23, 1781, to the Lady, Mary Teresa, herself:

"Yes, my dear niece, I shall continue to pray for your vocation, since you desire it. A little while ago, before your father's death, you longed to take Jesus Christ for your spouse; you then felt the greatest distaste for the world.

"I beseech Him to confirm you in these sentiments, for if you change them, it will be difficult for you to persevere in the grace of God. What I say to you, I have already said to all the noble young ladies who have come hither to consult me, showing them that if they settled in the world, it would not be easy for them to save their souls. So corrupt is the world of to-day, that, so far as I have been able to observe, ladies who mingle in society ordinarily lose the grace of God. Think not, then, of forsaking Jesus Christ for the world; that would be to lose Him and your soul by your own act. All my relations who died during my lifetime, have, God be thanked, died happily; and I comfort myself with the hope of rejoining them in paradise. I would have you also with me there."

God, who grants the desires of His saints, soon called the young Teresa to His immediate service. When only seventeen, she declared, with a spirit worthy of her cousin and namesake, Teresina, whose example had quickened the fervor even of a saint, that she would become a nun, and she insisted on following out her vocation immediately. Her guardian refused consent on the plea that, her father had declared, that, if she manifested this inclination, she must not put it in execution until she should have completed her twenty-first year. However, as the young lady incessantly importuned him, and easily won her uncle to her side, by convincing him that her attraction to the religious state was not a passing fancy but a real vocation, she speedily gained her point.

It is not allowable in Italy for a young lady to pass from the schoolroom to the novitiate; every boarder desirous of becoming a religious, must return to the world for a short time, that her vocation may be tested. But our saint would not allow his niece to return to her relations who seemed to have grown so worldly since the death of Don Hercules, that he feared she would lose the love of God, and her vocation among them. He therefore confided her to his penitent, the duchess of Bovino, who joyfully welcomed her. When she left the monastery (Feb. 16, 1781,) the saint wrote to her to recommend, as was his wont, divine love, holy modesty and detachment from earthly things. "Above all," he continues, "avoid going to public festivities. The duchess thinks as I do in this matter; consult her, and you will see how far she is from wishing to expose your soul to perils of this nature." The young lady never gave her protectress the least anxiety on this point; her sole desire was to return as soon as possible to the monastery of her choice, and the only favor she asked was to be permitted to visit her uncle at Nocera, and receive the blessing of a saint.

The duchess and her daughter accompanied Dona Teresa to Nocera, where the party remained three days. The aged saint evinced the greatest delight at seeing his dear niece, whose birth he had foretold, and whose name he had chosen, perhaps in memory of that young and lovely Teresina, who had set him the example of counting all things as loss for the love of the Lord Jesus, and who in a short time had fulfilled a long space.

For ten months, Teresa had been inconvenienced by a wound in her leg. The saint was greatly distressed on hearing it; and when she knelt to ask a parting benediction. "I bless you," said he, "as your uncle and as a bishop." When the wound was unbandaged that evening, it was found perfectly healed, as not only the duchess, but the surgeon and other members of her household testified. His parting gifts to this much cherished niece were copies of *Preparation for Death*, and his *Visits to the Blessed Sacrament*, with a relic, in a little box of no value.

The holy bishop desired that the ceremonies attendant on Dona Teresa's entrance into the convent and profession, should be conducted with as little pomp and magnificence as possible. But as her other guardians held different views all was arranged with reference to the birth and fortune of the only daughter of the illustrious Count Hercules di Liguori. The cream of the Neapolitan nobility deemed it an honor to be invited to these ceremonies. The ardent novice besought her holy uncle to come to her profession, but he was unable to gratify her: "Your last letter," he wrote, "has given me such comfort that I have not been able to restrain my tears. Sad indeed I am, to be unable to comply with your wishes. If God had granted me the favor of being present at your sacrifice, I should certainly have done nothing during the ceremony but weep tears of joy; but as He has been pleased to deprive me of this consolation, I shall not cease to recommend you to Jesus Christ that He may inflame you with His holy love, and that you may one day contemplate Him face to face in paradise. I beseech you to recommend me often to Jesus crucified, that He may give me the grace of a happy death, for my sins inspire me with great fear regarding my eternal salvation. I bless you; you are always before me in my memento. Every day in my communion I ask Jesus Christ to give you grace to be entirely His." It being customary then as now for the relations and friends of ladies about to make the vows to present them with some token of remembrance and congratulation, the saint forwarded to his niece a picture of the Blessed Virgin "to remind her to thank Our Lady, and implore her protection." He had always manifested a warm affection for this niece, and his joy was complete when he saw her consecrate herself to God in religion.

As to his nephew Joseph: when this young nobleman showed an inclination to enter the married state, the saint referred the matter entirely to the guardians, desiring them not to constrain him in any way, and to select for him a wife of exemplary life and suitable birth. When the choice was fixed, Don Joseph paid his uncle this mark of respect, that he went to Nocera to bring the news himself. "I bless you, and pray God to bless you," said the aged prelate, and then having added some good advice, he sent the youth away consoled and satisfied.

It was about this time that Alphonsus revised for the last time his *Moral Theology*, already well known in every civilized country. Seven editions of this most valuable work were published at Naples and Venice during his own lifetime. Most of his other works had been reproduced in almost every language of Christendom, and had in all cases been productive of untold good. Years, infirmities, and sorrows now began to proclaim more loudly than ever that his sun was about to set on earth: and Father Villani, fearful that the labors of the holy doctor might shorten the precious days during which his sons could still gaze on the venerable beauty of his emaciated countenance, and learn from his beloved lips the secrets of a love stronger than death, commanded him to lay aside his eloquent pen, and rest from his labors. But the "Most Zealous Doctor," who did not desire to know any rest on earth, prevailed on his director to allow him to write still, by way of relaxation; a request that could not easily be refused. Several of his smaller works belong to this epoch. Father Tannoia having one day remarked that he had written many beautiful things with the intention of honoring the saints, but nothing in particular for the souls in purgatory, he composed his charming little *Novena* for these holy souls, and to please and gratify his dear disciple.

In short, Alphonsus did not forget any class of persons; all souls were dear to him as ransomed by the Precious Blood of Jesus Christ; and, in the decrepitude of old age, he labored for them with all the ardor of youth, or rather more ardently than ever. He would have wished to annihilate sin in a sinful world, and change sinners into saints, for the glory of his divine Master. He can no longer go on missions as in days gone by, but he will not stand idle in his Lord's vineyard — his prayers, his tears, his sufferings, his writings — he is prodigal of all these, for *a necessity lieth upon him to preach the gospel.* And reverently be it added: When they saw these things, then did the people remember the words of the Prophet: *The zeal of Thy house hath devoured me.*

CHAPTER LXVII.

The severest trials of Alphonsus. — The protection afforded the Church by the mighty ones of earth. — Treachery. — The saint refuses to be convinced. Letters. — Father Villani conceals from Alphonsus the treachery of Majone. How the saint suffered from his friends. — Terrible scene. — Profound dejection of the holy Founder. — Letter. — Important document. — Letter to Majone. — Astonishing meekness of the saint. — Obstinacy of Majone. Unavailing efforts of the saint to restore concord. — Indignation of his subjects. — Alphonsus had foreseen all.

T HE MOST terrible trials of our saint were yet to come. Twice had he foretold that he would die a subject, but how this was to be brought about it is probable that the divine mercy veiled even from his prophetic eye. The preceding pages will have shown that his life heretofore was but a tissue of sufferings, hardly illuminated by the feeble rays of consolation which a loving Father doled out sparingly to the son he so severely chastened. But now the time is at hand when his own brethren and sons will disown him; when he will be regarded as a traitor to that cherished child of his brain and heart, and the power of God working by him, his beloved Congregation; yea, when the vicar of Christ himself shall condemn the saint of Unity, the doctor of Infallibility. Then it is that we shall behold Alphonsus di Liguori in all the grandeur of his sublime and heroic virtue. Wronged, outraged and defamed as saint never was before, no complaint issues from the lips of calumniated innocence. "My sins have deserved more than this, Lord, it is good for me that thou has humbled me!"

The devil, unable to annihilate the Congregation by persecutions from without, endeavored to stir up treasons within, the surest means of destroying a work that had evidently come from God.

As the government of Naples was ostensibly Catholic, it was necessary that each religious establishment should receive not only the papal approbation but also an official sanction from the king and his ministers. History demonstrates that this official protection or approbation from so-called Catholic governments, if it were not in all cases such protection as the wolf affords to the lamb or the hawk to the dove, usually consisted in raising all possible, and impossible, obstacles to the very existence of good works set on foot by saints and saintly persons, for the glory of God and the salvation of souls. And at best, dearly has the Church paid for any "protection" ever given her by the mighty ones of earth.

On the 24th of August, 1779, the royal approbation was graciously bestowed on several points of the rule. This was regarded as a favorable moment to ask a general approbation, which would prevent all troubles on this score for the future. The grand almoner, Monsignor Testa, promised to use his influence for the saint, provided some decrees relating to pecuniary matters were omitted. This being agreed to, Father Majone, one of the consultors, was entrusted with the management of the business. Majone under the pretext that the king might still refuse, and his refusal become known to their enemies, proposed, that the consultors should each take an oath to preserve secresy in regard to all concerning this affair, which was done. But under cover of this secresy, Father Majone and the consultor associated with him, Father Cimino, made such arbitrary changes in the rule as to give it altogether a new form.

Notwithstanding the precautions of these unfaithful men, or rather because of these precautions, suspicions were awakened in the minds of the subjects. They protested against all novelties, and assured the holy Founder of their wish to have the rule remain unaltered. The saint, incapable of any species of double dealing himself, could not suspect it in others. Moreover, Father Majone had on several occasions transacted the business of the Congregation at court and elsewhere, to the satisfaction of all concerned, and Alphonsus had made him understand that the points which he was empowered to yield to the king, if necessary, did not properly belong to the rule at all, being only questions as to revenue upon which probably no rule capable of universal application could be made. "My dear Antonio," wrote the saint to

Father Tannoia, "there is no truth in the report that the rules are being changed. Be tranquil, and tranquillize others; the rumors which have disturbed you are entirely false."

"I have heard," he wrote to Father Corrado, "that some of our subjects fear that new rules will be substituted for the old ones. I know not how such fears can be entertained, since all must know how jealous I have always been of maintaining the rule." "You cannot," says he, in another letter to the same Father, "suspect me of duplicity. Now I tell you I will not tolerate the least change in the rules. What more can I say? If you will not believe me, I must bear all in expiation of my sins." He wrote in a similar strain to the other Fathers who had expressed fears on the subject. Nevertheless, as appeals continued to come, the saint wrote to Majone, plainly stating that some innovation in regard to poverty and the community life was suspected, and that he would never agree to anything of the kind. Majone hastened to reassure him, saying: "As for what you have written to me touching community life, to do away with this regulation would be to destroy the Congregation. I hope that Divine Providence will punish all those who thus spread discord." With astonishing effrontery, he presented the regulations he had made to Alphonsus, assuring him that all was in conformity with the rule, save the point regarding property, already alluded to. The waning sight of the holy old man rendered him unable to decipher the small, illegible writing of his treacherous disciple, which was, moreover, covered with erasures and interlinings; so he handed the document to Father Villani, desiring him to examine it carefully. With one glance, he saw that the rule had been changed, and testified his surprise to Father Majone, who simply said: "The King does not wish to have vows. Besides, it is not for us to make the laws; we must receive them from the almoner, and if some slight changes must be made in order to obtain the royal approbation, it matters little."

Father Villani, overawed by the pompous bearing of Majone, who was now in favor with the higher powers, or fearing to embitter too much the few hours of life that still remained to an aged paralytic, deaf, nearly blind, and hardly able to articulate, said that all was well. The saint immediately entoned the canticle of holy Simeon in thanksgiving, and impatiently awaited the arrival of the royal approbation. Meanwhile, Majone returned to

Naples well satisfied with the result of his visit to Nocera. The favor of the King and the venerated name of Alphonsus obtained all he desired. The grand almoner and the rest of the council gave a unanimous vote, believing — they too had been deceived — that they were conferring a favor on the Congregation which would console the declining years of its saintly founder.

The crosses that galled the shoulders of our holy bishop from this period to his happy death, came to him chiefly from friends and brethren whom he had tenderly loved, and trusted with his whole heart. Majone had lived with him at St. Agatha as his faithful counsellor. Father de Paul had been called to the Congregation by an extraordinary vocation, and selected by its founder for the great work of establishing it in the Papal States. The grand almoner, Monsignor Testa, who had formerly been his companion and bosom friend, henceforth allied himself with the traitor Majone. By the divine permission, even the Sovereign Pontiff himself encouraged the enemies of the saint — Pius VI, who had given him such tokens of veneration and holy friendship, persuaded that his great intellectual powers were extinguished in a second childhood, contributed above all the rest to fill up the measure of the woes that embittered his days and broke his heart — Pius VI who, when later on he heard that Alphonsus Liguori was no more, exclaimed with tears: "Alas, I have persecuted a saint."

The mutilated rule having reached Nocera, with an official letter from the grand almoner; February 27, 1780, Father Villani did not open the documents, as the saint was extremely ill. But anxiety and consternation spread among the Fathers, they surrounded Villani, and insisted on seeing the rules about to be forced on them. Except Alphonsus, no one in the house slept that night. Before daybreak, he was aroused from his peaceful slumbers by his outraged children, who told him of the alterations made, and demanded that justice should be done them. The holy old man was stupified with amazement. He looked at the new rules: "It is not so!" he exclaimed, "it cannot be!" Then turning to Father Villani, he said reproachfully; "Don Andrew, I did not expect such deception from you." Afterwards addressing the community, he said: "I deserve to be dragged at a horse's tail, for I ought to have read everything myself, as I am superior." Then looking at the crucifix, he exclaimed: "My Jesus pardon me! I trusted to my confessor, in whom could I have more safely confided?" "You know," he said to the assembled brethren, "how much it costs me to write even a line," sobs and tears almost choked his utterance. "I have been deceived," said he, sadly. He passed the whole morning in a state of absolute dejection. Grief so completely overpowered him that it was with difficulty he was made to taste food, and what he ate was moistened with his tears.

"Ah Lord!" he repeated in doleful accents, "punish not the innocent, rather punish the guilty one who has destroyed thy work." His grief became so terrible that for several days and nights sleep never once visited his eyelids, and his life was in danger. Not knowing what to do, he was constantly sending now for one subject, now for another, hoping that some one would suggest a means of extricating the community from this extraordinary difficulty. He sent to Illiceto for the Novice-Master, F. Tannoia; then to Naples for Father Corrado. The first words he addressed to some missionaries who returned from Calabria were: "They have changed our rule!"

It was reported, but falsely, thank God, that Father Cajone, Rector of Benevento, approved of these alterations. "I wish, dear Father," wrote Alphonsus to him, "that you would seriously examine the changes Father Majone has made. Our first rule was examined by Mgr. Falcoia, who has wrought miracles; it was afterwards submitted to Cardinal Spinelli, and finally to Pope Benedict XIV, who gave it his approbation. Now all is changed, and I marvel how any one can think this change an improvement. It is not the king, it is not his secretary that has done this, it is the work of Father Majone. I believe his intention is good, but it is impossible to recognize the work of God in these alterations. As for me, I have but a little time to live, and all my desire is to die at the feet of Jesus crucified."

In April 1780, the saint wrote a document of considerable length to the houses of the Papal States, through Father Ficocelli. He details the alterations made, and contrasts the new rule with the old, in a clear, lawyer-like manner, which proves that as yet his intellectual powers had not undergone the slightest deterioration. As founder, theologian, and lawyer, the saint never wrote anything of its kind to surpass this production of his eighty-fifth year.

Majone, seeing that all the Congregation opposed him, put on an appearance of zeal, and feigning to pity Alphonsus, represented him to the grand almoner as sinking under afflictions in the midst of rebellious subjects. Consequently, this official dispatched a letter to the Congregation, which was afterwards discovered to be of Majone's composition, enjoining the holy Founder and his associates to follow the new regulations in every particular, from March 1, 1780. The style is exceedingly overbearing: "Your lordship," says this precious document, "as Founder and Superior-General of the Congregation, must inform each member in my name, that this regulation must be immediately enforced, without any alteration or retrenchment whatever, for it is now the only rule, and is binding in all and each of its parts, on all the members of the Congregation, present and future, superiors, priests, students and lay-brothers, without any room for reply or opposition." It is easy to conceive the universal indignation which this letter excited. Alphonsus, who had to bear the brunt of all the discontent aroused on every side, endeavored to calm the excitement, and reestablish peace, not wishing the death of his treacherous son who had caused all there disorders, but rather that he should be converted, and live and die among his children.

"I write to you, my dear Angelo," he says, (March 20) "at the feet of Jesus Christ, where I beg you to put yourself, in these days in which Jesus Christ sacrifices himself for love of us. Let us forget the past. I beseech you to retire to our house at Ciorani, but if you prefer any other house, I leave you free to choose it. Be sure that I will love you as heretofore, and even more; you will find it by experience. You shall continue consultor-general, and have a voice on all subjects important to the Congregation. Place your reputation in my hands; I shall never cease to defend it with your brethren and with strangers...I bless you and pray Jesus Christ to fill you with His holy love, that you may be all for Him as He desires."

On the same day, the saint wrote to Father Corrado: "I believe it my duty to use the greatest meekness towards Father Angelo, because such is the will of Jesus Christ, and it is in this manner He inspires me to act. I have besought him for the love of Jesus Christ to trample the past under foot, and to retire to Ciorani or any other house he pleases. Thus I shall continue to act until it please God to restore peace. In employing this means, which is certainly the most agreeable to Our Lord, I hope to obtain all. We must be patient, and recommend ourselves to Jesus Christ, and to Mary the Mother of peace."

Far from yielding to such loving entreaties, Majone became more inflamed than ever against Alphonsus and the Congregation. Seeing that his designs were thwarted, he resolved to petition the King to compel all Redemptorists to submit to his new rule or quit the Congregation. When the missionaries heard this, their indignation could scarcely be restrained within bounds. Alphonsus, to prevent the evil consequences of such a step, wrote to Naples revoking the procuratorship which he had conferred on Majone, and bestowing it on Father Corrado. "I have learned," he wrote to the new procurator, "that our friend, by making an unauthorized use of my name, has endeavored to procure an order, in virtue of which the subjects must accept *his* rules or leave the Congregation. In short the author of this document would make me the murderer of my brethren. If Monsignor Testa is not convinced of the deceit that has been practised on him, we shall obtain nothing; for he will say he has done all I wished, which is not the case...Try to make him comprehend the state of our Congregation. We have more than a hundred young men who have finished their studies, and who would honorably distinguish themselves at the Sorbonne or at Louvain; but Don Majone would see them all out of the Congregation rather than not attain his ends. Tell Monsignore Testa that I have not become imbecile, as this person reports; I have still my right mind, though he labors to make me lose my senses." On the same day, April 10, he wrote to the grand almoner himself, representing, with his customary eloquence, the treachery of which he was the victim, and describing the sordid spirit that actuated Father Majone, "who, to increase his own importance as consultor-general, seeks to deprive the rector-major of his rights, and has added to, or retrenched from, the regulations as his own fancy suggested."

The subjects, finding that they would be forced to obey a rule which they had never promised to observe, protested against the consultors, and even against the holy Founder himself, for having kept the affair secret. So great was their dissatisfaction that it weakened considerably the veneration which they had hitherto manifested towards him. The aged saint not knowing where to turn for aid or consolation, spent most of his time weeping and praying before his crucifix. He again addressed the grand almoner, and besought former friends, now occupying eminent positions, to aid him with their influence.

But Monsignor Testa, heretofore one of the warmest friends and most enthusiastic admirers of the holy Founder, now refused to annul what had been done, and maintained that the changes made by Majone in concert with himself were excellent, and must be rigidly enforced. This prelate seems to have been so completely duped by the unfaithful deputy whom Alphonsus had commissioned to bring matters to a close at court, that he no longer showed even common courtesy to so old a friend, a bishop like himself, and possessed of all possible titles to the consideration, or rather veneration, of every dignitary in the Church.

The saint had foreseen all this in a general manner as far back as January 25. 1780. At the close of his meditation that day, he exclaimed: "I forsee that the devil will do all in his power to overthrow us this year." He informed Father Caione of the revelation he had on this subject adding: "Your Reverence will therefore have the goodness to have the prayers indicated on the enclosed paper recited in common from the beginning of February till the end of May."

CHAPTER LXVIII.

Alphonsus takes a bold step. — He proves that his intellect is as sound as ever. Testa begins to relent. — A turbulent member. — A new conspiracy. Stormy scene. — The founder invited to resign. — His re-election. — He is calumniated at Rome. — Consequences. — Action of the Pope. — Ingratitude of some of the saint's children. — F. de Paul coolly accepts the office of general. Hypocrisy of Leggio. — Resignation of the saint. — His fearful temptations. His charming frankness.

ALPHONSUS having now but a choice of evils, took the bold and dangerous step of suspending the execution of the new regulations until the result of the deliberation of a general assembly of the Fathers, to be immediately convoked, should be laid before the King. "If we are permitted to recur to the prince," said he, "to ask an augmentation of his favors or to be enlightened to understand them better, I do not think any harm can be done by suspending these new rules until we shall have exposed to him our wants, and the result of our deliberations." Several eminent and learned personages, lawyers and canonists, whom Alphonsus consulted, approved of this plan. He immediately informed the grand almoner, but as he received no reply, he commissioned a Father then in Naples, to let that dignitary know all, and added that if this did not suffice, he would go himself to Naples, all paralyzed as he was, and should he find it impossible to obtain an audience, he would write a thousand letters to the Prime minister, and send a thousand petitions to the King himself. Now at least, the early friend of Alphonsus saw that his intellect was as clear and strong as ever, and that, as in his earlier days, no difficulties could deter him, no opposition deaden his resolution or weaken his efforts, where God's glory was concerned. He took the trouble to inform himself of the real state of the Congregation, and when he learned how egregiously he had been deceived, he presently showed some disposition to retrace his steps.

Inexpressibly consoled at this, the saint informed the Fathers of it, in a circular letter in which he fixed May 1st for the general assembly, and urged all to be tranquil in the interim and pray for the success of their cause.

While the saint was laboring to arrange all to the satisfaction of his sons in the kingdom of Naples, the devil endeavored to stir up dissensions in the houses of the Pontifical States. The house of Frosinone contained among its members one of those restless and turbulent spirits whom God sometimes permits to disturb the peace of communities. The name of this unmanageable individual was Leggio. A burthen to superiors and to his brethren, the Founder was constantly obliged to remove him from place to place as he did not wish to expel him from the Congregation, unless matters became so desperate as to admit of no other alternative. These changes were very displeasing to Leggio; he nourished a secret ill-feeling against the saint, and, as revolutions in states generally give bad men opportunities of displaying their abilities, he no sooner heard of the difficulties of the Neapolitan houses than he determined to take advantage of them to create discord between the houses of the States and those of the kingdom. Of course he was actuated by the most lively zeal — who could doubt it, when he only proposed rebellion against the founder, and separation from his government?

It is quite true that nearly all the Redemptorist Fathers, who had ever known Alphonsus, entertained for him the deepest veneration and the warmest affection. But when he was denounced as an accomplice of Majone, appearances certainly not being in his favor — since outside the kingdom nothing had transpired but that the consultor was the trusted friend of the founder and was authorised to act in his name — it was easy enough to persuade the majority, either that God had forsaken him in his old age, or that years, sorrows, and infirmities had robbed him of the brilliant mental powers which had once been sufficient to overcome those who would have been incapable of appreciating his higher and nobler qualities. It was therefore arranged that a general chapter of the subjects in the States should be convoked, to entreat the Pope to allow them to separate from their brethren in the kingdom, and give them power to elect a new superior-general, they having already deposed Monsignor di Liguori.

The circular letter of Alphonsus elicited no reply. He was therefore obliged, much against his will, to order the houses of the states to send their deputies, in virtue of obedience. This mandate was obeyed, but the deputies were accompanied by Leggio, who came firmly bent on carrying out the separation he had projected.

The meeting was opened on the twelfth of May, but Alphonsus saw he had no longer docile subjects to deal with; nearly all expressed in the strongest language, their indignation against Majone and his colleague, but instead of entreating the unhappy pair by the mildness and benignity of Jesus Christ, some insisted on their immediate expulsion, and others wanted to have them deprived of their offices. So great was the spirit of insubordination displayed at this assembly, that the holy Founder sincerely regretted that he had ever convoked it. "Some are for Jesus Christ," said he, "some for the devil, and I am between the contending parties." General dissatisfaction was expressed at the lenity with which he treated Majone and his colleague, and if these indocile spirits were not audacious enough to depose the Holy Founder of their Congregation, they compelled him to resign his office, which he willingly did, for he would gladly have given his life for the restoration of peace.

At a new election held May 26, the saint was re-elected superior-general, — as strong proof of the love and reverence with which he was still regarded — but of the six former consultors only Fathers Villani and Mazzini were re-elected, and these in consideration of previous services. Instead of Father Villani, Father Corrado was nominated vicar-general, but he declined so weighty and troublesome a charge. "I beseech you to accept the office to which you have been nominated," wrote Alphonsus to this father; "I conjure you on bended knees not to pain me by refusing." This did not suffice, the saint was obliged to use to the utmost the shadow of authority that still remained to him, and command the unwilling subject under pain of sin.

Powerless to avert impending evils, Alphonsus bewailed at the foot of the crucifix the deplorable state of his beloved Congregation. Some reproached him for one thing, some for another: some completely forgot the respect due to his person and character, and even dared to say with disdainful bitterness: "You have founded the Congregation, and you have destroyed it. We know not whether God will forgive you this sin."

The saint suffered all in silence, and far from showing the least resentment, redoubled, if possible, his gentleness and kindness towards every one, resolved to drink to the very dregs the chalice which his Father had sent to embitter the closing days of his long and weary pilgrimage.

As will be readily conjectured, Alphonsus now found his office of rector-major the merest sinecure. The spirit of insubordination had spread, and there were few even of the laybrothers that did not undertake to discuss the administrative affairs of the Congregation, and give opinions or rather decisions with more authority of voice and manner than the holy Founder had ever been known to assume. Still worse, there was no longer harmony between the houses in the kingdom and those of the states, diversity of opinion produced division of hearts; some blamed one party, some another, and hardly a voice was raised in defence of the common Father of all. Leggio repaired to Rome, and signalized his zeal before the Holy Father, by painting our saint in the colors of a hypocrite. The calumnies seem to have been very generally admitted, though no one could understand how a man, once universally recognized as a saint, could deviate in such a lamentable degree from the paths of rectitude.

As the court of Naples was then endeavoring to infringe on the prerogatives of Rome, the king ordered that no subject of his should write to the Pope, or hold any intercourse whatever with the Roman Court. To disobey openly the royal mandate would be to destroy the Neapolitan houses; hence the only resource of the Founder was to select subjects in whose integrity he could confide, and depute them to represent to His Holiness the real state of the Congregation. Meanwhile, it might easily have been believed at Rome that Monsignor Liguori, now overwhelmed with years and infirmities, was unable to cope with the difficulties of the times, and fearful of seeing his dear institute suppressed by the king, like that of the Jesuits, granted concessions and made alterations entirely at variance with the rules he had formerly presented to Benedict XIV for approval. Be this as it may, it is certain that God permitted the perfidious Leggio to work his worst upon a saint, whom he should have loved, revered and obeyed.

This unhappy traitor had the audacity to present himself before Pius VI, and having expatiated on the novelties introduced into the rules at Naples, claimed the Pope's protection for himself and for the houses in the Pontifical States. He had already ingratiated himself with the members of the sacred college, which explains the readiness with which he obtained that a decree should be forwarded to Cardinal Banditi, charging him, in the name of the Pope, to inform the members of the Congregation residing in his diocese of Benevento, that they should strictly observe the rules and constitutions approved for them by Benedict XIV, without making the slightest alteration. A similar decree was despatched to the bishop of Veroli, with reference to the houses of Scifelli and Frosinone.

This news gave great delight to Alphonsus: "God be praised," he exclaimed! "by this order from the Pope our brethren in the papal states, are deprived of the liberty to alter the rule. My Jesus, bless the work, for it is thy own!" He did not perceive that the first effects of an order, so desirable in itself, would be disastrous to his poor Congregation. As soon as it was generally known that the Pope had guaranteed the integrity of the rule in his States, several of the most promising of his subjects withdrew from Naples, and joined their brethren in the papal territories, without even consulting the saint, though he was still, nominally at least, Rector-Major of the Redemptorists. Deserted by the flower and hope of the Congregation, he bowed his head in resignation to the divine will, which had permitted this terrible blow to fall upon his devoted head. He besought his great friend, Cardinal Banditi, to protect the poor Congregation, giving him perfect freedom as to the means to be used in rectifying the disorders from which it suffered so grievously. "If your Eminence," he wrote, "wishes to release me from my office of superior-general, do whatever you judge before God to be for the best. I have no desire but to see peace restored to my poor children."

As the wicked are generally bolder to plan and more courageous to execute for the devil than the good are in the service of God, Leggio now assumed such airs that no one seemed able to resist him. His next exploit was to obtain that "separation" which rankled as a thorn in the breast of the aged saint during the short space of life that remained to him.

On the fourth of August, an order was expedited in the Pope's name to the bishops of Benevento and Veroli, to the effect that the Redemptorist houses in their respective dioceses had no further connection with those of the kingdom. When Alphonsus heard that some arrangements were being made regarding these houses, he immediately sent for their most ancient fathers to inquire concerning them, but they replied that, as he was no longer their superior, they were not obliged to obey him. These words pierced his heart. Though perfectly resigned to suffer whatever his good Father might permit to befall him, the sorrows he now endured almost cost him his life. Endeavoring to conceal what he suffered, he encouraged the faithful few who had not yet deserted him, and peacefully awaited the stroke of death which he thought must now come; but his chalice was not full, the most bitter ingredients had yet to be dropped in.

Concealing every circumstance that could tend to place the late Rector-Major in a favorable light, Leggio now strove to have a president elected or nominated for the four houses, and petitioned the sacred Congregation to that effect.

That venerable assembly, with its wonted prudence, desired to examine thoroughly the real state of affairs, and instructed the inter-nuncio at Naples to take secret information, and report the result faithfully. Alphonsus received an order from the prefect of the sacred Congregation to transmit to Rome all the acts drawn up at the last assembly, with an account of what had since taken place.

This order greatly perplexed the saint. As unpleasant relations still existed between Naples and Rome, he could not readily comply with it. Unwilling to disobey the Pope, he wrote to the cardinal (August 24) that he would send two fathers to Rome the following November to give the desired information. Lest this should not suffice, he wrote anew (August 28), exposing to his Eminence the critical circumstances in which he was placed, and his powerlessness to remedy such grave disorders in a moment. "My most terrible trial," he writes sadly, "comes from my own sons, especially of the house of Frosinone, who wish to divide the Congregation and establish a second general. Small is the importance I attach to my office as regards myself, for my death is at hand, but it is hard for me to see the ruin of our Congregation." But Leggio was beforehand with him. He exaggerated the pretended offences of his spiritual father, represented the delay sought for as a piece of chicanery on part of an able lawyer in order to gain time and thereby elude the commands of the Holy See, and multiplied his petitions urging the injury the absence of a head might occasion. He was supported by the house of Frosinone, for the relief of which Alphonsus had, a few months before, sold his four silver services, which had been kept for the use of the distinguished strangers who so frequently visited him, and he could scarcely be prevented from disposing of his carriage, and depriving himself of the very necessaries his years and infirmities required, lest his children there suffer want. He had now the bitterness of learning in detail how his benefits had been requited, and might well exclaim in the anguish of his heart: The sons of my mother have risen up against me!

The grave disagreements existing between the courts of Rome and Naples favored the private ambition of Leggio. The saint fell into disgrace with the Pope, whose next step was to declare him deposed from his office, adding what was still harder to be borne, that the Neapolitan houses no longer formed part of the Congregation. Father de Paul was nominated superior or president of the houses in the Papal States.

This Father must have known how untenable the grounds were, upon which the holy Founder was condemned, but he does not appear to have uttered a word in his defence, or made the smallest endeavor to explain the obscure and critical circumstances in which he had been placed since the discovery of Majone's treachery. De Paul quietly accepted the post of president, and was elected rector-major in 1785.[1] When the Pope and the king of Naples consented to a re-union of the Roman and Neapolitan houses in 1790, De Paul was deposed, and F. Blasucci elected Rector Major of the whole Congregation. But the happy days of re-union and restoration, our saint did not live to see.

When Fathers Tannoia and Gallo arrived in Rome as deputies of Monsignor Liguori, they learned the full extent of the mischief without being absolutely certain as to what means or combination of means had been employed to produce these disastrous results. Leggio pretended that he experienced the most

---

[1] The Father who so coolly accepted his master's pest in 1785, lived, let us hope, to repent of so easily taking the first place while the saintly Founder was alive. He died at Frosinone in 1814. – Editor's original note

acute sorrow at the orders which had lately emanated from the Pope. "I have done all I could to disabuse His Holiness, but he will not be persuaded that Monsignor Liguori was deceived, and is innocent of the charges made against him," was his hypocritical assurance to them.

But he soon threw off the mask. The representatives of the saint could not procure a hearing; the sacred Congregation held no sessions during this season, and the cardinals had retired to their country houses. He informed Tannoia that the Pope abhorred the very name of Alphonsus, and would not permit it to be mentioned in his presence. Having now no object in dissembling his real sentiments, he one day exclaimed with an air of triumph: "Bishop Liguori has been disappointed of his canonization," thus showing that his wretched malice would, if possible, pursue its saintly victim even beyond the tomb.

When they returned to Nocera with their sad tidings, they could not bear to make known to their beloved Father the whole extent of his misery. Next morning as he was preparing for mass, at which he was about to communicate, Father Villani told him all. The dreadful news seemed to freeze the life-current in his veins, but he rallied a little, and profoundly bending his head, said: "God alone is sufficient for me. His grace will not fail me. The Pope wills it thus: May God be praised!" He said no more, but quietly resumed his preparation, heard mass, and received Holy Communion. After his thanksgiving, as he went out in the carriage, the devil assailed him violently, representing the destruction of the Congregation as his own work, and as a punishment of his sins, that God had abandoned him, and that he might now renounce all hope of salvation. During this temptation, he humbled and abased himself, but his humility seemed as if it were false, his hope presumption, and the temptation increased in intensity. He immediately returned, and had no sooner gained the threshold, than he wept bitterly, and exclaimed in heart-rending accents: "My brethren, aid me, the devil wants to make me despair; it is my sins which have caused God to abandon our Congregation; come to my assistance; I do not wish to offend God." The struggles of the holy old man were terrible, but Fathers Villani and Mazzini succeeded in reassuring him, saying that God could never fail to protect innocence, and that he would assuredly not abandon his own work. Pale and trembling, he heard all the words of consolation those good Fathers spoke, and when the temptation passed away, a smile of joy lit up the emaciated lineaments of his noble countenance. "My Mother, I thank thee," said this ever-devoted son of Mary, "thou hast helped me just now, always aid me, oh my Mother! My Jesus, my hope, let me never be confounded!"

When the fathers assembled about him after supper, he said, with his accustomed serenity: "The devil has been tempting me to despair during the day, but Mary helped me and by God's grace I have not made a single act of diffidence." Our saint possessed that charming frankness of manner which is so endearing in a community. He rarely concealed any thing from his beloved sons, his pains, his difficulties, his temptations, — he spoke of all occasionally, and even wrote of them in ordinary intercourse with those whom, as he often declared, he loved better than father, mother, sister, or brother. This is how he won entire confidence as a superior, and was able to apply continually his extraordinary skill as director of souls. In proportion to the affection with which he cherished *his dear little Congregation,* was the sorrow he now felt at the strokes that fell thick and fast upon him from those whom he so tenderly loved, that he would have given his heart's blood for the least among them.

CHAPTER LXIX.

Alphonsus unconsciously justifies himself. — The last touches given to his sanctity. — The saint displays his most noble qualities. — His submission to the new Rector-Major. — His meekness towards Majone. — "Servant of the Church till death." — The Pope's words absolute. — He reads the Life of St. Joseph Calasanza. — He will not allow his sons to appeal to the king. — The respect and obedience he compels them to evince towards the Pope.

THE POPE had been made to understand that the late Bishop of St. Agatha cared little for pontifical decisions, and was far more anxious to secure his own authority than to inculcate among his subjects, respect for decrees emanating from Rome. Apparently there was proof enough of this: what defence could be made for a man who had set aside the rules arranged by himself, when his mental powers were in full vigor, and approved, not merely by eminent theologians and high dignitaries, but by the Pope himself, and by such a Pope as Benedict XIV? A superior who would compel his subjects to keep rules which they never promised God to observe, and who would increase and diminish, alter and mitigate, according to his humor, without even condescending to explain his vagaries to the higher powers, or attempt to account for them. Could the Pope have seen and heard him, he would not have waited till after his death to exclaim, with that bitterness of heart which we all feel, when we find we have wronged virtue and innocence, and that it is no longer in our power to make amends to the objects of our persecutions: "Alas, I have persecuted a saint."

This great trial was necessary to elevate Alphonsus to the highest pinnacle of perfection. We have already seen him loved for those endearing qualities which he possessed in so eminent a degree, revered for his extraordinary sanctity, and universally regarded as a prodigy of erudition. Unlike so many other saints, his great qualities and wonderful mental endowments, were fully recognized during his life, and bishops, cardinals and Popes delighted to honor him. Crowned heads had been among his correspondents, and these included the learned of all nations; the kings of Naples, through whose reigns his tedious pilgrimage extended, had prided themselves on possessing such a subject, and had invariably treated him with astonishing courtesy. But now a change has come. Kings do not know him; ministers and prelates are indifferent to him when they do not actually persecute him; his own sons rise in rebellion against him; some moved by pity have not quite deserted him, but respect, veneration, gratitude, have disappeared; children whom he begot in Christ and brought forth in pains and anguish, now treat him as if his mind were as feeble as his body, or rather as if he were too insignificant to merit the slightest notice; his day is past, he has become a burden in his own Congregation. Worse, he is driven from that Congregation; both he and the few who still surround him are no longer styled Redemptorists.

As our dear Lord was never more deserving of our love, than when His enemies had done their worst upon him, so no epoch in the life of our great doctor is more admirable than this. It is now that we find Alphonsus Liguori displaying in the most striking manner the heroic virtues honored on our altars. Naturally enough, when the sad events, which formed the climax of his misfortunes, were discussed in his presence, the poor subjects who found themselves suddenly cut off from an order in which they had sworn to live and die, ventured to allude to the injustice done to him and to them. But the gentlest of saints sternly silenced them saying: "The Pope deems it his duty to act thus; may God be blessed! The will of the Pope is the will of God." Father de Paul appears at last to have been moved with compassion at the thought of the sorrow the poor old man must feel at being ignominiously deposed from his office, seeing his beloved Congregation divided, and more than all, being actually expelled from it. He wrote to represent the regret he experienced at being constrained to displease him through the mandate of the Pope. "By God's grace, I have never lost my judgment," wrote the saint in reply, "I rejoice that your reverence is appointed superior; all is right, you must in every thing fulfil the will of the Pope." To a religious who testified great displeasure at the appointment of F.

de Paul, inasmuch as it was the expulsion of the Founder, he said: "I care little about being deprived of my dignity of rector-major; it suffices for me that they have not taken away Jesus Christ and my mother, Mary."

The saint immediately put himself under obedience to the new general, and even resolved to go to Benevento and live there as a subject for the rest of his days. To dissuade him from executing this project, Father Villani told him that it was impossible in such a state of health, and that, since the rule was observed throughout the kingdom, the Congregation still existed therein. "Whatever may be the state of things here," said he sadly, "the Pope no longer recognizes these houses as forming part of the institute." Only one reason caused him to desist: he feared that such a step would complicate still more the difficulties already existing between the Pope and the king. He quieted his conscience by writing to the new president to assure him of his entire obedience; nor was he satisfied till Father de Paul commanded him to remain at Nocera, assuring him that he should always belong to the Congregation. The saint invariably evinced towards this Father the respect and submission of a most docile subject, and never resented in the slightest degree his conduct during the late troubles. If Father de Paul ever coveted the generalship which had come to him by such unworthy means, he no doubt found thorns enough in the crown of superiority, were there no other than the having among his subjects such a man as Leggio, and owing his position to the same. As rector of Frosinone, he had given but little satisfaction to the holy Founder; he seems however to have been tolerably respectful towards him, on paper at least, during the few days that remained to him, for they never again met on earth. He survived the saint about a quarter of a century.

The decree of the Pope all but destroyed the Neapolitan houses. Several of the Fathers passed into the States without even visiting Alphonsus. The more docile asked his advice, which he gave in two words: *Obey the Pope.*

Many were shipwrecked in the tempest, and retired to the world. Among others, a student whom he tenderly loved joined Majone and his companions. This almost broke the affectionate heart of Alphonsus. The unworthy object of his affection subsequently became canon, and gained such an ascendency over

421

his bishop, that he disposed at his pleasure of all the offices in the diocese. But God did not bless his ways. While still young, he was suddenly summoned before the supreme tribunal of the Almighty Judge, having been found dead in his bed one morning.

With regard to the unfortunate Majone, all that Alphonsus desired was to see him converted. He could not bring himself to act harshly towards an old companion, who had been his domestic chaplain at St. Agatha, and whom he once loved so tenderly. Seeing the climax of the terrible evils he had done the Congregation — all happened during the first nine months of the year 1780 — Majone was ashamed to return among his brethren. After having recalled him several times, Alphonsus informed him that if he did not return before a given date, he would be excluded from the society. Shame deterred him from obeying, and he so far forgot his dignity of priest as to undertake to administer the temporal affairs of a baron. In the house of this nobleman he died a premature death, detesting his sins, and bewailing his unhappy fate. May God, whose mercy is above all his works, have received his late but sincere repentance.

The saint, through all these reverses, appeared insensible to the dreadful humiliation that had come upon himself; his great soul was entirely occupied with his beloved Congregation. To see the innovations of Majone done away with, and the houses once more under one head, this was all he coveted. To attain his end nothing was left undone. He wrote a full statement of the case to Cardinal Banditi, begging him to make all known to the Pope, and caused prayers, masses, and novenas, to be offered for success. This elegant and statesmanlike document showed that the lawyer and the saint had not yet lost the qualities which once elicited universal approbation. The Cardinal himself signed the letter, but it was God's will that it should not serve the holy Founder's cause.

"Alas," he wrote to Father de Paul, "if the Pope knew all, he would not blame me. In due time I will make everything known to him, and perhaps recover his good graces: for I have never lost the remembrance of the affection he once deigned to show me, notwithstanding my great unworthiness, and come what may, I will die his faithful servant, and the *faithful servant of the Church*."

His most grievous trial was the Pope's displeasure. "What shall we do to satisfy him?" he asks the president, "to obtain once more the faculties and privileges necessary to the success of the missions?" So extraordinary was his reverence for the Vicar of Christ, that he took all that proceeded from him as literally as possible, and would not allow any one to interpret his will. "If the Pope," said the Fathers, "speak of those who give up the rule, that cannot apply to us who have always observed it?" "It is not for us to judge," said the saint. "Who will dare to constitute himself judge between the Pope and us? Let us humbly bow our heads in submission. If the Pope has cast us down by one rescript, he can raise us up by another; we must under all circumstances obey, without ever seeking to put our interpretation on his will."

"The Pope did not, and could not, have you in view," said Monsignor Carafa to Father Tannoia at Rome, when this good Father complained to him. When this was related to Alphonsus by the poor Fathers, whom it had consoled, he replied: "I understand all; but it is Bishop Carafa that speaks, and not the Pope." The Pope subsequently confirmed what he had done.

"It is hoped at Rome," wrote the poor old man to Father de Paul, "that the Pope will re-establish me Rector-Major; but how little I care about that office! What grieves me is the privation of those faculties, without which we can be of little assistance to souls." He commissioned him to represent this to the Pope, and endeavor to obtain a restoration; and he urged Father Caione to the same effect. "If I were not absolutely incapable of undertaking the journey," he added, "I should be already on the road." Had the saint been able to present himself before the Pope, there is no doubt but he would have gained whatever he asked, but among those now influential with his Holiness he was unable to procure a faithful ambassador.

From a letter to Cardinal Banditi on the same subject, we learn that the saint was never more zealous in promoting the work of the missions. "We have not ceased to labor for the good of souls," he wrote; "we give a great many missions. That of Foggia may be counted as four, for it will last a month and a half, after which missions will be undertaken at Nocera and elsewhere."

Monsignor Bergamo, who loved Alphonsus as a father, having come to Nocera to console him, was so grieved for him, that he journeyed to Benevento, to use his influence in his behalf with Cardinal Banditi. This eminent man was greatly distressed on learning the true state of things, but he thought it was not then expedient to take any steps at Rome to rectify the past. What the saint feared most, was that charity might suffer in consequence of these unfortunate circumstances; "I strive to instil into all my brethren a perfect spirit of charity," he wrote to the president; "do you the same, my dear Father, for God loves those who love charity." His only consolation at this time was to weep and pray before the Blessed Sacrament, and meditate on the Passion of Christ. He read and re-read the Life of St. Joseph Calasanctius, who, towards the close of his long life, had been deposed from his office of superior-general, and his Congregation suppressed, and who died in disgrace with the Pope.

Alphonsus respected the very wishes and thoughts of the Pope. He would not allow his Fathers to claim the royal protection, or even to inform the king of what had been done in the States, chiefly, if not solely, by Neapolitan subjects; and when he learned that some subjects, growing disheartened and restive under ceaseless persecution, had determined to write to the king, fearing that this would lead to some complication dangerous or troublesome to His Holiness, he wrote to the acting superior-general, Father Corrado: "I know not how I could excuse from mortal sin any Father who, in this present conjuncture, would have recourse to the king." In a word, the respect and obedience he showed the Pope and compelled those under his charge to show him, edified and affected every one.

CHAPTER LXX.

Incessant efforts of the saint to bring about a reunion. — He appeals to the king, who grants his request. — The protection accorded by kings. — Letter to Leggio. — New Trials. — Arrogance of Leggio. — Scruple. — Division. The Pope calls Alphonsus a saint. — He does him full justice only after death.

THE EFFORTS of Alphonsus to bring about a reunion, through every alternation of hope and fear, were incessant. Knowing that if the evils done by Majone in Naples could be repaired, the great obstacle would be removed, he entreated the king to allow the Fathers to make an oath to do what they had been forbidden to do by vow, following the precedent of St. Joseph Calasanctius and his clerics. The king graciously granted all that was asked. Alphonsus learned this good news from a letter dispatched to him by his old and constant friend, the Marquis of Marco: "His Majesty, grateful for the zeal and indefatigable labors of the missionaries, and their success in preaching the jubilee, has deigned to grant all the favors you have asked: he permits (1) that the missionaries make oaths of a life in common, and of poverty; (2) the said missionaries may take the oath of perseverance; (3) they may accept some assistance from their friends and benefactors during the wheat and olive harvest."

Readers of this age, in the western countries at least, can scarcely imagine a state of things in which it was necessary to appeal ostensibly to a prince for such permissions. Fancy a religious Congregation asking the President of the United States for leave to keep its rules! Here is a specimen of the protection the Church was wont to receive from the secular power. The king was born a Catholic, and condescended to remain one, but he must in consequence reduce the power of the Catholic bodies in his kingdom to the merest shadow. Otherwise a harmless man, he must discuss in his cabinet the minutest details of conventual establishments, and impose his silly notions on religious, with an authority which the Pope himself has rarely assumed, imitating, according to his little capacity, the imperial sacristan of Vienna, his august contemporary. The unfortunate kingdom of Naples has had too many monarchs of this description.

As the saint could not get all he required, he was glad to take what he could get, and he notified all the houses to make fervent thanksgiving to God for these concessions, at the same time inculcating the most rigorous observance of rule. So important was this royal decree considered at the time, that the rector of Illiceto wrote to Alphonsus: "We cannot find words to express the sentiments of our hearts; our consolation surpasses the anguish we have endured; in spite of hell, we have been restored to life. God has now comforted us, and we conjure him to give us perfect peace." This joy passed outside the Congregation; its friends seemed as delighted as its members, and the people of Illiceto lit bonfires in their boisterous rejoicing.

All was now ready for a reunion; the Fathers of the kingdom longed to be placed on the same footing as their brethren in the States, and the Fathers in the States longed to be once more under the mild and affectionate rule of a saint. But they were not worthy of this great happiness. Alphonsus humbled himself so far as to write to Leggio himself: "I pray you to remember," said he, "that if you persevere in maintaining this division, you will never experience a moment of peace, for peace cannot be associated with the spectacle of a disunion of which you have been the author, and which you can no longer remedy. I beseech you, for the love of Jesus Christ, to consider this well at the foot of the crucifix; I embrace you, and beseech God to make known to you His holy will." But Leggio was far from listening to the prayers of the spiritual Father who had begot him in Christ. By some unaccountable means, he prepossessed almost every one against him: "Monsignore Liguori," said he, in a tone of contempt, "demands too much. He wants to enact the role of Pope, or to arrange matters quite independently of the Pope...The Pope does not receive the law, he gives it. We wish for the rule of Benedict XIV, not the reform of Monsignore Liguori."

Beset on all sides, the Pope confirmed the previous decisions. Only one voice, that of Cardinal Zelada, was in favor of Alphonsus in the Sacred College. When he heard of these sad and tiresome proceedings, he repeated with perfect resignation: "I will what God wills; the will of God can redress all wrongs." Nor did he ever despair of regaining the Pope's favor, or cease his efforts for a single day to bring about the coveted union. Always trying, never succeeding, still hoping, such was the record of the few days that remained to our Most Zealous Doctor. When his last effort failed, his degenerate son, Leggio, remarked with disgusting arrogance: "He played for his canonization, and has lost it." The news of this failure having reached him who was unconsciously *working,* not playing, for his canonization, he said: "For six months I have not asked anything of God but that his holy will might be accomplished. Lord, I will only what thou wiliest!" A few years after, when the minute examination of his virtues took place in the sacred Congregation of Rites, the calumnies of his adversaries redounded to his honor. Then did Pius VI issue a solemn decree containing these words: "We preserve the remembrance of the eminent piety of the servant of God, of his reverential submission to the Holy See, as his words, his actions, his writings testify."

Owing to the saint's extreme delicacy of conscience, he had another source of anxiety. Through love of holy poverty, he had engaged himself by vow to depend on the local rector like any other subject; but as the rectors of the Neapolitan houses were not lawful superiors, since the Pope did not recognize them as such, to whom was he to recur? Not daring to address the Pope, to whom he had been so grievously misrepresented, and who was so prejudiced against him, he entreated Father Corrado to obtain the Pope's decision for him. It was not to the Pope, however, but to the Cardinal Penitentiary, that the Father applied. His Eminence admired the extreme exactness of the saint, and directed that he should submit to the decision of his confessor.

It is somewhat singular that the Pope, even while giving decisions against Alphonsus and using the utmost severity towards him, never doubted his sanctity. When Cardinal Banditi and Monsignore Bergamo endeavored to exculpate him, the Pope remarked that it is not well to change the rule of a Congregation without the sanction of the Holy See. These good prelates explained that Alphonsus had made no change; the changes fraudulently made by Majone were repudiated by him as soon as he heard of them; he had since been making superhuman efforts to rectify the errors of the treacherous consultor, and had, thanks to God, almost succeeded. They enlarged on what was notorious, the sanctity of the holy old man and his devotion to the Apostolic See: "I know," returned the Pontiff, "that *Monsignore Liguori is a saint,* and that he has been most obedient to Christ's Vicar, but he has not done well in this circumstance;" and being asked to bless him, he said: "I bless him with all my heart, and I bless all the members of his Congregation."

When he, whose displeasure was most grievously felt, entertained so high an opinion of the old man, towards whom he showed such severity — a severity altogether foreign to the gentle and benign nature of Pius VI — what can we conclude, but that God inspired the Sovereign Pontiff to act in this seemingly unaccountable manner, in order that the last fine touches might be added to the wonderful sanctity of Alphonsus Liguori.

Although the Pope seems to have shown a little lenity towards him from this period, they were never fully reconciled. Pius VI did him ample justice, but not till he was already enjoying, among the just made perfect, the fruits of his heroic patience.

CHAPTER LXXI.

Prosperity of the Congregation. — Touching letters. — Alphonsus utters no reproach. — Paroxysms of grief. — Heroic confidence in God. — He is universally regarded as a saint. — Petition. — Audacity of Leggio. — The missionaries acquitted by the royal council after nineteen year's litigation. Gratitude of the saint — The most diabolical of all works. —The Sicilian subjects choose a general for themselves. — The Neapolitan Fathers elect a coadjutor for Alphonsus, with right of succession. — Change of sentiments. The last drop. — Perfect submission. — The German house. — Last days and deeds of Leggio.

D ESPITE the perpetual trials to which they were subjected, the Redemptorist houses prospered. The Pope this year (1781) established a hospice at the Church of St. Julian, near St. Mary Major, a foundation at Gubbio, and another at Spello, to supply the necessities of his States. The saint experienced the greatest joy on learning this, and wrote several letters to the Fathers in the States, congratulating them on their success, and testifying the lively joy he felt at the flourishing state of their novitiate. On hearing of the contemplated foundation at Ravenna, he prophesied that it would not take root, nor did it.

As life was slowly ebbing, the saint's mind continually turned towards his brethren in the States, and the messages he sent them from time to time show, not merely that he fully and freely forgave those among them who had wronged him so deeply, but rather that he entertained no recollection of any injury done him. Father de Paul having in a letter referred the good done by the Congregation to Alphonsus as Founder, the latter wrote:

"I thank God that he has made use of me to give birth to the good now effected by your reverence, with the sanction of the Pope." As the saint was at times scarcely able to dictate, Father Villani informed the president of the great consolation he experienced on hearing of the progress of the institute in the pontifical states. "I thank you," he wrote, "for the welcome letter by which you have made known to us the benedictions heaven showers upon you. I can assure you it has been a source of great consolation to us. Monsignore, our Father, is particularly delighted at the news; he blesses God for it, and speaks of it frequently. I may add, that he has desired me to write to you to this effect."

"Monsignore, our Father," wrote Brother Francis Anthony to the same, "has twice charged me to tell you that he embraces you tenderly, and that he desires you would pray, and make your community pray, for him. He will never more be well, and he wants me to tell you not to forget that he and you were once companions. I use the very words he desired me to employ."

Father de Paul seems to have shown all the kindness he now could show to the aged saint: "We do not fail," he wrote, "to remember you in all our common prayers, and you may rest assured that, when the Lord shall call you to himself, all the masses prescribed by the constitution shall be celebrated for you by the Fathers in the states."

The saint was so delighted with the promises contained in this letter, that with the touching gratitude which had always characterized his great heart, he would thank Father de Paul the very day he received it, June 21, 1782. His letter, like all he ever wrote to his brethren, overflows with the warmest sentiments of divine love and tender affection for his cherished children, but it is remarkable that he does not terminate it by giving his benediction to his correspondent, which, as a bishop, he might have done under any circumstances: "I pray Jesus Christ," he says, "to bless you and your houses and those who dwell in them." As he recognized the president for his superior, he simply subscribed himself, "Your affectionate and much obliged, BROTHER ALPHONSUS MARIA, of the Most Holy Redeemer."

His heart was filled with sorrow because his houses were deprived of the privileges and other favors formerly allowed by the Holy See, and during the crisis of a fever, brought on by mental sufferings, he would at intervals exclaim: "What! are we not of the Congregation of the Most Holy Redeemer? Do we not acknowledge the rule of Benedict XIV? If we observe that rule, why are we not of the Congregation? ...Perhaps they doubt whether we do keep our rules, and this is why we are rejected?

But God wills it, let us have patience." On being told that his sons were real Redemptorists he would instantly become calm. It was observed that during the deliriums, that occasionally supervened in the fevers his domestic calamities had brought on, he never uttered a word of dissatisfaction against the Pope, or showed in any way that he felt the slightest resentment against those who had injured him so deeply.

Some fathers who had just returned from a mission having gone to his room to beg his blessing, Alphonsus, as the same idea always filled his mind, said: "I cannot understand how it is that we do not belong to the Congregation of the Most Holy Redeemer, since the rule of Benedict XIV has always been observed by us, and is observed still." "Without doubt we do belong to it," said Father de Meo, "since the Pope and the king designate your Lordship as founder of the Congregation." "I wish not to be even named in this world," he returned, "but I desire it to be known that the rule observed by us is the very one we received from the Pope, and from which we have never departed." "True," said the father, "and it must always be acknowledged that the Congregation exists here, since the rule given by Benedict XIV to Don Alphonsus Liguori is kept here." "What does my name signify?" interrupted the saint. "All I care for is that it be known that we are subject to the Pope. Let us bless God for all he has done."

During the darkest hours, the holy Founder knew and felt that the work of his life was to endure: "Never lose confidence," he would say to his fainthearted sons, "Lazarus lay four days in the tomb before he was resuscitated. Only let us be what we ought to be in the eyes of God; he is all powerful, let us pray, and resign ourselves to his will." This remarkable confidence, or rather profound conviction, struck his friends as extraordinary, and ere long these sentiments were so extensively shared by the Fathers that all regarded the subsequent restoration of the privileges of the institute in Naples, and still later, the reunion of the Roman, Sicilian and Neapolitan houses, merely as the fulfilment of the oft-reiterated prophecies of a saint whose confidence in God no amount of misfortune, persecution, or trial, could shake or diminish.

It afforded no small consolation to the struggling houses of the Institute in the kingdom that, from first to last, the most eminent bishops and cardinals sustained and defended them. These dignitaries wrote and re-wrote in favor of missionaries, whom they regarded as their most potent auxiliaries, and used all possible influence to obtain an adjustment of their difficulties. Their letters, quoted at full length in the original memoirs of the holy Founder, show the high esteem in which the missionaries were held, and that Alphonsus was universally regarded as a saint.

The united petitions of cardinals, bishops, canons, princes, and congregations, could not fail to make some impression on the Pope, and Alphonsus was not slow in turning the favorable change to advantage. Careless though he was about his own reputation, the loss of the privileges formerly enjoyed by the Fathers cut him to the heart, because of the damage resulting to souls. Strong in his innocence, and confiding in the clemency of the Holy Father, he addressed to him the following petition.

"MOST HOLY FATHER! The bishop, Alphonsus Mary di Liguori, prostrates himself at the feet of your Holiness, humbly entreats you to grant to his missionaries all the graces, faculties, and privileges conceded by the Holy See to the venerable Congregation of Redemptorists in the Pontifical States."

This petition was forwarded in March 1783, and on the 4th of April following, the Pope granted to all members of the Congregation, present and future, the indulgences and other spiritual favors which the Redemptorist missionaries enjoyed in the States of the Church during missions, and all other exercises of their ministry. This rescript wounded the heart of the parricide Leggio, and knowing that it could not be gain-said, he forged a document, to which he had the audacity to affix the honored name of Tannoia, containing several questions, and praying that the graces conferred should be distinctly specified. Being himself on the spot, he hoped to reduce the pontifical favors to the faculty of blessing rosaries, but this time his intrigues failed. He was officially informed that the rescript was so clear as not to need any explanation.

Another consolation awaited the much-tried servant of God. The affair with the baron of Ciorani, and other existing difficulties, being brought for the last time before the royal council, Alphonsus was triumphantly acquitted, and his missionaries declared free from all contravention of royal decrees. A royal decree, dated April 10, 1784, approved of the proceedings of the council, and the missionaries and the Founder were fully exonerated: these affairs had been before the Neapolitan tribunals for nineteen years. Such auspicious events, following close upon each other, filled the heart of the old saint with joy and satisfaction. He immediately showed his gratitude to his "sweet Jesus," by ordaining that special thanksgivings should be offered to God and to our dear Lady for the *great miracle*. A miracle undoubtedly it was; but a miracle entirely due to the prayers and penances of the saint.

The archtraitor Leggio had not yet forsaken his evil courses. He was still successfully engaged in the most diabolical of all works, sowing cockle or discord among his brethren. The fruits of his miserable diplomacy soon appeared, and the reunion of the dismembered institute became more difficult than ever, when it was known that the Sicilian members had broken off from their brethren in the kingdom, and chosen a Rector-Major for themselves. The few that had heretofore been faithful to Alphonsus now trembled for their existence as a religious body; and lest his death, which might occur at any moment, should suddenly deprive them of a head, they elected Father Villani as his coadjutor and future successor.

Meanwhile, the hearts of his former children began insensibly to turn towards that dear father who had nurtured them in Christ. His heroic patience and charity, tried by every possible reverse, moral, material, and physical, could not long continue powerless to touch them, and they yearned for their Father's home, poor and insignificant as it had now become. Many of the Fathers of the Papal States, and two in particular who had been most obstinate in maintaining the division, now humbly begged to return to the holy Founder, adding that they would be content to take the lowest place if they could only live under his fatherly rule once more. This, though in itself a great consolation, became the occasion of adding the last drop to the bitter chalice which the saint had to drain to the dregs; for Father de Paul, seeing that his houses were becoming depopulated, asked the Pope if he could in conscience permit his subjects to return to their first allegiance, and received a negative reply. This was, perhaps, the rudest shock the saint ever experienced; but he received it with perfect resignation. "What the Pope wishes, I wish," said he; "the will of the Pope is the will of God, and the will of God turns all bitterness into sweetness."

Alphonsus had not only to bear these reverses himself: a far more difficult task was to reconcile his sons to them. Continual trials from within and without had wellnigh disheartened them; weary and fainthearted, they poured their complaints and repinings into the ear of their ever-indulgent father. And, alas for poor human nature, it is by no means improbable that these repinings were sometimes accompanied with threats of following the majority. But the saint never lost patience for a moment: "We will pray for our brethren in the states," said he, soothingly, "and they will pray for us, and thus we shall all, please God, attain sanctity. They will do good there, and you will do good here, and the will of God shall be accomplished by all."

The rector of Nocera having animadverted severely on the conduct of Majone, the primary cause of all these calamities, Alphonsus testified displeasure at his language. "That is his affair," said he; "our whole business is to think and to say, *God wills it.*" Nor would he permit a word against those men, now so sadly changed, who had once gloried in the title of his sons, or indeed against his worst enemies. It was in these adverse circumstances that all the grandeur of our saint's character became fully apparent. The extraordinary nobility of soul which he displayed seemed rather to belong to the state of the just made perfect, than to one who, however great his sanctity, was still encumbered with a perishable body.

About this time the fame of Alphonsus attracted from Austria the two first German subjects, Clement Hofbauer and Francis Hüble. They were admitted to the novitiate in Rome, and were so sanguine about the introduction of the Congregation into Vienna, that they would see no obstacles in the way. The Fathers laughed at the projected German foundation, but Alphonsus prophesied that the hopes of the fervent novices would be realized. "God will not fail to spread his glory by their means," said he; "the suppression of the Jesuits has left their fatherland almost destitute of evangelical workmen. Instructions will be more useful there than sermons, as the people must live among Lutherans and Calvinists. At the beginning, they should be made to say the

Credo, and then admonished to avoid sin. These holy men will do good, but God does not will that I should mingle in this affair. My sweet Jesus! humble me more and more, that thou mayest be the more glorified."

In consequence, partially at least, of the late prohibition, the lack of subjects soon began to be painfully felt in the kingdom. With a sad heart, Father Villani represented to the saint that the house of Illiceto was no longer able to maintain the *Studentat*, the other houses being, through extreme poverty, incapable of assisting it. "Alas," said the holy Founder, sighing, "our houses are now falling into decay; ah, Lord, thy will be done! May that happen which is most pleasing to thee!"

To afflict still more this poor old man, whose sorrows should have excited the deepest sympathy, the implacable Leggio asked the Holy Father to specify the existing houses of the Congregation, which was done in a brief, dated December 17, 1784, wherein the Pope declared that the only houses of the institute were those of Benevento, San Angelo, Scifelli Frosinone, Spello, Gubbio, and the hospice of San Julian in Rome. The last mentioned now became the principal or mother-house of the Congregation. The wickedly fertile brain and bad heart of Isidore Leggio planned still deeper humiliations for the hapless Fathers of the kingdom, but he paused, fearing lest his intentions might appear through his assumed zeal. His policy at this epoch was to render the saint contemptible. "Poor old man," said he to a prelate who had been inquiring about him, "he is in a pitiable state; his mind is so impaired that he is no longer a man. He has lost his senses, and is now in his second childhood." The mortal enmity of this wretched man reached still greater lengths. One day a young relative of the Liguori family having delivered a very eloquent speech, a prelate, who happened to call at San Julian, naturally felicitated the Fathers on the fact that the orator was related to their Founder: "When was Monsignore Liguori our Founder?" interrupted Leggio in a tone of undisguised contempt; "Bishop Falcoia is our Founder." The prelate, who could scarcely restrain his indignant astonishment at this absurd declaration, retorted with spirit: "It should be no small glory for you to claim as your Founder a man so eminent by his birth, sanctity, and learning, as Monsignore Liguori is universally admitted to be."

But Leggio went further. He tried to introduce into the Congregation of Rites the cause of the canonization of Bishop Falcoia, hoping to be able to secure to him the title of Founder of the Redemptorists. Proud of having contributed to establish the houses of Spello and Gubbio, his extravagances outstripped all rational bounds. "I am the real Founder," he said; "if the Order still exists, it is to me it is indebted, for I have sustained and still sustain it." The hatred of this deluded man followed the servant of God beyond the tomb; he lived to work in vain against the canonization of St. Alphonsus. At. length the eyes of the Pope were opened; and when the impostor endeavored to stir up discord between the Cardinals, and disquiet the Pope himself, he appeared in his true colors, and was promptly forbidden to approach the Vatican. Alphonsus had foretold that he would one day receive a great chastisement. Feared and despised by all, though powerless to inflict the injuries he had once dealt out with no sparing hand, he died suddenly, on the feast of the Most Holy Redeemer, 1801. No word of faith, love, or hope, was uttered by this dying renegade — no confession, no viaticum. When the agonies of death seized him, extreme unction was hurriedly administered — he had previously refused both physicians and sacraments, insisting that he required neither. Seeing that life was really drawing to a close, the persecutor of St. Alphonsus raised his hand, struck the bed violently, and died without uttering a word or making a sign which it would be a comfort to his friends, if he now had any, to remember.

CHAPTER LXXII.

The saint's marvellous gift of eloquence. — His continued interest in the missions. — In the Church in general. — His gratitude for being a child of the Church. — Gratitude for the hospitality shown the Jesuits by Catherine of Russia and Frederick of Prussia. — His conviction that the suppression would not continue long. — He defends them. — His hatred of the Jansenists. Arnauld. — The Blessed Eucharist. — "Mercy to sinners." — How to deal with sinners who come to confession badly disposed. — His perpetual sermon, Avoid sin. — His last visit to the nuns of Nocera. — Obedience. — His occupations. — His politeness. — Accident. — He sells his horses. Temptations.

SOME TIME before the fatal catastrophe of 1780, our saint was reduced to such a state of physical weakness that his life seemed but a prolonged agony, yet he continued to preach every Saturday on the glories and virtues of Mary, and to expatiate from time to time on the Passion of Jesus, and His real presence in the Blessed Sacrament. The faithful lovingly crowded around him, to gather, as they said, the last precious pearls that fell from his lips. But so much did these efforts of charity cost him, that the ever-faithful Father Villani, in concert with the doctors, forbade him to continue them. His zeal now found vent chiefly in prayer. His feeble voice no more resounded in the beautiful church of Nocera; his burning eloquence no longer thrilled the hearts of the pious crowd, so avaricious of gathering "the precious pearls that fell from his lips." Judged by its effects, his preaching must always have been something marvellous; he himself described it when he said that he liked preachers whose words did not pass directly from the head to the tongue, *but descended first into the heart*, to be inflamed by its fire before rising to the lips. Who thinks of brain, or head, or logic, when reading the instructions of St. Alphonsus? All fire, all unction, all devotion, all sweetness, — verily it was out of the abundance of his burning heart that his sacred lips, cleansed and consecrated, as we may well believe, by an angelic spirit, (like to him who touched with a fiery coal the lips of the prophet), spoke to the hearts of all.

To the last our wonderful saint manifested the greatest interest in the apostolic works of the Congregation. When his sons returned from missions, he welcomed them joyfully, and listened with ineffable delight to the glad tidings they brought him, of souls converted to God, or attracted to perfection. These recitals would at intervals cast a gloom over the great soul of this extraordinary missionary. "Alas!" he one day sighed, as visions of earlier days arose, when his harvests were greater than he and his brethren could gather in — "what do I do? I am useless, and even a burden to the Congregation." "Others labor now," said a Father soothingly, "and you, as Founder, participate in their labors." "Founder?" he repeated, "I am but a miserable wretch. I can do only evil. God alone founded the Congregation. I have merely been a worthless instrument in His hands."

His zeal for the general interests of the Church rather increased as he journeyed towards heaven. When strangers came, he was always inquiring about the state of religion, and he felt such keen sorrow if he heard the Church was persecuted or despised in any place, that Father Villani was obliged to tell those who were going to visit him, to say nothing of the dark picture Catholic Europe then presented, and to be particularly silent about the trials the Holy Father had then to endure from so many unruly sons and faithless subjects.

He loved to read the authors who defended the Catholic faith, and, like his great patroness, St. Teresa, he frequently, and with indescribable fervor, thanked God that he was a child of the Church. "Thanks to God," he would say, "that I was born in the faith, and in Italy, which is the centre of religion. O how wretched we should be if we were deprived of Jesus our hope!" He thanked God for every grace and favor he heard of, and rejoiced in the success of bishops and priests; but he testified particular gratitude to God whenever he learned that any good deed had been done by a sovereign. When he was told of the hospitality shown the Jesuits by the otherwise infamous Empress Catharine of Russia, and by Frederick of Prussia, he loved to magnify this princely hospitality, and never ceased to thank God that the good seed was preserved in these remote and uncongenial countries. At the time of their suppression, which he lamented almost more than themselves, he had said, "If there remains only one Jesuit on earth, the order can be restored;" and he had always the fullest confidence that these valiant soldiers of Jesus Christ would again take their rightful place in the armies of the Church. "Let us pray God," he would say, "for these holy religious, because their institute renders great service to souls, and is a powerful arm of the Church. People assert that they are schismatics! Verily, they are singular schismatics! Pope Ganganelli was God's instrument to humble them, and Pius VI is God's instrument to raise them up. It is God who kills and brings to life again. Let us pray to him, and he will not fail to bless them."

He was more uncompromising than ever with his old opponents, the Jansenists. "O blood of Jesus Christ!" he would exclaim, "how thou art trodden under foot by the impious, those wolves in sheeps' clothing, who pretend to revive among the faithful the spirit of the primitive Church! It was by a kiss of peace that Judas betrayed Jesus; it is by the same kiss of peace that these innovators to-day betray Jesus Christ and the souls he died to save!" Speaking of that unfortunate meeting of Bourg-Fontaine, he said with unwonted energy: *It was less an assembly of men than of devils.* The worst point of Jansenism in the saint's eyes was, that it practically closed up the greatest fountains of grace to fallen man — penance and the eucharist.

"Arnauld," said he, "could not find a more efficacious means of making the great sacrament inaccessible, than to exaggerate the dispositions which St. Paul requires for receiving worthily. I know that the angels themselves are unworthy of this sacrament, but our dear Lord has instituted it for men, to help their weakness. All our good comes to us from this sacrament; without it, we should be lost." He could never endure confessors who testified a sort of abomination for poor sinners. He was always inculcating upon his Fathers, and upon all the priests who placed themselves under his direction, or merely visited him, the tenderest compassion for great sinners. "Jesus Christ never showed anything else for them," said he. His instructions on this point are invaluable to all who have a care of souls. He was, and is still, admitted to be the greatest theologian of the day; his learning was extraordinary; his sanctity won him universal veneration; being almost a centenarian, his experience was necessarily vast; nevertheless his one cry is, MERCY TO SINNERS!

"The penitent," says he, "knows his state and detests it. He must not be left to his own strength; he must have the grace of the sacraments; this supplies what he cannot attain by his own strength. *It is a Jansenist doctrine to defer absolution.*" Again he says: "Many come to confession badly disposed; but when the confessor explains to them the hideousness of sin, the loss of paradise which it involves, the offence committed against God, they change their sentiments. The confessors themselves should endeavor to enkindle compunction in their penitents, when they are not contrite."

So our saint continued to the end the Most Zealous Doctor. He instructed all who approached him, by word and example. When secular gentlemen came to the convent to make the spiritual exercises, he would cause himself to be carried to the church that he might encourage them to avoid sin and devote themselves entirely to God. On one of these occasions he insisted on being brought thither, though he had just been bled. The effort of an hour's sermon on the love of Jesus and Mary reopened the wound, and blood flowed abundantly while he gave them his blessing. The audience reverently dipped their handkerchiefs in the oozing fluid, and ever after regarded them as relics. When priests made retreats in the house, he would always invite them to his room, and go through some spiritual reading with them. His great aim was to inspire them with devotion towards the blessed sacrament and the Blessed Virgin, horror of sin, *and mercy towards sinners* .

In June 1871, he paid his last visit to the nuns of the Convent of the Purity. He spoke as usual of the love of Jesus and Mary, of the benefit of a religious vocation, and the strictness with which religious should observe their rules. The nuns offered him a beautiful bouquet, which he accepted, and placed on Our Blessed Lady's altar. His solicitude for those who were more immediately his spiritual children seemed to increase in intensity. "It is certain," said he to them one day, "that God wishes you to be saints. I recommend to you poverty and obedience; obedience, were it even to the cook. He who fails in obedience fails in his duty to God, and God will drive him out of the Congregation. I regard failings against poverty and obedience as capital offences."

He was, if possible, more particular than ever about enforcing punctuality in all the common exercises. "I do not want great things," said he, "let them be little, provided they be constant." But he did not suffer the less spiritual matters to escape him, and was always sure to inform himself as to how his dear sons were treated with regard to food, clothing, and lodging. "We receive strangers hospitably," said he, "and are we to neglect our own?" He once gave his director, Father Villani, a very sharp reprimand for not making it his business to see that the Fathers and Brothers were supplied with all necessary for them; nor would he receive any excuse for neglect of duty in this particular. When unable to leave his bed, he was always reading, praying, or meditating; and if anything struck him as particularly worth remembering, he made it a point to tell it to the Fathers who came to sit with him after supper, that they too might be benefited.

The only thing about his infirmities that displeased him was that they made him burdensome to others. He could not bear to have his food brought to his room, until Father Villani commanded him, as it was impossible for him to go to the refectory. When a service was done him, he testified his gratitude with a gracefulness peculiar to himself, and he would not ask the smallest favor except in the humblest manner.[1] In short, he continued to be to the end, and in all his relations, what an admiring friend once described him, "the most perfect gentleman among the Neapolitan clergy."

His condition became unusually painful from September 19th, 1784, when an internal rupture took place as he was taking his daily drive. He was taken out of the carriage, brought to a neighboring house, and placed on a bed, to all appearance quite dead. The surgeons who were instantly summoned had great difficulty in repairing the effects of this new calamity, the rupture having become much worse by the jolting of the carriage, and he was brought home in a most alarming condition. Nevertheless he rallied a little, but as he could never again enter a carriage, the doctors ordered that he should be carried out in a sedan chair. The rector had to use all his authority to induce him to try this new vehicle, but after the first essay the saint had quite enough of it. "What!" he cried, "must I be carried on the shoulders of these

---

[1] His usual mode of requesting, and even commanding, was, "Have the goodness to oblige me," "Do this in charity for a poor old man," "For the love of our dear Lady gratify me in this," "Have compassion with a feeble old man, and obey for the sake of Jesus Christ," "I beseech you to give me this consolation, that you will do this for the love of God," &c. – Editor's original note

poor men? The thought of it made the going out yesterday more painful than salutary." The Fathers explained that these people had no repugnance whatever to carry his chair or litter, that they earned their bread by this kind of labor; but it was all useless, and not to distress him again in this respect, a wheel-chair was procured, which could be easily propelled up and down the corridor.

He now sent his horses to Naples to be sold, and introduced them to the nobility and gentry of that city by the following flattering description: "As for the horses, I do not wish to have any scruples about them: mention therefore that one of them suffers in the jaws and cannot eat hay or oats; the other, which is older, suffers from vertigo, and throws himself on the ground from time to time; his ears must be pulled in order to make him rise. Explain all this, as I wish to be free from scruples." Such rare candor did not add to the value of the horses. One was sold for the equivalent of eighteen francs; the other for six! Such was the inglorious fate which awaited the superb equipage pertaining to the aristocratic prelate of St. Agatha.

On Friday, November 25th, 1784, the saint celebrated mass for the last time. As he gradually became more infirm, Father Villani felt constrained to deprive him of this, his greatest consolation. But he continued to hear mass and receive Holy Communion daily; sometimes he heard five or six masses, and he was accustomed to remain before the blessed sacrament, rapt and motionless, five or six hours every day, as Brother Francis Anthony testified.

He now began to suffer all the anguish, scruples, terror, and perplexities, which are the martyrdom of privileged souls; he became the sport of diabolical temptations to such an extent that he quite lost his ordinary serenity. "Who knows," he would say, weeping, "whether I am in the state of grace, and whether I shall be saved? Ah! my sweet Jesus, do not allow me to be lost, for in hell I could not love thee. Punish me as I deserve, but do not cast me from thee!" He had also to struggle against the rebellion of his senses, and against thoughts of vanity, presumption, and incredulity. "There is not one of our mysteries," said Father Mazzini, "against which he was not tempted. I have been terrified at his temptations, but amazed at his courage in resisting them."

Only one thing could quiet him — the voice of his confessor. Hence when these awful temptations were unusually importunate, he would drag himself to the room of Father Villani to receive a word of consolation. If Father Villani were not within reach, he would tell his temptation or scruple to any priest he could find; and, as he always hesitated about disturbing or inconveniencing any one, it cost him incredible pain to address himself to a Father, at the unseasonable hours during which these mental struggles usually became most violent.

What will seem almost incredible is, that this aged saint, broken down with sorrows and wasted to a shadow with bodily infirmities — a saint, moreover, who had always led a life of angelic purity — should now be a prey to those sensual temptations which become so dreadful a cross to a soul that has chosen Jesus Christ as her only spouse. So violent were these horrible temptations that at times he could not distinguish feeling from consent; and then he would sigh, and groan, and strike his feet against the ground as one writhing in agony which, passing outside of the soul, convulsed the body also. "My lord," said a priest who called to see him one day, "you seem so melancholy, you who were never known to be other than cheerful." "Alas!" replied he, "I endure the torments of hell." Sometimes when unable to sleep at night, he would call the brother who usually waited on him, and the faithful Alexis who had followed him from St. Agatha, that they might aid him to dissipate his terrors, and not unfrequently were they obliged to summon Father Villani or Father Mazzini to his bedside.

Even in prayer he ceased to find conscious support. "I go to God," said he to his director, "and he repulses me. This morning I said: 'My Jesus, I love thee,' but a voice within me insisted: 'That is not true.' Alas! my Jesus," he sighed, looking towards the crucifix, "shall I not have the happiness of loving thee eternally? My dear Mother Mary, why must I not love thee forever?" When tempted against faith, he was heard to murmur incessantly: "I believe, O Lord, and I wish to live and die a child of the Church." Wonderful faith, but still more wonderful humility! A founder, a bishop, a theologian of European reputation, a master in Israel — his only boast, the only claim he makes on the Divine Mercy which he so loved to magnify is, not that he is priest, or bishop, or founder, or doctor, but a simple, docile child of the Church — a child such as Jesus took by the hand and set in the midst of apostles, saying: *Unless you become as* THIS LITTLE CHILD, *you shall not enter heaven.*

Temptations against chastity harassed him almost to the end. "I am eighty-eight years old," said he one day to Father Criscuoli, "and the fire of my youth is not yet extinct. My Jesus," he would exclaim, in these terrific straits, "grant that I may die rather than offend thee! O Mary, if thou wilt not assist me, I may sin worse than Judas! Alas," he sighed, "I have trodden under foot all my obligations; I no longer say mass or office; I neglect good works; my senses are rebellious, and I eat like a wolf. I cannot understand how God bears with me."

When his meals were brought to him, he could scarcely induce himself to eat, for fear of sinning, and after having commenced, he was seen to stop suddenly, fearful of the mere natural gratification which a hungry man takes in satisfying his hunger. One day he said to Father Villani: "I hear an interior voice saying: 'Thou hast forsaken thy God, and he has forsaken thee'." The Father enlarged on the goodness of God, who willeth not the death of a sinner, but rather that he be converted and live. "O my God!" exclaimed the saint, "how many times have I said these words to encourage sinners, and see how I have forgotten them myself!"

The thick gloom that shrouded his once brilliant mind used to increase in intensity as the hour of communicating approached. Love made him long to be united to Jesus Christ, but fear sometimes predominated. Several times he would not have approached the Holy Table if Father Villani had not come just in time to command him. One day he remained irresolute until noon, when his scruple suddenly passed away, and he cried out, shedding tears of devotion: "Give me Jesus Christ!" On another occasion, he was so intensely eager to communicate that moments appeared ages, and he repeated again and again with seraphic ardor: "When wilt thou come, my dear Jesus? I wish to satiate my love. I hope to love my Jesus eternally, although my sins have deserved hell."

While most grievously assailed by temptation, he petitioned to be brought to the church, saying that the devil left him in peace while he was before the blessed sacrament. Heavily as these desolations and obscurities weighed upon him mentally, and even

444

physically, he received all who came to consult him with his accustomed urbanity, resolved their doubts in his clear, incisive manner, and consoled them in their little afflictions as though he himself stood in no need of consolation. The mystery of direction in the Catholic Church! He could impart light though he was conscious only of darkness, and console others while he felt himself utterly abandoned by God! A cousin of his, member of a religious Congregation in Naples, who happened to be tormented by scruples and temptations, at the same time wrote to him for advice and received the following reply:

"Your Reverence tells me there are times when you believe yourself lost: let us console each other and be of good cheer, for I am often in similar straits. Although so near death, temptations do not leave me, and like yourself my only resource is the crucifix. Let us then embrace the cross, and keep our eyes immovably fixed on our dying Jesus. Thus shall we have ground to hope that he will not condemn us to hell, where we should be separated from him, which would constitute the hell of our hell. Let us therefore say to him continually: 'Lord, cause me to love thee, and then send me where thou pleasest. Chastise me as thou wilt — my sins deserve all — but do not deprive me of the happiness of loving thee.' ...Amid all these disturbances, do not forget to pray for poor sinners, especially towards the close of your meditations."

It is worthy of remark that despite all these scruples and desolations of spirit, our saint never omitted any of his devotional exercises. Prayer and spiritual reading divided his days. He read with particular satisfaction the Lives of St. Gregory Nazianzen and St. Francis de Sales, as they had both gone through trials resembling his own, and had come forth from the crucible unscathed and purified.

CHAPTER LXXIII.

Diabolical phantoms. — The Neapolitan missionary. — The phantom priest. Another temptation. — Heavenly favors. — Supernatural instinct. — The feast of the Blood of Jesus. — The mental power of the saint not impaired. — The act of love. — Saintly coachmen. — God glorifies the sanctity of his servant. The burning mountain. — The little children. — The saint's testimony to Father de Meo's sanctity. — Gift of prophecy. — Humility of the saint. — His heroic obedience. — His gentlemanly demeanor among his brethren. "Always crooked." — Advice to a young cleric. — Pious practices. — Vacant sees.

ORDINARY wiles not succeeding, the devil presented himself before the saint under the guise of strange phantoms. These apparitions came sometimes in one shape, sometimes in another, to alarm and annoy him. Once it was as a Neapolitan missionary who lauded his works to the skies, but Alphonsus humbled himself saying: "I have indeed done what I could, but all the good results from the divine assistance." "That is true," was the rejoinder, "but it will always be said they are your works, and you shall have the entire credit of the good effected by them." At this Alphonsus prayed and made the sign of the cross, upon which the phantom immediately vanished.

Another day the devil entered his room in the form of a priest, and endeavored to excite him to despair. "I have done nothing good of myself," said he, "I am incapable of anything good, I have no merits, save the merits of Jesus Christ." This humble confession quickly despatched the tempter. "Oh, these are only natural feelings, and therefore perfectly sinless," said the devil on another occasion, when Alphonsus was molested with a sting of the flesh. Although the malignant spirit had come in the form of one of the Fathers, Alphonsus resisted this impious doctrine with so much energy that he almost fell from his chair.

Again the demon approached the saint as a gentleman whom he tenderly loved: "What can you hope for," said he, "what can either of us hope for, if both are destined to be damned?" "Even in hell I will love Jesus Christ," returned the fervent lover; "I trust not in my works, but in his Passion and death." The cloven foot was made apparent by the effects of this confession, and its owner rapidly disappeared.

But our generous confessor was not left wholly without solace. Indeed his raptures and ecstasies were more frequent than ever during his latter years, and his more violent temptations were invariably followed by some precious heavenly favor. The Fathers who were honored by personal intercourse with him, love to expatiate on the ravishments of divine love which ever and anon irradiated the wasted lineaments of his noble countenance. Hours passed by unheeded when he knelt before the beloved of his soul, and in these intimate communications with his God, he already realized the perfect charity that casteth out fear. Even now was his hoary head decked with the halo of sanctity, and the darkness of night was often illumined by the celestial light which brightened his countenance. He knew by a supernatural instinct when the blessed sacrament was near, and on one occasion when Father Garzillo, who was ninety years old, had inadvertently passed from the memento for the living to the memento for the dead, the saint observed to the brother: "Father Garzillo has not consecrated to-day," and the servant Alexis who had served the mass, testified that this was the case.

Once on Wednesday in Holy Week, Alexis overheard him repeat ten times over, "Tomorrow is the feast of the Blood of Jesus." Brother Anthony went in and said: "True, to-morrow will be Holy Thursday, when commemoration is made of the body and blood of Jesus Christ." Alphonsus, perceiving that he had been heard, said no more. What made this a little remarkable is that for some time previous he had been unable to distinguish the months of the year or the days of the week. Nevertheless his mind was not in the slightest degree impaired. One day he asked the young clerics, who had come to pass the recreation hour with him, to explain a stanza of a hymn by St. John of the Cross. The mystical sense of this poem was too deep for students, but the saint explained it with such unction and eloquence, depth of learning and supernatural light, that both Fathers and clerics were mute with admiration.

448

Once when the saint had been bewailing that he was no longer able to serve God as of old, that he now satisfied none of his obligations, one of the Fathers, compassionating the genuine grief from which these lamentations exhaled, explained that his age and infirmities dispensed him from the pious exercises he had once performed with such fervent alacrity, and that an act of love would supply for all. "Teach me, then," he said with emotion, "to make an act of love." The father bent over him, and uttered the beautiful words which we learn in childhood, and hope to repeat with ever increasing fervor as the dark shadows of death thicken about us: "My God! I love thee with my whole heart!" "My God! I love thee with my whole heart," echoed the saint, and he repeated again and again this cherished aspiration, sucking sweetness out of every word till he was ravished in ecstasy.

Joseph di Mauro, one of the king's architects, having come to Pagani to examine the Redemptorist church, went to pay his respects to the saint, who, when the first salutations were over, asked whether the theatres were much frequented at Naples. Mauro having replied in the affirmative, he continued with still greater interest: "And the churches — are they much frequented?" "O yes," returned the architect, "and you cannot imagine the good that results from this. All classes, especially the working people, crowd them, and we have saints even among the coachmen." At these words the saint rose quickly from his recumbent position, and exclaimed in a tone of joy and triumph: "Saintly coachmen at Naples! *Gloria Patri!*" He could not sleep for joy at this intelligence, but during the night would frequently call to the brother or to Alexis: "You heard what Don Mauro said: 'Saints among the coachmen at Naples!' What do you think of that?"

During an eruption of Mount Vesuvius, God glorified the sanctity of his servant. The town in which the saint lived was in great danger, from its proximity to the burning mountain. The Fathers, terrified at the frightful spectacle, informed Alphonsus of their peril; and, unable to resist their reiterated entreaties, he looked towards the flaming summit, and said: "I bless thee in the name of the Father, and of the Son, and of the Holy Ghost." He had scarcely uttered these sacred words, when the fiery torrents took another direction, and the volcano vomited its burning matter into the gorge of a neighboring valley.

We have already remarked the tender affection which Alphonsus always manifested for children. While he was able to go out, mothers would hold up their little ones for his blessing, and on perceiving them, he always had the carriage stopped. If they were ill, he blessed them and prayed over them, and his wrinkled hands lingered lovingly on their pretty little heads. When he could no longer leave the house, the mothers still brought their babes to him, especially the sick, and the brother and servant who usually presented them declared that he effected thousands of cures on these innocent patients.

The gift of prophecy with which he was endowed manifested itself more frequently as his end approached. One day he remarked to the Fathers, that the Congregation was about to sustain a great loss. Shortly after, that prodigy of erudition and sanctity, Father Alexander de Meo, was struck with apoplexy while preaching at Nola, and died in the church. Alphonsus felt this loss keenly, as he loved the deceased Father most tenderly, and revered him as a saint. "Father de Meo," said he, "is such that he gives one an idea of the wisdom of God." Wonderful praise, from a savant to a savant, from a father to his son, from a saint to a saint!

To a young man who came from Naples to be cured by the saint, he said: "Pray to our dear Lady to assist you to die well." The youth understood him, took his advice, and in a few days was no more. Looking into futurity, Alphonsus in the spirit of a patriot and a saint, thanked God that he was not to live to witness the entrance of the French into his native city (1799). He often unconsciously gave evidence that he could read the secrets of hearts. A gentleman one day asked him to do something for his daughter, who was said to be possessed. "Possession!" he exclaimed, "let the girl make a good confession." She followed his advice, and immediately ceased to be possessed.

The saint disclaimed all power to work miracles. "If I had any such power," he said, "would I not heal my own crippled limbs, and my paralyzed body." Yet miracles he wrought almost every day of his life.

The faithful knew that God was with him, hence he never made his appearance without being surrounded. "Must I bless all these?" he once asked of Fathers Villani and Mazzini, his humility being alarmed at the gifts they attributed to him. The Fathers assured him that it was a bishop's office to bless, and that it would not be right to refuse. The children, above all others, delighted to surround him; they instinctively knew that he loved them dearly. "Look at these young sparrows around an old owl," he once said gleefully, as the little ones clung to his habit or gambolled at his feet. He sometimes scrambled to the convent door to get a little fresh air; on these occasions his little favorites never left him alone.

The obedience of the saint was so perfect that he literally did not wish to move, if possible, without permission. He obeyed even the servants who waited on him. They could make him do whatever they pleased.

His love of holy poverty grew stronger every day. If any one chanced to say, "your book," "your pen," he would gently observe that he had nothing of his own. The poorest fare pleased him best, and it was with difficulty he could be persuaded to use any other.

To the last, he showed himself a perfect gentleman in his intercourse with his brethren. He hated to enter his wheel-chair, because one of his sons, or his dear humble friend Alexis, had to draw it. Father Villani refused to allow him to dispense with this poor comfort. "But," objected the saint, "the noise of the wheels disturbs the Fathers on both sides of the corridor. There should be perfect silence while they write or study." He insisted so much on this that the rector compromised by consenting to have the wheels of the noisy vehicle covered with leather. So scrupulous was the servant of God in all that concerned religious modesty, that he would only allow his wounds to be dressed when commanded by his director.

As he was unable to inflict those corporal mortifications to which he had accustomed himself from youth, he adopted the equally painful though passive one, of remaining motionless in his chair from morning till night. Alexis having one day placed him in an uncomfortable posture, set about rectifying the mistake. "What is the use of my moving," pleaded the saint, smiling, "whichever way I turn, I am always crooked." The grand vicar Rubini had noticed at Arienzo that he often kept the same position for five or six hours together.

The love of God inflamed his heart to such a degree that he seemed to lead the life of a seraph. "By the divine mercy," said he to Father Villani, "I do not feel attached to anything terrestrial."

Very often his whole day seemed an uninterrupted transport of love. His sole delight was to receive Jesus Christ, or to remain, unconscious of the lapse of time, before the eternal lover of his soul in the tabernacle. Even during sleep, he could think only of Jesus and Mary: "O my sweet Jesus," he would exclaim in his dreams, "how beautiful art thou! How lovely art thou, O Mary!" So great was his love for Jesus crucified, that when he was no longer able to make the stations, he used to perform the way of the cross in spirit in his room, before a large crucifix.

To a young cleric who came to ask his blessing he said: "My son, if you wish to persevere, communicate several times a week, and be devout to the blessed sacrament and the Blessed Virgin." The youth longing for another blessing, again sought his father's room: "My son," said the saint at the second visit, "I recommend to you holy obedience. By obedience you will please God, and be loved in the Congregation; but I especially recommend you to be devout to Mary and the holy eucharist." And on a third visit, the saint received him with more kindness than ever, and said: "If the enemy of God tempts you to leave the Congregation, immediately have recourse to Jesus and Mary, and do not cease to invoke them till the temptation vanishes."

As he perceived his memory to be failing in some things, he made Brother Francis write some of his daily pious practices, lest he should forget them: "Ten acts of love; ten acts of conformity to the divine will; ten acts of love towards Jesus Christ; ten acts of love to the Blessed Virgin; ten acts of love to the blessed sacrament: ten acts of confidence in Jesus Christ; ten acts of confidence in Mary; ten acts of resignation in suffering; ten acts of abandonment to God; ten acts of abandonment to Mary; and ten prayers to do the will of God."

The same interest in the temporal concerns of his Fathers and brothers, the same solicitude for the sick, distinguished him to the end, but he was far more interested in their spiritual good. His zeal extended over the whole Church, and he might say with the apostle whom he resembles in many respects: "Who is weak and I am not weak? Who is scandalized and I am not on fire?" Tell him of some scandal or disedification, and it affected him so deeply that he could neither sleep nor eat; but recount some of the glories of the Church, and the aged invalid visibly grew young again. Hearing from Father Falcoia that the missionaries were

452

effecting much good in the Pontifical States, he testified the liveliest joy, and incessantly repeated, "God be praised forever! God be praised!"

When he heard there was a prospect of reconciliation between the courts of Rome and Naples, he seemed transported with gladness. The pretensions of the Neapolitan court caused many sees to be left vacant. "I am anxious that the bishoprics should be provided with holy prelates," said he, "for when sees are vacant, things go wrong, and souls are lost. Do you know what results from the absence of bishops? The loss of souls, without any notice being taken of it. This has caused me to weep before God for the past six months. The want of a bishop is the ruin of a diocese."

When the Bishops of Gaeta and Avellino came to inquire after his health, he replied: "I am as one who must soon appear before the tribunal of Jesus Christ." Then, with a touch of his old fire, he said to the former: "Now that you are going to Naples, I entreat you to send for Father N____ and tell him, from me, not to maltreat souls redeemed by the blood of Jesus Christ." This was a priest of Jansenistical proclivities. One day our most zealous doctor was accidentally overheard bearing to himself this magnificent testimony: "Lord, thou knowest that all I have thought, said, done, or written, has had no other end than thy glory and the salvation of souls." With regard to the habitual candor and sincerity of his language, he once let these words escape, when conferring with Father Villani on the state of his conscience: "I am a bishop, and I ought to tell the truth; I do not remember having ever uttered a deliberate falsehood, even when I was a child."

CHAPTER LXXIV.

God alone. — Incorrect conclusion. — Vigor of the saint's intellect. — His fear of God's judgments. — His exalted idea of the sacerdotal dignity. — His consummate tact. — Celebration of his ninetieth birthday. — Young men of ninety. — Foreshadowing. — Interesting details. — The saint is visited by his absent children. — "By thy words thou shalt be justified." — Visit of Count Joseph Liguori. — "Save your soul." — Parting benedictions. — Brother Gerard. — Delicate attentions of the Neapolitan bishops. — Universal grief for the hopeless condition of the saint. — Miracles.

WE NOW approach the term of our saint's long and weary pilgrimage. More than ever, *God alone* possessed his whole heart and soul, and nothing save what concerned the glory or service of God awakened within him the slightest interest. When people spoke in his presence of mere worldly matters, he would make his deafness an excuse for keeping silence, or assume an air of imbecility that made superficial observers imagine that the once bright intellect of the great doctor was now obscured by the dull mists of dotage. Yet when subjects were introduced which he considered worthy of his attention, he conversed as gracefully and intelligently as ever, and proved himself capable of grappling successfully with the more obscure questions of moral, mystical, or dogmatic theology. Those who consulted him on matters of conscience, had their doubts resolved and their difficulties cleared up as lucidly as he could have done it in the prime of life.

"Pray for me," said he to some priests who visited him, "I am about to present myself at the judgment-seat of God;" and this idea affected him so deeply that the priests withdrew in terror, saying: "If he trembles, what will become of us?" He had a most exalted idea of the sacerdotal dignity. Two newly ordained priests having come one day to pay their respects, he kissed their hands with devotion, and exclaimed: "O what a great dignity is the priesthood! You are now exalted above sovereigns, kings, and emperors!" He showed a ready tact in accommodating his conversation to his visitors. When Don Gaetano Celano and his wife, who were munificent benefactors of the Congregation, visited him a little previous to his happy death, he received them with his usual urbanity, and testified the liveliest gratitude for the favors they had done him. Then, determined that they should not leave him without receiving some spiritual benefit, he dexterously turned the conversation on the duties of the married state, and gave them some useful counsel, assuring them that their happiness depended on their having but one heart and one will.

His biographers give numerous other instances to show the acuteness of his fine mental powers to the very last. And not a few among the eminent men of Naples came at one time or another to test them; but it was not a wreck of genius they encountered, the saint, the scholar, the philosopher — he was all these, as in the heyday of youth and strength.

On the 27th of September, 1786, a solemn high mass was celebrated in the church of Nocera, in thanksgiving for the preservation of the Father and Founder for so many years. Father Villani and the community paid him an early visit, to announce to him that he had completed his ninetieth year, and offer their warm and sincere congratulations. The saint was deeply moved by this graceful attention, and shedding tears of joy he said: "I do not deserve such kindness; all comes from the divine mercy. I thank my dear Fathers and Brothers most sincerely. God himself will reward their charity."

When he heard of the death of his old friend, Father Garzillo, who was almost a hundred, he made an act of resignation, said a *De profundis*, and then jocosely remarked: "I am another of these young men." He knew that he would soon join the friends of his youth and the companions of his declining years, and he rejoiced in the thought. To a Carmelite father who was in the habit of visiting him every year, he said, in September, 1786: "Father Joseph, we shall not meet again next year." His words were prophetic. On the Feast of Our Lady of Mount Carmel, July 16, 1787, he observed in a joyful tone to his faithful attendant: "Brother, I have a new function to perform." He alluded to his approaching death.

Two days after, the gravest symptoms supervened. As the body became weaker, the soul increased in fortitude. Not a doubt, fear or scruple now disturbed the dying saint. "I was constantly beside him," wrote the affectionate and devoted Tannoia, "and I did not suffer the gentlest sigh of him who had loved me so well to pass unheeded."

Mass was celebrated in his room, and he communicated daily, as usual. It was crowded from morning till night. The Bishop of Nocera, Monsignore Sanfelice, came every day, as did all the neighboring priests and religious, anxious to gather some of the precious perils that dropped from the lips of the dying saint. To a Father who asked how he was, he said fleetly: "Recommend me to Jesus Christ." To a similar question from the faithful Brother Anthony, he merely said: "Thanks be to God."

When the same brother asked him to bless all the Fathers and Brothers, he said with touching tenderness: "And you too. You must pray to God and the Blessed Virgin for me," he continued, as he blessed his beloved children, and, fixing his dying eyes upon them with unspeakable tenderness, foretold them all manner of benedictions.

On the morning of the 24th, he frequently asked the surrounding Fathers to be quick in giving him holy communion. But there was some delay, and when the time for receiving came he was unconscious. The doctors now gave him over. When somewhat recovered, he was told to prepare for extreme unction, but remembering he had not communicated, he said; "I wish to have his body." He was again told to prepare for his last anointing, but his mind was full of one idea and he repeated, "give me his body." Fearing that he was not sufficiently conscious, his director did not comply with this request, but administered extreme unction, and then desired him as bishop and superior to bless the Congregation in the names of Jesus and Mary. Alphonsus raised his hand, and imparted to all his children the coveted benediction.

As soon as his life was despaired of, Father Villani notified the distant houses, and all the rectors and as many of the Fathers as could be spared, set out to visit him. This pleased him greatly, and his delight at seeing his dear sons once more, especially those of the States, lit up his wasting lineaments, as he blessed them with the sign of the cross.

"By thy words thou shalt be justified." Collecting the scattered sentences that escaped from this profoundly learned, eloquent, and holy man, during the closing days of his mortal career, we present a few to our readers as his most fitting panegyric. "My Jesus, I love thee with my whole heart, because thou didst die for me." "Give me my Jesus." "I offer all my sufferings to Jesus." "I believe all the Holy Catholic Church teaches, and therefore I have hope." "Is the eucharist coming?" "My Jesus, do not leave me." Such are the blessed aspirations that issued from the abundance of the burning heart of this earthly seraph.

His nephew, Don Joseph, came from Naples with his wife and her uncle, the Prince of Polleca, and on entering his room, said: "I have come to see you, and to ask your blessing." "I thank you," said Alphonsus, with the exquisite courtesy which always distinguished him; but when the young nobleman asked for some good advice, the dying man repeated impressively: "SAVE YOUR SOUL." The young wife, Donna Gusmana, having come in with her uncle, Alphonsus blessed them also. Joseph desiring to hear more words of wisdom from the saint who had watched over his childhood, and guided his boyish steps in virtue, came closer, took the cold and clammy hand, and reminded the dying saint that he was his nephew. The saint pressed his hand, and held it for some time, after which he endeavored to raise his feeble arm in benediction over the heir of his dear, deceased brother; but finding that the party still lingered, he said: "Be satisfied; it is finished; you can go now." SAVE YOUR SOUL was the alpha and omega of his advice to his relatives on all occasions.

Temptations of most violent character now assailed him at intervals, but the voice of his confessor, or a pious ejaculation, sufficed to disperse them. The Fathers would suggest, as occasion required, acts of every virtue, which he repeated distinctly. Once he asked suddenly: "What must I do to merit?" "Do the will of God," rejoined a Father. Then the saint remained silent. Sometimes he would fix his eyes lovingly on a picture of Our Lady of Sorrows. Every morning many masses were celebrated in his presence, the Fathers being anxious to gratify him in every particular; and to say or to hear mass he had always regarded as his greatest privilege and delight. Brother Francis Anthony asked him to bless the houses of the Papal States, which he did in a loud voice, and with evident emotion. He gave his parting benediction to his former diocese, and in particular to the nuns who had loved him as a Father. Then he said with emphasis: "I bless the king, all the generals, princes, and ministers, and all the magistrates who administer justice."

Although the saint's advanced age gave little hope of his recovery, yet prayers ascended to heaven without intermission, for that intention, from convents, churches, religious congregations, and the poor. When one of the Fathers placed in his hand a picture of his dear son, Brother Gerard, to whom he had much devotion, guessing the intention of the donor, he said sweetly: "God does not will that Brother Gerard should cure me."

Though the news of the change for death could not excite much surprise, it caused universal grief. It was only now that priests and people realized how much they loved him. Prayers were offered all over Naples, that God might give him a happy passage; and the town of St. Agatha rivalled his native city in demonstrations of grief and affection. Many of the bishops of the kingdom ordained that the collect *Pro infirmo* should be said at every mass until the purified soul of his distinguished colleague should have passed to a brighter world.

The wound in the saint's throat from which he had suffered so much at Arienzo, reopened some days before his death, and rendered his condition intensely painful; but his patience and resignation under this new affliction could not fail to enhance his crown. God again glorified his sanctity by miracles. His touch and his blessing restored hearing to Father Samuel, ex-Provincial of the Capuchins; healed the inveterate ulcer of Father Buonopane; and enabled the crippled canon, Dominic Villani, to throw away his crutches, and spring about with all the agility of his youthful days.

Although Alphonsus had prophesied that his death was at hand, and appearances fully justified the prediction, his sons could not accustom themselves to the idea of losing him. Prayers were offered day and night, that he might be left with them just a little longer; and, not to neglect human means, they summoned two eminent physicians from Naples. But, as the departing saint himself observed, it was not God's will to restore him. Towards midnight on the 25th of July, he became so faint that the attendants thought his chastened spirit had already passed the blessed portals of death. Masses succeeded each other in his room, from two in the morning of the 26th until noon. At the *Sanctus* of the first mass, he opened his eyes and looked at the celebrant; at the *Elevation* he did the same, and moved his lips as if in prayer. Absolution was pronounced over him at three A.M., and the prayers for the dying commenced, but he revived during the litanies. Six of the students having come from Ciorani for his last benediction, he recognized them, though in his agony, and appeared pleased to see them. Twice over he blessed these dear children of his heart.

At a later mass he communicated, and during a following mass made his thanksgiving. The Fathers who tried with all their ears to distinguish every word he pronounced, now seized only these: "I hope so," but his lips continued to move in inaudible prayer. He asked for his beads, and having received them, commenced to recite the rosary, but so gently that his breathings no longer formed audible words.

On the twenty-seventh, his sufferings were intense. Unable to find rest in any position he cried out at intervals, "Help me," "unbind me," "place me on the ground." During these terrible spasms, he often exclaimed: "My Jesus!" Mortification having already set in, a poultice replaced his bandage; but, when he felt the infirmarian applying it, he said with tears: "They have touched me." Being informed that it was only Brother Leonard, who had been with him about half a century, he appeared satisfied.

Next morning, being asked how he felt, he replied: "I am dying." Then perceiving the solicitude evinced by the Community and the medical men, he said: "It is finished." Being asked whether he would like to hear mass and communicate, he joyfully signified his assent and began his preparation. This was on Saturday. It was the last time he received Jesus his love, in the Blessed Sacrament, to which he was so tenderly devoted.

CHAPTER LXXV.

Details. — "Give me the Madonna." — The saint can no longer articulate. He is visited by our Lady herself. — Answer to his prayers. — The crucifix. His prayer to die among his beloved brethren. — It is beautifully answered. He dies in an ecstasy of love. — His soul among the seraphim. — His personal appearance. — Character. — Obsequies. — Veneration of all classes, especially the clergy. — Funeral honors, devised by the Bishop of Nocera, dispensed with. Masses celebrated without intermission. — The funeral. — Miracles.

TO A LAST inquiry of his medical friend as to how he felt, the saint replied: "My hour approaches." Fearing that mental and bodily weakness might prevent his raising his heart to God by aspirations of love and oblation, he begged the Fathers to suggest pious affections, and he repeated in a faint tone every ejaculation they uttered. Once, when they ceased, fearing to fatigue him, he said in a tone of loving reproach: "Have you no more holy thoughts to suggest to me?" When he seemed about to expire, the blessed candle was placed in his hands, and the beautiful prayers with which Holy Mother Church soothes and sanctifies the last breathings of her children, were once more affectionately recited. After a while, a picture of Our Blessed Lady was given him; he opened his eyes, and joined his hands in an attitude of prayer. Then having kissed the picture, he recited distinctly the *Ave Maria*, His mind now seemed agitated by conflicting emotions, and pressing his hand to his forehead, he exclaimed: "My thoughts, will you not let me rest?" Next morning he took the crucifix, raised it to his lips, opening and reopening his eyes to contemplate it. When told to place himself in the hands of Mary, he stretched out his arms to signify that he offered himself to his dear Mother.

Next morning a picture being placed in his hands; he looked at it attentively, and said: "Is this St. Joseph?" "Yes," returned a

Father, "recommend yourself to him." The servant of God continued to gaze fixedly on the image, and gently murmured some words, the sense of which the attendant Fathers could not catch. When the devoted Alexis inquired whether he wanted anything, he replied: "All is over." Then he said: "Give me the Madonna." When a picture of Our Lady was put in his hands, he began to invoke her, and recommend himself to her protection. In the evening the death rattle commenced, and it never left him. About nine (July 29th),[1] the prayers for the dying were again said, and the holy sufferer being asked to bless the Congregation once more, moved his head in acquiescence, being no longer able to raise his hand. He had frequent fainting fits next day, but to rouse him to consciousness it was sufficient to repeat the sacred names of Jesus and Mary. A Father having offered him the picture of St. Michael which hung at the head of his bed, he kissed it, and gazing on it with affection, recommended himself to the blessed archangel. To the acts of faith, hope, and charity suggested, he murmured assent, but almost inaudibly. Ere long he could not articulate anything, but he continued to respond to each pious affection, either by opening his eyes, or moving his lips.

Our Lady herself consoled him in his last moments. At the close of day, the two Fathers who assisted him saw his face suddenly become resplendent, and a sweet smile overspread his lips. He held a picture of Our Lady which a Father had put in his hands, reminding him to invoke her for a happy death. As soon as the sweet name of Mary was mentioned, he opened his eyes and looked at the picture. About seven, he appeared to have another interview with the Queen of Heaven, as his biographer Tannoia has left on record.

Then was the life-long prayer of the servant of Mary answered. "O Consolation of the afflicted," he exclaims, "do not abandon me in my last hour! Obtain for me the grace of invoking thee often, that I may expire with thy sweet name, and that of thy divine Son, on my lips. Pardon my boldness, O my Queen; come thyself to console me with thy presence before I expire. I am a sinner, it is true, and therefore do not deserve this favor; but I am thy servant, I love thee, I have great confidence in thee.[2] O Mary,

---

[1] The original manuscript incorrectly stated "Aug 29th"

[2] Visits to the Blessed Sacrament – Editor's original note.

I hope in thee; do not refuse me this consolation...Thou hast bestowed it on many others; I also long for it. If my boldness is great, thy goodness is greater, for it seeks out the most unworthy to console them."[3]

The dying prelate wished to have a crucifix continually in his hand, and, as every one desired to possess one that had been used by him, a new one was substituted every few minutes for the one he held. He had always longed and prayed to die among his beloved sons. "O my God!" he exclaims in his PREPARATION FOR DEATH, "I thank thee now for the favor thou wilt one day grant me, of dying surrounded by my dear brethren, who will have no anxiety but for my eternal salvation, and who will all assist me to die well." God gave him this consolation most munificently. The Fathers crowded in from all the houses, and like another Jacob he died surrounded by a numerous progeny. It was not in a death struggle but in an ecstasy of love that the great spirit of Alphonsus di Liguori passed from earth. No pain, no sigh, no sorrow, marked its exit. The martyr of love fell asleep in the arms of Jesus and Mary as the *Angelus* bell was ringing. The body, chastised and brought under subjection, lay in the solemn and venerable beauty of "precious death;" the soul might now be sought among the seraphim. He at last rested from his labors, an eternal rest; his works still follow him.

The great Neapolitan saint exchanged exile for paradise on the 1st day of August, 1787, at the age of ninety years, ten months, and five days. The Congregation had then entered its fifty-fifth year, and more than twelve years had elapsed since the saint had resigned the episcopate.

Alphonsus di Liguori was of middle size, and was remarkable for personal beauty; his head was rather large, his complexion fresh. A broad, lofty forehead, piercing, but tender blue eyes, an aquiline nose, and a small mouth often relaxing in a heavenly smile, were his most attractive features. His hair and beard had been jet black; but sorrows and labors blanched them while he was still in his prime. Being naturally short-sighted, he usually wore glasses, except when preaching, or conversing with women. His voice was clear and sonorous; it was capable of filling the most spacious edifice, and it never failed him till the last. He had

---

[3] Glories of Mary. – Editor's original note

an imposing mien, but his manners, though somewhat grave, were exceedingly frank and gracious. From infancy to old age, he always made himself amiable and agreeable to every one. His judgment was subtle and penetrating, his memory prompt and tenacious, his mind precise and methodical. His life was one of continued application; a fulfilment of his vow *never to lose one moment of time.*

He was by nature courageous and enterprising, and he usually succeeded even beyond his own expectations, because his confidence in God never failed. Not to be cast down by adversity, he was never unduly elated by prosperity.

His reprimands were energetic, but he softened their severity by his habitual gentleness. Unpitying towards himself, he was all charity towards others. Such is the description biographers concur in giving of our saint.

The obsequies[4] of the great doctor were solemn and beautiful, such as he himself would have desired; tears, devotion, veneration — such were the manifestations of all who came to pay him the last duty. The Bishop of Nocera, Monsignore Sanfilice, ordered that every possible respect should be shown to the sacred remains of his illustrious colleague; and by his order, the bells of all the churches in Nocera responded to the solemn tolling which, from the belfry of the Redemptorist convent, announced that the magnanimous soul of the holy Founder reposed in the bosom of the Father.

The city and the adjacent country poured out their inhabitants to give a last look at the calm and beautiful face, so familiar to them all in its aspects of suffering and resignation, of sweetness and benignity. So great was the concourse that a detachment of the royal cavalry was required to preserve order. Every one wished to touch the sacred body; rosaries, scapulars, and other objects of devotion were constantly being applied to it, and whatever was sanctified by contact with this emaciated frame, so long the tabernacle of the Holy Ghost, was ever after treasured as a relic. The bier was surrounded by starlike lights, emblematic of his faith, *the victory that overcometh the world,* and covered with the fairest blossoms which the beautiful gardens of Nocera

---

[4] Funeral rites

yielded, fitting types of the purity and innocence of his life, and the "good odor of Christ Jesus" which he was, and is, to the world.

The priests, regular and secular, of the diocese of Nocera, relieved each other all day in chanting the office and the *Libera*,[5] for one who so long had been their father, their doctor, their saint, their pride. His extraordinary erudition had made him an oracle among them for more than half a century; his undoubted sanctity had challenged their admiration; his wonderful sweetness had won their hearts, and disarmed the petty jealousies which poor human nature is sometimes weak enough to show, when there is question of virtue and talent almost above its own comprehension.

Alphonsus de Liguori was always extremely beloved by every order of the clergy. As he surpassed all his contemporaries in learning, so he surpassed them in humility; and in their intercourse with him, instead of being dazzled by his wonderful mental gifts, they were invariably captivated by the genuine goodness of his heart. He loved his own Congregation, but he loved, too, every congregation, every order, every priest, every religious, that labored for Jesus and Mary. Nothing small, mean, or ignoble, ever sullied the expansive soul of our most zealous doctor; he was a thorough gentleman in his intercourse with the clergy and, in his dealings with them, self-interest never entered into his calculations. He was edified by their virtues, he took pride in their learning, he gloried in their success! Far from confining his zeal or his sympathies within the limits of his own Congregation, he would have all to be preachers, prophets, saints — *Redemptorists*, in the sense that every priest is the co-laborer of the great Redeemer, *with whom there is mercy and copious redemption.* Hence the extraordinary affection and veneration shown him by all orders of the clergy, especially those to whom he was personally known.

It was arranged that the blessed corpse should be carried in procession through the town, resting during the chanting of the *Libera* in the church of the saint's dear daughters, the Poor Clares, and giving a similar consolation to his equally dear nuns of the Purity; the cortège to return, in the same order in which it set out, to the Redemptorist convent. But the gentlemen of Pagani, or the

---

[5] Part of the office for the dead, chanted after the *Requiem* Mass and before the burial, asking God to have mercy on the deceased on the day of Judgment.

lower town, would not hear of this arrangement, fearing that by some pious stratagem the bishop would seize the blessed remains for his cathedral. Vainly did Monsignore pledge his word that nothing of the kind was intended; it was only when the Fathers themselves assured the excited people that no such project was contemplated, that they became calm, the bishop, fearing a tumult, dispensed with the elegant arrangements he had projected for the funeral, and decided that everything should be conducted with the greatest simplicity.

Although on this account no invitations were issued, the church and convent of the Redemptorist Fathers were crowded with ecclesiastics of every grade. Temporary altars were erected for the accommodation of the numerous priests who wished to offer up the holy sacrifice in presence of the blessed remains, and masses succeeded each other without intermission from dawn till noon, each day while the holy body remained unburied, in that church doubly consecrated by the preaching, the prayers, the tears of a saint.

Crowds besieged the church from daybreak, the inhabitants of the neighboring villages insisting upon offering their homages to "the saint." The clergy, regular and secular, of the city and the adjacent towns, formed as it were a guard of honor around the blessed bier, praying rather *to* a saint than *for* a saint. The mothers, as usual, presented their children to touch and kiss the blessed body, and Brother Francis Anthony and the ever faithful Alexis "suffered them to come," remembering the delight which their beloved master had always taken in being surrounded by the precious little innocents, and that he had never shown himself weary of the importunity of the eager mothers who presented them.

At a signal from the bishop, Monsignore Sanfelice, the funeral procession began to form. Six gentlemen of Nocera begged the honor of carrying the relics of the saint, but the rectors of the four Redemptorist convents in the kingdom of Naples refused to relinquish their prior claims. The precious burden was therefore placed upon their shoulders; canons held the corners of the pall, and six gentlemen surrounded the coffin bearing lighted torches. The Fathers of St. Francis of Paula, the Carmelite Fathers, the Redemptorist priests, students, and lay-brothers and the Cathedral Chapter, preceded the bier; the Bishop of Nocera followed, and behind him, the military and the townspeople. The procession did not enter the town, but merely described an immense semicircle before the church and monastery, going out by the great door of the latter and returning through the principal gate of the former. When the rectors laid down the sacred remains, the canons chanted the office, after which a grand requiem mass was celebrated. The funeral oration was pronounced by the celebrated Don F. Pinto, afterwards Bishop of Tricarico. To satisfy the surging mass of people who could not find room in the church, the pulpit was placed near the main entrance.

At eleven o'clock A.M. (Aug. 2) a celebrated artist of Naples came, without being at all invited, to take the likeness of the saint. All trace of pain and suffering had vanished from the noble countenance, which now appeared full of vigor and manly beauty, more expressive than ever of the two great qualities which preeminently distinguished the most celebrated of our modern bishops, sanctity and intellectual gifts. When the cast was removed, part of the skin of the left nostril adhered to it, and the bright blood which issued from the wound was eagerly but reverently gathered by the pious multitude.

Whole communities of monks were hourly arriving, with clergy of every order, to the number of several hundreds, from all quarters. The space in front of the church was thronged with the carriages of the nobility, who vied with the poor, the dearer children of the "good bishop," in testifying their affectionate veneration. Every one begged to have something that he had touched, but it was impossible to gratify the pious avidity of so many thousands. At seven in the evening, the bishop, fearing that some disorder might occur in such an immense concourse, or that some disagreement might take place between the people and the soldiers on guard, ordered that the holy body should be buried. It had remained on the catafalque[6] for over thirty-three hours, yet notwithstanding the oppressive heat of the weather, it emitted no unpleasant odor. It was deposited in a leaden chest, sealed with the seals of the bishopric of Nocera, the municipality of Pagani, and the Congregation of the Most Holy Redeemer. This chest was fastened with three keys, one of which was given to the

---

[6] A raised bier or platform that supports the coffin or the body of the deceased.

mayor of the town, the second to the saint's relative, the Prince of Polleca, who attended in the name of the Liguori family, and the third to the Rector of Pagani. The chest was deposited at the left angle of the high altar. Several beautiful epitaphs were composed for a mausoleum which the Fathers intended to raise to their saintly Founder, but as this project was not carried out, the door of his vault was closed with a simple marble slab, bearing a concise Latin inscription, of which the following is a translation:

HERE REPOSES THE BODY
OF THE
MOST ILLUSTRIOUS AND REVEREND LORD
ALPHONSUS DI LIGUORI,
BISHOP OF
SAINT AGATHA OF THE GOTHS,
AND FOUNDER OF THE CONGREGATION OF THE
MOST HOLY REDEEMER.

In those days when neither steam nor telegraph had come to annihilate space, the news of our saint's happy translation to eternal glory was slow in reaching the more distant towns and hamlets which he had formerly evangelized. Many of the people of these places, especially the peasants — for Alphonsus di Liguori, patrician as he was by birth, had always been, like all our great and holy churchmen, the friend and Father of the working classes and the poor — thronged the church for many days subsequent to the funeral, to pray beside his tomb and touch it with their scapulars and rosaries. And the little children loved to testify their affection and veneration for the gentle Father to whom their innocence and candor had endeared them, by kneeling near his sacred relics, and kissing, with humility and devotion, the sepulchral stone which enclosed "the saint."

Miracles immediately began to glorify the memory of the humble servant of God. Wherever he was known or had ever been heard of, the sick and the sorrowful were inspired on a sudden with an extraordinary sentiment of his power before God; and they felt that he who had always testified such tender compassion for the corporal and spiritual miseries of poor human nature, *could* and *would* relieve their sufferings. Hundreds of well-authenticated miracles prove that the new saint did not disappoint the confidence of his clients. As an appropriate and touching tribute to the wonderful innocence of his long life, his boisterous friends, the little children, universally styled him "the saint." And this praise literally proceeded also from the mouths of infants and sucklings, for a child of a year old, who had just been cured of a mortal illness by Alphonsus, on being shown his picture, raised his little hands and eyes to heaven, and exclaimed several times: "The saint is in heaven! Alphonsus the saint!" The infant had never before uttered a syllable.

CHAPTER LXXVI.

Honors shown to the saint's memory. — Testimony of the Archbishop of Palermo. — Of Cardinal Benediti. — Of the Archbishop of Amalfi. — Letter of Monsignore Lopez. — Magnificent obsequies. — Letter from the Bishop of Nusco. — The Superior-General of the pious workmen. — Mother Raphael. The modern Francis de Sales. — Cardinal Spinelli. — The Archbishop of Salerno. — Other distinguished testimony. — Alphonsus a model for all orders of the clergy. — His extraordinary sweetness towards sinners. — His life-long propensity to magnify the mercy and goodness of God.

ALL THE Redemptorist houses, both in the kingdom of the Two Sicilies and the Papal States, vied with each other in the posthumous honors they showered on their sainted Founder; but reverence and affection for the great Bishop were by no means confined to his more immediate children. All the religious congregations to which he had ever been affiliated, now proudly claimed him as a brother, and no royal personage was ever honored with obsequies as magnificent as were everywhere spontaneously celebrated for the most zealous doctor. Music, painting, poetry, and oratory, of the first order, were brought into requisition to commemorate one who excelled in all these departments. The most distinguished literary men of the day delighted to consecrate their worthiest efforts to him whom they had long looked upon as their greatest glory and honor. A mere collection of the orations in which his virtues were extolled, and his intercession invoked, would fill a larger volume than we have been able to devote to his life. As a testimony of the universal veneration in which he was held, we shall here make a few extracts from the numerous letters of condolence which flowed in upon the Fathers of Nocera, when it was known that the saint had passed from earth, entirely omitting those which were written by his own sons, the Redemptorist Fathers.

"Let us fearlessly assert," wrote Monsignore San Severino, Archbishop of Palermo, "that we stand in need of the prayers of the saintly bishop, who has now received the reward of his labors, his struggles, and his virtues…As for me, I expect great assistance from him, because he always loved me during his mortal life. He will obtain of God, that I may lead a better life henceforth, and belong wholly to Him." "The loss of Monsignore Liguori," wrote Cardinal Banditi, "has been felt by me with a keenness proportioned to the great love I bore him. The particulars of his death have affected me to tears, and the miracles he continues to work in all directions prove that he will one day be numbered among the saints whom the Church delights to honor."

"I pray," wrote Monsignore Puoti, Archbishop of Amalfi, when he heard that his saintly brother in the episcopacy was dying, "that when the venerable Bishop Liguori shall have gone to enjoy the Divine beauty, he will, through the great kindness he has ever shown me, remember me, and obtain for me a double share of his spirit, that I may perform well my laborious and difficult ministry, and finish my course in the peace of Christ."

The following is from Monsignore Lopez, Bishop of Noia, who was afterwards viceroy of Sicily:

"My soul has been filled with the most lively sorrow at the sad tidings of the death of Bishop Liguori. I grieve for his loss as much as his venerable Congregation do; if they weep for a father and a founder, I weep for a man, worthy of the greatest respect for his holiness and learning; but the bitterness of my sorrow is tempered by a firm confidence that God has crowned him with the glory of the saints, and that he is now our most charitable intercessor in heaven."

The Fathers having gratefully acknowledged the respect shown to their illustrious Founder by Monsignore Amato, Bishop of Lacedogna, who had magnificent obsequies celebrated in his cathedral, he answered Father Villani, September 22, 1787:

"I have only performed a duty. I wished to honor the memory of our saintly and admirable prelate; and though fully persuaded that he needs not our suffrages, I feel bound to have many masses offered, to satisfy in a trifling degree the great obligations I am under to him."

"I feel my confidence in his powerful intercession increase," wrote Monsignore Bonaventure, Bishop of Nusco, "and I more than ever invoke him in my spiritual wants. His picture I wear around my neck, and I long above all things to possess the relic you promised me. God is wonderful in his saints...I hope, despite my extreme misery, to obtain everything through the intercession of him whose death we unite in deploring, although it is less a subject of grief than of joy."

Father Antonio, Superior-General of the Congregation of Pious Laborers, wrote: "I have always regarded Don Alphonsus Liguori as a saint, and every member of my Congregation shares my sentiments. You ask me to procure prayers for him, but you should rather advise me to recommend myself and my brethren to him, that he who loved us on earth may continue to protect us in heaven."

"The sad news of our common Father's decease has produced in my soul conflicting sentiments," wrote that dear daughter of our saint, Mother Raphael, superior of the nuns of the Most Holy Redeemer at St. Agatha, "sorrow because of the loss he will be to the world, and joy from the firm conviction I feel that he now lives in the mansions of glory, where he will become our intercessor with God."

Don Mariano Arcieri, who is so celebrated for his virtues that it is hoped he may one day be raised on our altars, was not at all astonished at the miracles which followed the holy bishop's death: "I have always considered him a saint," said he, "and as such I have recommended myself to him even during his life." Arcieri was so charmed by the excessive meekness of the saint that he never called him anything but the modern St. Francis de Sales.

Indeed, Alphonsus had been regarded as a saint for almost three quarters of a century. Cardinal Spinelli wrote of him to one of the great Roman Congregations, in 1748: "We can truly assert that Don Alphonsus Liguori, a Neapolitan chevalier, professor of theology, and an indefatigable missionary, merits, as much through his rare piety as his extraordinary erudition, especially in ecclesiastical matters, to receive from the Holy See permission to read and retain the works of all prohibited authors." Monsignore Rossi went so far as to accept the archbishopric of Salerno at his request. Alphonsus having once asked a certificate for some person: "I would not have granted it to any one else," said the archbishop, "but my conscience can repose on your word in perfect security." The same prelate designated Alphonsus to Pope

Benedict XIV as a man of wonderful learning, unvarying uprightness, consummate prudence, and angelic life.

The aged Monsignore Giannini sought to be directed in all things by the holy Founder, and was wont to style himself his son, and beg the reluctant saint to treat him as a son. The Bishop of Caserto used to call him a perfect mirror of justice. Bishop Rosa was accustomed to say: "We have a true saint on earth in Don Alphonsus Liguori." Canon Barba, who was more or less connected with the saint for many years, bore him this splendid testimony: "In all the varied intercourse I had with him, I saw that his life resembled the Lives of the Saints whom the Church honors on her altars. He always reminded me of a Francis de Sales or a Philip Neri."

The celebrated Don Joseph Jorio once wrote to some ecclesiastics who begged him to give a mission in their territory: "I entreat, I exhort, I most earnestly beseech you, to engage Father Alphonsus to undertake this work, for he is the first missionary in the kingdom for learning and sanctity."

Monsignore Kalifati, the learned Bishop of Osia, in one of his works describes his brother prelate "as very celebrated in the Church of God and in the republic of letters, for prudence, zeal, piety, and vast learning, and for his excellent works, all which rendered him deserving of unbounded praise."

The learned authors of the Historical Dictionary of Illustrious Men (Venice, 1796) style him a truly apostolic man, a perfect ecclesiastic, an accomplished model for bishops, and a most powerful defender of Christian morality; and speak of his works with unbounded enthusiasm.

The Archbishop of Morreale, in his "Vera Sposa," says: "Monsignore Liguori is the hero of our age. A priest after God's own heart, a man of truly apostolic character, an elegant orator, an excellent superior, a tender father, a bishop like those of primitive times. The Holy Ghost has ever been his guide. In imitating his Divine Model, he never relaxed. All who knew him concur in saying that he was a lively and faithful copy of Our Lord Jesus Christ."

The same prelate, in another of his works, styles him, "a man of the greatest piety, a most useful writer, a judicious and irreproachable theologian, a celebrated founder, a truly great bishop, and the apostle of his age." And addressing his clergy he continues: "Study then this bishop, so highly elevated above his contemporaries by the nobility of his birth, his faith, his charity, his erudition. His room was like to that which the Shunamite woman prepared for the Prophet Elias. A bed, a table, a chair, and a lamp, comprised all its furniture. His food was frugal, he retrenched all superfluities that he might have wherewith to give in alms...The poor of Jesus Christ were his only riches, and the joy of his heart." Even in Rome, which the saint never visited but once, his name had more weight than the names of all the illustrious and distinguished scholars that crowded its colleges.

From every country in Europe testimonials highly honorable to the saint reached Nocera. His mission was far from being confined to his age or country, and this was readily seen by the most enlightened of his contemporaries. He was set in the Church as a burning and shining light, to enlighten the people of his day and all coming generations, and to inflame the cold or tepid hearts of men with love for the Divine and Eternal Lover of their souls. He opened anew the life-giving sacraments to all Christians, and encouraged them to draw waters with joy from the fountains of the Saviour. He has instructed with the glowing eloquence inspired by his heroic charity, the rich and the poor, the learned and the ignorant, men and women of every age and condition. Penetrated to the very marrow of his bones with a life-long horror of sin, he lifts up the fallen, he presses the most wretched to his innocent heart, he calls the slave of a thousand vices, *My brother!* Only be resolved to sin no more, and he shows you Jesus awaiting you with outstretched arms, and even pressing forward to meet his guilty child. It is always Jesus — an inexhaustible fountain of mercy, love, and goodness — that he preaches. He indeed reminds us of the worm that dieth not, and the fire that is never extinguished, and the smoke that ascendeth forever and ever; still more does he expatiate on the rapturous bliss which our own God has prepared for those who love him, glory unutterable which the eye hath not seen, the ear heard, the heart of man conceived; but the only hell which this ardent lover could fear was to be separated from Jesus, and the only heaven he yearned for, was to repose in the bosom of the Father. No wonder then, that the great and good of his time vied with each other in testifying affection and veneration for this seraph of earth. The saint of unity, the saint of infallibility, the saint of Jesus and Mary, the saint of penance, the saint of the eucharist, the man after God's own heart — what other saint has so many claims upon Christians? His sweet and touching words resound through the universal Church everywhere and forever:

"My brother, cease to sin, avoid the occasions of sin; our sweetest Lord will help you by His grace; His grace is always to be had for the asking; *ask and you shall receive*; pray, strive to love Jesus more and more; come to Him by confession, receive Him in communion. He loves you, He loves you with an eternal love, He longs for your love; if you be holy, become still more holy; if a sinner, a relapsing sinner, yea, a sinner covered with the filth of every abomination possible to human depravity incited by diabolical ingenuity — though your sins be red as scarlet He will make them white as wool; He willeth not the death, but the conversion, of the sinner; His mercy is above all His works. *My brother!* come to the Lord Jesus! He cannot spurn the penitent. See His hands and feet fastened to a gibbet; it is love for you, my brother, that renders the omnipotent God powerless to hurl His thunderbolts on your guilty soul. A man of sorrows and acquainted with infirmity, He will understand your griefs, your struggles, for we have not a high-priest who cannot compassionate our miseries."

O how well does our great bishop follow the counsel of his prototype: *An ancient man rebuke not, but entreat him as a father; young men as brethren; old women as mothers, young women as sisters*: he rebukes none, all are his fathers, his mothers, his brothers, his sisters — they are more, they are his children. *My little children of whom I am again in labor till Christ be formed in you!* Verily, it is easy to comprehend the wonderful effects which this great voice of one crying in the desert of this world must have produced, when he depicted, to surging multitudes, the love borne to sinners by Him whom we find true when all other loves die or prove false! *Can a mother forget her son? And even if she should, I will not forget thee.* Even now, from the cold, dead page, do not his words of fire burn into our hard, unthankful hearts, disarming criticism with their unearthly beauty; echoes of the communings of the Creator with his virgin creatures in the paradise of pleasure, or of the divine words with which the Incarnate Wisdom of the Father consoles the sad hearts of His fallen, but not rejected, children: *Come to me, all of yon that labor and are burdened, and I will refresh you. My yoke is sweet and my burden light.* Foolish and slow of heart to believe must we be, if the words of this friend of publicans and sinners stir not the deepest depths of our hearts. Rather may they revive in us faith and hope, that we may exclaim with the lepers of the Gospel: "Jesus, Master, have mercy on us," and that, being grateful recipients of that mercy which our saint never tires of preaching, we may return Him love for love, to the end that our many sins may be forgiven us, because we love much.

CHAPTER LXXVII.

Alphonsus as a child. — His three great sins. — Early sympathy with the humbler classes. — As a priest. — "Keep your rules." — As superior. Remarkable instances of his kindness and compassion. — A model for bishops. His excessive clemency. — His love for his subjects. — His unbounded confidence in them. — Instance. — Alphonsus as a theologian. — His attachment to his clergy. — Their love for him. — Instances. — Accused of laxity. — Characteristic defence.

W E SHALL conclude our sketch of the servant of God by glancing at him once more, in the different roles in which Providence placed him during his prolonged and varied career.

Alphonsus was, as we have seen, a child of benediction. Wherever saints pass they leave blessed traces, and as an infant he had been caressed, and fondled, and blessed, by the sainted Jesuit who afterwards shared with him the honors of canonization, and who prophesied that he would be a bishop and do great things for Jesus Christ. He had a saintly mother, and it is to her teachings and example that he was wont to attribute anything good in him as a child. The office of his festival declares that he never sullied his baptismal robe by mortal sin, but his confessors believed that he scarcely committed even a wilful venial sin. Yet he was naturally proud and high-spirited, as the very faults into which he fell prove. His three great sins, as he used to style them, have been already recorded. The first was characteristic. Hearing his father scold a poor servant unmercifully for some trifling omission, his natural generosity of soul and *sympathy with the humbler classes* tempted him to reproach the Count with making a great noise about nothing, a liberty which the haughty noble could not brook and for which he struck him a blow before several guests. Again he bewailed a relaxation of fervor; and, as the greatest of his sins, he wept over the excess of dejection to which he had yielded through wounded vanity, when he failed in the last lawsuit he undertook. As a child, as a boy, as a young man living amid the gayeties of the world, he is a model to all youths, especially those of gentle blood like himself, or rather absolutely to all.

But still more resplendent is the example he gives to priests. His life so pure, so holy; his labors, his penances, his hours of prayer before the Blessed Sacrament; but above all, his incomparable zeal — the Lord Jesus had spoken to his heart, and what he heard in the ear, he preached on the house-top. In industry, few of the saints of God equal him, and perhaps none surpass him; his vow, *never to waste a moment of time,* gives some feeble explanation of the life-long toil, for the blessed results of which we thank God today. As a student, he might be considered slow. In some particular instances, when he had any doubt as to whether his views were the exposition of the divine law, he would write to all the learned men of his acquaintance, especially those of the Roman Congregations; but above all, he would *pray.* As a priest, he was always to be found at the altar, in the confessional, by the bedside of the sick and dying, or instructing with tongue or pen the souls which Jesus died to save.

Next, we have St Alphonsus as a religious, *Keep your rules;* this is the burden of all his discourses: *Fear nothing but sin:* this is the epitome of all his warnings. There is no instance recorded of our saint having ever broken a single rule, and this cannot but give us the highest idea of his sanctity, since a great pope has not hesitated to declare that a religious who faithfully observes his rule is fit for canonization.

It is chiefly as Superior that all the beauty of the saint's character comes out. He was more a father than a ruler, more a mother than a father. No one was sad that he did not console; sick, that he did not relieve. The troubles of his children were his troubles; be made his own of their gains and their losses; he invited them to come to him at all times; he corrected them but rarely, and his words were full of sweetness and compassion. His whole aim was to make them realize that the yoke of the Lord is sweet and his burden light, that a day spent in his courts is preferable to years passed in the tabernacles of sinners.

He was always urging them, but with ineffable sweetness, to become saints. They were his joy and his crown. His heart followed them everywhere, and in all their labors they were strengthened by his blessing and his prayers. His letters, of which we have hundreds, show that they were never absent from his mind, and that, if possible, he never ceased for a moment to interest himself about their welfare. Their vocation he was always trying to strengthen and confirm; their studies he encouraged and directed; their pains of mind and body he relieved. In writing to rectors, he was always insisting on the importance of having the rules perfectly observed — for his first care was, that his children should become saints, and he feared the slightest wilful fault more than a hundred persecutions. But sweetness and kindness continually mingle with his instructions. "I beseech you to govern with all possible meekness," he writes to the Rector of Caposele; "treat every one with affability and politeness. I recommend this to you with the greatest earnestness." And the same he continually repeats in one shape or another. "I love you, I esteem you, and if I have sometimes found a little fault with you, I have never doubted your good-will," he writes to another rector, who had given him grave cause of displeasure. "Treat N. with great kindness," he writes to the novice-master, "because he is tormented by temptation; keep up his courage. And now that the weather is so warm, lessen the exercises of the novices, make them go out often, and do not ask them to study so much." The saint sometimes speaks sternly enough in the circular letters he addresses to his dear children, but the severity is sweetened by such phrases as these perpetually recurring: "God knoweth that each one of you is dearer to my heart than my brother and even my mother. Each one of you is the object of my peculiar affection, for whom I am ready to give my blood and my life." "Be attentive to Brother N., and see that he is not exposed to cold." "I rejoice at what you say of Brother Nicholas, but do not allow him to do much until his health is completely reestablished." "Make Brother B. go out every day, and show him the best road." "I do not wish Brother M. to study, for fear of a relapse. Make him take outdoor exercise." "Tell Father de Meo to beware of fatiguing himself; I hear his chest is affected." "I beseech you not to expose yourself to contract any sickness. Endeavor to preserve your health, it is most necessary that you should."

But we should not soon have done were we to transcribe all our saint wrote concerning the temporal, and far more, the spiritual welfare of his brethren. As a superior we find him always on the alert to support, counsel, and befriend them, and this he evidently considers his first and dearest duty. No father, no mother, ever showed more patience with wild, unreasoning children, than Alphonsus showed towards the least edifying of his subjects. In their regard, he was all patience, all goodness, all hope. He never expelled a subject who had not previously expelled himself; he could, though not very readily, see their faults, and correct them; but he was powerless to cast one of his children from him. In this respect, it seems to us, that he surpassed every other saint that governed a community. Even when they yielded to the tempter, and, in the heat of passion or temptation, asked to go, his policy was to gain time, that he might, in some way or other, dispel the illusion.

To a young Father, who for some trifling cause had asked a dispensation, he pleasantly wrote:

"St. Paul the hermit said to St. Anthony, who asked him to open the door, if he did not wish to find him dead before it, 'Verily a beautiful way of begging; you beg with a menace!' I say the same to you. You say, 'Let me do this, otherwise I ask to be released from my vows.' But who will release you? For the love of God, my dear father, do not be so carried away any more. I have compassion on you, for *it is not you who speak, but the temptation which agitates you.*"

To Father Tannoia, the novice-master, who seems to have been a very strict disciplinarian, he wrote the following note, which will explain itself:

"Once a subject is in the novitiate, he must not be sent away without grave reasons; and if he have made his vows, the reasons must be still graver, and the subject incorrigible; *otherwise one sins mortally in dismissing a subject.*"

To Father Villani, who showed, in a few instances, an inclination to severity, he wrote on the same subject: "To justify expulsion, the faults of a subject must be real, deserving of no compassion, and leaving no room to hope for amendment."

Verily, that sweet spirit St. Alphonsus *would not have been half as lax had he been but half as holy!*

We will now quote an instance of forbearance unexampled in the annals of religious orders, at least in modern times.

482

The lay-brother, Francis Tartaglione, being one day in the refectory of the Redemptorist house at Nocera, became so angry at some remark another brother volunteered, that he dashed a glass with its contents in his face. Here was an unheard-of outrage. The older Fathers were not long in deciding on the course to be pursued; but, fortunately for the delinquent, Father Alphonsus happened to be at Nocera. Previous services rendered to the Congregation, and the virtue which he knew this poor brother to possess, despite a fiery temper which he had worked hard to subdue, inclined the saint to recommend delay; and the end of it was that the brother, instead of being expelled, was seen humbly performing a course of penance, and was heard from time to time blessing the kindness and charity of the good Father who knew so well how to pity and forgive his erring but repentant son.

Alphonsus ever showed the greatest respect and esteem for his sons, and was not ashamed to let them see how tenderly he loved them. In his letters he generally addresses them by their Christian names. Even Father Villani is simply called, "My dear Andrew," but those whose birth entitled them to the aristocratic *Don* usually received it from the urbane Rector Major, whether in speaking or writing.

The confidence he placed in his Fathers and Brothers was literally unbounded. A miracle of truth and candor himself, he was incapable of suspecting the opposite qualities in others; he was even faulty, or at least obstinate, in this respect. Witness his conduct with regard to Majone. The whole Congregation saw through his duplicity, while the saint refused to credit the evidence that convinced others, and would not believe, till the document was placed in his hands which showed him that the Congregation was wellnigh ruined. This was the immediate cause of the troubles which clouded his latter years. Majone's intentions were so glaringly evident, that it was easy to convince the inimical or the indifferent that the saint was himself a party to the changes his treacherous son wrought in the rules, in direct violation of his commands.

As a bishop, Alphonsus is a perfect model for every personage raised to that exalted office. This will be readily seen by the few details we have given of his life at St. Agatha. Other prelates, who assuredly were competent judges, used to style him a new St. Charles Borromeo. He was completely at the service of his clergy;

he wished each of them to recur to him, as to a tender, indulgent father, in every emergency, and he always made them understand that his chief business was to advise, instruct, assist, and console them. His purse was always at their disposal, and he seldom accepted even his ordinary dues. His vigilance was miraculous; nothing escaped it. The common opinion was that an angel or a devil made known to him every scandal that was attempted in his diocese: and, once known, he would not rest till the evil was eradicated. As a superior, and consequently a judge, no human being ever surpassed him in lenity to the accused. He gave them the benefit of every doubt. He insisted on hearing the sentiments of all who had means of knowing the truth. When asked, a little before his death, to give consent, as Rector Major, to the dismissal of a subject, he inquired whether all those who ought to be consulted had consented, "for," he continued, "*if there be a single one of a different opinion, I must hear his reasons.*"

He governed his priests by loving them, by devoting himself entirely to their interests; and never was a bishop more passionately beloved by priests and people. Even those whom he had withstood with all the apostolic boldness of a perfectly fearless character, acknowledged the justice of his proceedings, and were foremost in bewailing his resignation of his see. As for human respect, if it be possible for human nature to be wholly free from it, he was. When there was question of ordaining clerics, or bestowing benefices, he settled the matter according to his own conscience, and all the kings of earth could not induce him to abate one iota in the qualifications he required. Both as bishop and as superior, mercy was his prevailing characteristic; at the least sign of repentance, he anticipated a returning prodigal, and assumed the greater part of the penance himself. When Father Villani insisted on expelling a subject who had given him much anxiety and trouble, the saint wrote: "I have compassion for this poor Father. I know he has done very wrong; but if he repents, we cannot send away a man who humbles himself sincerely." The poor Father wisely opened his whole heart to Alphonsus, who in turn procured his pardon from Father Villani. "I have read," wrote the saint to this dear child of his heart, "all that you have written to me of your troubles. Now then, do all you have promised, and be assured that God will more willingly accept the little you do amid so much anguish, than if you did it in sweetness and consolation. You have made great progress, and I bless God for having given you such strength…Go, then, and place yourself in the heart of Jesus. I tell you for certain that Jesus and Mary love you."

It is true that the saint was strict in driving away sin, and all occasions of sin, from his subjects; zeal against sin was, as has been already said, his most salient characteristic. It is no less true that he insisted that the spirit of the priesthood should always and under all circumstances be, as it were, palpable, in the favored priests of whom he was the tender father and watchful shepherd; it is true, that being himself among the most industrious students that ever lived, he required that his priests should continually study the divine law of which they were the exponents; that, having an acquaintance with the sacred Scriptures as intimate, perhaps, as any theologian ever attained, if not more so — and his works fully bear out this assertion — he insisted that his priests should continually inculcate that *all Scripture is profitable, to teach, to reprove,* and that a priest ignorant of what he ought to know, or a priest who in the matter of sacred learning would ever say, *It is enough,* should be unheard-of in the flock confided to his pastoral care. The man that minutely, laboriously, and conscientiously examined, and even quoted nearly eight hundred Christian authors, and not a few pagans, for the composition of a single work, could not sanction any undue recreation for his clergy; but, despite all this, and despite his own life of innocence almost unsullied and penance so severe as to cause him to be likened to St. Peter Alcantara, St. Alphonsus Liguori is the largest-hearted of saints, the most readily understood of theologians, and the easiest and sweetest master that repenting sinners can choose. "In the spirit of the divine Lord, who forgave all who had faith to come to Him, not exacting of them more than the least of that which his sanctity inflexibly required, St. Alphonsus drew to the fountains of the most Precious Blood all who had need — the most stained, hardened, and outcast— exacting of them only the least which the sacrament of penance imposes as the condition of our pardon."

During his life, he was frequently accused not only of laxity of doctrine, but also of excessive indulgence, even of weakness, so notorious was his lenity in all the relations of life. Indeed he himself saw this, and he admitted it, when reproached for what seemed a sort of stain on an otherwise perfect character. His defence is characteristic of the whole man. In our imperfect state we are scarcely capable of invariably recognizing the golden mean; with the best of intentions, we easily glide into either extreme. The saint, knowing this, readily pleaded guilty. "But," said he, "if I must err, let it be on the side of mercy and charity, of meekness and compassion. If I must be punished in the next life, let it be for too much indulgence, rather than for excessive rigor." Verily, a worthy disciple of Him whose mercy is above all his works!

CHAPTER LXXVIII.

Miracles attest the sanctity of Alphonsus. — Magdalen de Nuncio.— Francis de Octajana. — Antoinette Tarsia. — The nun of Salerno. — The saint's countrywoman, Dona Giordani. — Miracle wrought on the Lady Louisa Palatella. — Two processes. — The saint declared Venerable. — Proceedings suspended. — Alphonsus is beatified. — Canonization. — Indulgences granted. The city of Naples chooses him for patron. — Respect paid to him by the Royal family and people of Naples. — High esteem of several popes for Alphonsus, especially Pius IX. — Raised to the Doctorate. — Conditions. — The excellences of all the Doctors reunited in our saint. — Extraordinary pomp and splendor of the saint's beatification and canonization. — Decree.

THE SAINT had no sooner accomplished his happy transit from earth to heaven, than hundreds of miracles attested his power with God. Several of these are mentioned in the bull of his canonization, as the instantaneous and perfect cure of Magdalen de Nuncio, who, being at the point of death, a great portion of her breast having been amputated on account of a gangrenous ulcer, invoked Alphonsus, and immediately arose, perfectly healed, her breast having become whole again; the cure of Francis de Octajana, of the reformed Minors, who, being in the last stage of consumption, his life despaired of, prayed to Alphonsus for several days, and was suddenly cured, every trace of the malady instantaneously disappearing; of Antoinette Tarsia, who, having fallen, loaded with a heavy burden, from a high place, was on the point of dying of the injuries received, but having earnestly implored the aid of Alphonsus, suddenly arose entirely cured.

Others equally striking are recorded. Doña Catherine Biscotti, a Benedictine nun of Salerno, after suffering for fourteen months from a grievous malady, was declared to be dying. The doctor thought mortification had already set in. While in this state she exclaimed: "Alphonsus Liguori, prove to me that you are really a saint, as is everywhere proclaimed; you must cure me of this illness, and as the process of your canonization will have to be drawn up, I promise to bear witness to my cure juridically, and to have a mass and a *Te Deum* sung in thanksgiving." Having said this, the nun fell asleep, and on awaking found that she was perfectly cured.

Another miracle evinced the affectionate confidence of a client of our saint. Don Julian Jourdain,[1] a lawyer of Lucere, was sick unto death of a violent fever. His sister, who tenderly loved him, was heart-broken at the prospect of his death. Rushing into his chamber, she fell on her knees before a picture of Alphonsus, and cried out: "My holy countryman, I, a poor stranger, have recourse to you. You must spare me my brother, I *will* obtain this favor." She then seized the picture with faith and confidence, and gave it to her brother, who simply said: "Monsignore, succor me!" Instantaneously the fever ceased, and the sick man's recovery was complete and lasting.

When the Lady Louisa Palatella of Foggia was in momentary danger of death, the physicians having pronounced her case hopeless, Father Tannoia suggested to her to have recourse to Alphonsus. She did so, and holding his picture with devotion, made a vow to offer him a number of waxlights, and to support an abandoned girl if he would assist her. Her confidence was rewarded, and she was safely delivered, though her child had been dead for several days.

The miracles wrought by the servant of God are so numerous that many volumes would be required to contain a concise account of all. "The Lord was truly lavish of such favors towards His servant, in order, undoubtedly, the sooner to illuminate the Church, his tabernacle among men, by causing him to be placed on her altars as a burning and shining light."

Two verbal processes were speedily drawn up: one at St. Agatha, which loved the memory and gloried in the heroic virtue of its former bishop; the other at Nocera, which had been blessed by the sanctity of his latter years, and still possessed the treasure of his relics. These processes were signed by eighty-seven witnesses, all distinguished for learning and piety, who deposed on oath to the sanctity and miracles of the great doctor. The acts of these processes were then forwarded to Rome, to obtain the introduction of his cause. Four hundred and eight petitions to this effect immediately followed, from cardinals, archbishops, bishops,

---

[1] The Jourdain (Giordani) family were originally from Nocera. -Ed.

collegiate establishments, religious bodies, magistrates of the highest standing including one from Ferdinand IV, King of the Two Sicilies.

As early as July 9, 1794, Cardinal Archinto was appointed reporter of the cause. Despite the troubles that disturbed the Holy See towards the close of the last century, this cause progressed, and on the 4th of September the servant of God was declared *Venerable*. On the 14th of May, 1803, the Sacred Congregation decided, after a rigid examination, that nothing in the printed or manuscript works of the Venerable Alphonsus di Ligouri deserved censure. On the 25th of June, 1803, Pope Pius VII granted a dispensation from the decree of Urban VIII, which forbids any special examination of the virtues of a servant of God to be undertaken until fifty years have elapsed after his death. On the 7th of May, 1807 being the feast of the Ascension of Our Lord, the Holy Father published the solemn decree on his virtues, proclaiming that Alphonsus Maria di Liguori had possessed the theological and cardinal virtues in a heroic degree. The extraordinary examination of his miracles was appointed for 25th September, 1809, but the invasion of Rome and the captivity of the Holy Father suspended the proceedings, which were not resumed until February, 1815.

The Feast of the Seven Dolors of Our Lady, which fell that year on the 17th of September, the Octave of the Nativity, was selected for publishing the decree on the miracles, on account of the great devotion which he had ever displayed towards the sorrows of Mary. On the 26th of September, 1816, his holiness signed the brief of beatification, which conferred the title of *Blessed* on the illustrious doctor, declaring him to be most assuredly in the enjoyment of eternal glory, and that his relics and pictures might be exposed to the veneration of the faithful, and authorizing the dioceses of St. Agatha and Nocera, and the Congregation of the Most Holy Redeemer, to celebrate yearly in his honor the mass of the beatified. The ceremony of the beatification was celebrated nine days later, with extraordinary pomp and splendor, little more than twenty-nine years having elapsed since the precious death of Alphonsus.

After the beatification, God continued to manifest the glory of his blessed servant, by many extraordinary miracles. Pius VIII approved of two of these in particular (December 3, 1829), and declared, with the usual formalities, that the solemn canonization of the blessed Alphonsus Maria di Liguori could safely be proceeded with (May 16, 1830). This holy pontiff dying some months later, was succeeded by Gregory XVI; but political and other reasons, which it is unnecessary to enumerate, delayed the solemn canonization till Trinity Sunday, May 26, 1839. On this auspicious day, Alphonsus Maria di Liguori and four other servants of God were solemnly declared saints, the ceremonies being conducted with a pomp and magnificence heretofore unequalled even in the Eternal City itself.

Besides the special indulgence for the canonization our Holy Father granted in perpetuity, Jan. 10, 1840, to each and all of the faithful of both sexes, who, being truly contrite, shall, after having confessed and communicated, devoutly visit one of the churches of the Congregation of the Most Holy Redeemer on the Feast of St. Alphonsus, August 2d, or during the octave, a plenary indulgence, applicable to the souls in purgatory, on the usual conditions of praying for peace among Christian rulers, for the extirpation of heresy, and for the exaltation of the Holy Catholic Church. The same holy pontiff prescribed that the Feast of St. Alphonsus should be celebrated throughout the world by all who are obliged to say the breviary, and by the faithful in general, under the rite of *duplex minor*, and inserted his name in the ecclesiastical calendar.

The city of Naples declared her most illustrious son her patron, jointly with St. Januarius, July 4, 1839, with the sanction of the king and the ecclesiastical authorities. The fête on this occasion lasted nine days. A silver statue of the saint, in which was enclosed a relic, was presented to the native city of their holy Founder by the Redemptorist Fathers. It was carried in procession to the cathedral, with extraordinary pomp, and placed beside the statue of St. Januarius, the first patron of Naples. During this fête, all Naples, and thousands of the inhabitants of the neighboring towns, paid their willing homage to this new glory of the Neapolitan Church, the king and queen, the queen-mother, the prince and princess of Salerno, and the younger members of the royal family mingling with their subjects on this occasion, and edifying all by their truly religious deportment and their affectionate veneration for the august prelate whose noble head was now resplendent with the aureola of sanctity.

The vast and profound learning of Alphonsus, joined to his eminent sanctity, had fixed on him, even during life, the suffrages of the Catholic world; and devotion to him, and appreciation of his doctrine, have but increased with time. Every pope, from Benedict XIV to Pius IX, has been lavish of praises of this great son of the Church. Benedict XIV, whose extraordinary learning won him the praises even of a Voltaire, quotes Father di Liguori as an authority in one of his elegant and erudite works. To this great pontiff the saint dedicated his "Moral Theology," and the compliment was not unappreciated, as an elegant letter from the Pope to the priest eloquently testified. When Clement XIII, who compelled him to accept the mitre, had seen and conversed with him, he remarked to a prelate of his court: "At the death of Monsignore Liguori, we shall have one saint more." Clement XIV would never allow him to resign his bishopric, saying that he could govern his diocese from his dying bed, and that a single prayer of the holy bishop was worth more than a hundred ordinary episcopal visitations.

Pius VI, even when permitted by Providence to be numbered among those from whom the heaviest crosses of the aged Founder proceeded, habitually called him a saint, and was wont to kiss his picture with devotion. He ordered his cause to be introduced immediately after his death and kept on his table some of his works to read, whenever he had a moment of leisure. Pius VII called him a most brilliant star in the firmament of the Church, and deemed it an honor to celebrate the beatification of so great a saint. Leo XII ordered the canonization of the Blessed Alphonsus to be proceeded with before all others, and sent a special blessing, a letter, and a medal, to the publisher of his complete works, which he graciously permitted to be dedicated to himself. The great canonist, Pius VIII, during his short pontificate, published the important decree which declared that the canonization of the Blessed Alphonsus Liguori might in all safety be proceeded with. Gregory XVI loved to praise the profound learning and eminent sanctity of Alphonsus. He placed his name in the ecclesiastical calendar, and extended his mass and office to the universal Church. "He is resplendent," said that great Pope, "even among the brilliant lights that adorn the Catholic Church."

Our reigning pontiff, Pius IX, has declared that the works of the saint are of the greatest utility, not only to the simple faithful, but also and chiefly, to ecclesiastics, and to all who are charged with the direction of souls; and has, moreover, graciously responded to the petition of 39 cardinals, 10 patriarchs, 135 archbishops, 544 bishops, 4 right reverend abbots, 25 generals of orders, 4 faculties of theology of universities, 15 metropolitan chapters of cathedrals, three congregations of missionary priests, and all the parishes of the kingdom of Naples, by declaring St. Alphonsus a Doctor of the Church — a distinction which had not been conferred on any ecclesiastical writer or theologian for six centuries.

The conditions which the Church requires for this rare and honorable distinction are: eminent knowledge, great sanctity, and the declaration of the Church. Now our sainted prelate has not only fulfilled the necessary conditions, but seems also to have reunited in himself the peculiar excellences of the most celebrated among the doctors: the spirit of penance of St. Jerome; the apostolic boldness of St. Ambrose; the divine unction of St. Augustine, the tender piety and love of Mary which distinguished St. Bernard; the devotion to the Church and zeal for the clergy which characterized St. Peter Damian; the lofty intellect and angelic meekness of St. Thomas Aquinas; and the lively faith and ardent love which gained for St. Bonaventure the beautiful title of *Seraphic Doctor*.

The style of St. Alphonsus is eminently his own; yet in his devotional works there is some resemblance to the vehement and fiery, but sweet and tender style of the *Last of the Fathers*, the honey-tongued St. Bernard, to whom, as a lover of Mary, our saint was especially devoted.

The beatification, canonization, and elevation to the doctorate of Alphonsus were conducted with singular splendor. The beatification took place in the basilica of St. Peter. In front of this glorious church floated a magnificent standard representing the Blessed Alphonsus in glory, with a Latin inscription, commemorative of the innocence of his life, his burning love of God, and his unflagging zeal in the divine service. A beautiful picture of the miracle of Foggia, representing the rays of light issuing from the image of Our Lady and reflected on the forehead of the preacher while he was in ecstasy, hung over the chief entrance of the majestic portico, which was decorated at various points with inscriptions referring to incidents, in the life of the saint, or miracles performed by him. St. Peter's Church, by far the largest and grandest edifice in the world, was hung with the richest damask embroidered with gold. Above the chair of St. Peter, radiant with waxlights innumerable, was an oval picture representing the serene and beautiful countenance of the beatified. When the brief was read, the picture of the saintly prelate was exposed to the multitude, amid the music of bells and the deep bass of artillery, all present falling on their knees to offer him the first public homage. The glorious *Te Deum*, sung by hundreds of the finest voices on earth, was but a poor expression of the gratitude and delight of the enthusiastic multitude.

Towards evening, Pius VII himself was seen prostrate before the picture of the beatified, the whole Sacred College praying with the august Head of the Church on earth. When the Holy Father arose, the postulator of the cause, Father Vincent Giattini, a worthy son of blessed Alphonsus, presented to the Vicar of Christ and each of the illustrious members of the Sacred College, a copy of the life of the blessed Founder of the Congregation of the Most Holy Redeemer.

At the canonization of Alphonsus, the decorations of the great basilica occupied several thousands of people for weeks. On the eve of the eagerly desired day, cannon boomed from the castle of San Angelo, and all the bells in Rome rang out their merriest peals, to announce its approach to the eager people. At midnight, the trumpets of the guards resounded through the town, and music burst forth in every direction; at four in the morning, a hundred cannon were fired in honor of the festal day.

Rome was filled with strangers from every clime under the sun, and, as on the day of Pentecost, there was not a man who could not hear his own language in the beauteous city of the popes. This august dynasty rules not the church of a nation or an empire, but the Catholic Church, whose maternal bosom nurtures every tribe and tongue and people and nation, and makes them to her God a kingdom. The vast square before St. Peter's was but a mass of human beings; perfect order being preserved by the grenadiers and guards of Rome, in their showy but elegant uniforms.

At six o'clock A. M. a procession which could be formed only in Rome, wended its way towards St. Peter's. First came the cross — the badge, the glory, the standard of Christian Rome. The well cared for orphans of the great charitable institutions and the schools of Noble children; religious orders with their gorgeous banners and quaint but picturesque costumes — Alcantarines, with brown habits and blue cords; barefooted Augustinians in their heavy, though not ungraceful robes; Capuchins, with flowing beards and sandalled feet; Carmelite monks, in white and brown; the white habit of the Brothers of Mercy and the ample black robe of the Benedictine; the flowing white and black costume of the son of St. Dominic; the red and blue crosses of the Trinitarians; the sombre brown of the Maronite habit, and the celestial blue of the Coptic monk — canons of cathedrals, collegiate establishments, confraternities, the members of the Congregation of Rites, the secular clergy, citizens bearing torches, the banners of the new saints. The pennant of St. Alphonsus was supported by a venerable white-haired man, whose noble bearing and military air attracted many a reverential gaze. This was a nephew of the saint, who had received the sacrament of confirmation at his hands; he was now a general in the royal army of Naples, and the group of handsome young officers who attended him were grandnephews[2] of Alphonsus. The Pope's heralds, his court, the singers of the Papal chapel, bishops, mitred abbots, cardinals, the prefect of Rome, the chief civil officer, and the Pope, surrounded by the principal personages of his household and followed by the generals of orders — this imposing array of the dignitaries and sons of the Church, with its august head, awakening so many historic associations and holy recollections naturally, as it were, marshalled itself into perfect order, as it slowly advanced through the surging mass of human beings, the sombre garb of high civilization contrasting with the bright and varied costume of the light-hearted Italian peasants who had travelled many a weary mile, and faces of every hue, red, yellow, brown, and from black to white.

The immense basilica was superbly decorated and brilliantly lighted, the sun being completely shut out by the gorgeous

---

[2] Several descendants of the saint's brother, Count Hercules Liguori, and of his sister Teresa, Duchess of Presenzano, still glory in claiming as their collateral ancestor, the great bishop and doctor. Like most of the old families of Naples, thy have considerably declined from their former wealth, power, and consequence. Those of the family who were present at his canonization, had the gratification of seeing his statue honored with a niche in St. Peter's. -Ed.

damask hangings of the windows. Golden lustres and chandeliers swung from the roof, and candelabra of exquisite workmanship supported the airy bubbles of light that glistened before the pictures of the new saints. The glare of more than four thousand waxlights was sufficient to illumine the greatest temple ever raised by man to the Divinity. In a tribune near the papal throne were the kings of Naples and Bavaria, Don Miguel of Portugal, and the Queen of Sardinia. *This elegant work of art is a miracle of taste and genius, wrought by the first artist of the day, in the purest white marble. It is almost thirty feet in height, a perfect colossus. The likeness to the saint is striking — those who knew him in life have testified to this. The mitre and crosier are held by a cherub.*

The grandest part of this magnificent ceremony was when the assembled thousands rose as one man, and listened with subdued mind and tear-bedewed eye to the INFALLIBLE VOICE, which proclaimed, *ex cathedra,* the sublime holiness of the five servants of God associated in this august ceremony. Seated in the chair of Peter the 258th successor of him who was appointed *to confirm his brethren* spoke, in simple but majestic language, his final judgment as Supreme Doctor and head of the Catholic Church, his sonorous tones thrilling through every heart:

"In honor of the Most Holy and Undivided Trinity, for the exaltation of the Catholic faith and the increase of piety among Christians, by the authority of Our Lord Jesus Christ, of the blessed apostles Peter and Paul, and by our own, WE, after mature reflection and oft-repeated invocation for the divine aid, and after having consulted our venerable brethren the cardinals of the Roman Church, the patriarchs, archbishops, and bishops of this capital, decide and pronounce, that the blessed Alphonsus, blessed Francis of Jerome, &c., are saints; we number them among the saints, and ordain that their memory shall be annually honored by the worship of the Church on the day of their birth,[3] namely, that of Alphonsus on the 2d of August, &c. In the name of the Father, and of the Son, and of the Holy Ghost. Amen."

The clear and thrilling tones of the Vicar of Christ now gave out the *Te Deum,* in which thousands of voices were quickly blended. The cannon of San Angelo, the innumerable bells of

---

[3] The Church calls the day of their death their birthday, as commencing their new and blessed life as saints in heaven. -Ed.

495

Rome, the sound of trumpets, the joyous burst of military music — all combined to render the scene one of triumphant and bewildering splendor. Mass was celebrated by the Holy Father himself, who had previously chanted the prayers of the office of the newly declared saints. This being over, His Holiness bestowed from the *loggia* the pontifical benediction on his children of every clime and color, who in tens of thousands knelt with bowed head and reverent mien to receive it, and on the still more numerous children of his paternal heart, who were denied the privilege of assisting at that great day's celebration, *urbi et orbi.*

A far rarer honor than canonization was decreed our saint by our present illustrious pontiff, which has associated the already honored and venerated name of Alphonsus Maria di Liguori with the greatest event of our time, the Vatican Council. The following is a translation of the decree which placed his name in the category of the Doctors of the Church:

"Among those who have done and taught, and whom our Lord Jesus Christ has declared should be great in the kingdom of heaven, is rightly counted Saint Alphonsus Maria di Liguori, Founder of the Congregation of the Most Holy Redeemer, and Bishop of Saint Agatha of the Goths. He shone as a watch-light on its tower, giving examples of all virtues to those who follow Christ and are of the household of God. Already, because of the brightness of his light, he has been reckoned among the saints, the domestics of God. But what he reduced to practice in his holy life, he taught also in word and by writing. He stands distinguished for dispelling and clearing up the lurking-places of unbelievers and Jansenists, so widely spread. And, over and beyond this, he has cleared up questions that were clouded, he has solved what was doubtful, making a safe path, through which the directors of Christian souls may tread with harmless foot, between the involved opinions of theologians, whether too loose or too rigorous.

"And besides this, he has signally cast light on the doctrines of the Immaculate Conception, and of the Infallibility of the Sovereign Pontiff teaching *ex cathedra*, and he strenuously taught these doctrines, which, in our day have been defined as of faith.

"He has finally made clear dark passages of the Holy Scriptures, both in his ascetic writings, which are freighted with a celestial odor, and in a most salutary commentary, in which, for the nourishment of piety and the instruction of the soul, he has given expositions of the Psalms, as well as of the hymns recited in the divine office, for the benefit especially of those obliged to its recitation.

"Pius VII, of holy memory, was greatly moved by the exceeding wisdom of Alphonsus, and spoke in his praise, as follows: 'In the midnight of the world, he has shown, by his voice and his writings, the road of justice to the wandering, by which they may pass from the power of darkness to the light and kingdom of God.'

"Nor were less remarkable words used by Pope Gregory XVI, of holy memory, when he raised by decretal letters, St. Alphonsus to the honors of canonization. Pope Gregory XVI said that there was in the writings of the blessed Alphonsus 'a wonderful force, an abundance and variety of doctrine.' But in our days the 'Nations declare his wisdom, and the Church shows forth his praise,' so that very many cardinals of the Holy Roman Church, almost all the prelates of the whole Catholic universe, the generals of religious orders, the theological faculties of the most celebrated universities, illustrious chapters of canons, and learned men of every ecclesiastical body, have presented petitions to our Holy Father Pius IX, Supreme Pontiff, in which they express their common desires that St Alphonsus Maria di Liguori may be adorned with the title and the honors of *Doctor of the Church*. His Holiness, graciously accepting these prayers, committed to the Congregation of Rites, according to custom in matters of this kind, the examining of so very grave a question. Consequently, in ordinary meetings held at the Vatican on the day below mentioned, hearing the most Eminent and Reverend Cardinal Constantine Patrizi, Dean of the Sacred College, prefect of the said Congregation, and reporter of the Cause, full attention having been given to the animadversions of the Rev Father D. Peter Minetti, Promoter of the Holy Faith, with the answers of the Promoter of the Cause; and also the opinions of theologians not engaged in the cause (*pro veritate*); and finally, all relating to the matter on the one side and on the other having been most severely weighed, the most Eminent and most Reverend Cardinals of the Sacred Congregation of Rites have judged, by unanimous consent, that it should be answered:

" 'To give counsel to His Holiness in favor of the granting, or declaration, and extension to the whole Church, of the title of *Doctor*⁴ in honor of Saint Alphonsus Maria di Liguori, with special office and mass, the *Credo*; the antiphon *O Doctor* at the *Magnificat* of the First and Second Vespers; the *Sapientiam* [from the Common of Doctors], for the lessons of the First Nocturn; and the *In Medio Ecclesia*, for the Responsory of the Eighth Lesson. Dated March 11, 1871.'

"Presently, a faithful account having been made of all and singular the above, to our Most Holy Lord Pope, Pius IX, by the undersigned Secretary of the said Sacred Congregation, his holiness approved and confirmed the rescript and of his supreme authority ordered that a General Decree, urbis et orbis should be sent forth, on the twenty-third day of the same month and year. CONSTANTINE, CARD. PATRIZI,

Bishop of Ostia and Villetri, Prefect of the Sacred Cong. of Rites. [L. S.] D. Bartolini, Secretary of S. C. R.

---

⁴ In eighteen centuries the title of Doctor of the Church had been conferred only on seventeen. St Bonaventure, Card. Archbp. of Albano, who died in 1274, closed the illustrious category until March 23, 1871, when St Alphonsus was elevated to this rare dignity. -Ed.

CHAPTER LXXIX.

The undying characteristic of St. Alphonsus — The work most cherished by Alphonsus. — Sketch of the early days of the order in Northern Europe. — A prophecy and its fulfilment — Vocation of F. Hoffbauer. — Hübl. — Various persecutions. — Splendid testimony. — Prisons and death. — Death of the second General. — His successors. — Jealousies of the Neapolitan government Present state of the Congregation. — Father Passerat — His holy death. Prayers and prophecies.

THE GREAT and life-long characteristic of St. Alphonsus was zeal against sin. "And what," asks one of the most eminent prelates of our day, "is the Congregation of the Most Holy Redeemer, but this burning zeal against sin, incorporated and made perpetual in the Church of God?"[1] We have already sketched the hopes and fears, the favors and crosses, which checkered the earlier days of the institute founded in so sublime an idea, and for such a glorious mission. Although it is chiefly as priest, bishop, and doctor, that Alphonsus di Liguori is known and loved by the zealous and the pious, yet it is evident from his rules and his letters, that he regarded the Congregation which he founded as the great work of his life; the work, by excellence, *which his Father had given him to do*, the work destined to perpetuate even to the day of doom, his uncompromising zeal against sin and worldliness with his unfailing benignity and inexhaustible compassion for sinners. Hence a life of St. Alphonsus would seem incomplete without a slight glance at the fortunes of the Order which has the honor to claim him as its founder.

Twelve houses of the Congregation were in successful operation at the date of his happy death, 1787, namely those of Ciorani, in the diocese of Salerno, about seven leagues southeast

---

[1] Archbishop Manning, in his sermon on The Mission of St Alfonso, delivered in the Redemptorist Church, Clapham, Aug. 2, 1864. -Ed.

of Naples; Nocera del Pagani, a city of some 7,000 inhabitants, a few miles from Ciorani; Illiceto, a little town in the diocese of Bovino; and Caposele, a mere village in the diocese of Conza, all in the kingdom of Naples; Girgenti, a flourishing city in Sicily; San Angelo, Benevento, Scifelli, Frosinone, Rome, Gubbio, and Spello, all except the Eternal City, unimportant places in the Papal territory.

The petty and despicable jealousies of the Neapolitan government, so liberal towards freemasons, had early endeavored to make such arrangements for the Congregation of the Most Holy Redeemer as would confine its workings within the limits of the kingdom of the Two Sicilies, but nothing was farther from the views of the holy founder. Seeing that its development under such auspices must be cramped and stunted, he was particularly anxious to plant it in more genial soil, and seized with gratitude and delight the first opportunities that offered of establishing his sons under the fatherly sway of his nearest royal neighbor, Pope Pius VI.

Alphonsus had prophesied that his Congregation, so far from becoming a prey to the enemies who employed their best energies for its destruction, would survive even to the judgment-day, and that, after his death, it would spread into many countries, and be most successful in procuring the glory of God and the salvation of souls, especially in the more northern regions. He had seen with delight, in 1784, the arrival in Rome of the two men[2] destined to propagate the Congregation in these very regions, Clement Mary Hoffbauer, a simple peasant of Moravia, a baker by trade, and Thaddeus Hübl, a youth of Bohemia, likewise of the humblest class.

---

[2] When Hoffbauer reached Rome, he accidentally, as it were, wandered into the little church of St. Julian, and being greatly struck by the deportment of some religious who were praying before the altar, he asked a little boy to what order they belonged. "They are Fathers of the Congregation of the Most Holy Redeemer," answered the child, "and you, sir, will one day belong to their institute." Clement, astonished at this, asked for the Superior, and hearing that the Redemptorists were the religious of the world-renowned Monsignore Liguori, he immediately joined them, to the dismay of his friend and companion Hübl, who was still undecided as to what order he would embrace. Instead of retiring to rest that night, Clement prayed till morning that his dear friend Thaddeus might obtain of God a vocation to the Congregation. The prayer was granted. Hübl called upon him early next day, and begged to be admitted among the novices. -Ed.

Scarcely had our saint gone to his reward, than his prophecies began to be verified. Towards the close of 1787, the very year of his death, Hoffbauer and Hübl, both subjects of Austria, but unable, because of the miserable laws of Joseph II, to make a foundation in any of his hereditary States, set out to evangelize the abandoned Catholics of Courland and Livonia, in the Empire of Russia, on the invitation of Monsignore Saluzzo, Apostolic Nuncio of Poland.

When the Fathers arrived at Varsovia, the Nuncio concluded that, as the wants of the Catholics were scarcely less pressing in Poland than in Russia, he would appeal to the Sovereign Pontiff for leave to detain them, which was readily granted. The king of Poland welcomed them with the most utmost cordiality, and bestowed on them the church of St. Bennon. From this first establishment the Polish Redemptorists have been called Bennonists.

The happy reunion of the houses of Naples, Sicily, and the Roman States was not consummated till 1791, when Father Blasucci was elected rector major of the whole Congregation. Blasucci may be regarded as the second General, as neither Father de Paul nor Father Villani exercised any authority beyond the political boundaries of the States in which they respectively dwelt, if we except the single house of Varsovia, which was under the jurisdiction of Father de Paul. As communication by letter or otherwise between Poland and Italy was difficult and uncertain, the new general appointed Father Hoffbauer his Vicar General for the northern countries.

In 1794, a house was founded at Mittau, in Courland, where the Fathers became so popular that all the denominations sought to benefit by their ministrations, and before many months elapsed, they had completely gained the hearts of the people. But in 1798, the government forbade the Redemptorists to hold any communication with their brethren outside the Russian dominions, and some time after suppressed the establishment. The Prussian Government, under which Varsovia had fallen, commanded that no subject should be admitted to profession under twenty-four years of age. This led to the closing of the convent at Mittau, to the intense regret of the inhabitants, and the Vicar General was obliged to send all the novices to Iestetten, in Switzerland, in 1803. Foundations were made at Lukow and

Radomyn, but persecution followed the Fathers everywhere. The novitiate seems to have been especially aimed at, for we find it driven from one spot to another — in 1805 at Triberg in the depths of the Black Forest, and, after several futile attempts to settle in 1807, at Viège, in Valais. Despite extreme poverty and frequent persecution, God blessed abundantly the labors of the Fathers. The nuncio, writing to the General, then residing at Rome, said: "I tell your reverence for certain, that among all the religious bodies with which I am acquainted, the subjects of your Congregation are the most distinguished for their exemplary lives and remarkable modesty."

It was especially at Varsovia that the fruits of their mission were apparent. Monsignore Litta, afterwards cardinal, wrote to Father General Blasucci, January 11, 1800: "On my return from St. Petersburg, I passed through Varsovia, where I sojourned more than a month. I observed, to my great consolation, that the Convent of the Most Holy Redeemer flourishes more and more, by the acquisition of new workmen, by the incessant concourse of people, and by the great fruits which result from preaching, and from the administration of the sacraments of penance and holy communion. The church was literally full from morning till night, and from morning till night masses, preaching, confessions, or benediction of the blessed sacrament filled the hours. I do not exaggerate. There are four sermons a day, two in the morning and two in the evening, alternately in Polish and German. The fruit of these continual labors is easily seen in the edifying lives of the people. Great as are the exertions of the Fathers, I do not call them excessive, because I see that they are necessary, and I dare not counsel moderation, in view of the immense fruit produced, lest I should oppose the will of God and injure his work."

But this happy state of things did not long continue. In 1807, the amiable and gifted Father Hübl, still in the prime of life, died the death of the just. The Vicar General had called him the Mother of the Congregation, because of his tender solicitude for his companions. Hardly had Father Hoffbauer ceased to bewail this dear son and brother, when a persecution arose which desolated the fair province of which such glowing accounts have reached us. The treaty of Tilsit altered once more the political aspect of Poland, and the accusations of the freemasons and Voltairians were so readily admitted under the new régime, that as early as June, 1808, the flourishing establishment at Varsovia was suppressed. The other foundations speedily shared its fate.

The poor Fathers were kept close prisoners in the fortress of Kustrin, and it is pleasant to record that the Protestant gaolers and other officials of that gloomy habitation treated them with affectionate reverence. The people loved to linger under their heavily barricaded windows, as their deep, melodious voices blended in the hymns and canticles of the Roman ritual — truly the songs of the Lord in a strange land — and their sweet wailings, borne afar on the evening breeze, were inexpressibly touching, both to the simple peasants and to the refined aristocrats. The dismal prison had become a house of praise and prayer, and a peace and happiness, which perhaps it had never before known, now reigned within its grim walls.

After several weeks, the Polish Fathers were commanded to return to their families, and Father Hoffbauer was permitted to retire to Vienna, where the archbishop appointed him pastor of the Italian Church. The same year, 1809, all the houses in the Papal States were suppressed, except Scifelli, which escaped, no one knew how or why. Only the establishments of Rome and Frosinone were ever restored. In 1815, Father Hoffbauer, at the request of the proper ecclesiastical authorities, sent a small band of his scattered sons to Bucharest, where they labored zealously and with fruit, until the Greek revolution made them wanderers once more.

After vicissitudes of every species, the Vicar General succeeded in establishing a foundation at Vienna, but he did not live to see the success of this work. Full of years and merits, he passed happily to our Lord, March 15, 1820.

In our own day, the cause of Clement Mary Hoffbauer has been introduced, and our present illustrious pontiff has declared him *Venerable.*[3] The witnesses since examined with a view to his beatification included bishops, priests, physicians, lawyers, artists, aristocrats, peasants, merchants, Lutherans, and one Jew, all of whom were eye-witnesses to the facts to which they subscribed. The cause of Father Passerat has been introduced into the Sacred

---

[3] Clement died at Vienna on March 15, 1820. He was canonized by St. Pius X on May 20, 1909. He is co-patron of both Vienna and Warsaw. The shrine of St. Clement Hofbauer is in the church of Maria am Gestade in Vienna, Austria. – SDP

Congregation; also that of Brother Dominic Blasucci, who died during the lifetime of the holy founder, at the age of twenty. Blasucci has been styled the Aloysius of the Congregation. The lay-brother, Gerard Majello, called the Thaumaturgus[4] of the Congregation, also a disciple of Alphonsus, has been solemnly beatified. Blessed Gerard died in 1755, aged twenty-nine.

Father Joseph Passerat was the worthy successor of the venerable Clement Mary Hoffbauer. It was he who introduced the Congregation into France, at the suggestion of the august daughter of Louis XVI, an exile like himself, but this foundation was not completed as rapidly as the piety of that unfortunate princess desired. It was not till 1820 that the Redemptorists were installed in their house near Strasburg. This establishment has been suppressed, and reopened, and suppressed again in our own day. In short, this order was accurately described by the holy founder when he said: "Our Congregation is like the grass of the meadow; it sprouts up, it is cut, but it does not die." Prisons, banishment, and even death, with alternations of glory and success, comprise the history of the Redemptorist order. Perhaps for its time it has been more persistently persecuted than any of the great companies that form, as it were, the flying artillery of the Church.

In 1816, shortly after the beatification of St. Alphonsus, Father Blasucci died,[5] second General of the Congregation, which he governed for a quarter of a century. He was succeeded by another disciple of the saint, Father Nicholas Mansione, who, when rector of Nocera in 1787, had the honor and happiness of administering the last sacraments to the dying founder. During his generalate and that of his immediate successors, Father Celestine Cocle (1824) and Camillo Ripoli (1832), the Congregation was considerably cramped by the petty jealousies of the Neapolitan government, which, as usual, attempted to regulate the business of the rector major. It is true that in 1841, Pope Gregory XVI divided the Congregation into six provinces, and commanded Ripoli to transfer to Rome the seat of his government, but in consequence of the senseless opposition of the

---

[4] "Miracle worker." St. Gerard Majello was canonized by Pope St. Pius X in 1904. – SDP

[5] Father General Blasucci was a younger brother of the venerable Dominic Blasucci, "the Aloysius of the Congregation." -Ed.

Neapolitan government, this project was not fully carried out until after the election of his successor, Father Nicholas Mauron (present rector major) in 1855, from which date, the Neapolitan government being no longer able to impede its progress, the Congregation has spread into almost every civilized country, and been signally blessed by God.

It now (1873) consists of nine provinces, the Roman containing six houses, the French twelve, the Austrian eleven, the Belgian eight, Upper Germanic eight, Dutch six, Lower Germanic six, all on the European Continent. Several of these establishments have been suppressed or confiscated by the robber-king Victor Emanuel and the infidel Bismarck.

The Congregation was introduced into the United States in 1832, the missionaries being sent thither by the venerable Father Passerat, who for twenty years had been seeking an opportunity to plant his order in America.[6] The American province now contains fourteen houses, of which the oldest is Rochester, and the last founded, Boston.

The Redemptorist Congregation was introduced into England in 1851, into Ireland in 1853, and into Scotland in 1867. It has been blessed with signal success in these kingdoms.

The Redemptorist houses of Central America are dependent on the Roman province. The total number of houses of this order is about eighty, besides which there have been several temporary missions.

The year 1848 was peculiarly disastrous to the Congregation in Europe. Four houses in the kingdom of the Two Sicilies, six in Austria and Modena, were among the victims of the revolution, which showed, either that favored Europe was not yet fully reclaimed from barbarism, or that she had relapsed into it. A mob of our modern exponents of liberty and equality attempted to sack the establishment at Scifelli, and one of their number quietly ran his bayonet through the body of a poor lay-brother, who had, rashly or courageously, attempted to close the door against the sacrilegious robbers. The Fathers of the flourishing house of Vienna were compelled to enter close carriages, and conducted

---

[6] There is a story current, we know not upon what authority, that St Alphonsus, seeing a sailing vessel bound for New Orleans, prophesied that his sons would yet possess flourishing establishments in that city, and there become the instruments of the perfection and salvation of innumerable souls. -Ed.

under a guard into the country, as far as their captors chose. They were then dropped in the forest, and left destitute of food and shelter, with the strictest injunction not to return to the city. The saintly and venerable Father Passerat was one of the victims of this outrage. A decree of the diet at Frankfort suppressed, throughout the whole Germanic Confederation, Jesuits, Redemptorists, and Liguorians. It is unnecessary to remark that the second and third terms are synonymous, though these learned lawmakers were not aware of that obvious fact. Incessant toil and persecutions told upon the vigorous frame of the saintly Father Passerat, now in his seventy-seventh year. He resigned his office of Vicar General, and retired to Tournai, where he died ten years later, October 30, 1858. No man ever knew better *how to abound and how to be brought low* . Tried by the highest prosperity and the depths of adversity — now waited on by emperors, again hooted by the rabble — he was unchanged in every vicissitude; to the very last he fully bore out the character his superior, the Venerable Clement Hoffbauer, had given of him to the rector major, Blasucci, in 1811:

"Father Passerat is a man of singular prudence and piety; he exacts of all great fidelity to the rule and constitutions. One may say he is patience personified; his zeal is incomparable; he refuses no labors; he braves all dangers. He has travelled on foot over twelve hundred miles. Twice he has visited me at Vienna, urged solely by the love of God and the interest of his community. In a word, the Congregation possesses in him an accomplished model of all virtues."[7]

The last words of this wonderful missionary are characteristic: *Grant me, O Lord, eternal rest, and let perpetual light shine on me!* Rest eternal! Perpetual light! The two great cravings of the creature's heart, whether saint or sinner.

Joseph Passerat was almost the last link that bound the Congregation to the days of its founder. Several Fathers trained by him still live to perpetuate the traditions he so faithfully taught and exemplified. Those who have barely seen him deem it a grace, and love to recall his benign features and his holy deportment.

We may appropriately add here the following words of the holy founder, for the world has seen them verified:

---

[7] Fr. Passerat was declared *Servant of God* in 1901 and *Venerable* in 1980. – SDP

"I am certain that Jesus Christ regards lovingly our little society, yea, that He regards it as the apple of His eye. Daily experience proves this, since, amid so many persecutions, He never ceases to protect us and render us worthy of laboring for His glory in so many places, and multiplies His graces towards us."

"I have," he says elsewhere, "a firm conviction that our little flock will continue to increase with time, not in honors and riches, but in efficacious means of procuring the glory of God, and laboring to cause Jesus Christ to be known and loved. We shall one day be reunited in heaven, never more to be separated, and there we shall meet hundreds of thousands who were once strangers to Jesus Christ and who, by our ministry, restored to grace, will love Him and contribute eternally to our glory and happiness. Let us, then, have unbounded confidence in our dear Lord; He has selected us to be among the great ones of His court, as is evident from the protection He affords our Congregation in general, and each of its members in particular."

This seraph of earth frequently bursts into the most sublime petitions which a founder could make for his institute, a father for his children: "O Jesus, increase Thy divine love more and more in the hearts of all who live, and ever will live, in this Congregation, that, in heaven, burning like the seraphim, they may eternally praise Thee and magnify Thy mercies towards them!"

"O Lord Jesus," he again exclaims — and we humbly and devoutly echo his beautiful prayer — "O Lord Jesus, perfect Thy work; grant that we may be wholly Thine, and spend ourselves for Thy glory, in such a manner that all the subjects of this Congregation, until the judgment day, may be perfectly pleasing in Thy sight, and gain Thee an infinite number of souls! Amen."

THE END

Slaying Dragons Press Classics

Slaying Dragons Press Classics is a new endeavor though one which has long been a desire of the Slaying Dragons Apostolate. In particular, there has been a desire to bring into print the marvelous and largely forgotten works of the master of morality and the spiritual life, St. Alphonsus Liguori.

With the desire to bring back into print many of his excellent writings, there has also been a felt need to make these writings intelligible to the modern Christian mind, often under-catechized and very much immersed in a worldly and secular culture. Many Christians, even among the devout, have been deprived of the traditional teachings of the Church in the modern era. Great Christian writers such as St. Alphonsus Liguori are, therefore, greatly needed by the modern Church.

Slaying Dragons Press Classics intends to bring back many of his writings, presenting them in a way that preserves the integrity of the original and also presents some helpful analysis to assist the reader in remembering the key teachings.

This effort of bring back into print lost and marvelous writings of St. Alphonsus Liguori will not, God willing, be limited to this great Doctor of the Church alone. It is the hope that this effort will be able to present many more lost spiritual treasures to the faithful of today.

Slaying Dragons Press

Slaying Dragons Press, founded in 2021, is the fruit of a spiritual work begun in 2016 which sought to find new ways to bring people the joy and beauty of the Catholic Faith. By God's Providence, what began under the name *The Retreat Box* has grown into *The Slaying Dragons Apostolate* and *Slaying Dragons Press.*

This work is a grassroots apostolate which thrives on support and endorsements from those who enjoy these books. As a result, fans of the books and supporters of the mission help increase the reach of *Slaying Dragons Press* by telling friends, family, priests, religious, and Bishops about these books.

Please consider supporting this work in any way that you can. While *Slaying Dragons Press* is *not* a non-profit, financial support is always welcome. Please visit SlayingDragonsPress.com for ways to support this apostolate. If you do not have a copy of the other celebrated books we have published, get one today!

*Support this work on **Patreon!**
     ~patreon.com/**theslayingdragonsapostolate**

*Subscribe to the author's website for discounts and news!
     ~SlayingDragonsPress.com/pages/**Subscribe**

Popular *Slaying Dragons Press* Titles

The Occult Among Us: Exorcists and Former Occultists Expose the Nature of This Modern Evil

The Rise of the Occult: What Exorcists & Former Occultists Want You to Know

Slaying Dragons: What Exorcists See & What We Should Know (also in Spanish – *Matando Dragones*)

Slaying Dragons - Prepare for Battle: Applying the Wisdom of Exorcists to Your Spiritual Warfare

Swords and Shadows: Navigating Youth Amidst the Wiles of Satan

Come Away By Yourselves: A Guide to Prayer for Busy Catholics

Slaying Dragons Press